# Long Before Stonewall

# Long Before Stonewall

*Histories of Same-Sex Sexuality in Early America*

EDITED BY

*Thomas A. Foster*

*with an Afterword by*
*John D'Emilio*

*New York University Press*

NEW YORK AND LONDON

NEW YORK UNIVERSITY PRESS
New York and London
www.nyupress.org

Library of Congress Cataloging-in-Publication Data
Histories of same-sex sexuality in early America / edited by
Thomas A. Foster.
p.   cm.
Includes bibliographical references and index.
ISBN-13: 978-0-8147-2749-2 (cloth : alk. paper)
ISBN-10: 0-8147-2749-2 (cloth : alk. paper)
ISBN-13: 978-0-8147-2750-8 (pbk. : alk. paper)
ISBN-10: 0-8147-2750-6 (pbk. : alk. paper)
1. Homosexuality—United States—History—18th century. 2. Gays—
United States—History—18th century.   I. Foster, Thomas A.
HQ76.3.U5H57 2007
306.76'6097309033—dc22            2007000134

New York University Press books are printed on acid-free paper,
and their binding materials are chosen for strength and durability.

Manufactured in the United States of America
c 10 9 8 7 6 5 4 3 2 1
p 10 9 8 7 6 5 4 3 2 1

For Marlon

# Contents

# Acknowledgments

This project has been enormously gratifying to work on. I owe a debt of gratitude to the many people who helped along the way by offering suggestions for authors, pointing me to relevant essays, giving general advice, and sending emails of encouragement and expressions of enthusiasm for the project.

I thank the departments of history at the University of Miami, Rice University, and DePaul University for institutional support while I worked on the volume. In particular, I would like to thank Holly Grieves of DePaul University for scanning the reprinted articles to create electronic files. A grant from the University Research Council of DePaul University helped defray some of the production costs.

This book would never have been possible without the efforts of the contributors. I would also like to thank Debbie Gershenowitz who carefully guided and advised at every point.

# Introduction

## *Long Before Stonewall*

### *Thomas A. Foster*

In mid-eighteenth-century Massachusetts, the engraving featured on the cover and on the facing page, published in the *Boston Evening Post*, depicted the Freemasons of Boston engaged in anal penetration with a wooden spike or treenail. Treenails were commonly used in ship-building in the eighteenth century and joined timbers by becoming engorged when wet. Thus, the very object being used for penetration was a multilayered phallic symbol. The image also included the figure of an "ass" (furthering the anal emphasis) that brayed "Trunnel him well, brother." A poem accompanied the engraving and depicted the Masons as romantically and sexually interested in one another. It only added to the focus on the phallus (note that the word "trunnel" was highlighted with capital letters) and the posterior with the lines: "I'm sure our TRUNNELS look'd as clean / As if they ne're up A—se had been; / For when we use 'em, we take care / To wash 'em well, and give 'em Air, / Then lock 'em up in our own Chamber, / Ready to TRUNNEL the next Member." Sodomy was, of course, still a capital crime in eighteenth-century Massachusetts, yet the story managed to muster humor about the act by calling on a cultural association of depraved and inferior manhood with same-sex sexual interest.[1] That by the eighteenth century an all-male secret social club could raise the specter of homosexuality is significant. We might even speculate that the satirist was referencing molly houses of London, which were reported on in local newspapers.

Traditional scholars might argue that the engraving displays the scatological, not the sexual. But to draw too fine a line around the sexual limits our understanding of ways in which the erotic, romantic, intimate, reproductive, and physical join together with so-called nonsexual areas of life and society in early America. The anal "intimacy" depicted in the image necessarily raises the possibility of sodomy, enabling us to speak of same-sex sexuality without actually locating the term sodomy in this discussion.

This book, a collection of reprinted and original ground-breaking work, uses history, anthropology, psychology, literary criticism, political theory, and sociology to tease out various histories of same-sex sexualities in early America. Parts one and two chart the contours of same-sex sexuality in colonial societies, including interactions among Native Americans and Europeans. Parts three and four examine new meanings of same-sex sex in the early United States. Collectively, these essays demonstrate that long before the modern era, individuals came together to express their same-sex romantic and sexual attraction. Some reflected on their desires in quiet solitude. Some endured great hardship for their words or actions that expressed homosexual interest.[2]

The eighteenth century in particular was a critical period in the development of traditions of sexuality. These languages and ideas around sex and personhood were only in the late nineteenth and early twentieth centuries officially enshrined in the professional terms of the then-relatively new fields of psychology and sexology. *Long Before Stonewall* exposes the deep foundations that modern sexual political movements and identities are built upon.

Reconceptualizing sexuality in preindustrial America has broader implications for our understanding of the development of the modern subject or self. Studying same-sex sexuality can also tell us something about life in early America, in particular something about connections of sex and reputation and character. Sexuality in early America was not as cordoned off into a realm of "private" behavior as it is today. The distinction between private and public was not so starkly drawn yet and therefore sex and sexuality affected more "nonsexual" arenas than has generally been understood. Indeed, the modern propensity to view sex as part of one's private life has led to its teleological absence from studies of public life. Early American society was agrarian and localized. Face-to-face interactions established one's personal reputation in the community. In colonial America, troublemakers always ran the risk of being pushed out or worse. But we should keep in mind that character and reputation were about more than simply being able to hold one's head high. The entire economic system, of both credit and household economies of barter, was based on character and reputation. In an era before depersonalized credit scores, what one did with one's self (drink too much? engage in extramarital sex?) —male or female, elite or ordinary, could play a vital role in securing one's livelihood and status in the community.[3]

This general emphasis on character and reputation is familiar to students of early America. What is less well understood, however, is the extent to which personal behaviors regarding moral behaviors played an important role in establishing one's social and economic position. Taking into account sexual behaviors raises questions about the extent to which sexuality was part of that broader public reputation. It is within this context that a discussion of same-sex sexuality in early America must be situated.

## Lesbian and Gay History

Charged by the modern gay liberation movement, activist-scholars set about to develop a broader and deeper sense of history for gays and lesbians. In 1976, Jonathan Katz first compiled cases of sodomy and legal pronouncements and other writings in his ground-breaking volume *Gay American History* which was quickly followed by an equally important volume, *Gay/Lesbian Almanac*. Both volumes included a comprehensive survey of what documentary evidence existed for the study of homosexuality in colonial America. By culling from the historical record those cases focused on same-sex sexuality, the book underscored gay history as a field of inquiry.[4]

Early scholarship on same-sex sexuality in early America made good use of legal statutes and court records. Given this methodological emphasis on court records, our understanding of early American same-sex sexuality is greatest for male homosexuality in the seventeenth century and specifically for New England—the time and place that because of its court system and emphasis on policing moral and sexual behaviors left the most pronounced documentary evidence for historians to sift through. Despite the relative involvement of seventeenth-century New England courts, the absence of a very large number of sodomy cases even in that locale has led to two very different interpretations. Were there few cases because the population thoroughly embraced the official revulsion to same-sex sexual behavior? Or, was it because many managed to either avoid detection or were not actively taken to court by a sympathetic network of kin and community?

The scholarship on seventeenth-century New England has also had an unintended consequence. The draconian anti-sodomy pronouncements of court and church have been assumed to accurately reflect the broader lay understanding of sentiments toward sexual intimacy between members of the same sex. The focus on sexual acts, sinful or criminal, has been taken to reveal the broader cultural understanding of sodomy as only an act, fully disconnected from personhood and identity. Moreover, the emphasis on the seventeenth century has led to incorrect assumptions about lay opinions. Additionally, the Puritan milieu has come to stand for the broader preindustrial American history. While early scholars sought to say something definitive about Puritan society, many readers have extrapolated from this narrow time and region and concluded that these findings could stand in for findings on early America more generally. To date, much less has been written about eighteenth-century same-sex sexuality.[5]

The gulf in the history of same-sex sexuality in eighteenth-century America is all the more pronounced, given the body of literature that exists on much of the early modern world. Scholarship on Renaissance and early modern Europe and Latin America has deepened our understanding of sodomy and same-sex sexuality before the nineteenth century. Scholarship on Renaissance texts has demonstrated how sodomy figured in broader discussions of state power, family formation, lineage and patriarchy, aristocratic corruption, and early modern masculinity. Scholarship on early Latin America has also shown important connections between masculinity and gender and same-sex sexuality. Other works have shown how sex between men in classical and early modern Mediterranean cultures, for example, provided culturally sanctioned space for sexual and romantic relations among men and boys.[6]

## Same-Sex Sex in Early America

In 1565, at St. Augustine, Florida, the Spanish established the first permanent European settlement in what would become the United States. According to research by Jonathan Katz, the earliest legal case of sodomy took place in Florida in 1566, when the Spanish condemned to death a "sodomite," a French Lutheran interpreter. Reports of sex between men among indigenous peoples date as far back as 1528, however, when Cabeza de Vaca wrote about "one man married to another" while living as a captive among the Indians of Florida. Other such statements in the sixteenth century came from observations by Europeans in California and later from Illinois.[7]

From early studies, we know a fair amount about early American official and ministerial teachings against sodomy and expressions of sexual desire between anyone other than husband and wife. Virtually all colonies outlawed male same-sex sexual activity and punishments ranged from ostracism, fines, whippings, and castration, to execution. But sodomy was not handled in the same manner everywhere. Among, as the above cases suggest, Native Americans, it was generally not considered a crime. In the seventeenth century, however, when Europeans established New France, New Spain, New Netherland, and New England, in all locales sodomy was criminalized. In colonial Spanish North America, in some cases individuals were exiled from communities. In colonial New England in 1629, the first recorded punishments for sodomy occurred on the ship *Talbot* in Massachusetts. The result was not execution but rather the "5 beastly Sodomiticall Boys" were returned to England for their crime. As previously acknowledged, in New England, courts took the most active role of any region in policing the population and therefore the majority of cases come from this time and place. Broadly construed, same-sex sexual intimacy was criminalized, as "sodomy" stood for a host of sexual transgressions. In New Haven, its own colony until the late seventeenth century, William Plaine was executed in 1646 for masturbating with "a great part of the youth of Gilford—above 100 tymes." In New Netherland in 1646, Jan Creoli, a slave who admitted that he had committed sodomy in the West Indies, was executed for forcibly sodomizing a ten-year-old African, one Manuel Congo. Creoli was strangled and then burnt at the stake. The boy, for taking part in the sinful act, was beaten. By 1664, the time of the English takeover of New Netherland, the Dutch had executed three individuals for sodomy. In the seventeenth-century British mainland colonies, men were executed in Virginia, New Netherland, and New Haven.[8]

Although courts in established colonies over time took a decreasingly active role in monitoring and enforcing norms of sexual behavior, well into the eighteenth century policing sodomy was one tool of the colonial project. Europeans used sodomy in an emblematic effort to destroy perceived wickedness among indigenous populations. But for some the focus on sodomy and other Christian sins was also a means to reform and civilize a supposedly heathen population. Elsewhere, Jonathan Goldberg has shown how this was part of the Spanish model of colonization. Tracy Brown's essay in part one looks at one particular case from eighteenth-century New Mexico and finds it to be part of the same colonial project.[9]

Broadly construed, sexuality in early British America shifted in the eighteenth century. As historian Richard Godbeer argues, sexuality in general made a shift in the eighteenth century that mirrors the well-charted course alteration American society made from community to individual. The explosion in print sources and rise of authorities and discourses outside of the church, and the broader diversification of the population and the economy, all combined to make the eighteenth century markedly different from the seventeenth-century British American colonies.[10]

Given the Enlightenment emphasis on individual rights and liberties, in the era of the American Revolution many crimes were removed from capital status. Although his plan was rejected, Thomas Jefferson proposed that sodomy in Virginia be punished by castration not execution. In 1777, Georgia's legislature also resisted making it noncapital. But in 1787, the Pennsylvania legislature made sodomy punishable by imprisonment, not death. Other states removed sodomy from the list of capital crimes in the long wake of the American Revolution: New York and New Jersey, for example, followed suit in 1796, Massachusetts in 1805, New Hampshire in 1812, Delaware in 1826, North Carolina in 1869, and South Carolina in 1873.[11]

## Sources for Studying "Hidden" Histories

In the 1960s, the historical profession began to explore the lives of ordinary people and lay individuals, a move nurtured by the liberation movements of the 1970s and identity politics of the 1980s and 1990s. Like the fields of African-American history, women's and gender history, working-class and labor history, and social history in general, the history of sexuality has benefited from studying history from the bottom-up (by looking at the lives of ordinary Americans), as well as from the top-down (focusing on official rhetoric and the lives of elites). It is this move away from official pronouncements of court and church that have had the greatest impact toward revising our understanding of same-sex sexuality in early America.

In many ways, the sources available to scholars of same-sex sexuality are no different from those available for other studies. Although court records provide the most obvious location, in colonial America, given the relative absence of cases, scholars, almost by necessity, have begun to look elsewhere. Clare Lyons in her examination of eighteenth-century Philadelphia, reprinted in part two, used not only imported literature but also lists of book borrowers to trace the transatlantic circulation of ideas of same-sex sexuality. Print culture offers one of the richest veins for examining imported ideas. Newspapers can provide evidence of both regional cases and awareness of those from afar. But Lyons also brilliantly employs "reading silences" in the historical record, for what one doesn't say often reveals as much as what one does articulate. Finally, personal papers provide glimpses of experience and identity.

Richard Godbeer's fresh examination of one of the earliest cases of sodomy, also reprinted in part two, draws heavily on court testimony and importantly charts the distinction between popular and official views of sex between men. Informed by the relatively recent emphasis on the lives and views of ordinary people, Godbeer turns his focus on the testimony of those involved in the court hearing of Nicholas Sension. By listening to what Sension's neighbors, servants, and townsmen had to say about his behavior, and their assessment of the man, himself, Godbeer moves us away from simply hearing the legal and religious absolutism. Indeed, Godbeer finds only shades of gray. Community members knew of Sension's sexual interest in servants and more often than not, turned something of a blind eye.

Even in his acknowledgment of the severe possible penalties for sodomy, Godbeer reminds us that Sension was not punished harshly by the courts. Relative leniency by the courts in New England is a story fairly familiar to scholars of colonial America. Works by Cornelia Dayton, Mary Beth Norton, and others have shown that colonial courts were interested primarily in securing communal harmony and in protecting social hierarchies of status, race, and gender, rather than enforcing the letter of the law. Juries consistently hesitated to convict middling white men of crimes, instead saving their harshest punishments for cultural outsiders, including men of color, transients, and poor men and women.[12]

Although court records and personal papers figure prominently in many of the essays here, print representations and the role of print undeniably played a critical role in the formulation of eighteenth-century American understandings of same-sex sexuality. Unlike the discourse of medical and psychological orientations that were fashioned from case histories and disseminated by medical treatises, eighteenth-century society developed an understanding of same-sex sexuality through a variety of popular print media.

## Acts and Identities

The essays in this volume situate same-sex sex in the legal, social, and cultural setting—but at the same time recognize that in colonial America and the early United States, it was at moments distinguishable and separable. What distinguishes the preindustrial world from the modern world is this ability of same-sex sexual desire and behavior to at times be similar to other sinful acts, that all individuals could be capable of, and at other times to appear distinct and unusual. In the modern world, same-sex sex becomes more consistently and firmly, if still inconsistently, attached to personhood and identity.

Nearly all scholars of preindustrial Europe and Latin America find that same-sex sexuality could be understood to be a part of a person's identity and conceptual categorization. In this way, sodomy as a simple, discreet, sinful "act" does little to describe the richness of sexual expression and identity in the early modern era. This calls into question the accuracy of the traditional manner of describing that difference between the modern and early modern world as a development of a same-sex sexual identity. Although psychological models for same-sex sexuality, and the terms *homosexual* and *heterosexual* are indeed modern, dating only from the late nineteenth and early twentieth centuries, the essays here indicate that the *acts-versus-identities* pronouncement is an oversimplification made from the vantage point of modernity and focusing on psychological models at the expense of others. Long before Stonewall, the history of same-sex sexuality took root and began establishing cultural precedents that later medical models drew upon.[13]

Just as today, there were a variety of ways that one's sexual behavior could influence one's identity in early America. Some saw it as a religious failing. Well-known Puritan and Harvard instructor, Michael Wigglesworth viewed his sexual desires for male pupils with disgust and horror. He saw this interest as a signal that he had not achieved spiritual favor and longed to purify himself of his lusts. But others saw it as part of a general interest in pleasures. Most would have recognized the dominant idea that self-control was absent in those who gave over to interest in a member of the same sex.[14]

All of the individuals discussed in this volume, in some measure, resisted social conventions of sexual expression and instead followed their own path to sexual, emotional, physical, or romantic satisfaction. Individuals punished by the courts resisted social restrictions by their very actions. Other records suggest that some Americans claimed an unrepentant defiance of norms of the day. But unlike today, although some groups of individuals did engage in group sex, generally there is little evidence that many stood together in open collective defiance of condemnation of the day. In part four, Stephen Shapiro's original reading of *Ormond*, however, challenges even this notion by pointing to novelist Charles Brockden Brown's emphasis, indeed strategy, for *collective* defiance of heteronormative social norms.

We also know that early Americans were aware that cooperative defiance was occurring in mother England. In eighteenth-century London and in other European cities, men had been congregating in "molly houses," semipublic clubs for socializing, sexual intimacy, and conviviality. A series of raids on these inns and popular public cruising spots led to numerous arrests and trials of men for sodomy. In some of the court records, individuals express outrage at their being harassed and view themselves as perfectly within their rights to seek out members of the same sex for sexual and romantic interactions. London newspaper accounts of molly house raids were selected to be reprinted in eighteenth-century newspapers in Massachusetts. While those colonials reading about these arrests may not have seen molly houses as part of American urban life, they would have learned that same-sex intimacy could be more than simply a wicked sinful act, it could be an expression of intimacy between members of the same sex, who defiantly chose to eschew normative patterns of integrating romance and sexuality into their lives.[15]

Private papers, court testimony, lay literature, popular print culture, and lives lived all show that same-sex sexual interest did in many cases come to characterize an individual's interior self. Individuals would not have understood their sexual interest in members of the same sex in the same way that early twentieth-century psychological models of sexuality created. Nonetheless the early modern interests in character and reputation and in connections between private vices and public virtues reveal much about the significance of sexual behavior outside of the "acts" rhetoric of the church or the courts.

## Long Before Stonewall

In part four, Mark Kann's examination of prison reform in the new nation underscores how sodomy could be a singular concern and part of a host of vices and sins. In the founding era, the shift away from punishing the body to reforming the self gave voice to notable concerns about same-sex sexuality, and in particular, sex between adult men and male youths. Kann finds that even in the early nineteenth century acts and identities as models for understanding sodomites vied for cultural play. The discourses of prison reform in the new nation importantly remind us that the development of sexual orientations has not only long roots—but also an uneven pattern of growth.

Some scholars have noted with concern the frustratingly high burden of evidence placed on scholars of sexuality and of same-sex sexuality, in particular. These scholars argue that historical figures are heterosexual until proven otherwise (beyond a shadow of a doubt). Elsewhere, current scholarship on several prominent historical figures innovatively reads clues and signals of same-sex sexual and romantic interest and argues that there may never be a "smoking gun" to locate the sexuality of such individuals. Work by Bob Arnebeck on Washington DC architect, Pierre L'Enfant, and first-son, Charles Adams, child of John and Abigail Adams, argues that records suggest both men may well have been homosexual. Similar work by William Benemann argues that Lewis of the famed exploratory team Lewis and Clark was likely homosexual, again by a preponderance of tantalizing evidence. The essays in this volume may focus more on cultural and social discourse about same-sex sexuality, than the behaviors and interests of individuals, but nonetheless share a similar concern with Arnebeck and Benemann in finding a history of same-sex sexuality by reading old sources in original ways.[16]

Scholars of same-sex sexuality have ground various lenses for viewing their subject. Some have argued that an exclusive focus on genital contact is either anachronistic or overly simplistic or both. In the early nineteenth century intensely romantic same-sex relationships for men and women were both commonplace and celebrated. The relationships arguably provided the sanctioned private opportunity for sexual relationships. Essays in part three demonstrate that studying homosocial relations can bring richness to our understanding of romantic and sexual relationships of the past. A reprint of Caleb Crain's examination of the close personal relationship of two men in the late eighteenth century, finds that intimacy in early America need not involve a record of genital expression. Similarly, an excerpt from Lillian Faderman's classic 1981 work, *Surpassing the Love of Men*, uses the novel *Ormond* to locate eighteenth-century same-sex relationship standards. Finally, in her original essay, Lisa Moore takes the pastoral poem of one early Republic woman and asks what it means that she wrote this poem, complete with female imagery and depictions of intimate relationships between two women, for a close female friend of hers. All of these examples tell us a great deal about opportunities for close personal bonds between members of the same sex.[17]

Several of the essays in this volume pay particular attention to racial discourses. Although the scholarship tends to privilege the study of Euro-Americans, in part because of the availability of sources, essays here both examine Anglo-American racialized homoerotics and shed light on same-sex sexuality within communities of color. Tracy Brown demonstrates that a legal case of sodomy in Spanish colonial New Mexico can be read for understandings of sodomy and intimacy not only between men in official Spanish colonial society but also among Pueblo Indians. Gunlög Fur's inquiry into Delaware Indian nation culture moves away from focusing on Anglo-American culture and takes up the question of what sodomy, same-sex sexuality, and homoeroticism meant to eighteenth-century Native Americans living in the northeastern American colonies. Ramón Gutiérrez begins this volume with an original essay that challenges the fundamental and widely held understanding of the berdache. Gutiérrez's controversial essay will likely spark more debate around how to interpret the figure. Was the berdache a figure of celebrated sexual and spiritual status and hence a historical role model for a queer movement today? Or has our historical knowledge of the berdache been misinformed by contemporary concerns seeking a positive queer history? In part four a reprint of John Saillant's examination of the homoerotics of abolitionist imagery suggests additional examples of racialized understandings of same-sex sexuality. Finally, Stephen Shapiro's discussion of Brown's gothic novel, *Ormond,* recognizes the racial boundaries that Brown plays with as being implicated in his examination of categories of gender, class, and sexuality.

The essays in this volume also shed light on early American associations of same-sex sexuality and gender. In particular, several essays question early American notions of transgender and transexuality. This theme is present in Brown's *Ormond,* which is discussed by both Faderman and Shapiro, and it is also raised by Gunlög Fur and by Tracy Brown as she probes court testimony for evidence that individuals believed one of the men involved in the sodomy case she examines, might have been a berdache. The subject of biological sex, same-sex sexuality, and gender performance is handled directly by Elizabeth Reis in her original examination of hermaphrodism.[18]

Others have looked outside of what might be considered same-sex to shed light on the history of same-sex sexuality. In her essay in part two, Anne Myles, for example, argues that we can learn much about the history of same-sex sexuality by studying how deviant religious practices in colonial New England mirror the marginalization of sexual practices. Her essay on the controversy over Quakers in Puritan New England asks what studying historical challenges to dominant models of family and sexuality can show us about the roots and trajectory of the position of homosexuals in later society.

Myles and others also demonstrate how queerness and sodomy could figure in cultural "othering" whereby same-sex behavior, or deviant sexual behavior in general, served to demarcate outsiders while simultaneously underscoring shared values and practices of the in-group. The sodomite as outsider or cultural other in this way could serve as a repository for concerns about the stability of the early American family, the foundation of the early American state, the strength of patriarchy, or the sexual power and prowess of white heterosexual manhood.

Some scholars have begun a history of *heterosexuality* that has dramatic implications for the history of homosexuality. Jonathan Katz's book on the nineteenth-century "invention of heterosexuality" has important implications for the development of homosexuality as he sees it. Laura Mandell's original essay in part four uses newspaper discussion of bachelorhood and marriage to plum the norms and ideals of heterosexuality in the new nation.[19]

My own work on heterosexuality, specifically on manliness and sexual incapacity, used seventeenth-century divorce records from New England, coupled with imported household and reproductive manuals to examine a discourse of marital sexuality and normative male sexuality in early New England. In addition to arguing for a standard of manliness that took into account sexual performance and virility, thereby enhancing our understanding of early modern masculinity by turning away from an exclusive focus on politics and commerce, the study also challenged the "acts versus identities" paradigm, given the evident connections between manly self and sexuality. By looking at understandings of impotent men, as sexually and socially different in disposition and body, the study found early modern sexuality—one that looked more modern than not.[20]

In June 1969, gay men, lesbians, bisexuals, and transgender individuals at the Stonewall Inn, a bar in New York City, refused to quietly comply with what had become commonplace harassment at gay bars, the police raid. In those days, kissing, holding hands, and cross-dressing could all justify a charge of indecency. But on this particular night and for several days, they violently resisted. Newspapers carried the story of the "Stonewall riot" (a local gay organization dubbed the event as "The Hairpin Drop Heard Round the World") and within a year's time gay rights organizers marked the occasion with reverence as the beginning of the modern gay rights movement. Ever since then, cities and towns around the country (and now around the globe), in ever increasing numbers, have celebrated the moment of resistance with summertime gay rights parades and celebrations. Stonewall became a symbol for the birth of a gay rights movement—a movement that for some, seemed to come out of nowhere.[21] Although Stonewall symbolically marks the start of the gay rights movement, a political movement had been building for nearly a century. And for centuries, Americans generated records that point us to those who held intimate and romantic desires for members of the same gender.

The essays in this volume sketch out same-sex sexualities in early America, particularly of the late colonial and early national periods, at the time of the nation's founding. But these histories should also give readers cause for reflection on the various ways that sex, sexuality, gender, race, class, and power are conceived of today and in their own lives. Regrettably, we will never know how many well-meaning family members destroyed the intimate same-sex confessions (or proud boastings) written in personal papers and in private diaries. Even in the early twentieth century some sexually explicit court records were sanitized before being transcribed and reprinted. But the scholars featured here continue the painstaking work of combing through extant papers and reading between the lines to recover long lost feelings, desires, and relationships.

### NOTES

1. Thomas A. Foster, *Sex and the Eighteenth-Century Man: Massachusetts and the History of Sexuality in America* (Boston: Beacon Press, 2006), 96–7, 169–73.

2. On the history of homosexuality in modern America see, for example, George Chauncey, *Gay New York: Gender, Urban Culture, and the Making of the Gay Male World, 1890–1940* (New York: Basic Books, 1994); John D'Emilio, *Sexual Politics, Sexual Communities: The Making of a Homosexual Minority in the United States, 1940–1970* (Chicago: University of Chicago Press, 1983); Lillian Faderman, *Odd Girls and Twilight Lovers: A History of Lesbian Life in Twentieth-Century America* (New York: Penguin, 1991); Jonathan Ned Katz, *Gay American History:*

*Lesbians and Gay Men in the U.S.A.* (New York: Thomas Y. Crowell, 1976); Katz, *Gay/Lesbian Almanac: A New Documentary* (New York: Harper & Row, 1983); and Elizabeth Lapovsky Kennedy and Madeline D. Davis, *Boots of Leather, Slippers of Gold: The History of a Lesbian Community* (New York: Routledge, 1993).

3. On sexuality in early America, see, for example, Sharon Block, *Rape and Sexual Power in Early America* (Chapel Hill: UNC Press for OIEAHC, 2006); Cornelia Dayton, *Women before the Bar: Gender, Law, and Society in Connecticut, 1639–1789* (Chapel Hill: UNC Press for the OIEAHC, 1995); Kirsten Fischer, *Suspect Relations: Sex, Race, and Resistance in Colonial North Carolina* (Ithaca: Cornell University Press, 2002); Foster, *Sex and the Eighteenth-Century Man*; Richard Godbeer, *Sexual Revolution in Early America* (Baltimore: Johns Hopkins University Press, 2002); Clare A. Lyons, *Sex Among the Rabble: An Intimate History of Gender and Power in the Age of Revolution, Philadelphia, 1730–1830* (Chapel Hill: UNC Press for the OIEAHC, 2006); Merril D. Smith, ed., *Sex and Sexuality in Early America* (New York: NYU Press, 1998); Roger Thompson, *Sex in Middlesex: Popular Mores in a Massachusetts County, 1649–1699* (Amherst: University of Massachusetts Press, 1986).

4. Katz, *Gay American History*; Katz, *Gay/Lesbian Almanac.*

5. On sodomy in the seventeenth century see, Alan Bray, "To Be a Man in Early Modern Society: The Curious Case of Michael Wigglesworth," *History Workshop Journal* 41 (1996): 155–65; Richard Godbeer, " 'The Cry of Sodom': Discourse, Intercourse, and Desire in Colonial New England," in this volume; John M. Murrin, " 'Things Fearful to Name': Bestiality in Colonial America," *Pennsylvania History* 65 (1998): 8–43; Robert Oaks, " 'Things Fearful to Name': Sodomy and Buggery in Seventeenth-Century New England," in *The American Man,* eds. Elizabeth H. Pleck and Joseph H. Pleck (Englewood Cliffs, NJ: Prentice Hall, 1980), 53–76; Colin L. Talley, "Gender and Male Same-Sex Erotic Behavior in British North America in the Seventeenth Century," *Journal of the History of Sexuality* 6 (1996): 385–408; Roger Thompson, "Attitudes Towards Homosexuality in the Seventeenth-Century New England Colonies," *Journal of American Studies* 23 (1989): 27–40; Thompson, *Sex in Middlesex*; Michael Warner, "New English Sodom," *American Literature* 64 (March, 1992): 19–47.

6. On the Renaissance see, Josiah Blackmore and Gregory S. Hutcheson, eds., *Queer Iberia: Sexualities, Cultures, and Crossings from the Middle Ages to the Renaissance* (Durham: Duke University Press, 1999); Alan Bray, *Homosexuality in Renaissance England* (New York: Columbia University Press, 1995); Gregory W. Bredbeck, *Sodomy and Interpretation, Marlowe to Milton* (Ithaca: Cornell University Press, 1991); Louise Fradenburg and Carla Freccero, eds., *Premodern Sexualities* (New York: Routledge, 1996); Jonathan Goldberg, *Sodometries: Renaissance Texts, Modern Sexualities* (Stanford: Stanford University Press, 1992); Goldberg, *Queering the Renaissance* (Durham: Duke University Press, 1994); Michael Rocke, *Forbidden Friendships: Homosexuality and Male Culture in Renaissance Florence* (New York:

Oxford University Press, 1996). On colonial Latin America see the excellent collection by Pete Sigal, ed., *Infamous Desire: Male Homosexuality in Colonial Latin America* (Chicago: University of Chicago Press, 2003). On early modern Spain and New Spain see Federico Garz Carvajal, *Perceptions of Manliness in Andalucia and Mexico, 1561–1699* (Amsterdam: Amsterdamse Historische Reeks, 2000).

7. Jonathan Katz, *Gay American History*; Katz, *Gay/Lesbian Almanac*.

8. Ibid.

9. Carvajal, *Perceptions of Manliness in Andalucia and Mexico, 1561–1699*; Godbeer, *Sexual Revolution in Early America*; Jonathan Goldberg, *Sodometries*, 179–222.

10. Jonathan Katz, *Gay American History*; Katz, *Gay/Lesbian Almanac*.

11. Kathleen Brown, *Good Wives, Nasty Wenches, and Anxious Patriarchs: Gender, Race, and Power in Colonial Virginia* (Chapel Hill: UNC Press for OIEAHC, 1996); Dayton, *Women Before the Bar*; Fischer, *Suspect Relations*; Godbeer, *Sexual Revolution in Early America*; and Mary Beth Norton, *Founding Mothers and Fathers: Gendered Power and the Forming of American Society* (New York: Vintage Books, 1997).

12. On "acts versus identities" see, for example, Michel Foucault, *The History of Sexuality: An Introduction*, trans. Robert Hurley (New York: Pantheon Books, 1978); and John D'Emilio and Estelle Freedman, *Intimate Matters: A History of Sexuality in America* (New York: Harper & Row, 1988). Kim M. Phillips and Barry Reay, eds., *Sexualities in History: A Reader* (New York: Routledge, 2002). Scholarship on sexuality in early modern Europe has offered significant challenges to this paradigm, while studies of early America have not.

13. Edmund S. Morgan, ed., *Diary of Michael Wigglesworth, 1653–1657: The Conscience of a Puritan* (New York: Harper & Row, 1965).

14. On molly houses, see Alan Bray, *Homosexuality in Renaissance England* (New York: Columbia University Press, 1995), 89–104; Randolph Trumbach, *Sex and the Gender Revolution: Volume One, Heterosexuality and the Third Gender in Enlightenment London* (Chicago: University of Chicago Press, 1998); Stephen Shapiro, "Of Mollies: Class and Same-Sex Sexualities in the Eighteenth-Century," in *In a Queer Place: Sexuality and Belonging in British and European Contexts*, eds. Kate Chedgzoy, Emma Francis, and Murray Pratt (Burlington, VT: Ashgate, 2002), 154–76.

15. Foster, *Sex and the Eighteenth-Century Man*.

16. See Bob Arnebeck's work at http://www.geocities.com/bobarnebeck/LEnfant .htm; William Benemann on Lewis and Clark http://www.law.berkeley.edu/library/ staff/benemann/Text02.doc

17. Carroll Smith-Rosenberg, "The Female World of Love and Ritual: Relations between Women in Nineteenth-Century America," *Signs*, 1 (Autumn 1975), pp. 1–29.

18. Joanne Meyerowitz, *How Sex Changed: A History of Transsexuality in the*

*United States* (Cambridge: Harvard University Press, 2002); Susan Stryker and Stephen Whittle, eds., *The Transgender Studies Reader* (New York: Routledge, 2006).

19. Jonathan Ned Katz, *Invention of Heterosexuality* (New York: Penguin, 1995).

20. Thomas A. Foster, "Deficient Husbands: Manhood, Sexual Incapacity, and Male Marital Sexuality in Seventeenth-Century New England," *WMQ* 56 (October 1999): 723–44. On eighteenth century see, Foster, *Sex and the Eighteenth-Century Man.*

21. Hairpin quote from Martin Duberman, *Stonewall* (New York: A Dutton Book, 1993), as cited by D'Emilio, *Sexual Politics, Sexual Communities,* 232.

# Part I

# Colonial Native Americas

# Chapter 1

# Warfare, Homosexuality, and Gender Status Among American Indian Men in the Southwest

## Ramón A. Gutiérrez

For the last forty years, and particularly since the height of the gay libera-tion movement, there has been a rather prolific scholarly project commit-ted to a quest for the historical roots of contemporary homosexuality. In this search for older forms, alternative patterns, and cultural variants of signification of sexual behavior between and among men, one can point to the absolutely catalytic documentary history that Jonathan Katz edited. In his massive and foundational *Gay American History: Lesbians and Gay Men in the U.S.A.* (1976), Katz chronicled patterns of homosexuality in what is now the United States from pre-Columbian times to the present. Among the many things that he uncovered were the shards of a Native American tradition that was known only to a few anthropologists, and be-fore that, to a number of early sixteenth-century European explorers and missionaries.[1] Called berdache by Europeans and by a more complex set of indigenous terms in the Americas, these men who had sex with other men were particularly fascinating. Not only did they offer exclusive sexual service to members of their own sex, but they also were transvested as women and performed women's work.

A number of historians and anthropologists were fascinated by this dis-covery and set out to chronicle the berdache tradition. They saw in it a po-tential model for childhood socialization that might ultimately lead to gay liberation, and if not that, at least a path toward a more gender tolerant society for tomboys and sissies to develop into lesbians and gays. While American scholars have called the berdache a "third sex," a "fourth sex," "two-spirited persons," and "man/woman," to the Zuñi Indians they were *la'mana,* to the Tewa they were *quetho,* and to the Navajo they were *nadle.*[2] The berdache putatively embodied both the masculine and the feminine, moved easily between the segregated worlds of indigenous men and women, and offered moderns an alternative, more natural and less constrained way to live and love. Anthropologists like Will Roscoe and Walter L. Williams celebrated the berdache, situating them in mystical New Age worlds, heralding their primitive premodern ways, unfettered by homophobic cultures, and free of rigid masculine and feminine gender roles.[3] Many of these unwitting projections backward of the then contemporary gay liberation moment's politics of yearning profoundly distorted the history of the berdache. As will be argued below, what we mainly know about the history of the berdache has them located in warps of masculine power, in warfare, slavery and exploitation, not in worlds of egalitarian possibilities and of gender harmony and accord. The lives of the berdache were lives of humiliation and endless work, not of celebration and veneration.

Here we will study historically how the berdache were first described by European colonial soldiers and priests in the 1500s, where they were located socially in the gender division of labor; and whom and how they served. Clearly these European observers came with a set of biases that were hard for them to overcome, but they nevertheless were intent on trying to understand indigenous social organization in order to conquer and eventually exploit the natives, or in the case of the missionaries, to Christianize.

While this historical excursion will be limited primarily to those areas previously under Spanish control that ultimately became part of what is today the American Southwest, larger hemispheric patterns and longer historical trends will also be noted. Native American berdache still exist among many tribal groups in North and South America. Here we reference their experiences particularly as they illuminate larger historical patterns and permutations of longer institutional histories.

When Spanish soldiers and missionaries first saw Native American men pressed into impersonating females, forced to perform women's work, dressing as women, and offering receptive sexual service only to men, they asserted that these individuals were living in *bradaje. Bradaje* as a word was derived from the Arabic *bradaj,* which means male prostitute; hence the English word berdache. *Bradaje* was something Europeans were quite familiar with in the fifteenth and sixteenth centuries, having inherited it themselves from East Asia and Islamic Africa where it was extensive. When they found men so employed in Florida and New Mexico, in central Mexico and in the highlands of Peru, they were not particularly surprised and described in a rather matter of fact fashion what they saw. Missionary moralists on campaigns to propagate Christian marriage quite naturally expressed great revulsion over what appeared to be "marriages" between men. In the ecclesiastical lexicon of the day, what was being practiced was clearly the sin against nature, or sodomy, which inhibited marriage and the propagation of children, which after all was the only real purpose of human sexuality.

One of the earliest descriptions of *bradaje* is found in the narrative of Alvar Núñez Cabeza de Vaca, published in 1542, recounting events from 1528 to 1536. Núñez Cabeza de Vaca was second in command of the 1528 expedition of Pánfilo de Narvaez, which had sailed from Hispaniola to conquer Florida. The conquering party failed miserably, stranding Núñez Cabeza de Vaca and his compatriots in Florida. Fashioning makeshift rafts to return to Cuba, they were instead swept by Caribbean currents to the shore of Louisiana. From there they walked in a westward direction across what is now Texas, New Mexico, and southern Arizona for some five years, before turning south into northwestern Mexico. There, in 1536, near Culiacán, Sinaloa, Spanish slave-raiders encountered Alvar Núñez Cabeza de Vaca and three lone survivors of the expedition. Recalling what he had seen on the northeastern coast of Texas, Núñez wrote: "I saw a wicked behavior (*diablura*), and it is that I saw one man married (*casado*) to another, and these are effeminate, impotent men (*unos hombres amarionados impotents*). And they go about covered like women, and they perform the tasks of women, and they do not use a bow, and they carry very great loads. And among these we saw many of them, thus unmanly as I say, and they are more muscular than other men and taller; they suffer very large loads."[4] When Núñez Cabeza de Vaca noted the berdache dressed as women, he himself stood completely naked among indigenous male warriors, who were themselves naked.

Commenting further on marriage and the division of labor among the Yguaces, a neighboring indigenous group, Núñez stated, "when these Indians are to marry, they buy women from their enemies, and the price that each one pays for his is a bow, the best that can be found, with two arrows, and if by chance he has no bow, then a net. . . . Among these people, the men do not burden themselves nor carry anything of weight, rather, the women and the old people, who are the ones they value the least, carry it. . . . The women are very hardworking and endure a great deal, because of the twenty-four hours there are between day and night, they have only six of rest, and the rest of the night they spend in firing their ovens in order to dry those roots they eat. And from daybreak, they begin to dig and bring firewood and water to their homes, and put in order the other thing of which they have need. . . . There are some among them who practice sodomy (*pecado contra natura*).[5] From these descriptions womanhood was associated with a virtual state of slavery. Women were purchased cheaply and made to work cooking and hauling loads endlessly, activities that warriors in their prime refused to do.

Ten years after the Núñez account of his travels in Texas and New Mexico was published in Spain, it became one of the main sources Francisco López de Gómera relied on for his own widely read and cited *Historia de las Indias* (1552). López de Gómera concluded two things about the transvested men who married other men. First, they were "impotent or castrated" (*impotents o capados*). Second, they were denied access to the instruments of war, "for they could neither carry nor shoot arrows," though clearly marched into battle with warriors, hauling their load and servicing their needs.[6] Fixating on the fact that the berdache were "more muscular than other men and taller," López de Gómera concluded that what Núñez had described were eunuchs. For when men were castrated in youth, it was not uncommon for them to grow taller and more muscular.[7] When a century later the Jesuit priest Andrés Pérez de Ribas described some transvestites he had observed in the northwestern Mexican state of Sinaloa, their basic social location and role in the division of labor remained unchanged. Pérez de Ribas affirmed that the berdache "do not use the bow and arrow; rather, some of them dress like women."[8]

Among the many things Alvar Núñez Cabeza de Vaca told the viceroy of New Spain in 1536, about his trek across Texas, New Mexico, and Arizona, was that he had heard that the Pueblo Indians of New Mexico and Arizona had cities of gold. Determined to conquer them in 1540, Francisco Vásquez de Coronado led a grand expedition north into the land of the Pueblo Indians, where he found little except large cities made of mud. Pedro de Castañeda, the official chronicler of the Coronado expedition, presents one of the most extensive descriptions of the geographic distribution of berdache. As the conquering party marched northward up the western coast of Mexico toward the Gulf of California, Castañeda describes finding men transvested as women around Culiacán, Sinaloa, among the Tahus of southern Arizona, among the Pacaxes in the foothills of the Sinaloan Sierras, among the Indians near the mouth of the Colorado River, and in the Suyo Valley on the border of Arizona. All these people were "grand sodomites," attested Castañeda, with men enjoying sexual service from other men.[9]

Not far from New Mexico Castañeda described a 1540 berdache initiation he had witnessed that began in a male ceremonial chamber, or *kiva*, by transvesting the male in female garb. Then,

> the *dignitaries* came in to make use of her one at a time, and after them all the others who cared to. From then on she was not to deny herself to any one, and she was paid a certain established amount for the service. And even though she might take a husband later on, she was not thereby free to deny herself to any one who offered her pay.[10]

Hernando de Alarcón, also a soldier with the Coronado expedition, further reported that the berdache "could not have carnal relations with women at all, but they themselves could be used by all marriageable youths." Indeed, it was such sexual service that led the Spaniards to also refer to the berdache as *putos* or male whores.[11]

As was just noted, in Pueblo Indian gifting practices, anyone who wanted to have sex with the chief's berdache was expected to pay. Recounting what he had seen during the conquest of New Mexico's Pueblo Indians, Gaspar Pérez de Villagrá wrote in 1610 that "the natives brought a great number of beautiful many blankets, which they gathered together, hoping to entice with them the Castilian women whom they liked and coveted." The Indian men desired sexual intercourse not only with the Spanish women that accompanied the soldiers, but also with the young male soldiers. "If a youth in our company had not cried out for help, he would have been attacked," noted Villagrá, because "these people are addicted to the bestial wicked sin [of sodomy]."[12]

Three hundred years later, in 1852, Dr. William A. Hammond, the United States Surgeon General, traveled through New Mexico and was particularly fascinated by the transvested men he met at the pueblos of Laguna and Acoma. Calling the berdache "*amujerado,*" literally a person made woman-like, he described them as the persons used "in the saturnalia or orgies, in which these Indians, like the ancient Greeks, Egyptians and other nations, indulge. He is the chief passive agent in the pederastic ceremonies, which form so important a part in the performances. These take place in the Spring of every year."[13]

Hammond added that when a man was transvested and pressed into a berdache status sexually serving other men: "he is at once relieved of all power and responsibility, and his influence is at an end. If he is married, his wife and children pass from under his control."[14]

That the berdache were consistently described as men abnormally tall and heavy led Fray Juan Agustín de Morfi in the 1770s and Dr. Hammond in the 1850s to wonder if they were eunuchs. Morfi pondered the matter and admitted uncertainty. Hammond, the rational scientist that he was, decided to explore the "facts." Hammond asked to perform a physical exam on a berdache from Acoma Pueblo. While an Indian male undoubtedly would have protested if a similar request had been made to examine a wife or daughter, in this case the town chief agreed, brought his berdache to Hammond, and remained there throughout the examination. Reporting what he had learned in this and in a similar examination at Laguna Pueblo, to his great amazement, neither was a hermaphrodite. Both had scant pubic hair, small penises ("no larger than a thimble," "not . . . over an inch in length"), and small testicles ("the size of a small filbert," "about the size of a kidney bean"). More significant were the comments Hammond elicited from the Acoma berdache: "He informed me with evident pride, [that he] possessed a large penis and his testicles were '*grande como huevos*'—as large as eggs."[15]

Our next ethnographic descriptions come from more recent times, from Zuñi Pueblo in western New Mexico, between 1830 and 1930. Here three female American anthropologists—Matilda Coxe Stevenson, Elsie Clew Parsons, Ruth Benedict—described the activities of a berdache named We'wha and a number of men who were known locally as *la'mana*, who were similarly transvested, doing women's work, and servicing men. Matilda Coxe Stevenson described We'wha in 1904 as "the tallest person in Zuñi; certainly the strongest." During an 1890 fracas with American soldiers from Fort Wingate, We'wha was apprehended fighting alongside Zuñi's governor and members of the warrior society (the Bow priests). When Zuñi men staged their own religious rituals, observed Elsie Clew Parsons in 1916, the *la'mana* dressed like a woman, styled his hair like a woman, and then personified a woman in dance. Yet, when a *la'mana* died, the corpse was dressed like a woman except that "under the woman's skirt a pair of trousers are put on." *La'mana* were always buried among the men. Indeed, the Zuñi would say of We'wha, "she is a man."[16] Matilda Coxe Stevenson observed in 1904 that "the men of the family . . . not only discourage men from unsexing [that is, becoming *la'mana*] . . . but ridicule them." Parsons noted a similar fact about Zuñi's *la'mana* in 1916: "in general a family would be somewhat ashamed of having a *la'mana* among its members." Of a *la'mana* named U'k, Parsons attested that, "U'k was teased . . . by the children." During one of the sha'lko dances Parsons witnessed at Zuñi, the audience "grinned and even chuckled" at U'k; "a very infrequent display of amusement during these sha'lko dances," Parsons confided. After the dance ended, Parson's Cherokee hostess asked her: "Did you notice them laughing at her [U'k]? . . . She is a great joke to the people."[17]

In Pueblo Indian religious ideology all rituals and all ceremonial roles within these rites have supernatural antecedents that are said to originate in mythic times in the actions of the gods. Aware of this fact both Stevenson and Parsons were told that the Zuñi myth, known as "Destruction of the Kia'nakwe, and Songs of Thanksgiving," explained the origins of the *la'mana*. As Stevenson explained, "in the Zuñi dramatization of the *kia'-nakwe* dance of thanksgiving for the capture of the gods the one impersonating the Kor'kokshi wears women's dress and is referred to as the *ko'thlama*, meaning "a man who has permanently adopted female attire." Parsons was told in 1916 that the reason the *la'mana* performed in the *kia'-nakwe* dance was "because together with other *ko'ko* [gods] he [the *la'-mana*] was taken prisoner by the kia'nakwe."[18]

Both Stevenson and Parsons observed that the *la'mana* who personified Kor'kokshi during this ceremonial not only wore female clothes, but also had blood smeared between his thighs. As women, Stevenson and Parsons were predisposed to assume that a man dressed as a woman with blood between his thighs signified menstruation. But Pueblo men greatly feared menstruating women and believed that they had the power to pollute male ritual. For four days before and also during their own male rituals they abstained from having sex with women, but clearly had sex with men. It thus seems highly unlikely that men would have been representing a menstruating woman in their rites. Rather, since the Kia'nakwe dance is about the capture and vanquishment of enemies, the blood might be explained more adequately as coming from a torn anus due to homosexual rape or from castration.[19]

Stevenson transcribed the myth "Destruction of the Kia'nakwe, and Songs of Thanksgiving," which recounts the details of a war between the Zuñi gods and a group known as the Kia'nakwe. On the second night of what would be four days of fasting, U'yuyewi and Matsai'lema, the Zuñi Twin War Gods, the principal deities of warfare in this pueblo, were dispatched to Ko'thluwala'wa. As the myth states:

To implore the Council of the gods to cause rainfall, that the A'shiwi bow-strings, which were made of yucca fiber, might be made strong, and the bowstrings of the enemy, made of deer sinew, might be weakened. The A'shiwi secured their arrows for the engagement with the Kia'nakwe on Ko'yemshi mountain. The prayers of the A'shiwi brought heavy rains on the third morning and again they met the enemy. This time their forces were strengthened by the Kok'ko, present at the request of U'yuyewi and Mat-sai'lema, who were now the recognized Gods of War. Again Ku'yapalitsa, the Cha'kwena [Warrior Woman], walked in front of her army, shaking her rat-tle. She succeeded in capturing one [??] of the gods from Ko'thluwala'wa—Kor'kokshi, the first born of Si'wulutsiwa and Si'wulutsitsa; It'tsepasha (game-maker), one of the nine last-born; a Sa'yathlia (blue horn, a warrior god); and a Sha'lako (one of the couriers to the u'wannami (rain-makers). These gods succeeded in making their escape, but all were captured except the Sha'lako, who ran so like a hare that he could not be caught. The Kia'-nakwe had a dance in which the prisoner gods appeared in celebration of their capture. Kor'kokshi, the first-born, was so angry and unmanageable that Ku'yapalitsa had him dressed in female attire previous to the dance, saying to him: "You will now perhaps be less angry."[20]

This exhaustive survey of the textual evidence we have on the history of the berdache tradition in Mexico's north and in what became the American Southwest, provides enough glimpses to answer the question of whether *bradaje* was a celebrated and permissive gender role that encom-passed both the masculine and the feminine. Was one socialized to this role? Was it freely chosen? Or was it a status of subordination and humili-ation individuals were forced to accept? From the Spanish colonial sources presented here, berdache are first and foremost encountered in the battle-field, in campaigns against enemies. They were unarmed, hauling loads, cloaked as females, cooking, and offering sex to men, and thus essentially doing women's work. That berdache were generally described as biological males who were stronger and taller than most, who were forced to carry enormous burdens, and who dressed as women in the company of naked warriors, as Núñez attested in 1536, further illuminates their status as rooted in the logic of the battlefield and the heat of war. Wearing clothes, particularly those of women, marked the berdache's subordinate status and their enslavement, as again Núñez suggests when he described the Yguaces of Texas. And if there is still any doubt about the origins of ber-dache status, the Zuñi myth about the "Destruction of the Kia'nakwe, and

Songs of Thanksgiving" is explicit and unequivocal. The myth as ritualized in ceremonial, attested Matilda Cox Stevenson's informants, was a celebration about the conquest and imprisonment of male enemy gods who were undoubtedly homosexually raped or castrated—recall the blood between their thighs—and then further humiliated by having to dress as women and do their slavish work. The evidence here indicates the *la'mana* of Zuñi, the *amujerados* of Acoma and Laguna, and the *bradaje* of northern Mexico were far from celebrated or revered individuals on the battlefields or in local affairs. Rather they were laughed at even by local children, deemed foolish, and considered jokes. They lost their social standing and their family and serviced the whims of their master said Dr. Hammond.[21]

In the Old World and in the New, there was a rather universal gender representation of conquest: victors on vanquishing their enemies asserted their virility by transforming losers into effeminates. We know that heterosexual rape was a common habit of war. What we are only now starting to admit is that men defeated in war were similarly treated and forced to perform demeaning forms of sexual service for other men, allowing themselves to be anally mounted and fellating their new lords. Thus, it does not matter much whether we examine slave male prisoners of war among the Zuñi or the Arawaks, the Aztecs or the Incas, to understand what is so graphically depicted on those numerous pre-Columbian Moche potter figurines from northern Peru that depict slaves in women's clothes being passively penetrated in homosexual intercourse. Status inversion marked through gender symbols has rather universally been associated with defeated men.[22]

Conquest narratives, travelers' accounts, and ethnographies indicate that the social status of the berdache had meaning primarily in the sociopolitical world of men. Berdache were reported as being under male ownership; it was the town chief after all that presented his berdache to Dr. Hammond for examination in the 1850s. Taken from the battlefield and brought into the center of political society, the berdache were always kept in the ceremonial chambers within which men lived and in which they performed the rituals that kept rival factions in a community from tearing the town apart.[23]

Until quite recently, residential segregation by sex was the rule in every Pueblo Indian town in New Mexico and Arizona. Pedro de Castañeda, one of New Mexico's first explorers, observed in 1541 that the "young men live in the *estufas* [kivas or male ceremonial lodges] . . . it is punishable for the women to sleep in the *estufas* or to enter them for any other purpose than to bring food to their husbands and sons." Diego Pérez de Luxán reiterated this point in 1582, as did Fray Gerónimo Zárate Salmerón when he wrote in 1623: "The women and young children sleep in the [houses]; the men sleep in the kiva."[24]

Segregated from women in their *kivas,* men practiced the religious or political lore that kept the community at peace with itself and with its gods. Women's rituals, centered in the household, celebrated their feminine powers over seed life and human reproduction. Their powers to bring forth life were immense and predictable. Men's magical powers over war, hunting, curing, and rainmaking—the basic preoccupations of Pueblo Indian life—were always more unpredictable and precarious, and thus more elaborately ritualized. From men's perspective, women's capacity to produce, indeed to overproduce, was the problem that threatened to destroy the balance that existed in the cosmos between femininity and masculinity. Only by isolating themselves in ritual and placating the gods would men keep potent femininity from destroying everything. Women constantly sapped men of their energy. Men had to toil in the fields that belonged to their mothers and wives, they had to protect the village from internal, external, natural, and supernatural enemies, and they constantly had to give semen to their voracious wives. Men got nothing in return from women in this agricultural society, for even if women bore children, until puberty those children belonged to their mothers.[25]

It is in this isolated and fragile world of masculine political ritual that we must place berdache, the *amujerados,* and the *la'mana.* Male Pueblo rituals were highly stratified. Men who became war chiefs were persons with enormous political power by virtue of their physical strength, their cunning, and their psychological acumen. No doubt this is why many berdache wearing dresses were described as big and strong; clearly they were defeated prisoners of war. It should thus not surprise us that the men who were pressed into berdache status were there primarily to service and delight their conquering chief. Recall that 1540 description offered by Pedro de Castañeda recounting how in the male ceremonial chamber he had witnessed a recent prisoner of war first sexually mounted by the dignitaries, then offered as a sign of generosity to other males who wished to have him, and finally pimped by his master to anyone willing to pay.[26] Some three hundred years later the berdache were still playing a comparable ritual role, noted Dr. William A. Hammond in 1851. The *amujerado* was the "the chief passive agent in the pederastic ceremonies."

In Pueblo life, unmarried bachelors and junior men spent most of their time in the kivas. Ostensibly this was so that they could master religious lore, but in reality, it was also to minimize conflicts between juniors and seniors over access to female sexuality that only adult married men enjoyed. Sex with a berdache not only serviced the personal erotic needs of junior men, but it was also an assertion of power by these young men that served a religious (political) end. So long as bachelors were having sex with the berdache, their village was not beset with conflicts between men over women. For as Hernando de Alarcón would note in 1540, berdache "could not have carnal relations with women at all, but they themselves could be used by all marriageable youths." This may have been the reason why the Spaniards also referred to the berdache as *putos,* or male whores. European prostitutes, both male and female, initiated young men to sexuality and gave married men a sexual outlet without disrupting power relations among senior men over family, marriage, and patrimonies. Male prisoners of war pressed into prostitution in women's clothes were living testaments to their conqueror's virility and prowess. When a berdache was offered to guests as a gesture of generosity and hospitality, this too testified to the master's power. And like every slave historically, the berdache became economic assets when pimped and sold to other men, so that they too could play out their fantasies of domination.[27]

In thinking about the meaning of the berdache among American Indians we can enormously expand our understanding by studying gender as a status rather than a role. It is equally important that when we pluck out an individual from their cultures, be it We'wha, U'k, or the countless other berdache and *la'mana* that once lived, it is our responsibility to place them in that context of power that gender differences represented, be they born of nature or of war. As for gay liberationists who seek a less rigid gender hierarchy in which to grow and prosper, the berdache status as a gender representation of power rooted in war is not the place to find it. When facts are misinterpreted with the goal of finding gay models of liberation where they do not exist, we perpetuate on We'wha, U'k, and all the berdache that once existed yet another level of humiliation while shrouding their enslavement and rape, their pimping and their pandering in romantic webs of obfuscation.

### NOTES

1. Jonathan Katz, *Gay America History: Lesbians and Gay Men in the U.S.A.* (New York: Crowell, 1976).

2. Elsie Clew Parsons, "The Zuñi La'Mana," *American Anthropologist* 18 (1916): 521–28; Sue-Ellen Jacobs, "Berdache: A Brief Review of the Literature," *Colorado Anthropologist* 1 (1968): 25–40; W. W. Hill, "The Status of the Hermaphrodite and Transvestite in Navaho Culture," *American Anthropologist* 37 (1935): 273–79; E. W. Gifford, "Cultural Elements Distribution: XII Apache-Pueblo," *University of California Anthropological Records* 4 (1940): 4–90; Jesse Walter Fewkes, "A Few Tusayan Pictographs," *American Anthropologist* 5 (1892): 9–26.

3. Will Roscoe, *The Zuni Man-Woman* (Albuquerque: University of New Mexico Press, 1991), and *Changing Ones: Third and Fourth Genders in Native North America* (London: Macmillan Press, 1998). Walter L. Williams, *The Spirit and the Flesh: Sexual Diversity in American Indian Culture* (Boston: Beacon Press, 1986).

4. Álvar Núñez Cabeza de Vaca, *The Narrative of Cabeza de Vaca*, edited, translated, and with an introduction by Rolena Adorno and Patrick Charles Pautz (Lincoln: University of Nebraska Press, 1999), pp. 131–32. Cyclone Covey's translation and edition of Cabeza de Vaca's *Adventures in the Unknown Interior of America* (Albuquerque: University of New Mexico Press, 1983), translates "*hombres amarionados impotents*" as "eunuchs" and explicitly refers to their sexual mutilation; see p. 100. Covey clearly had consulted López de Gómera's 1552 *Historia de las Indias,* which largely glossed Núñez Cabeza de Vaca's statements.

5. Núñez, *The Narrative of Cabeza de Vaca,* pp. 106–07.

6. Francisco López de Gómera, *Historia de las Indias* (Madrid: Atlas, 1946), p. 182.

7. Richard C. Trexler, *Sex and Conquest: Gender Construction and Political Order at the Time of the European Conquest of the Americas* (London: Polity Press, 1995), p. 67.

8. Andrés Pérez de Ribas, *Páginas para la historia de Sinaloa y Sonora; triunfos de nuestra santa fe entre gentes las mas barbaras y fieras del Nuevo Orbe,* 3 vols. (Mexico City: 1944), vol. 1, p. 132, as quoted in ibid., p. 66.

9. George Hammond and Agapito Rey, eds. and trans., *Narratives of the Coronado Expedition, 1540–1542* (Albuquerque: University of New Mexico Press, 1940).

10. Hammond and Rey, *Narratives of the Coronado Expedition,* pp. 147–48.

11. Ibid.

12. Gaspar Pérez de Villagrá, *History of New Mexico, Alcalá, 1610,* trans. Gilberto Espinosa (Los Angeles: Quivira Society, 1933), p. 141.

13. Hammond and Rey, *Narratives of the Coronado Expedition,* pp. 147–48.

14. Harry Hay, "The Hammond Report," *One Institute Quarterly* 6 (1963), p. 11.

15. Fray Juan Agustín Morfi as cited in W. W. Newcomb, *The Indians of Texas from Prehistoric to Modern Times* (Austin: University of Texas Press, 1961), p. 74; William A. Hammond, "The Disease of the Scythians (*Morbus Feminarum*) and Certain Analogous Conditions," *American Journal of Neurology and Psychiatry* I (1882): 339–55, quotes from 334–36.

16. Parsons, "The Zuñi La'mana," p. 529.

17. Matilda Cox Stevenson, *The Zuñi Indians: Their Mythology, Esoteric Fraternities, and Ceremonies* (Washington, D.C.: Smithsonian Institution, 1904), p. 37; Parsons, pp. 526–28.

18. Ibid.

19. Stevenson, *The Zuñi Indians*, pp. 36–37; Parsons, "The Zuñi La'mana," p. 525.

20. Stevenson, *The Zuñi Indians*, pp. 36–37.

21. Hay, "The Hammond Report," p. 11.

22. Richard Trexler, *Public Life in Renaissance Florence* (New York: Academic Press, 1980).

23. On berdache as shamans see Williams, *The Spirit and the Flesh.*

24. Hammond and Rey, *Narratives of the Coronado Expedition*, pp. 254–55; George Hammond and Agapito Rey, eds. and trans., *The Rediscovery of New Mexico, 1580–1594* (Albuquerque: University of New Mexico Press, 1966), p. 178; Fray Gerónimo Zárate Salméron, *Relación, an account of things seen and learned by Father Gerónimo de Zárate Salmerón from the year 1538 to year 1626* (Albuquerque: Horn and Wallace, 1966), paragraph 74.

25. H. Haeberlin, *The Idea of Fertilization in the Culture of the Pueblo Indians* (New York: American Anthropological Association, 1916); Jane Collier, *Marriage in Classless Societies* (Stanford: Stanford University Press, 1988).

26. Hammond and Rey, *Narratives of the Coronado Expedition*, pp. 147–48.

27. Ibid.

# Chapter 2

# Weibe-Town and the Delawares-as-Women

## Gender-Crossing and Same-Sex Relations in Eighteenth-Century Northeastern Indian Culture

### Gunlög Fur

*European Encounters with Indian Practices of Gender and Sex*

In the morning we soon came to a Women's Town (Weibe-Town) of 5 to 6 huts, where none but unmarried womenfolk live, who do not want to take any husbands.

In May 1770, Moravian missionary David Zeisberger was acutely discomforted when he came upon a "Women's Town" on the banks of Beaver Creek in northwestern Pennsylvania. Zeisberger's company had paddled up the river to find a good location for a new mission site when they encountered a village of unmarried women. Zeisberger spent most of his life among Indians in eastern North America and his diaries and historical accounts of Indians demonstrate both his understanding of and struggle against cultural expressions that he deemed alien. His encounters with Delaware, Mohican, and Iroquois Indians introduced him to radically different gender perceptions and norms of sexual conduct than his own. Many of these he found completely unacceptable. References to this women's town are tantalizingly meager, yet it is clear that its location hindered Christian men from choosing this area for a settlement. There are reports from other tribes that berdaches camped together at some distance from their countrymen. Is it possible that this was a village of female berdaches?[1]

Native American sexuality caused comment, consternation, and condemnation widely among European travelers, missionaries, and colonial

administrators from the very first occasions of contact and onward. Sometimes comments were clearly based on stereotypical expectations, such as
when Peter Lindeström wrote about Lenape and Susquehannock Indians
who inhabited the region surrounding the New Sweden colony along the
Delaware River that they "have their mixing together with father and
mother, brother and sister like soulless beasts, no one quite knowing, who
is the father of the child." At other times, however, real encounters and
specific observations of practices and rhetoric introduced European colonists to Indian practices of organizing gender and sexuality. This essay
uses missionary diaries and diplomatic minutes from encounters between
Europeans and Delaware and Iroquois peoples in eastern North America
during the eighteenth century to discuss interpretations of gender crossing and deviant sexual behaviors among Indians. But it also attempts to go
behind the fascination and judgment to ask what these sources can tell us
about Indian understandings and practices of gender and same-sex relations. Studying gender and sexuality in Native American contexts leads us
to question binary divisions into male/female and masculine/feminine, as
well as hetero/homosexual.[2]

German pietists, known as Moravians, began in the early 1740s to establish a string of Indian missions across Pennsylvania and into Ohio and
appeared, for a while, to be most successful in converting Delaware, Mohican, and other Indians in the region. At the same time, constant negotiations over land and trade embroiled these peoples in interactions and conflicts with Pennsylvania officials and with the Iroquois confederacy. In
both these settings practices and talk about sexuality and gender perceptions entered into the encounters and left their mark on the source material. There is much evidence of cultural (mis)understandings surrounding
gender and gender crossing, some of which is explicitly linked to same-sex
sexual practices. One of the most remarkable cases of gender crossing in
eastern North America was the metaphor of women used for the entire
Delaware nation during a large portion of the eighteenth century. Contemporary reactions and ensuing scholarly debates surrounding this usage
reveals fears regarding feminized masculinity and homosexuality. Similarly, although in a much more obscure way, the occurrence of *Weibe-
Town* produced anxiety about gender inversion in contemporaries.

There exists a large body of evidence from Native North America regarding gender variation, recognized by specialized vocabulary and descriptions of combinations of male and female tasks and clothing. Often
these descriptions included open or veiled references to homosexual sex.

When Spanish colonists arrived in the New World they reacted strongly against the sight of men dressed in women's attire and having sex with men. In sixteenth-century Spain vigorous efforts went into combating sodomy, which was perceived as connected to Moorish enemies. Now they found same-sex acts to be prevalent also in this hitherto unknown world. Early Spanish visitors and chroniclers commented on sexual behaviors, imagery, and cross-dressing, and marveled at how these practices appeared to have religious connotations. Later, French and English observers equated sodomists with hermaphrodites, which their reports said were common among American Indians. By the early eighteenth century, the term "berdache" crept into the language used to describe these people, a word adapted from an Arabic and Persian term for the younger partner in a male homosexual relationship. This underscored that for Europeans sexual behavior defined these people more than their labor or vestments did. Europeans were not necessarily unaccustomed to men in women's clothes, or men who shared sex with other men, but what seemed to differ in North America was the respect afforded to these people.[3]

In an exhaustive survey Will Roscoe found alternative genders to be "among the most widely shared features of North American societies." A male berdache—or two-spirit—role has been reported from over 150 different tribes, while among barely half that number there are observations of a female counterpart. Roscoe also found that what he calls third and fourth gender identities also involved sexual relations between individuals of the same physical sex but not necessarily of the same gender. So far scholars have not identified two-spirit identities among the Delawares, but there are good reasons to argue that they recognized such gender variance. At least one early eighteenth-century source records the existence of a "hermaphrodite" in a town inhabited by Conestogas, Delawares, and Shawnees. Among the Delawares all of the preconditions necessary for more than two genders existed. Women wielded substantial influence both as individuals and as a collective, in terms of production, distribution, and in rituals. Religious beliefs and mythology offered space for individuals to seek and follow their own visions, at the same time as each individual existed in a web of kinship obligations to the collective. Three was a holy number and their eighteenth-century political organization recognized three clans (wolf, turkey, and tortoise) that represented carnivorous, herbivorous, and omnivorous beings. During creation the omnivorous tortoise mediated between water and land and female and male and only members of this clan could be elected as chiefs of the entire nation. The historical context of the mid-eighteenth century was one of constant pressure from white settlement, disease, war, and removal from ancestral homelands. In this situation several visionaries, many of them women, emerged offering revitalization of traditional life-ways and hope that the onslaught of white influence could be stopped. At the same time women's political influence was ignored by colonial administrators and officers, and curtailed in arenas of conflict and negotiation that favored men and warriors.[4]

Native American understandings of the origins and organization of gender suggest that gender need not be viewed as emanating from or dependent upon biological sex. There are many ways in which societies deal with the experience that male and female are not tidy categories and that not all individuals can be assigned to one or the other. Anthropologist Jay Miller suggests a way to think of the problem in his discussion of three as a basic number in many cultures. He discusses male and female as examples of extremes in need of mediation by a third entity. The berdaches could "tap supernatural reserves of power or energy by virtue of this mediating status. . . . These mediators provide a three-dimensional framework for the flatter relationships between the inclusive and exclusive, usually represented by the metaphors of men-right/women-left in the overall scheme of cultural life." That said, it is vital to stress that the many different peoples known collectively as Indians represent a vast variety of cultures, languages, and economies. Men's and women's roles could take different shapes. Few other places on earth seem to have offered European colonists as much consternation concerning gender categories as early America.[5]

With these things in mind, let us return to *Weibe-Town*. Zeisberger described stopping there where he saw a "beautiful large piece of land" but, he added, "since this Town is so close we continued on." For the Moravian missionary the town represented a forbidden neighborhood and therefore he could not settle there despite a suitable habitat. In order to try to understand why Zeisberger regarded it as a threat, let us focus on his assertion that these women did not want to take husbands.

These women were not merely unmarried, but elected to remain so. A village of independent women who chose not to marry embodied many of the traits which the German missionary saw as obstacles to his (and God's) attempt to convert and civilize the Delawares. European Protestants viewed unmarried women with suspicion, accepting no such institution as the convent and arguing that marriage was a woman's highest calling. Indeed, even widowed women were thought to exist in a limbo in which their sexual drive could be hazardous to men's spiritual well-being. The village consisted of an entire "family" of only women, with the exception of "their father" who lived with them. Presumably there were also children in the village as among the Delawares children followed their mother and belonged to her lineage. How the women were related is not made clear in these records, but the six to eight houses suggest a sizable population. The neighboring town of Kaskaskunk, where one of the most influential Delaware leaders lived, had twenty houses. All in all, a village run by women, who were in no need of men, represented a distillation of all that which had to be overcome in order for the Delawares to become successful converts.[6]

Single-sex native communities raised several concerns for Europeans like Zeisberger. First, there was the issue of authority. Women who acted independently from the men they lived with, and even exercised power over them, outraged the missionaries' sense of propriety and civilization. Second, women's independence in their sexual expressions created worry about both heterosexual and homosexual relations. After over forty years of missionary work among the Delaware and other Indians in Pennsylvania and Ohio, Zeisberger compiled his experiences and knowledge into a *History of the North American Indians.* Regarding their general attitudes toward marriage and sexual relationships, he wrote that "it is safe to say that one does not learn to know them well until they become concerned about the well-being of their souls and confess the evils that weigh on their consciences. One may be among them for several years and, not knowing them intimately as stated, but regard them as virtuous people. Far from it. Impurity and immorality, even gross sensuality and unnatural vice flourish among them, according to the testimony of the Indians themselves." He reiterated his frustration at the influence of Native women and described Delaware women in particular as liars and gossips and meant that they only appeared to be meek and modest when in reality they practiced all sorts of vices, such as adultery, stealing, and deception. Throughout almost half a century women had been expelled from the Moravian missions for adultery, chastized for demanding too much labor from their husbands, and for creating a destructive environment for the young through their depraved sexual initiatives. Yet, there was worse. Zeisberger concluded his list of their shortcomings: "There are traces of unnatural sins among them, hardly known to any except to those such as missionaries who have learned to understand the people well." It is impossible to know if it was a suspicion of "unnatural sins" that haunted the

missionary as he avoided the town full of unmarried women, but his encounter with them came at a time when he saw his work among the Indians threatened by Delaware women's opposition. He raged in his diary
that he had "not found elsewhere among the Indians that the women are
such instruments of Satan and so influential among the people."[7]

Much of the hostility toward women stemmed from what Zeisberger
and other Europeans viewed as unnatural loyalties and family configurations among Indians. Indians grew up with a multitude of links and responsibilities toward lineage and clan, which required them to work and
pray in close proximity with people other than those with whom they
were related by marriage. These ties were often stronger than those that
connected a man and a woman. In this respect, *Weibe-Town*, a single-sex
community, would not have been unusual. Women separating themselves,
particularly for ritual purposes, such as all women did during their menstruation, was practiced among Delaware people. Women and men spent
large parts of the year in separate pursuits and same-sex workgroups was
often the norm. Men also abstained from women's company and from
sexual relations with women during certain periods, or permanently, as
was the case with some of the more powerful healers described in the
1620s by Dutch colonist Nicolas Wassenaer. "The ministry of their spiritual
affairs is attended to by one they call Kitzinacka. . . . This priest has no
house-keeping of his own. He . . . must not eat any food prepared by a
married woman. It must be cooked by a maiden or old woman. He never
cohabits with them, living like a capuchin [a monk]." This priest was also
exempt from war efforts, placing him closer to women in terms of gender.[8]

Zeisberger noted the intense relationships that could evolve between
men: "Two comrades who have been reared together or have become attached to one another will be very close and constant companions. . . . It
seems almost impossible for either of them to live without the other." Such
friendships could also develop within the bounds of the Moravian towns.
The Delaware convert Michael lived for many years in the house of unmarried brothers in Bethlehem and took every opportunity to express
his pleasure in this arrangement. He developed a particularly strong bond
of friendship with one of the Moravian assistants, Andreas. Zeisberger
offered no such accounts of female friendships, but women frequently
shared subsistence work in single-gendered groups, or traveled through
the woods in the company of other women. Sabine Lang writes about
these strong, often formally sealed, same-sex friendships that have been
described from different parts of North America that they were "not

identical with homosexual relationships, but they may well include at least a homoerotic component" and suggests that an "even better term might be 'homoemotional.'"[9]

There were also mythical references to all-women villages. Zeisberger related how Indians critical of his message told him how they had visited heaven to see what it was like. Among other things they described two large towns, "in one of which there were only women, of extraordinary size." Such separation of the sexes may have caused anxiety also among Delawares because at the same time mythological stories cautioned against refusing marriage. A woman rejecting the advances of in turn a beaver, a skunk, and an owl by calling them ugly eventually finds herself in trouble and dies because none of these animals will help her. But Delawares also spoke in awed terms about a woman who withdrew from her village "from some cause or other." In that account, just as in *Weibe-Town*, there was a child, but no mention of a husband.[10]

It is not surprising then that neighboring Indians did not seem disturbed by this village and interacted with its inhabitants. It was the Indians in the neighborhood who gave the town its name and when Zeisberger held a gathering at another town in the vicinity, the father from *Weibe-Town* visited and expressed his pleasure at the presence of the Moravians. Later discussions with local Delawares revealed that the area was indeed suitable for a mission village. Whatever the missionary might have suspected, it is unlikely that this was a community of same-sex loving women. It would have been much easier to form such relationships in any regular village. Records regarding sexual relations between Native American women are particularly scarce, but Paula Gunn Allen hypothesized in 1986 that lesbians would have existed in tribal societies and that their relationships were integral to tribal life, since women spent most of their time in single-sex groups. In her discussion of "cross-gender females" based on a review of ethnographic observations, Evelyn Blackwood found that "[h]omosexual behavior occurred in contexts within which neither individual was cross-gender nor were such individuals seen as expressing cross-gender behavior. Premarital and extramarital sexual relations were also permissible. . . . Sexuality clearly was not restricted by the institution of marriage." Sexual abstinence appears not to have been the only reason for women to abstain from marriage in eastern North America. French Jesuit Lahontan described a group of women among the Illinois called *Ickoue ne Kioussa* or "hunting women." These joined men in hunting and claimed that they could not stand the yoke of marriage, did not manage to bring up children, and were too impatient to endure the long winters in the village. Hunting women did not necessarily forego sexual contacts, and their eventual children were brought up as "legitimate heirs" by relatives. Zeisberger also mentioned the existence of "hunting women" among the Delawares. Based on hunting women's refusal to marry and their participation in the male subsistence activity of hunting, Will Roscoe suggests that "*ickoue ne kioussa* were true female berdaches."[11]

Until and if we uncover further, and more extensive, sources there is no way of knowing what *Weibe-Town* represented in the Delaware world of the late eighteenth century. Two things we may conclude from the sources surrounding this occurrence. One is that Delawares recognized practices of sexuality and organizations of relationships between men and women that appeared as completely alien and ungodly to German missionaries. The other is that the latter reacted against these, particularly as they concerned influence and independence of women, thus revealing their own underlying conceptions of sex and gender. *Weibe-Town,* whatever it was, and the occurrence of "hunting women" represented a range of possibilities and obligations in place for Delaware women. Sexuality, gender, and desire thus come together in complicated ways in the historical material, confounding contemporary observers and subsequent scholars with their roots in Western, Christian cultures alike. We shall now turn to an example that bring these threads together in a particularly tantalizing and intricate manner.

### Feminizing Nations in War and Ritual

You will remember that you are our Women; our Fore-Fathers made you so, and put a Petticoat on you, and charged you to be true to us, and lie with no other Man; but of late you have suffered the String that tied your Petticoat to be cut loose by the French, and you lay with them, and so become a common Bawd, in which you acted very wrong, and deserve Chastisement.[12]

With this accusation an Iroquois speaker harangued the Delaware tribe at a council held at Easton in Pennsylvania in 1756. The fluidity of gender and sexuality as evidenced by the story of *Weibe-Town* was not the only instance involving Delawares in colonial America. For much of the colonial period the Delaware Nation as a whole was known in diplomatic contexts as "women." Popularized in the nineteenth-century writings of novelist James Fenimore Cooper, the image of Delaware men made into women by Iroquois conquerors elicits both curiosity and disgust. The designation, as described by him, degraded the status of Delaware men by placing them in a political position subordinate to manhood. It also raised the specter of homosexuality by placing men in the position of women. This made perfect sense in the nineteenth century, but what did it mean to Delaware men and their contemporaries from other nations during the time it was in use?

In the late 1600s, diplomatic records from Pennsylvania report references to the Delawares as "women." By next midcentury, Tamaqua, one of the leaders of the Delawares who had removed to Ohio, told the Iroquois representatives in a council that "I still remember the Time when You first conquered Us and made Woman of Us, and told Us that You took Us under your Proection [sic]." Another Delaware spokesman explained in a council at Sir William Johnson's home in the Mohawk Valley in 1756 that "We are looked upon as Women, and therefore when the French come amongst us, is it to be wondered that they are able to seduce us." At another session with the French commander at Fort Duquesne at the fork of the Ohio and Allegheny Rivers in 1758 Tamaqua made an even more tantalizing assertion: "I have not made myself a king. My uncles have made me like a queen, that I always should mind what is good + right, + whatever I agree with, they will assist me."[13]

By the middle of the eighteenth century, the metaphoric description of the Delawares as women appears to have been common usage and Iroquois spokesmen invoked this designation in a manner that established themselves as men who had authority over women and they proceeded to officially order Delawares off their own land. This served the Pennsylvania government well and Jane T. Merritt argues that making the Delawares into metaphorical women "not only confirmed Pennsylvania's purchase of Delaware land from the Iroquois but helped assert a patriarchal authority on people whom they thought lacked the gender hierarchies common in Euramerican homes." In order to do so the Iroquois borrowed a European concept of gender "to delineate Delawares' subordinate position in terms that Euramericans would clearly understand."[14]

As the initial quote demonstrates, this feminization of Delawares was entwined with sexuality as well. In July 1742, a council was held between representatives of the Iroquois Six Nations, Delaware Indians, and Pennsylvanians. In a highly charged atmosphere of contention over land in eastern Pennsylvania, the Six Nations representative, Canassatego, rose to speak before the congregated Indians and colonists. He turned to the Delawares present and argued that they had been wrongful in charging the Pennsylvanians with land fraud. He finished scathingly:

> We conquer'd You, we made Women of you, you know you are Women, and can no more sell Land than Women. . . . Your Ears are ever Open to slanderous Reports about our Brethren. You receive them with as much greediness as Lewd Woman receive the Embraces of Bad Men. And for all these reasons we charge You to remove instantly.[15]

Canassatego's language constructed the Delawares not just as women, but as sexually active women who belonged to Iroquois men. Their perfidy consisted in infidelity as they received other men "with as much greediness as Lewd Woman receive the Embraces of Bad Men." Moreover, the words of Tamaqua and the unidentified Delaware king seem to indicate that the Delawares agreed and viewed themselves as feminized men, made so by (sexual) conquest by the Iroqouis. Then, as sexually active "women" they were open to the enticement from other men, such as the French.

Gendering the Delawares as females thus had both gender and sexual implications. Historian Richard Trexler identifies an "inveterate male habit of gendering enemies female or effeminate" in the ancient as well as early modern world and argues that sources repeatedly proclaimed the Delawares to be "'effeminates,' even 'half-men,' because of their war-induced dependency." Another historian, Nancy Shoemaker, ended a thorough examination of gendered terms of abuse and alliances in Northeastern intercultural negotiations with a question: Why is it that English and Indian men are so united in their use of gendered terms as metaphors for hierarchy and domination? She identifies a common characteristic in Indian-gendered insults: "it was always sexuality . . . that explained what it meant for one nation to dominate another." Sexuality, she finds, was used as an analogy to explain dominance and submission. Her conclusion, like Trexler's, points to the one great similarity between Indians and whites, "that men went to war and that women did not." While Shoemaker regards heterosexual sexuality as the template for dominance and subordination, Trexler uses homosexual rape as the model for denigration of (male) enemies and argues that such patterns determined the scorn levied at men who placed themselves in a passive sexual position, like berdaches did.[16]

The evidence from councils and interactions between enemies across North America seems convincing: male warriors berated other men for weakness and dependence by calling them "women" and referring to female genitalia and passive homosexuality. This allowed Joshua Goldstein to suggest that the berdache offered "[a]merindian cultures . . . a ready category for men who become women (and thus inferior), which was easily adaptable to humiliating enemies." To regain one's honor, then, men must remove their drag and resume the habits of real men. Thus, in 1756, when Sir William Johnson sought to enlist the aid of the Delawares, he ended a treaty with them "by taking off the Petticoat, or that invidious name of Women from the Delaware Nation." A year later, the Delawares seemed to have done so, as a Mohawk Indian, Little Abraham, reported. The Delawares, he said, "looked upon themselves as Men, and would not acknowledge no Superiority that any other Nation had over them." He went on to relay a threat directed at English colonists, that unless they left the country the Delawares would "cut off your private Parts, and make Women of you, as you have done of us."[17]

However, there are elements in the metaphor of Delaware-as-women that do not easily fit into an interpretation of gender hierarchy and male domination. David Zeisberger's account of how the Delawares were established as women is telling in its detail concerning the ceremonial context surrounding the institution. Zeisberger reported that the Delawares had told him that at a meeting between representatives of the Six Nations and Delawares—a meeting not witnessed by a European—the Iroquois ceremonially declared that the Delawares should now be women and "dressed them in a woman's long habit, reaching down to the feet." This was tied around them with a wampum belt, further emphasizing the ceremonial and spiritual significance of this alteration. The Iroquois then gave them a corn-pestle and hoe and a calabash filled with oil. These symbolized women's work as agriculturalists and their role as peacemakers. The Delawares were now enjoined to "heal those who were walking in foolish ways that they might come to their senses and incline their hearts to peace." Making Delaware men into women thus involved a change of clothing, employment, and ritual responsibilities. The connection between dressing a man in a petticoat and the various berdache traditions of two-spirit people seems quite obvious and it is somewhat startling that it is often absent from the discussions of the Delaware-as-women. Did the Delawares, in fact, become a nation of berdaches, and did the Iroquois make them so by conquering them (sexually)?[18]

Daniel Brinton, a nineteenth-century scholar, who meticulously worked to capture Delaware language and culture stories and had access to Zeisberger's manuscripts, wrote that some young Delaware males "apparently vigorous and of normal development, were deprived of the accoutrements of the male sex, clothed like women, and assigned women's work to do." This differed distinctly from the otherwise highly honored work and comportment of women, said Brinton, who claimed that these men "were treated as inferiors by their male associates. Whether this degradation arose from suspicious rites or sodomitic practices, it certainly carried to its victim the contempt of both sexes." Of more recent writers, C. A. Weslager concluded that the Delawares being made women was "the outstanding recorded instance of its kind in the East. It is probably the only time that the rite was so institutionalized as to affect the status of an entire tribal group." Generally, however, neither scholars discussing the Delawares, nor those dealing with the concept of berdache and multiple genders discuss the instance in which an entire tribe was constituted as women.[19]

There are good reasons to take a closer look at the connections between men in female clothing, genders, sexualities, and the role of the Delawares. It is patently obvious in Brinton's quote above that it was gender crossing (or gender mixing) that he deemed to be abhorred, not women in their performance of proper feminine occupations. To Brinton any association with femininity in a male, or with sexual inversion, proved devastating to that man's character. In a European context words like effeminate and emasculated spelled degradation. Brinton made an explicit connection between effeminate behavior in a male and immoral subordination, demonstrated through aberrant sexual acts. It is significant that such a connection emerged in England at the beginning of the eighteenth century. Randolph Trumbach identifies in this period a marked shift in the perception of the effeminate fop, in which the word *effeminate* underwent an alteration and became exclusively associated with adult sodomites. By the first decades of the century, men who desired other men sexually were described as "a new society" of "men worse than goats, who dressed themselves in petticoats." It was the purported passivity of the sodomitical role that other men judged to be a deplorable sign of femininity, and dress and mannerisms emphasized this connection. The later part of the century saw a simplification of men's clothes and a restriction on physical familiarity between men. Trumbach argues that a new masculinity now required all males "to be active at every stage of life" in order to avoid any contamination of feminine or sodomitical passivity.[20]

Interestingly, Indians appeared to concur. In 1720, an embassy from Illinois and Missouri Indians visited France. Jean-Bernard Bossu, who traveled in North America at midcentury, reported meeting people who still remembered their visit to the great European city. One man described how he had in several public places noticed "men who were half women, with curled hair, earrings, and corsages on their chests. . . . This American spoke with the great scorn of these people, whom we call *petits maîtres*. They are born with the natural weakness and coquetry of women. Nature seems to have started to make them women and then forgot and gave them the wrong sex. . . . Our Indian said that such effeminate manners dishonor a respectable nation."[21]

Sources from the eighteenth century thus point toward conflicting interpretations of the role and standing of effeminate men in Indian societies. In situations of war and strife men could be insulted by charges of feminine behavior, and often explicit linkages were made between male domination and homosexual penetration. In other situations, however, berdaches could be held in high regard and their roles linked to spiritual power and shamanism.

Where in all this does the designation of the Delawares as women fit in? If one looks at the arguments presented by some of the Delaware leaders themselves in numerous conferences and councils throughout the eighteenth century, a sharp divergence becomes evident between two different discourses on gender, one deployed by the Iroquois and English participants which seems to fit neatly with Trumbach's conclusions, while the other fell back on a tradition of gender roles which were not ontologically connected to either biological sex or sexual desire. These Delaware (male) representatives did not deny being women, but they consistently emphasized the ritual underpinnings of this role. The gendered language used by and between Delawares was not a language of oppositionary relations between sexes, not a language describing unrelated males and females, and not a language of copulation. Nor was it expressing subordination. Instead, it was primarily a language of family and kinship. Sexual restrictions were severe, as European observers commented, between related individuals. Sexual relationships were not acceptable between uncles and nieces or brothers and sisters. Abusive sexual language in the context of war and conflict is certainly found in some council exchanges, sexual taunts that evoked images of sexual conquest of males as well as females. But the ceremonial language of the institution of the role that the Delawares took on is a different one. In many ways it resembles the definitions of the role of berdache.

The metaphorical language of the councils emphasized that the Delawares were women and held a role connected to the ritual obligations of actual female matrons. When Tamaqua said that he had been "made . . . like a queen," the term signified a woman of high standing in Delaware society. What Tamaqua and others referred to when they designated themselves as women, was the ritual role of women in peacemaking, a role of honor and obligation that had been confirmed through solemn ceremonies. While the role had a ceremonial origin it did not mean that Delaware males were perpetually occupying a third gender identity. Instead, as several instances make clear, war captains and sachems employed the position as suited the occasion, sometimes throwing off the petticoat and at other times wrapping it tightly around themselves. However, the occurrence of gender roles other than male and female, and understandings of gender as acquired not by biological necessity but guided also by dreams and visions, facilitated the adoption of a female role also by those with other-than-female bodies. Undoubtedly, though, the cruelty of intercultural clashes and conflicts over land convinced some Delaware men that it was through emphasizing male power and dominance that their people would defend their place in the colonial world. The implications were clear in the words of the warriors who threatened to cut off the private parts of both English and Iroquois, unless they treated them as men.[22]

The Delaware-as-women should be separated from the more common and general sexual abuse connected to warfare. This was a different institution existing alongside that of sexual conquest, and not necessarily in opposition to it, but one that demonstrates that gender and sex could have a lot of different meanings. It suggests a subtlety of gender movements not easily comprehended in a binary universe. One understanding was that the combination of genders—such as when a male individual adopted female garb—gave powers that transcended either of the two genders. Yet it is also clear that this notion was not uncontested. The status of ritual women was deeply entwined with ideas concerning lineage, kin, friendship, and connection, while a corollary status (or opposite) of men incorporated notions surrounding war, individual courage, killing, and death. The Delawares contrived to maintain the balance by gendering their universe to the extreme. Yet this was a losing battle in the face of a world where war, death, and disease filled Delaware as well as English and Iroquois everyday experiences, and the scale easily tipped in favor of patriarchal notions of maleness, connected to prowess and war. The surface similarity between berdaches and the emerging English discourse on sodomites in petticoats also lent itself to a ready condemnation of the berdache role, even though in Native understanding it carried a far different meaning. Thus, it is likely that not only the Delawares' own understanding changed over time, but also that the Iroquois, who at one time participated in a ceremony with political implications of peacemaking and kinship, later came to find it possible and perhaps even advantageous to insult the manhood and sexual capacity of Delaware men.

European visitors to and settlers in North America brought their cultural expectations on how to interpret sexual behaviors to their descriptions of Native American societies. While the Spanish clearly expressed revulsion, unsurprising considering the strident efforts to eradicate sodomy within Spain, northern Europeans, like the Protestant Moravians, were more reticent. This did not spell acceptance of Indian sexual and gender mores, as is clear from their reactions to nonhierarchical gender systems, women's influence, and sexual independence. Sex in Indian ways confused, disgusted, and enticed European men, and it has been my intention in this chapter to tease apart their gut reactions from actual observations in order to illuminate aspects of gender and sexuality in Native American societies. Whether overtly or obliquely, the specter of same-sex acts haunted European concern about Indian practices. Feminine men in women's clothing, and women in no need of men, made America a strange land to many of these observers.

Same-sex couplings were part of the Native American past, and undoubtedly individuals also had sex together. Some of these acts took place between individuals who thought of themselves as different genders, but with the same anatomical sex, others had sex in the way we would call homosexual. (In Raymond Hauser's words: "It is probably true that not all berdaches were homosexual, and certainly not all . . . homosexuals were berdaches.") It is hard teasing apart different strands of influence in the historical record: third and fourth gender people were both abused and respected, homosexual sex was both frowned upon and accepted, European writers and administrators were both appalled and puzzled and perhaps intrigued. So much is shrouded in darkness, and perhaps, that is as it should be. But in societies that valued highly spiritual intervention and tied individual choices and actions to visions and dreams it is likely that roles relating to gender and sexuality would be suffused by spiritual responsibilities as well. Whether certain individuals approved of others' gender and sexual behaviors or not, they would be bound to accept them.[23]

The records from encounters between Europeans and Indians in colonial America remind us that the human species is characterized by its capacity for variation and construction of new forms and meanings. Among Indians in the Northeast, individuals could choose other roles than what commonly followed on their biological sex. The definition of a person as "woman," "man," or "berdache" depended less on biology than on the roles they chose to shoulder. *Weibe-Town* on the Beaver Creek and the symbolic role of male Delawares as women demonstrate, in all their mysteriousness, that Indian norms for women's and men's expected and possible behaviors and choices offered a range of human possibilities, for women as well as for men and for those who saw themselves as both-and. The women's town was not a requisite for "lesbian" relations—by all accounts such occurred as easily in regular towns—but all-women communities occasioned anxiety in both white and red men, as is evidenced by the accounts of mythological all-women villages, and stories of the dangers of marriage refusals. The metaphorical use of a female designation for the entire Delaware tribe did not mean that they took up a collective berdache role or that they all practiced passive homosexual sex. Yet, the existence of two-spirit people, and the acceptance of gender variance based on spiritual injunctions and established through ceremony, supplied the template for the recognition of Delawares as women. However, both Indian and white contemporaries worried over the meaning of feminine men and same-sex sexual behavior. The increased violence marking interracial relations in eastern North America over the course of the eighteenth century also marked a more violent language regarding gender crossing and same-sex sexuality. While some men held on to notions of gender as a concept designating complementary responsibilities open to all bodies, others clearly argued for male dominance in sex as well as in politics.

NOTES

1. Quote from Box 137, F.1, "Lagundo-Ütenunk (Friedenstatt) Diary," 5/3/70, *Moravian Archives* (*MA*); Walter L. Williams, *The Spirit and the Flesh: Sexual Diversity in American Indian Culture* (Boston: Beacon Press, 1986), 81.

2. Peter Lindeström, *Geographia Americae with an Account of the Delaware Indians,* trans. Amandus Johnson (Philadelphia: The Swedish Colonial Society, 1925), 109.

3. Williams, *The Spirit and the Flesh,* 131–140; Will Roscoe, *Changing Ones: Third and Fourth Genders in Native North America* (New York: St. Martin's Press, 1998).

4. Roscoe, *Changing Ones,* 9–10; Will Roscoe, "How to Become a Berdache:

Toward a Unified Analysis of Gender Diversity," in *Third Sex, Third Gender: Beyond Sexual Dimorphism in Culture and History*, ed. Gilbert Herdt (New York: Zone Books, 1991), 371; *Minutes of the Provincial Council of Pennsylvania* [*MPCP*], ed. Samuel Hazard (10 volumes Harrisburg, Pa, 1838–1852), III, 149–152.

5. Jay Miller, "People, Berdaches, and Left-Handed Bears: Human Variation in Native America," *Journal of Anthropological Research* 48:3 (Fall 1982), quote from 286; Patricia Albers and Beatrice Medicine, *The Hidden Half: Studies of Plains Indian Women* (Lanham, Md.: University Press of America, 1983), 276.

6. Box 137, F.1, "Lagundo-Ütenunk (Friedenstatt) Diary," 5/13/70, 6/3/70 (*MA*); Kenneth Johansson, 'Mannen och kvinnan, lusten och äktenskapet—Några tidstypiska tankegångar kring gåtfulla ting,' in *Jämmerdal och fröjdesal. Kvinnor i stormaktstidens Sverige*, ed. Eva Österberg (Stockholm: Atlantis, 1997), 34–35; Merry Wiesner, *Women and Gender in Early Modern Europe* (Cambridge: Cambridge University Press, 1993), 23, 253.

7. David Zeisberger, *History of the Northern American Indians* [hereafter *Zeisberger's History*], ed. Archer Butler Hulbert and William Nathaniel Schwarze (Ohio State Archaeological Society, 1910), 20, 124–125; Box 135, "Goschgoschünk Diary, 1768–1769," 7/15/68 (*MA*).

8. Nicholaes van Wassenaer, "From the 'Historisch Verhael,'" in *Narratives of New Netherland 1609–1664* (hereafter *NNN*), ed. J. Franklin Jameson (New York: Charles Scribner's Sons, 1909), 68, 80; Margaret M. Caffrey, "Complementary Power: Men and Women of the Lenni Lenape," *American Indian Quarterly* 24:1 (winter 2000), 44–63; Regula Trenkwalder Schönenberger, *Lenape Women, Matriliny, and the Colonial Encounter: Resistance and Erosion of Power (ca. 1600–1876)* (Bern: Peter Lang, 1991).

9. *Zeisberger's History*, 119; "Kirchen-Buch der Gemeine in Bethlehem," vol. II: 1756–1801, July 1758 (*MA*); Sabine Lang, *Men as Women, Women as Men: Changing Gender in Native American Cultures* (Austin: University of Texas Press, 1998), 329.

10. "David Zeisburger[*sic*?] Journal," *Ohio Archaeological and Historical Publications* 21 (1912), 85, 103; John Bierhorst, *Mythology of the Lenape* (Tucson: The University of Arizona Press, 1995), 51, 106–107; John Heckewelder, *An Account of the History, Manners, and Customs of the Indian Nations; Who Once Inhabited Pennsylvania and the Neighbouring States* (Philadelphia: Abraham Small, 1819), 200–201.

11. Paula Gunn Allen, *The Sacred Hoop: Recovering the Feminine in American Indian Traditions* (Boston: Beacon Press, 1986), 67–80; Evelyn Blackwood, "Sexuality and Gender in Certain Native American Tribes: The Case of Cross-Gender Females," in *The Lesbian Issue: Essays from SIGNS*, ed. Estelle Freedman et al. (Chicago: University of Chicago Press, 1985), 35; Roscoe, *Changing Ones*, 75; *Zeisberger's History*, 85.

12. Treaty at Easton, 1756, in *Indian Treaties Printed by Benjamin Franklin, 1736–1762*, ed. Julian P. Boyd and Carl Van Doren (Philadelphia, 1938), 148.

13. King Beaver, 1754: *MPCP* VI, 156–157; Delaware King: *Documents relative to the Colonial History of the State of New-York* VII, gen. ed. E. B. O'Callaghan, vol. ed. J. R. Brodhead (Albany 1856), 157; "The Journal of Christian Frederick Post" (1758), *Early Western Travel Journals 1748–1765,* ed. Reuben Gold Thwaites (Cleveland: The Arthur Clark Company, 1904), 273; also "Journal of Moses Titamy and Isaac Hill to Minisinks, 1758," *Pennsylvania Archives [PA],* ed. Samuel Hazard et al., 9 series, 122 vols. (Harrisburg and Philadelphia, 1852–1935), III, 504–508; *MPCP* VI, 363.

14. Jane T. Merritt, *At the Crossroads: Indians & Empires on a Mid-Atlantic Frontier, 1700–1763* (Published for the Omohundro Institute of Early American History and Culture. Chapel Hill: University of North Carolina Press, 2003), 220–223.

15. *MPCP* IV, 577–582.

16. Richard Trexler, *Sex and Conquest: Gender Construction and Political Order at the Time of the European Conquest of the Americas* (Cambridge, Mass.: Blackwell, 1995), 1, 72–79; Nancy Shoemaker, "An Alliance between Men: Gender Metaphors in Eighteenth-Century American Indian Diplomacy East of the Mississippi," *Ethnohistory* 46:2 (1999): 239–263, quotes from 245, 254–255.

17. Joshua S. Goldstein, *War and Gender: How Gender Shapes the War System and Vice Versa* (Cambridge: Cambridge University Press, 2001), 360; Trexler, *Sex and Conquest; Documents relative to the Colonial History of the State of New-York,* 119; *Indian Treaties,* 178.

18. *Zeisberger's History,* 35.

19. Daniel G. Brinton, *The Lenâpe and Their Legends; With the Complete Text and Symbols of the Walam Olum* (New York: AMS Press, 1969) [1885], 109–110; C. A. Weslager, "The Delaware Indians as Women," *Journal of the Washington Academy of Science* 34 (1944), 381. Debates among scholars have hinged upon whether the Delawares had indeed been conquered by the Iroquois and whether the position as women was one of honor or one of disgrace. Authors have expressed ambivalence toward the conflation between the categories of men and women, and it becomes apparent that the need to salvage the reputation of Delaware males hinges upon denunciation of women and of feminized masculinity.

20. Randolph Trumbach, "The Birth of the Queen: Sodomy and the Emergence of Gender Equality in Modern Culture, 1660–1750," in *Hidden from History: Reclaiming the Gay and Lesbian Past,* ed. Martin Bauml Duberman, Martha Vicinus, and George Chauncey, Jr. (New York: New American Library Books, 1989), 129–140, quotes from 135, 139.

21. Jean-Bernard Bossu, *Travels in the Interior of North America, 1751–1762,* trans. and ed. Seymour Feiler (Norman: University of Oklahoma Press, 1962), 84. I am grateful to Nancy Shoemaker for introducing me to this source.

22. Roscoe, *Changing Ones,* 130–136; Lang, *Men as Women, Women as Men,* 247–257; Box 131, F.3, "Friedenshütten, Pa (Wyalusing) 1765–1778," 7/8/66; Box 137,

F.1, 5/5/70, 7/11/70, 7/14/70; Box 144, F.6 "Gnadenhütten, Ohio 1773–1778," 3/26/76; Box 177, F.5, "White River, Ind. 1800–1806," 2/21/1803, *MA; PA* V, 335; Heckewelder, *History, Manners, and Customs,* xxvii–xxviii, 56–65.

23. Raymond Hauser, "The *Berdache* and the Illinois Indian Tribe During the Last Half of the Seventeenth Century," *Ethnohistory* 37:1 (winter 1990): 45–65. Reprinted in *American Encounters: Natives and Newcomers from European Contact to Indian Removal, 1500–1850,* ed. Peter C. Mancall and James H. Merrell (New York and London: Routledge, 2000), 119–136. Citation is from reprint edition, 124; A present-day Native American scholar of colonial America offers an explanation from an Indian perspective: "Much toleration of individualism in many Indian societies derives from the sacredness of an individual's personal mission in life." Opposing another person's sacred mission would even have dire consequences. "If the Great Spirit chose to create alternative sexualities or gender roles, who was bold enough to oppose such power?" Duane Champagne, "Preface: Sharing the Gift of Sacred Being," in *Two Spirit People: American Indian Lesbian Women and Gay Men,* ed. Lester B. Brown (New York and London: Harrington Park Press. An Imprint of The Haworth Press, Inc., 1997), xviii, xix, xx; Williams, *The Spirit and the Flesh,* 91.

# Chapter 3

# "Abominable Sin" in Colonial New Mexico
## Spanish and Pueblo Perceptions of Same-Sex Sexuality

### Tracy Brown

In June 1731, two Pueblo Indian men, Antonio Yuba and Asensio Povia, were accused of committing an "abominable sin" ("pecado nefando," or, in this case, anal intercourse) in a pasture outside of Santa Fe.[1] Yuba, from the pueblo of Tesuque, and Povia, from the pueblo of Nambé, were literally caught in the act by Manuel Trujillo, a Spanish resident of Santa Fe and the owner of the pasture in which Povia and Yuba were discovered. The two men had gone to Trujillo's pasture to tend cattle for the local mission. It was there that Trujillo came upon them. He was so angry at his discovery that, according to his testimony, he spontaneously whipped the two men with the reins from the horse that he was riding. He then denounced them to the local Spanish civil authorities, which investigated the matter. In the end, after much testimony, both Yuba and Povia were whipped and then banished to remote pueblos for their transgression.

Placed within the broader context of colonial New Mexican society, the investigation conducted by civil authorities into Asensio Povia's and Antonio Yuba's actions sheds light upon several issues which will be addressed in this chapter. Most generally, a close study of the investigation reveals attitudes that both Spaniards and Pueblo Indian peoples held concerning same-sex sex and masculinity in eighteenth-century New Mexico. Spanish civil and Catholic Church authorities perceived of such activity as an "abominable sin" in New Mexico as they did in the rest of the New World. All sexual activity, in fact, was in some way marked by Spanish moral codes; but some sexual activity was seen as being far more problematic than others. Sex between men fell into this latter category. The meager evidence concerning Pueblo attitudes concerning sex shows that they did not share this perspective concerning sex between men at contact; but by the eighteenth century, some may have adopted such beliefs as their own. The investigation thus illustrates how a clash in belief systems might occur in New Mexico, and what happened as a result.

A detailed study of the investigation also illustrates the methods Spanish authorities used to police Pueblo sexuality and to impose proper moral codes concerning sex, sexuality, and gender. The imposition of such moral codes concerning sexuality was part and parcel of the colonial project in New Mexico: Spanish civil and Church authorities sought to police Pueblo peoples in numerous arenas of their lives, and sex was one of those arenas. In the seventeenth century in New Mexico, missionaries were at the forefront of this policing; but after the Pueblo Revolt of 1680 and the reconquest of New Mexico beginning in 1692, civil authorities took over the role from the Church. Church power had weakened considerably by the eighteenth century due to a number of interrelated factors. After the revolt, officials in Mexico City decided that the only reason Spaniards would return to New Mexico would be to create an outpost of Spanish authority on the northern frontier. Conversion of Indian peoples in New Mexico was no longer a priority in, or a justification for the existence of, the colony as it had been in the seventeenth century.[2] Thus, it is not surprising to find that all eighteenth-century sexual misconduct cases involving Pueblo Indians in New Mexico were prosecuted by civil, not Church, authorities.[3]

Such policing was obviously a form of social control, but as this case demonstrates, it may not have been that effective. Pueblo peoples attempted to negotiate and even resist the imposition of Spanish moral codes, sometimes with the assistance of defense attorneys (or protectors, as they were called) assigned to them by the authorities investigating cases. As I demonstrate below, both Povia and Yuba denied that sex ever occurred; and their protectors offered numerous and varied explanations for what it was they were doing when Manuel Trujillo discovered them. The end result is, I argue, a muddying of the facts of the case: to the point that the governor himself expressed doubts about the veracity of the evidence. Despite this, the governor of New Mexico imposed punishment upon both Povia and Yuba. We should not read this as a triumph of Spanish over Indian power, at least in the realm of sexuality, however. Civil authorities prosecuted only two cases involving Pueblo sexual misconduct in the entire eighteenth century. The other case, which involved an adolescent charged with having sex with an animal, is discussed briefly below. In addition, there is some slight evidence that civil authorities attempted to police Pueblo marriage practices "extrajudicially" or informally, outside of the Spanish court system.[4]

There are a number of possible explanations for the existence of such a small number of investigations concerning Pueblo sexuality. Spanish civilians and authorities might have policed Pueblo sexuality extrajudicially. It is also entirely possible that the records of other investigations were destroyed; New Mexico has a long history of record destruction and loss.[5] But, one must also take into consideration that state power in New Mexico was "fledgling" at best throughout the colonial period. There simply were not enough governmental officials to carry out many investigations into Pueblo life. Therefore, these officials had to choose their battles where Pueblo people were concerned. If one looks at the documentation concerning Pueblo communities for the entire eighteenth century, it is clear that civil authority kept closer tabs on those activities it deemed an immediate security threat to the Spanish populace such as unauthorized movements of groups of Pueblos, rumors of secret meetings or revolts in Pueblo communities, and, to some extent, heretical or sacrilegious activities that promoted the maintenance of traditional spiritual practices. But, overall, it is clear that sexual practices were not as vigorously policed as were other arenas of Pueblo life.

In this chapter, I have been careful to use the terms "same-sex sex," "same-sex sexuality," and sodomy to discuss anal sex between men, however awkward or wordy these terms may be, rather than "homosexuality." The term "homosexuality" denotes, as Richard Trexler and others have argued, a distinctly contemporary phenomenon: "the notion of a 'gay' lifestyle shared by everyone participating in homosexual behavior."[6] Serge Gruzinski argues that such a community may have existed in colonial Mexico City, but there is no evidence of the existence of such a community in New Mexico.

## The "Pecado Nefando" and Eye-Witnessing Sodomy

Criminal investigations in the Spanish New World were typically conducted in three main phases: the sumaria (or fact-gathering phase); the plenario, where defendants or their representative offered a defense of their positions; and sentencing.[7] In the Yuba/Povia investigation, which followed standard investigational procedure, Spanish civil authority seemed

intent neither to establish the guilt of the accused nor who was most culpable. Assuming the guilt of the accused was a common practice in the
northern frontier regions, especially in cases involving an accusation of a
Spaniard against an Indian person.[8] In addition, Yuba, the older of the two
men involved, was assumed to be culpable for the act due to his age; thus,
Spanish authorities did not spend a lot of time attempting to determine
culpability in this case. The issue that authorities were most focused on
delineating in the trial was what sort of behavior the two men were actually engaged in and whether or not a sex act had been completed. In investigating this issue, attitudes about same-sex sexuality in colonial New
Mexico are revealed.

The sumaria, or fact-finding, phase of an investigation typically began
with an accusation of a crime or at least the notification of local officials
that a crime had been committed.[9] In the case of Yuba and Povia, Manuel
Trujillo, their accuser, appeared before Lieutenant General Perez Velarde
on June 25, 1731 to denounce the two men. The accusation was very brief,
and states only the barest facts of the case as they were told to Perez Velarde by Trujillo. As noted in the first paragraph of this chapter, Trujillo
accused Asensio Povia and Antonio Yuba of committing the "pecado nefando" after he discovered them together in his pasture in June of 1731.
Trujillo's unmediated response to this discovery provides an initial insight
into how Spaniards viewed sex between men. Trujillo was so angry at his
discovery that he spontaneously dismounted from his horse and whipped
both men with the reins.[10] Yuba, in fact, claimed that he whipped both he
and Povia four times.[11] What caused Trujillo to act in such a manner—to
take punishment into his own hands in this way before even denouncing
them to the authorities or allowing them to be prosecuted by the law?
Clearly, as Trujillo himself explained, he believed that they were violating
Church law (he stated he was "punishing them for what they were doing
against God").[12] But his spontaneous reaction can also be tied to commonly held beliefs concerning proper gender roles and sexuality.

## The "Pecado Nefando"

The term "pecado nefando" can, again, be literally translated as "abominable sin." Spanish authorities had been involved in the search for, and
prosecution of, "pecado nefando" since contact and colonization of the

New World began in 1492; in fact, many chroniclers of the conquest, as well as civil and Church authorities, suspected that the New World was "infested" with the practice.[13] In Spanish-occupied parts of the New World, it was applied to a various assortment of activities ranging from anal sex between men to fellatio. In other words, the term might be applied to anything that could be defined as nonreproductive sex;[14] however, male-male anal intercourse seems to have been the focus of much of the prosecution of "pecado nefando."[15] The term's English equivalent is "sodomy": it is often used interchangeably with "pecado nefando" in the historical and anthropological literature on the subject, or, more frequently, to stand for the term.[16] This is the tradition I follow in this essay.

As Trujillo's comments make clear, sodomy was considered a crime against God in the New Mexican Catholic Church. At the time of conquest, the Church defined all forms of sexual activity as sinful; it was, simply, that some sexual activity was more sinful than others. Vaginal sex within the institution of marriage, and which led to reproduction, was seen as the least offensive form of sexual activity in which one could engage. All other type of activity was condemned to one degree or another and the Church sought to regulate this behavior.[17] In fact, in Counter-Reformation Spain, "churchmen and secular officials in Seville increasingly prosecuted people accused of adultery, bigamy, fornication, love magic, sodomy, and soliciting sexual acts on the streets and in the confessional."[18] Church officials sought to impose a "gendered moral order" and those who broke that order by committing an act of sodomy were accused of "undermining the reproductive function of sex and the formation of the core social unit, the family."[19] Such acts were "against nature": they "offended the gender prescriptions of God's holy order in the nature that he had created."[20]

Sodomy was considered to be such a serious crime that Church and civil officials reserved the most severe punishments for it in both Spain and the New World. *Las Sietes Partidas,* the legal code in place in Iberia at the time of conquest,[21] stipulated that those who committed crimes against nature be put to death, except where compulsion or young age prevented a person from engaging in the activity freely.[22] Exile was also a common punishment.[23] The Spanish Inquisition punished sodomy in a similar fashion, according to historian William Monter. Mid-seventeenth-century Holy Office guidelines stipulated that "if the accused was under the age of twenty-five when he committed the crime, or if he had only done a 'close attempt' rather than fully consummated anal sex, he could not be executed." A "close attempt" could mean many things, of course; here, it seems to have meant any sexual or sensual activity apart from anal penetration with ejaculation. If the accused confessed to sodomy, " 'his contrition and simplicity provoked much clemency.' "[24]

These attitudes were imported to the New World after conquest. They shaped the ways in which the Church dealt with sodomy and other "unnatural" sex acts that it encountered there. For example, the first bishop of Mexico wrote a primer on Catholic doctrine that was published in 1543. This document, *Doctrina breve muy provechosa,* condemned sodomy, especially the male-male form of sodomy. "Zumárraga (author of the primer) concluded that the male-female form of sodomy was less sinful than sodomy between two males."[25] Such attitudes remained in place through the end of the colonial period, although it appears as though Inquisition prosecution of sodomy cases in Mexico dropped off after 1700.[26]

Civil authority in the New World, too, labeled such activity a crime and, as Asunción Lavrin correctly argues, Church and state had overlapping interests in the regulation of sodomy because both understood "the need for concerted control for the sake of social order."[27] Martin Nesvig argues that civil law "reviled sodomy for the same reasons as the theologians: homosexuality was a crime against nature, God, and the Crown." But beyond knowing this it is difficult to outline how civil authorities typically treated the crime in the New World due to, simply, a lack of documentation.[28] Iberian law codes may have provided colonial authorities with guidance on how to deal with the crime, but it is very likely that many had not read the codes or possessed copies of the codes.[29] This is most certainly the case for New Mexico, which lacked not only copies of such codes, but also lawyers formally trained to carry out such investigations and prosecutions.[30] A close analysis of the case at hand will reveal how Spanish civil authorities in New Mexico prosecuted sodomy. However, Ramón Gutiérrez argues that at least at the level of popular opinion, attitudes about sex, and about sodomy in particular, conformed to those held by Church and civil authorities in the rest of the New World. New Mexico Spaniards believed that "normal" intercourse involved the man lying on top of the woman. It was unnatural and wrong for a woman to be on top of a man during intercourse because "he [became] submissive by the very fact of his position, and the woman being above [was] active."[31] Sodomy not only undermined the reproductive function of sex, but for a man to take the submissive position in sex also violated gender prescriptions.

### *"Vido Ocularmente": The Importance of Eye-Witnessing Sodomy in Colonial New Mexico*

After hearing Trujillo's accusations concerning the "abominable sin," Perez Velarde immediately issued an order for Yuba's and Povia's arrest and imprisonment. Trujillo, accompanied by soldiers from the Santa Fe presidio, went back to the location where he had caught Yuba and Povia committing sodomy. The two men were still in the pasture and were immediately taken into custody. All of this took place on June 25, 1731—the same day that Trujillo discovered them in his pasture.[32] The swiftness with which they were imprisoned points not only to the serious nature of the accusation, but also to the fact that the authorities believed Yuba and Povia were guilty of what they were accused. Once in custody, the two men were shackled and kept separate from one another so that they could not communicate with each other.[33] Clearly, the authorities were afraid that they would corroborate on testimony if left to their own devices.

On the following day, June 26, Trujillo's official declaration was taken. In his declaration, Trujillo stated the same thing as he had in his initial denunciation of the two men, adding not only that he was very angry with Yuba and Povia for what they had done but also that he had seen them committing the act with his own eyes ("vido ocularmente"). He explained that he had denounced them so that their act would not go unpunished, which again points to Trujillo's anger at what he had witnessed. Since Trujillo was asked numerous times during the investigation if he had witnessed the crime with his own eyes, it is clear that the authorities wished to establish that the crime had, indeed, occurred.[34] It appears that Perez Velarde was aware that, in crimes as serious as sodomy, it was necessary to do so. As Charles Cutter states concerning the northern frontier, "carnal relations between persons of the same sex and bestiality . . . created public scandal by violating accepted standards of behavior, and magistrates took measures to halt such activity. In these matters, provincial judges evidently proceeded with caution, for in the very few cases that exist, they required clear proof of the crime."[35]

But of course having eyewitness testimony was difficult in these types of crimes: and that is what became the central problem of this case, as the next events in the investigation illustrate.

### *"For God's Sake, He Was Unable to Get Erect!"*<br>*Povia Denies That Sodomy Occurred*

The two declarations of Yuba and Povia closed out the fact-finding phase (or first stage) of the case. Povia, the younger of the two, was questioned first on June 29. When asked if he knew why he had been imprisoned, Povia responded that he and Yuba were caught by the Spaniard lying on the ground "belly to belly."[36] He also explained that Yuba had grabbed his "virile member" and pulled it to his "posterior part" but that Povia was unable to get an erection. Seeing this, Yuba continued to touch him but he still could not get erect. It was at this point that "the Spaniard" caught the two, Povia on top of Yuba, belly to belly; the Spaniard then removed Povia from Yuba.[37] Povia again insisted, "for God's sake, he was unable to get erect!"[38] By insisting that he could not get erect even after Yuba's numerous attempts to stimulate him, he implied that he was not interested in engaging in sexual activity with him and that he might have even been forced to do so.

It is obvious that Perez Velarde did not believe Povia's claim, because in the next question, he demanded to know if Povia was speaking the truth since Trujillo said they were committing the "pecado nefando." He also asked Povia to reconfirm that he and Yuba were "belly to belly" when discovered by Trujillo. Clearly, Perez Velarde understood that the whole case would fall apart if Povia's claims were true, and he was attempting to marshal as much evidence as possible against Povia's claim. Since he believed that the position in which the two men were discovered was proof that sodomy had occurred, he focused on that in his questioning of Povia. In addition, his insistence that a Spaniard, Trujillo, had seen the two Indian men "belly to belly" points to a classism and racism that underwrote colonial New Mexican society: a Spaniard's word held more weight than a Pueblo's in such proceedings. To counter such attitudes, Povia insisted that he "told the truth," and that "he was a Christian."[39] By stressing his conversion to the faith of the colonial authorities, as well as his honesty in the context of a legal procedure that required truthfulness on the part of participants, he presented himself as someone who was a successful part of the colonial project in New Mexico—not as someone who was a less than valued member of colonial New Mexican society. And certainly, not someone who would commit the "pecado nefando."

Yuba had a different version of events. In his interrogation on June 30, he claimed that Povia was the aggressor in the case: that Povia "was forcing himself upon" Yuba when Trujillo arrived and told Povia to "get off" of Yuba.[40] Upon hearing this, Perez Velarde repeated to Yuba what Povia had told him in order to emphasize the difference between their two stories: that he and Povia were "belly to belly" and that he had grabbed Povia's penis and pulled it to his posterior part; but finding that there was "no activity" he grabbed Povia's penis again to excite him. Yuba then admitted that he had, indeed, grabbed Povia's penis, but that it was only to "scratch" ("rasguñaba") it.[41] The use of the verb "scratch" (as opposed to, for example, "stroke" or "caress") implies that the activity that was occurring was, at the very least, nonsexual in nature. Given that Yuba claimed Povia was forcing himself upon him, it strongly implies that their interaction was aggressive: that Yuba was attempting to injure ("scratch") Povia in some way. Yuba wished to argue that the contact between the two men was not consensual, and that Povia—not Yuba—was the aggressor in this scenario. On the critical issue of whether or not Povia was erect, Yuba was silent.

## Age and Culpability

With the completion of the interrogation of Yuba and Povia, the "fact-finding" phase of the trial was concluded. The second phase, or plenario, began with ratification of testimony. Charges were then leveled at both Povia and Yuba and their defenders (called Protector de Indios) presented formal defense petitions.[42] After both of the accused ratified their testimonies, insisting that they had nothing new to add and that they had told the truth in their original declarations, Yuba was formally charged on July 4. The document restates Povia's version of the events, not Yuba's: that the two men were "belly to belly" and that Yuba grabbed Povia's penis in an effort to have anal sex. When Povia could not get erect, the document continues, Yuba "touched it to cause activity."[43] The statement read to Povia on July 5 states only that he is being charged with committing the "pecado nefando" with Yuba.[44] These statements of charges raise several issues. First, Perez Velarde says nothing about Povia's inability to attain an erection in either of the two statements; by ending the description of what happened at Yuba touching Povia to "cause activity," this summarization of events leaves one with the impression that "activity" did eventually occur (and thus sodomy). In other words, Perez Velarde did not believe Povia's claims that he could not attain an erection. Second, there is no consideration given to the idea that one of these two men did not consent to the activity that occurred. Perez Velarde clearly believed that the activity had occurred with the consent of both the parties involved.

Finally, Perez Velarde made it clear that Yuba was, in the eyes of the law, the one who was most culpable in this criminal act. In not repeating Yuba's version of events in either statement of charges, there is no counterbalance to Povia's accusations; Yuba's version of events is erased from further consideration from this point on in the trial. Later in the investigation, Perez Velarde simply states that Yuba was most culpable, providing no explanation as to how he arrived at this conclusion. Again, it was common practice to assume the accused was guilty in northern frontier communities during the colonial period. In addition, based upon the way in which the Inquisition and civil authority in Spain sentenced people convicted of sodomy, Perez Velarde was most likely also influenced by the fact that Yuba was the older of the two men (Yuba was 30 years old; Povia appeared to be 18).[45] Recall that *Las Sietes Partidas,* the legal code in place in Spain at the time of the conquest, stipulated that those who committed sodomy be put to death except where compulsion or young age prevented a person from engaging in the activity freely. Youth was seen as a factor in clear decision-making, as well as the ability to consent to sexual (or other criminal) activity. Perhaps such attitudes influenced Perez Velarde in his handling of this case. Certainly, such beliefs influenced the defenders of the two Pueblo men, as we see in the next section of the investigation.

### "It Is Not Clear What They Were Doing": The Defense of Yuba and Povia

In his written defense of Yuba, Juan Manuel Chirinos argued that Yuba ought to be released from prison for two reasons: first, because the two men were simply "playing around" ("jugar"), on top of each other with Yuba grabbing Povia's penis to "scratch" it, when Trujillo arrived and "recklessly denounced them."[46] In other words, Trujillo misconstrued what was going on: the two men were not engaged in sodomy, but were merely wrestling about in a nonsexual manner. Notice that Chirinos' recounting of the events differed from Yuba's: here the use of the verb "jugar" to describe what Yuba and Povia were doing implies that they were playfully wrestling when Trujillo happened upon them. Chirinos does not argue, nor does he even imply, that Yuba was forced into the activity—which is of course what Yuba told Perez Velarde happened during his interrogation on June 30. Despite the fact that Chirinos provided an explanation of what Yuba and Povia were doing, he next stated in his defense of Yuba that authorities needed to make clear (to "certify") what exactly was going on in cases such as these since the charge of sodomy was so serious. Since it was not clear what the two men were doing, Chirinos insisted that the charges be dropped. Finally, Chirinos argued that Yuba "was newly converted to [the Catholic faith]" and therefore ought to be treated with "clemency and mercy." In other words, even if Yuba was engaged in sodomy, he could not have known it was a sin or a crime because "he was newly-converted to the Catholic faith."[47]

Chirinos' defense of Yuba is a rather haphazard affair, attempting to address all possible explanations for the behavior of the two men and then refute any argument that might point the finger of responsibility at Yuba.[48] His statement is contradictory, first arguing that the two men were not committing sodomy so the charges should be dropped, and then stating that it was not clear what they were doing, so the charges should be dropped. Chirinos then goes on to concede that while sodomy might have occurred, Yuba could not have know it was wrong because he did not understand the tenets of the Catholic faith as a new convert.

In his brief defense of Povia, Antonio de Ulibarri repeated that Povia could not complete the act because he could not get erect. He stressed that Povia "did not consent to the crime" and that, as a minor, "he was not corrupted by carnal desire."[49] He was, according to Ulibarri, an "incapable boy."[50] This defense parallels Spanish Inquisitors' argument that an attempt at sodomy was not the same as carrying out the act; and that youthful indiscretion must be taken into account. Ulibarri not only argued that no sodomy occurred; he also insisted that Povia was incapable of sodomy due to his age (he was not "corrupted" by carnal desire). Because he was so young, Ulibarri argued, Povia was unable to perform or to even have the desire to perform sodomy. Thus, in looking at the two defenses together, explanations of what Povia and Yuba were doing range from the outright denial that sodomy occurred; to the argument that it was not clear that sodomy occurred; to finally an acknowledgment that sodomy might have occurred, but no one was to blame for it due to ignorance of Christian doctrine.

### *"His Posterior Part Was Wet": The Visual Evidence of Sodomy*

Normally, at this point in an investigation, papers would be remitted to the governor who would then issue a sentence (the third phase of the investigation). But in this case, Governor Cruzat y Góngora returned the papers on July 17 to Perez Velarde, requesting that he reinterview everyone involved in the case.[51] No explanation for the change in procedure is provided in the court records, but based upon the questions that Cruzat y Góngora directed Perez Velarde to ask Trujillo it appears that the governor was not convinced that sodomy had actually occurred. He ordered Perez Velarde to ask Trujillo if he saw Povia and Yuba "without pants and with their clothes raised"; he also directed him to ask Trujillo "if he saw them consummate the pecado nefando or [other] movements with his own eyes."[52] These questions reflect the governor's desire to unearth exactly what type of activity Yuba and Povia were engaged in on the day they were discovered in Trujillo's pasture. This is not surprising, given the belief that an "attempt" at sodomy was far less serious a matter than actual penetration with ejaculation ("fully consummated anal sex"). Civil authorities in New Mexico held attitudes that were similar to the Spanish Inquisitors: that sodomy accusations needed to be proven beyond a shadow of a doubt.

Perez Velarde provided no information that would enable the governor to determine which of the two scenarios had occurred (an "attempt" or full consummation). At this point in the trial, the only evidence that had been presented was Trujillo's insistence that he had found Yuba and Povia in a compromising position ("belly to belly") in his pasture, both Yuba's and Povia's assertion that they were struggling with each other and that Povia could not get erect, and the defense of the two men which pointed to many different possible explanations for what Trujillo had seen. The strongest piece of evidence that sodomy had occurred was the position in which the two men were found. Perez Velarde's noting the position of the two men frequently in the documentation, as well as pressing declarants about the matter, reflects his belief that this piece of evidence was perhaps enough to convince the governor that sodomy had occurred. Over the course of the investigation, the position of the two men was discussed or at least mentioned twelve times after Povia's and Yuba's initial declarations were taken. This evidence did not convince the governor, however, resulting in the return of the papers to Perez Velarde and further investigation into the matter.

On July 19, Perez Velarde asked Manuel Trujillo, Povia's and Yuba's accuser, to appear for a third time to answer more detailed questions about what exactly he had seen. He was asked whether or not the two men were clothed; if he saw the act completed with his own eyes or what actual movements he saw; and, if, after lifting Povia off of Yuba, there was any evidence of a completed act. Trujillo declared that when he found the two men, he pulled Povia, the smaller of the two, off of Yuba "by the hair." When he lifted Povia, he "opened" Yuba's legs to see if Yuba "was a man or a woman." He discovered "he was a man and that his posterior part . . . was wet."[53] He noted that the two men "had no pants on," and that what clothing they were wearing was "raised up."[54] He also said that he saw them moving about, indicating that they were having sex.[55] These details—especially the one concerning the state of Yuba's "posterior part"—point to the completion of a sexual act. By providing this particular detail, Trujillo emphasized to Perez Velarde that ejaculation had, indeed, occurred. By doing so, he provided both Perez Velarde and Cruzat y Góngora the information they sought: that Povia and Yuba had not simply attempted sodomy but had had "fully consummated" anal sex.

On July 20, Perez Velarde ordered Yuba to reappear to answer more questions because "he was the most culpable" in the criminal act.[56] The questions asked clearly point to Perez Velarde's need to prove that Yuba and Povia had engaged in a completed act of sodomy. In this second interrogation, Yuba was first asked why he was in the pasture to begin with. He responded that he had gone to "help care for the sheep of the local convent." When asked how many times he had had sex with Povia, he replied only on the day "he was struggling with the said Asensio." He was then asked if he had ever "executed the sin" with anyone else, to which he responded no.[57] It was at this point that Perez Velarde began to really pressure Yuba: he demanded that he tell the truth, because Trujillo had seen with his own eyes "that his posterior part was wet."[58] To this, Yuba exclaimed, "for God's sake it is not so, Trujillo lied and that for Saint Maria he did not do such a thing and that he was not a woman for doing such a thing!"[59] Perez Velarde pressed further, demanding again that Yuba tell the truth because Trujillo had seen them "wiggling." Yuba replied that it was true that they were struggling and playing ("luchando y jugando") belly to belly as he had already declared.[60]

While Perez Velarde acquired the tidbit of information that he was looking for—that established that sodomy had, in fact, occurred—there are still obvious questions left unanswered by his investigation. For example, neither Povia nor Yuba is ever asked to explain what they were doing together, if they were not having sex. Yuba says that they were "playing" together, but it is not clear what this means. Both Povia and Yuba assert early in the proceedings that coercion was involved. Was this "play," then, rape? If some elaboration upon these statements were provided, Yuba's position that no sodomy had occurred might be strengthened. Second, while Povia asserts that he never got erect, Yuba is not asked at any point in the trial whether or not this is true. He is never given the opportunity to elaborate upon this bit of evidence. If he had been given such an opportunity, he may have also said that Povia could not get erect, strengthening his case that sodomy had not occurred. Finally, there is no investigation into Povia's and Yuba's relationship prior to the day they were found together in Trujillo's pasture—except for one brief question about whether or not the two had had sex on previous occasions. This type of information might provide some background against which to analyze their actions. But Perez Velarde did not ask such questions; and, a search of the eighteenth-century documentation turns up no other cases or documents that address their relationship.

My point is that Perez Velarde's investigation into the matter is filled with gaps. He did not ask obvious questions because he assumed the guilt of the accused from the beginning of the investigation—as was normal procedure in eighteenth-century New Mexico. He did not need to ask about whether or not Povia had an erection because he knew that sodomy had occurred. Nor did he need to investigate what Yuba meant by statements that the two men were "playing" or their prior relationship, because he knew sodomy had occurred. The weight of the Spanish system of justice, as well as Spanish beliefs and attitudes toward same-sex sex, shaped this investigation from its inception resulting in gaps in information.

Yuba's statements, on the other hand, are contradictory: while he appears intent on denying that sodomy had occurred ("I did not do such a thing!"), he also adds immediately that he was "not a woman for doing such a thing." Here he seems to admit that sodomy did occur, but that this did not make him any less of a man. Furthermore, rather than simply saying "never" when asked how many times he had had sex with Povia, he replied "only on the day he was struggling with Asensio." Yuba was of course under a considerable amount of pressure during this interrogation, and thus he may have missed the fact that Perez Velarde was asking him a leading question ("how many times have you had sex with Povia?"). The declaration that he was "not a woman for doing such a thing," however, seems to have been blurted out of context. There was no reason for Yuba to make such a declaration, to insist to Spanish authorities that he was "womanish" for doing what he did. It is therefore important to analyze this slip of the tongue, for it will provide insight into the ways in which Pueblo peoples viewed masculinity and sexuality after Spanish contact and colonization.

### *"I Am Not a Woman for Doing Such a Thing":* *Passivity and Same-Sex Sex*

It is interesting that Yuba was most upset about being perceived as a woman, as opposed to a sodomite. Notice that he did not exclaim, in the heat of the moment, that he was not a sodomite for engaging in sex with Povia; he exclaimed that he was not a woman for doing such a thing. That he was concerned about being called a woman, as opposed to something else, ought to therefore be carefully considered here. There is evidence from the documentary record that indicate that Spaniards questioned Pueblo masculinity in the colonial period, and that this upset Pueblo men greatly. In 1709, for example, a number of San Juan and Santa Clara men went on an expedition against the Apaches without asking for a license from Governor Peñuela to do so. When asked why they had done such a thing, Captain José Naranjo and the other men who accompanied him explained that their alcalde mayor[61] Juan de Ulibarri "gave them much shame" for initially refusing to go on an earlier, similar expedition. He had told them that they "were not men [and] that they give the arms to the women and they take the mantas and metates" [women's clothing and corn grinding implements] and that "the Jemez and Zia were more manly [literally "mas hombres"] because they killed the Apaches."[62] In other words, they were weak like women for not going on the expedition. Therefore, Naranjo and the others had gone on an unauthorized expedition against the Apaches in order to prove they were warriors.

In this context of "pressured" masculinity, Yuba perhaps felt compelled to deny the effeminacy that his actions with Povia implied. Gutiérrez argues that in New Mexico, "to be buggered was a symbolic sign of defeat equated with femininity; to bugger was an assertion of dominance and masculinity.... Any man who did not assert his sexuality ... ran the risk of being labeled tame, assumed castrated, and thereby lacking ... honor."[63] As noted at the beginning of this essay, any New Mexican man who willingly took the passive role in sex was also seen as emasculated. It is quite possible that Yuba had absorbed these attitudes prior to the investigation and was concerned that his behavior made him look weak and nonmasculine in the eyes of Spanish authorities. As a newly converted Catholic, he may have been exposed to Spanish attitudes through the Church. And, of course, many Pueblos had daily contact with Spaniards; Yuba certainly could have picked up on Spanish attitudes through such daily, casual contact. Or, perhaps Spanish officials taunted Yuba during the proceedings— while he was in custody or during questioning—but those comments were not included in the final recording of testimony and interrogation.

### Pueblo Perspectives on Same-Sex Sex and Masculinity

It is of course possible that Pueblo attitudes toward sexuality were also a source for Yuba's concerns. Perhaps something in Yuba's upbringing or his life at Tesuque shaped his perception of masculinity and sexuality in addition to Spanish attitudes to which he was no doubt exposed. There is very little evidence of Pueblo perspectives on sexuality and sex in the New Mexican documentary record. References to sodomy or to any other type of sexual practice in Pueblo communities in the colonial New Mexican records are almost entirely absent (the Yuba/Povia investigation is a notable exception to this statement). There is, however, the matter of the berdache,[64] which, if handled sensitively, might shed some light on Pueblo perspectives concerning same-sex sex and passivity in sex. The evidence for berdache in New Mexico is sparse until the mid-nineteenth century when anthropologists such as Matilda Coxe Stevenson and Elsie Clews Parsons began to document their presence in Pueblo communities.[65] Both Stevenson and Parsons indicate that berdache were not denigrated in Pueblo communities. Stevenson writes that when the famous berdache We'wha died unexpectedly in late 1896, his death was "'regarded as a calamity'"[66] because he was a "'conspicuous character'" of Zuni because he was a very good potter and weaver, accomplished in the "domestic arts," and "was known for his command of Zuni religious knowledge and practice."[67] Elsie Clews Parsons, too, noted in 1916 that she encountered a generally positive attitude toward berdache at Zuni. Although she did write that there was some resistance to the practice in one family at Zuni, "in regard to the custom itself there seemed to be no reticence in general and no sense of shame."[68] Of course, it is problematic to assume that eighteenth-century attitudes toward berdache were the same as in the nineteenth. However, assuming that attitudes concerning the berdache would have most likely declined (rather than improved) with time and increased contact with Europeans, there is at least some reason to believe that Pueblo communities did not denigrate berdache at the time of the Yuba/Povia investigation.

However, Walter Williams, who does not write specifically about Pueblo communities but about native North America more generally, argues that assuming the passive position in sex was acceptable only as long as the person on the bottom was a berdache. North American indigenous societies did not prohibit or denigrate same-sex sex as long as it occurred between a masculine and feminized male (or berdache), with the berdache assuming the passive position. Sex between two "masculine" men (i.e., neither inhabiting the social role of a woman), or sex where a berdache was "on top," however, was not always acceptable. Sometimes, Williams acknowledges, passivity in the sex act was kept a secret so as not to put one's partner's masculine identity in jeopardy.[69]

If, for a moment, we assume that Pueblo peoples held similar beliefs concerning passivity in same-sex sex (the "passive" in same-sex sex could not be of the masculine gender), then Yuba's comment about not being "womanish" for engaging in sexual activity with Povia makes sense: being caught assuming the passive position with another man when one was not a berdache had the potential to make one "womanish." The only way that Yuba would not be perceived of as "womanish" in this scenario was if he was a berdache. There is no evidence in the trial that either Yuba or Povia was a berdache, however. While the investigation has many gaps in information, it does provide a description of the clothing that both men were wearing at the time that they were discovered. Since cross-dressing is now considered to have been a central characteristic of berdachism (along with sexual activity with men),[70] evidence that either Yuba or Povia were dressed in women's attire would strongly indicate that one of them was a berdache.

If either Yuba or Povia had been dressed as a woman, Manuel Trujillo, their accuser, most certainly would have made that known to Perez Velarde. Trujillo only indicated in his testimony that both men were "without pants." However, in his second and final defense of Yuba, Chirinos argued that the fact that the two men were without pants was not convincing evidence of a completed sex act, since "Indians do not wear pants, but mantas or gamusas."[71] "Gamusa" is a term that means hides or chamois; "mantas" refers to a square piece of fabric made of cotton or wool that the Pueblos wove for their clothing.[72] Anthropologist Matilda Coxe Stevenson indicates that women wore blankets or mantas attached over the right shoulder and under the left arm and cinched with a belt around the waist. Men, on the other hand, wore longish shirts of cotton, wool, or deerskin; woven breech cloths [loincloths] of cotton or wool and long leggings of buckskin with an "overlegging reaching up to the knee formed of a straight piece of skin wrapped around the leg and held on by a woven garter below the knee."[73] Since the incident occurred in June, we may perhaps assume that neither Yuba nor Povia were wearing the long leggings but only a shirt and short breech cloth. Thus, when Chirinos explained that they did not wear pants, I assume him to mean that in the *summer* they did not wear pants, but only a short "kilt" or loincloth.[74] Chirinos' discussion of the clothing the two men were wearing tells us that neither was dressed in women's clothing, which would have been evidence that one of the men was a berdache.[75]

While the issue of berdachism is never mentioned in the trial record, it is possible that the Spaniards involved were at least dimly aware of the practice. Recall that Trujillo, in his second more detailed declaration, indicated that when he came upon Yuba and Povia in his pasture he lifted Povia off of Yuba by the hair to see if the person on the bottom was a man or a woman. In other words, Trujillo was unsure of the passive person's sex. Given the strong patriarchal, heterosexist, and Christian environment of New Mexico at this point in time,[76] it is quite odd that Trujillo did not simply assume that the person underneath Povia was female. What made him question Yuba's sex? There are many possible answers to that question, of course. But perhaps Trujillo, seeing two Pueblo personages engaged in intercourse and knowing a bit about the existence of berdachism among them, understood that he could not assume that the person on the bottom was female.

Given all the evidence discussed, I argue that it is quite possible that Yuba's comment that he was "not a woman" for engaging in sex with Povia stemmed from a combination of beliefs—some Pueblo in origin, some Spanish. There is evidence to support the assertion that Yuba feared how Spanish authorities perceived him; the possibility also exists that Pueblo communities sanctioned "masculine" men that took the passive position in sex with other men. If this is true, Spanish ideologies concerning sex overlaid Pueblo beliefs and worked to highlight or perhaps even exacerbate already-existing rules and codes. Yuba's comment illustrates how the clash of European and Indian ideologies—so characteristic of colonial domination in the New World—manifested itself at the individual, everyday level.

### *"It Is Not Possible to Commit Sodomy in the Manner Described": Chirinos' Final Defense of Yuba and Governor Cruzat y Góngora's Sentence*

The last substantial document in the trial record is Chirinos's second defense of Yuba, received by Perez Velarde on July 23. He begins by noting the inconsistencies between Trujillo's first and second declarations: that in the first, Trujillo never mentioned checking to see if Yuba's posterior part was wet. This detail, notes Chirinos, "prejudiced" his client greatly.[77] Chirinos clearly believed that Trujillo concocted the detail when it became clear that the governor did not believe the sex act had occurred. Further evidence that the act did not occur, Chirinos reasoned, was that it was not possible to commit sodomy in the manner described (i.e., "belly to belly").[78] Neither, Chirinos argued, was the fact that the two men were without pants convincing evidence of a completed sex act, since "Indians do not wear pants, but mantas or gamusas."[79] In light of these facts, Chirinos concluded that the evidence against Yuba was inconclusive, and therefore, he should be absolved of his guilt or punished only lightly.

The papers of the investigation were remitted to Governor Cruzat y Góngora on July 24, initiating the third phase of the investigation—sentencing. The governor handed down his decision on August 1. While acknowledging that there appeared to be little justification for the investigation, the governor still exiled both Yuba and Povia to remote pueblos for four months as part of their punishment for their crimes. They were also whipped 200 times (in addition to the four lashings already given to them by Trujillo) and told never to communicate with each other again.[80] Since exile was a common punishment for this type of activity in Iberia at the time of conquest, Cruzat y Góngora seems to have followed tradition to some extent in his sentencing of the two men. Despite Perez Velarde's insistence that Yuba was more culpable, both received similar sentences—

with the difference that Yuba was sent to a more remote pueblo (Zuni) than Povia (San Felipe).

There is no explanation provided for the governor's statement that there appeared to be little justification for the investigation. However, there were many explanations offered for the actions of the two men, ranging from denial that sodomy occurred to arguing that even if it did occur, one of the participants (Yuba) was newly converted and therefore would not have understood that what he was doing was a sin. Perhaps so many explanations placed a seed of doubt in the mind of the governor. Yet he did impose punishment, including ordering the two men never to communicate with one another again—which implies that he believed on some level that sexual activity had occurred and he wanted to ensure that it never happened again. He sought to cover all the bases by acknowledging that the evidence was weak, but punishing the two men anyway.

It should be noted that this was not the first time that Cruzat y Góngora used this tactic in deciding a case. In June 1731 (the same month that Yuba and Povia were investigated), the governor had Perez Velarde investigate Melchor Trujillo of Isleta for the suspicious death of his wife by drowning. In that case, the governor banned Trujillo from Isleta for two months but stated that he reserved the right to reopen the case should more information be forthcoming.[81] As with the Yuba/Povia case, the governor felt as though the case was not fully or satisfactorily investigated. Perez Velarde was his lead investigator in both cases, which implies there was some question as to Perez Velarde's competence in investigating them. Thus, again, to cover all the bases, Cruzat y Góngora imposed some form of punishment on Trujillo but voiced concerns over the guilt of the accused.

The punishment meted out by Cruzat y Góngora seems mild in comparison to the punishment that Jose Antonio, a boy who lived at Taos in 1775, received for committing bestiality with a calf in a local corral.[82] In that case, neither the fact that Antonio was also newly converted (like Yuba) or was only 13 years old and living in a "rustic" state, deterred the governor from imposing quite a harsh sentence on the boy: he was held in prison for eight days and whipped 12 times each of those days. He was also forced to burn the calf alive with his own hands, and then sent to live in a "house of known virtue."[83] While he was being whipped, he was repeatedly told the cause of his punishment in order to force him to "leave from his idiotism and barbarism."[84]

## Conclusions: Sex, Masculinity, and the "Weak" State

I have used the Yuba/Povia investigation in this article as a vehicle to un-earth colonial New Mexican society's attitudes toward same-sex sex and sexuality. I have also sought to place these attitudes in a broader frame-work—that of colonial Latin and North American ideologies and prac-tices—to give readers a sense of the backdrop against which Pueblo and Spanish New Mexicans formed their opinions about sex and masculinity. The investigation also demonstrates the ways in which Spanish civil au-thority in New Mexico policed Pueblo sexual practices. While this type of policing occurred with less frequency than crackdowns on revolt rumors or suspicious meetings, or at least did not surface as often in the official documentation concerning Pueblo communities, when civil authority did investigate Pueblo sexual practices they were guided by long-held, norma-tive assumptions concerning gender roles and sexuality. Finally, the inves-tigation demonstrates that Pueblo people were not immune to Spanish efforts to impose such normative assumptions. Both Povia and Yuba un-derstood that Spaniards took a dim view of same-sex sex and sodomy. Whether or not either was in agreement with them is, of course, a matter of debate. But, as I have demonstrated here, Pueblo views may have inter-sected with Spanish on the matter of passivity in sex, but diverged as far as the acceptability of sodomy and same-sex sex was concerned.

The lack of official policing of sexuality can be attributed to the fact that the Spanish state was "weak" in peripheral areas of empire like New Mexico. State power was literally embodied in the governor of the prov-ince and his assistants. Institutions and offices of the state that operated in other more central areas of empire such as Mexico City did not operate in New Mexico. Furthermore, the number of personnel that existed in a province like New Mexico was never enough to police the indigenous pop-ulace fully. Spanish civil authority had to pick its battles; and, in the case of New Mexico, that meant focusing on that activity that most threatened the stability of the colony. This fact may help to explain the persistence of same-sex sex and sodomy into the eighteenth century and the berdache in some Pueblo communities well into the nineteenth century.

Evidence of homosexual activity unrelated to the berdache status can be found in native North American cultures. This trial may be evidence that same-sex sex ocurred outside the berdache status in Pueblo commu-nities. Serge Gruzinski in fact argues that a homosexual subculture existed in Mexico City and Puebla in the seventeenth century. Men engaged in promiscuous sex and even arranged meetings in which such activity could easily occur; there were bathhouses; cross-dressing; some prostituted themselves in pulquerías. Gruzinski argues that this was a "subversive" environment that had a secret geography, "its network of information and informers, its language, its codes."[85] It is interesting to note that, overall, a majority of the men who were accused in the particular case that Gruzinski references in this study were Indian. Gruzinski writes that it is difficult to know why twice as many Indians as Spaniards were accused, but suggests that "sociopolitical considerations could have protected certain sectors" of the populace.[86] But one also wonders if berdachism in native communities did not lead those who had moved to urban centers to participate in such a subculture. I do not believe that the Yuba/Povia investigation is evidence of a homosexual subculture in Pueblo communities. However, I do think it is evidence that alternative sexualities and masculinities existed in Pueblo communities at contact, and continued to exist well into the colonial period.

## NOTES

1. The case is at Spanish Archives of New Mexico (SANM) 6: 830–890.

2. Ramón Gutiérrez, *When Jesus Came, the Corn Mothers Went Away: Marriage, Sexuality, and Power in New Mexico, 1500–1846* (Stanford: Stanford University Press, 1991), 146.

3. Even if Church power had remained strong in New Mexico, it is not clear that missionaries would have prosecuted such cases. Jurisdiction over such cases was muddied by the fact that the Church was under the control of the Crown in the New World. For a brief overview of Church-State relations, see, for example, Mark Burkholder and Lyman Johnson, *Colonial Latin America* (New York: Oxford University Press, 1990), 70–97; for how muddy jurisdictional boundaries impacted colonial New Mexican life, see Frances Scholes *Troublous Times in New Mexico, 1659–1670* (Albuquerque: University of New Mexico Press, 1942) and *Church and State in New Mexico, 1610–1650* (Albuquerque: University of New Mexico Press, 1942). Sodomy cases were handled by civil authorities in other areas of colonial Latin America according to Chad Black (personal communication).

4. SANM 6: 1056. The case concerns accusations against an alcalde mayor (local Spanish official) in 1732 that he abused members of Pueblo communities under his jurisdiction. Mateo Trujillo, a lieutenant at Jemez, claimed that the alcalde mayor had ordered him on several occasions to patrol his pueblo for anyone committing adultery. This same alcalde mayor also investigated a man at Zia for com-

mitting adultery in 1727, SANM 6: 524, and made it clear in his declaration concerning the case that he had patrolled Zia, SANM 6: 525.

5. See Henry Beers, *Spanish and Mexican Records of the American Southwest: A Bibliographical Guide to Archive and Manuscript Sources* (Tucson: University of Arizona Press, 1979), for a discussion of the destruction of New Mexico archives over time.

6. Richard Trexler, *Sex and Conquest: Gendered Violence, Political Order, and the European Conquest of the Americas* (Ithaca: Cornell University Press, 1995), 184n.19.

7. See Charles Cutter, *Legal Culture of Northern New Spain, 1700–1810* (Albuquerque: University of New Mexico Press, 1995), 105–146, for a general overview of these three phases.

8. Ibid., 131–132.

9. Ibid., 113.

10. SANM 10: 831, 836.

11. Ibid., 849.

12. Ibid., 831.

13. See Trexler, *Sex and Conquest,* for a comprehensive overview of Spanish definitions of, and attitudes toward, the "pecado nefando."

14. Geoffrey Spurling, "Honor, Sexuality, and the Colonial Church," in *The Faces of Honor: Sex, Shame and Violence in Colonial Latin America,* ed. L. Johnson and S. Lipsett-Rivera (Albuquerque: University of New Mexico Press, 1998), 45–47, 64 fn. 3; Peter Sigal, "(Homo)Sexual Desire and Masculine Power in Colonial Latin America: Notes toward an Integrated Analysis," in *Infamous Desire: Male Homosexuality in Colonial Latin America,* ed. Peter Sigal (Chicago: The University of Chicago Press, 2003), 5; Walter Williams, *The Spirit and the Flesh: Sexual Diversity in American Indian Culture* (Boston: Beacon Press, 1992), 9–10, 132; Asunción Lavrin, "Sexuality in Colonial Mexico: A Church Dilemma," in *Sexuality and Marriage in Colonial Latin America,* ed. A. Lavrin (Lincoln: University of Nebraska Press, 1989), 51.

15. Geoffrey Spurling, "Under Investigation for the Abominable Sin: Damián de Morales Stands Accused of Attempting to Seduce Antón de Tierra de Congo," in *Colonial Lives: Documents on Latin American History, 1550–1850,* ed. R. Boyer and G. Spurling (New York: Oxford University Press, 2000), fn. 1, 125; Richard Trexler, *Sex and Conquest,* 1; Richard Trexler, "Gender Subordination and Political Hierarchy in Pre-Hispanic America," in *Infamous Desire,* ed. Peter Sigal, 88.

16. The Real Academía Española's eighteenth-century dictionaries that one can search on-line (www.rae.es) in fact define the pecado nefando as sodomy. From 1734: "Pecado *nefando:* Se llama el de sodóma, por su torpeza y obscenidad."

17. Sigal, "Gendered Power, the Hybrid Self, and Homosexual Desire in Late Colonial Yucatan," in *Infamous Desire,* ed. Peter Sigal, 103, and Nesvig, "Complicated Terrain of Latin American Homosexuality," *Hispanic American Historical*

*Review* 81(3–4): 694–695; for a succinct overview of what sex acts the Church viewed as acceptable see Lavrin, "Sexuality in Colonial Mexico," 52–54, 73.

18. Mary Elizabeth Perry, *Gender and Disorder in Early Modern Seville* (Princeton: Princeton University Press, 1990), 118; see also Spurling, "Under Investigation," 112.

19. Spurling, "Under Investigation," 112.

20. Perry, *Gender and Disorder,* 118. Church and civil prosecution of sodomy in Spain did not, of course, begin with the Counter-Reformation. As Trexler points out in *Sex and Conquest,* 38–63, the Iberian Peninsula witnessed a long history of the prosecution of sodomy preceding the conquest of the New World.

21. Peggy Liss, *Mexico Under Spain, 1521–1556: Society and the Origins of Nationality* (Chicago: University of Chicago Press, 1984), 5.

22. Perry, *Gender and Disorder,* 123. See also Trexler, *Sex and Conquest,* 45–46 and Henry Kamen, *Inquisition and Society in Spain in the Sixteenth and Seventeenth Centuries* (Bloomington: Indiana University Press, 1985), 207–208.

23. Spurling "Under Investigation," 112.

24. Monter, *Frontiers of Heresy: The Spanish Inquisition from the Basque Lands to Sicily* (Cambridge: Cambridge University Press, 1990), 297.

25. Nesvig, "Complicated Terrain," 693–694.

26. According to Nesvig, it is not clear why prosecution dropped off after 1700, ibid., 710–712.

27. Lavrin, "Introduction: The Scenario, the Actors, and the Issues," in *Sexuality and Marriage in Colonial Latin America,* ed. Asunción Lavrin (Lincoln: University of Nebraska Press, 1989), 3.

28. Nesvig, "Complicated Terrain," 700.

29. Ibid., 697.

30. Marc Simmons, *Spanish Government in New Mexico* (Albuquerque: University of New Mexico Press, 1990), 85, 159–192; Charles Cutter, *The Protector de Indios in Colonial New Mexico, 1659–1821* (Albuquerque: University of New Mexico Press, 1986), 75; Cutter, *Legal Culture,* 105.

31. Gutiérrez, *When Jesus Came,* 212.

32. SANM 6: 831–833.

33. Ibid., 834.

34. Ibid., 836; ibid., 868.

35. Cutter, *Legal Culture,* 136.

36. "Porque lo cojio Español a este confesante con el otro yndio estando en el suelo barriga con barriga." SANM 6: 845.

37. "Y que el referido yndio presso cojio aeste confesante el miembro viril y se lo arrimaba ala parte posterior, y que no se alboroto para meterlo, y que el referido yndio selo estaba manoseando para q se alborotara, y que no pudo alborotarlo . . . y que estando este confessante sobre el otro ynido barriga con barriga, llego el Español." Ibid., 845–846.

38. ". . . y que por Dios no se le alboroto." Ibid., 846.

39. Ibid.

40. Ibid., 849.

41. Ibid., 850.

42. Indian peoples involved in criminal actions were assigned a Protector de Indios (or defense attorneys in more contemporary parlance) throughout Latin America during the colonial period. See Charles Cutter, *Protector de Indios,* for a comprehensive overview of how and when the office functioned in New Mexico, and a discussion of all cases involving Protector de Indios extant in the New Mexico archives. See Cutter, *Legal Culture,* for a more general discussion of the legal culture of the northern frontier of Mexico.

43. SANM 6: 857.

44. Ibid., 860–62.

45. Ibid., 845, 847. Perez Velarde estimated their ages; neither knew their exact age.

46. ". . . que estaba jugando con el dho asensio pobia quien estaba sobre el dho mi parte barriga con barriga quien lo rasguño y el dho mi parte procuro aser lo mismo y que de cojio el miembro biril para rasguñarlo." Ibid., 859.

47. Ibid.

48. In 1737, Chirinos defended a friar at Laguna against accusations of neglect of duties. SANM 7: 562–605. Cruzat y Góngora characterized his defense as "frivolous and without any value." Ibid., 602.

49. "Que como menor de edad no esta bisiado en el [adsero?] carnal." SANM 6: 864.

50. The phase is "muchacho eyncapas." Ibid.

51. Ibid., 867.

52. Ibid., 868.

53. "Se quito el yndio mas pequeño q. estaba enzima y que este locojio de los cabellos . . . y para desengañarsse de si hera hombre, o mugger el que estaba debajo le abrio las piernas, y vido q hera hombre y que en la parte posterio vido que estaba mojado." Ibid., 869–870.

54. "Estaban sin calzones y estaba ropas lebantada." Ibid., 870.

55. "Estaban meneandose." Ibid.

56. Ibid., 871.

57. Ibid., 873.

58. Ibid., 874.

59. "Dijo q por Dios que no es asi que mentío el dho Manuel Trujillo, y que por Santa María no hubo tal cossa, q no hera este confessante mujer para hazer tal cossa." Ibid.

60. Ibid.

61. Local representative of Spanish civil authority. All Pueblo communities had alcalde mayores living nearby.

62. Biblioteca Nacional of Mexico (BNM) legajo 6, #4, p. 30 of unnumbered document.

63. Gutiérrez, *When Jesus Came*, 210.

64. An anatomical male who typically assumed female dress and work roles in many native cultures throughout the New World. They often played important religious and economic roles in their respective communities according to Williams, *The Spirit and the Flesh*, 2–3; Gutiérrez, *When Jesus Came*, 33–34; Roscoe, *The Zuni Man-Woman* (Albuquerque: University of New Mexico Press, 1991), 2. The term "berdache" is Arabic in origin; by the sixteenth century, Spaniards had adopted the term to denote a "passive partner in male-male sexual intercourse," Robert Fulton and Steven Anderson, "The Amerindian 'Man-Woman': Gender, Liminality, and Cultural Continuity," *Current Anthropology*, 33, 5 (1992): 603. Spaniards then applied the pejorative term to Indian men dressed in female garb after they arrived in the New World, Fulton and Anderson, "The Amerindian 'Man-Woman,'" 604. When anthropologists and historians use the term today, it is not meant to carry any pejorative meaning.

65. See Will Roscoe, *The Zuni Man-Woman,* for a complete overview of all evidence concerning berdache in Pueblo communities both before and after Spanish contact and colonization.

66. Ibid., 123.

67. Ibid., 52.

68. Elsie Clews Parsons, "The Zuni La'mana," *American Anthropologist* 18, 4 (1916): 523.

69. Williams, *The Spirit and the Flesh*, 96–97.

70. It should be noted that how berdache are defined is debated. Not everyone agrees that sex in the passive position was a defining characteristic of the berdache; nor, for that matter, that the issue of sexuality or sexual "orientation" [to whom the berdache were attracted] was central to the lives of berdache as, for example, Williams argues in *The Spirit and the Flesh*. Some theorists argue that berdache played central economic roles in their tribes, see Harriet Whitehead, "The Bow and the Burdenstrap: A New Look at Institutionalized Homosexuality in Native North America," in *Sexual Meanings: The Cultural Construction of Gender and Sexuality*, ed. S. Ortner and H. Whitehead (New York: Cambridge University Press, 1981), while others argue that their primary role was spiritual, see Fulton and Anderson, "The Amerindian 'Man-Woman,'" or some mixture of economics and spirituality, see Roscoe, *The Zuni Man-Woman*.

71. SANM 6: 882.

72. Ross Frank, *From Settler to Citizen: New Mexican Economic Development and the Creation of Vecino Society, 1750–1820* (Berkeley: University of California Press, 2000), 15–16.

73. Matilda Coxe Stevenson, "Dress and Adornment of the Pueblo Indians," *The Kiva*, 52, 4 (1987[1911]): 280. These observations are based on late nineteenth-

century Pueblo life, although in the section of the article from which this quote is drawn is titled "Original Daily Dress."

74. I can find no source that indicates men wore mantas. Perhaps he meant the term loosely to refer to manta-like clothing, such as robes—which Pueblo men did wear in "prehistoric and early historic times" according to Charles Lange, *Cochiti: A New Mexico Pueblo, Past and Present* (Albuquerque: University of New Mexico Press, 1959), 75.

75. There are a number of photographs of berdache dressed in just such a manner. See Roscoe, *The Zuni Man-Woman,* 80–92.

76. See Gutiérrez, *When Jesus Came,* for a discussion of colonial New Mexican culture.

77. SANM 6: 881.

78. Ibid., 882. Of course, Chirinos is wrong.

79. Ibid.

80. Ibid., 886–887.

81. Case is at SANM 6: 804–828; Cruzat y Góngora's sentence is at frames 826–827.

82. Case is at SANM 10: 832–851.

83. SANM 10: 851.

84. SANM 10: 847.

85. Gruzinski, "The Ashes of Desire: Homosexuality in Mid-Seventeenth-Century New Spain," in *Infamous Desire,* ed. Peter Sigal, 209.

86. Ibid., 203–204.

# Part II

# Colonial British America

# Chapter 4

# "The Cry of Sodom"
## *Discourse, Intercourse, and Desire in Colonial New England*

### *Richard Godbeer*

Nicholas Sension settled in Windsor, Connecticut, around 1640, married in 1645, and became a prosperous member of his community during the ensuing years. Sension's marriage was childless, but his life appears to have been otherwise unexceptional save in one regard: in 1677, he appeared before the colony's General Court, charged with sodomy.[1] The frank and detailed testimony presented to the court by neighbors and acquaintances left no room for doubt that Sension had made sexual advances to many men in his community over a period of three decades. These advances, deponents claimed, had often taken the form of attempted assault:

> I was in the mill house . . . and Nicholas Sension was with me, and he took me and threw me on the chest, and took hold of my privy parts. [c. 1648] I went out upon the bank to dry myself [after swimming], and the said Sension came to me with his yard or member erected in his hands, and desired me to lie on my belly, and strove with me, but I went away from him. [c. 1658][2]

On other occasions Sension had offered to pay for sex: "He told me," claimed Peter Buoll, "if I would let him have one bloo [blow] at my breech he would give me a charge of powder."[3]

Town elders had investigated Sension's behavior and reprimanded him informally on two occasions, first in the late 1640s and again in the late 1660s. Both investigations were prompted by complaints from relatives of young men who had been approached by Sension.[4] Yet no formal action was taken against him until 1677. Fortunately for the defendant, although several men came forward at the trial to describe his unsuccessful overtures, only one claimed that Sension had actually "committed the sin of sodomy."[5] Because this was a capital crime that required two witnesses for a conviction, Sension could be found guilty only of attempted sodomy. He was sentenced to a severe whipping, public shaming by "stand[ing] upon a ladder by the gallows with a rope about his neck," and disfranchisement. His entire estate was placed in bond for his good behavior. Sension died twelve years later. No information survives to indicate whether he changed his ways as a result of the prosecution.

Nicholas Sension's experience raises many questions about attitudes toward sex in early New England and the effects of illicit sexual behavior on social relations in local communities. This article explores sodomy as a sexual category and as a social issue in colonial New England.[6] In seeking to understand sodomy and its place in the sexual culture of the northern colonies, I make two assumptions that underlie recent theoretical and historical scholarship. First, sex as a physical act must be distinguished from sexuality, the conceptual apparatus that men and women use to give meaning and value to sexual attraction and its enactment.[7] People never simply have sex; at some level of consciousness, they interpret their behavior in terms of their own and their culture's attitudes toward sex. Sexual acts are thus always "scripted."[8]

Second, the meanings ascribed to sex vary from one culture to another, from one place to another, and from one time to another. Although members of different societies may experience similar physical impulses and engage in similar acts, they understand them differently. Sexual categories have no universal signification; they are cultural products, emerging from and contingent on their specific context. Thus, if we are to understand past people's experience of sex, we need to jettison our own notions of sexuality in favor of the categories that they used. Indeed, we cannot assume that sexuality or even desire functions as an independent causal agent in all versions of human subjectivity. Sex acquires meaning in many cultures only as a function of political, economic, social, and religious ideologies.[9]

Theological and legal formulations in early New England, which together constituted the region's official discourse, had no place for desire or sexual orientation as distinct realms of motivation. Puritan thinkers condemned sexual "uncleanness" in general and sodomy in particular as sacrilegious, disorderly acts that resulted from innate depravity, the expression of which did not have to be specifically sexual. The word "lust" denoted any "fleshly" impulse that distracted men and women from "spiritual" endeavors; illicit sex, drunkenness, and personal ambition were equally lustful in Puritan eyes. Official statements on sodomy were sometimes inconsistent in their details, but two fundamentals united them: neither ministers nor magistrates thought of sodomitical acts as being driven by sexual orientation, and they were unequivocally hostile toward those who committed sodomy.

While some ordinary people (by which I mean those who were not invested with clerical, legislative, or judicial authority) doubtless perceived and judged sodomy along lines similar to those advocated by their leaders, others ascribed to it somewhat different meanings and values. The attitudes of colonists toward sodomitical behavior as it occurred in their communities are much more elusive than the legal and theological viewpoints promulgated through sermons, laws, and judicial decisions. Even more obscure are the ways in which people who were attracted to persons of the same sex viewed their own physical impulses. Legal depositions do survive that embody such responses, however, albeit in fragmentary and often oblique form. Whereas ministers perceived sodomy as one of many acts, sexual and nonsexual, that expressed human depravity, some lay persons apparently recognized a specific inclination toward sodomitical behavior in certain individuals. The extant sources reveal a few occasions on which New Englanders, sensing that official discourse was of limited use in making intelligible their actual experiences and observations, created what seemed to them more appropriate categories and frameworks of meaning. This informal and inchoate discourse did not go so far as to invoke a "homosexual" identity as such, but it does seem to have posited an ongoing erotic predilection that transcended the acts themselves. Villagers and townspeople were, moreover, seldom willing to invoke official sanctions against sodomy, despite theological and legal denunciation. Whatever their leaders' expectations, they viewed and treated sodomy on their own terms.

The purpose of this essay is to show that attitudes toward sodomy in colonial New England were more varied than has been assumed, in two ways. First, while religious and legal statements match scholarly impressions of premodern sexual discourse as focused on *acts* rather than *identity,* popular perceptions of sodomy sometimes appear closer to the latter, though we should take care not to invest them with a modern sensibility.[10] Second, not all New Englanders shared the virulent horror of sodomitical acts expressed in official discourse.[11] Some appear to have found other, nonsexual aspects of a person's behavior more significant in determining his or her social worth. What emerges most clearly from the surviving evidence is that, as in so many aspects of their lives, New Englanders were pragmatic in their responses to sodomy, focusing on practical issues rather than moral absolutes.

Responsibility for "put[ting sex] into discourse"[12] in early New England rested with the clergy. It was they who provided the official lens through which colonists were supposed to view sexual impulses. Ministers did not perceive sex as inherently dangerous or evil. Rejecting with scorn the "popish" advocacy of a single and celibate life,[13] Puritans on both sides of the Atlantic taught that God had ordained sexual relations between husband and wife not only to procreate but also to express marital affection.[14] "Conjugal love," wrote Samuel Willard, should be demonstrated through "conjugal union, by which [husband and wife] become one flesh." This oneness was "the nearest relative conjunction in the world . . . follow[ing] from a preference that these have each of other in their hearts, above all the world."[15] Clerics did, however, condemn sexual relations in any context other than marriage. All variants of nonmarital sex, they argued, desecrated the bodies and endangered the souls of the perpetrators. "Uncleanness," warned Samuel Danforth, "pollutes the body, and turns the temple of the holy ghost into a hog-sty, and a dog's kennel."[16]

Clerical condemnation of sex outside marriage was not indiscriminate. When New England ministers addressed their congregations on the subject of sexual uncleanness, they were careful to distinguish between different kinds and degrees of offense. Speaking in 1673, Danforth argued that "abominable uncleanness" could be "expressed by and comprehended under these two terms, *fornication,* and *going after strange flesh.*" Danforth explained that *"fornication"* was to be "taken in a large sense" to include four offenses: "whoredom" ("the vitiating of a single woman"), adultery, incest, and "self-pollution." The second category, *"going after strange flesh,"* incorporated sodomy ("filthiness committed by parties of the same sex") and bestiality ("when any prostitute themselves to a beast").[17] Willard, discussing the Seventh Commandment in a 1704 sermon, used different terminology to make a similar distinction. He told his congregation that "unlawful and prohibited mixtures" could be "ranked under two heads": "natural" and "unnatural." Sodomy and bestiality, he claimed, were "unnatural" because of "the species and sexes" involved, whereas "fornication" (sex "between persons who are single"), adultery, polygamy, and incest were "(in some sense) more natural" because they came "within the compass of the species and sexes."[18]

Danforth and Willard classified sexual acts in terms of those involved and their relationships to each other: their marital status, sex, and species. They and other commentators made a clear distinction between illicit sex performed by a man and woman and that between either two persons of the same sex or a human being and an animal.[19] Clerics believed that women as well as men might engage in sodomitical acts. John Cotton referred to the "unnatural filthiness . . . of man with man, or woman with woman," Thomas Shepard to "secret whoredom, self-pollution, speculative wantonness, men with men, women with women," Charles Chauncy to "unnatural lusts of men with men, or woman with woman," and Samuel Whiting to "unnatural uncleanness . . . when men with men commit filthiness, and women with women."[20]

Those who pursued "strange flesh" disrupted the natural order and crossed scripturally ordained boundaries between sexes and species. Such behavior was thus more clearly sinful and disorderly than was uncleanness between a man and a woman. Sodomy, argued John Rayner, was "more against the light of nature" than other sexual offenses between human beings and therefore "needed the more to be restrained and suppressed."[21] Clerical denunciations of sodomy were harsh and unequivocal. New England, wrote Chauncy, was "defiled by such sins."[22] These were, declared Cotton Mather, "vile . . . unutterable abominations and confusions." They should be punished "with death, without mercy."[23]

Although ministers defined sodomy as involving two persons of the same sex, the notion of sexual orientation had no place in their discourse; nor did they evoke desire as an independent agency that gave rise to sexual acts. They explained sodomy just as they did all other sins, sexual and nonsexual: it was driven by the innate corruption of fallen humanity and embodied disobedience to God's will. Sodomy did spring from a particular frame of mind, but that mental state was not specifically sexual. When William Bradford described the uncleanness that apparently swept through Plymouth Colony during the early 1640s, he divided the illicit acts into categories and clearly saw some as more egregiously sinful than others, but he made no distinction among them when accounting for their incidence. They all derived from "our corrupt natures, which are so hardly bridled, subdued and mortified."[24] Because sodomitical uncleanness was founded in universal corruption, the temptation to commit sodomy afflicted everyone. Even those who remained innocent of particular sinful acts were guilty in their hearts if not in deed. Shepard reminded his congregation that they were all guilty of "heart whoredom, heart sodomy, heart blasphemy, heart drunkenness, heart buggery, heart oppression, [and] heart idolatry."[25]

Ministers reminded their congregations of the fate suffered by the citizens of Sodom in order to warn against "all the sins" in which the Sodomites had engaged, not specifically their sexual offenses.[26] When Jonathan Mitchel referred to "the Apple of Sodom" in 1653, he combined two potent images to invoke not any particular sin, but general depravity and its fruits.[27] In 1673, Willard interpreted "Sodom's overthrow" as an admonition against "security and degeneracy" in all their manifestations, sexual and nonsexual.[28] Sodomy itself figured in the clergy's moral universe as one of many sins that fed on each other in a devilish symbiosis. Just as pride, gluttony, drunkenness, sloth, disobedience, evil company, irreligion, and profanity constituted "the very fodder and fuel of the sin of uncleanness," Danforth taught, so unclean acts would in turn encourage all manner of sin by "pollut[ing] the noble faculties of the soul, the mind, and the conscience." Sinful acts were, then, best understood in association with each other.[29]

Yet for New England clergymen, sodomy was far from being the "utterly confused category" to which Michel Foucault alluded in discussing premodern sexuality.[30] Throughout the seventeenth century, ministers were quite unequivocal in their definition of sodomy: Shepard and Chauncy in the 1640s, Whiting in the 1660s, Danforth in the 1670s, and Willard at the turn of the century referred to sodomy as sex between men or between women.[31] Ministers did not discuss the possibility that anal sex between a man and a woman or nonprocreative sex in general might constitute sodomy.[32] They focused on the violation of boundaries between the sexes, not rectal penetration or sodomy's nonreproductive character.[33] The word had for them a distinct meaning, even though the phenomenon to which it referred should, they insisted, be understood in tandem with, not in isolation from, other sins.

New England laws against sodomy generally followed clerical example in defining the crime as an act that involved "parties of the same sex."[34] The legal codes, however, focused much more specifically on male sex than did clerical pronouncements. The Plymouth, Massachusetts, Connecticut, and New Hampshire laws quoted verbatim Leviticus 20:13: "If any man lyeth with mankind, as he lyeth with a woman, both of them have committed abomination; they both shall surely be put to death."[35]

Rhode Island adopted the language of Romans 1:26–27, defining sodomy as "a vile affection, whereby men given up thereto leave the natural use of woman and burn in their lusts one toward another, and so men with men work that which is unseemly."[36] There were two exceptions to this male-oriented view of sodomy on the part of New England's would-be and actual legislators. A code drawn up by John Cotton in 1636 at the request of the Massachusetts General Court described sodomy as "a carnal fellowship of man with man, or woman with woman."[37] Cotton's formulation was consistent with those produced by his fellow ministers, but the court declined to follow his lead and omitted women from the Massachusetts law against sodomy. New Haven's law, passed in 1655, did include sex between women as a capital offense and cited Romans 1:26 as justification for doing so.[38]

New Haven's sodomy law differed in other respects from the codes adopted elsewhere in New England. Much more detailed and including a broad range of sexual acts, its definition of sodomy incorporated sex between men and between women, anal penetration by men of women and children, male or female ("carnal knowledge of another vessel than God in nature hath appointed to become one flesh, whether it be by abusing the contrary part of a grown woman, or child of either sex"), and vaginal penetration of a girl prior to puberty ("carnal knowledge of . . . [the] unripe vessel of a girl"). Each of these acts was to be treated as a capital crime. The law added that masturbation "in the sight of others . . . corrupting or tempting others to do the like, which tends to the sin of sodomy, if it be not one kind of it," could also justify death, "as the court of magistrates shall determine." The sexual acts encompassed by the New Haven law had two common characteristics, as the law itself explained. Each was nonprocreative, "tending to the destruction of the race of mankind," and each was "unnatural . . . called in scripture the going after strange flesh, or other flesh than God alloweth." Unlike clerical formulations and the laws enacted elsewhere in New England, the New Haven code viewed sodomy as a range of acts that frustrated reproduction, not simply as uncleanness between members of the same sex. The Assistants interpreted biblical references to strange flesh and unnatural sex as referring to the misuse of genital organs, not the gender of the persons to whom they were attached. Seen from this perspective, sodomy became a catchall term for any nonreproductive and therefore unnatural act committed by human beings. The act need not even involve a penis, since the law also encompassed sex between women.[39]

On only two known occasions did women appear before New England courts on charges of "unclean" behavior with each other. In 1642, Elizabeth Johnson was whipped and fined by an Essex County quarterly court for "unseemly practices betwixt her and another maid."[40] Sara Norman and Mary Hammon, both of Yarmouth, Plymouth Colony, were presented in 1649 for "leude behaviour each with other upon a bed."[41] In neither case does the brief court record suggest that the magistrates categorized the offense as sodomitical or, indeed, that they categorized it at all save as "lewd" and "unseemly." The use of these vague adjectives may reflect judicial uncertainty about the classification of sexual intimacy between women as well, perhaps, as a reluctance to describe the acts in question.[42]

Except for New Haven's, New England sodomy laws referred only to sex between men. Yet magistrates were sometimes ready to broaden their conception of sodomy, especially during the first few decades of settlement, which were avowedly experimental. In 1642, the Massachusetts General Court considered treating vaginal sex between a man and a prepubescent girl as sodomy. Dorcas Humfry, the daughter of a Bay Colony magistrate who lived in Salem, had charged three men with having "used her" over a period when she was between six and ten years old.[43] The court faced a serious problem in that the crimes had been committed before the enactment of a law against rape. The Assistants were reluctant to apply the law retroactively and, in any case, it did not apply to children under the age of ten. In the absence of an appropriate law, the magistrates contemplated defining the abuse of Dorcas Humfry as sodomy. They did so on the grounds that Scripture prescribed death for that crime, whereas the rape of a child "was not capital by any express law of God." Thus, the three men could be executed for sodomy with scriptural mandate as a justification, regardless of whether the General Court had passed a law against the crimes in question.[44] John Winthrop, writing in 1641, had argued that sex between a man and "a girl so young, as there can be no possibility of generation" should carry the death penalty since it was "against nature as well as sodomy and buggery." From this perspective, any nonreproductive act might be equivalent to sodomy.[45] The court eventually decided that Humfry's ordeal should be defined as rape. This effectively precluded capital punishment, and so the Assistants handed down sentences far short of execution.[46] But its willingness to consider sodomy as a possible label for sex between a man and a girl suggests that the term was flexible and need not apply only to acts between members of the same sex.

While magistrates were sometimes uncertain about the range of sexual couplings that sodomy might incorporate, they were much more liable to confusion over issues of proof. Sex between men was incontrovertibly sodomitical, but on neither side of the Atlantic did sodomy laws specify the point at which physical intimacy became a capital offense. There was no consensus among English legal experts as to whether penetration was necessary for conviction.[47] In Massachusetts, this question was debated at the 1642 trial that resulted from Dorcas Humfry's accusations. The General Court sought the advice of ministers and magistrates throughout the northern colonies, asking them *"an contactus et fricatio usque ad effusionem seminis sit sodomia morte plectenda* [whether physical contact and friction leading to ejaculation should be punishable by death as sodomy]." According to Winthrop's account, "most of them answered negatively, and that there must be such an act as must make the parties one flesh."[48] Yet the surviving answers given by three of the ministers from Plymouth, along with Bradford's summary of the colony's responses as a whole, illustrate the broad range of interpretations that the laws against sodomy could accommodate. Although the ministers were consistent and confident in their general definitions of sodomy, their formulations became just as varied and equivocal as those of court officials once they had to determine what constituted a sodomitical act in concrete terms.

John Rayner defined sodomy as "carnal knowledge of man or lying with man as with woman, *cum penetratione corporis* [with penetration of the body]." However, he continued, "full intention and bold attempting" could be as damnable as actually performing the act. Moreover, *"contactus* and *fricatio usque ad effusionem seminis"* might be "equivalent to penetration" if performed frequently and over an extended period of time. Like Rayner, Charles Chauncy argued that not only penetration but also "all the evident attempts thereof" might be capital offenses. He suggested that "lying with" could signify both copulation and "other obscure acts preceding the same." Meanwhile, Ralph Partridge wrote that there were several reasons to doubt this broad reading of the law. Partridge held that "the intended act of the Sodomites (who were the first noted masters of this unnatural art of more than brutish filthiness)" was expressed in Genesis 19 "by carnal copulation." Moreover, penetration was crucial to the act of sodomy "among the nations where this unnatural uncleanness is committed." (Partridge did not specify the nations.) Finally, he claimed that indictments in English sodomy cases spoke explicitly of penetration.[49] Others in Plymouth Colony must have agreed with Partridge's narrower view, since Bradford, writing to Governor Richard Bellingham on behalf of his colleagues, argued that while "high attempts and near approaches" in capital crimes may be "as ill as the accomplishment" in God's eyes, yet it was doubtful whether they were punishable by death according to law: "So in sodomy and bestiality, if there be not penetration."[50]

Definitions of the crime and of the criteria for conviction doubtless varied from one magistrate to another and from one case to another, so that generalizations are problematic.[51] But one broad feature does seem fairly clear: courts rarely accepted either intent or physical intimacy short of penetration as grounds for execution.[52] They took care to distinguish between sodomy, attempted sodomy, and other acts tending to sodomy.[53] Ejaculation without penetration did not constitute sodomy in their view of the crime, although it was indicative of intent and could substantiate a lesser charge of sodomitical filthiness.[54] This interpretation of the laws reflected the rigorous standards of proof that the New England judicial system sought to enforce in all capital cases. It was also consistent with the treatment of sex in official discourse, whether legal or theological, as a specific physical act rather than as a form of desire.[55] Magistrates and ministers referred to "sodomy" and "sodomitical" activity but not to "sodomites" or to any specifically homoerotic impulse.[56]

Securing evidence that would justify a conviction for sodomy was no easy matter. Most courts had only circumstantial evidence on which to base their deliberations: deponents may have seen the accused in compromising circumstances, but they rarely claimed to have witnessed penetration itself. The two-witness rule made conviction even less likely, and so in most cases the court could find only that relations to some degree sodomitical had taken place. Edward Michell of Plymouth Colony, for example, was whipped in 1642 for "his lude & sodomiticall practices tending to sodomye with Edward Preston."[57] A year earlier, William Kersley, also of Plymouth Colony, had been presented for "uncleane carriages towards men that he hath lyen withall." The indictment made no mention of sodomy itself, presumably because the court did not anticipate finding any concrete proof. Kersley's case does not appear to have proceeded further, suggesting that the testimony available against him was too flimsy to substantiate even a crime of lesser degree.[58]

Given these problems, it is not surprising that only two individuals, William Plaine and John Knight, are known to have been executed for sodomy in seventeenth-century New England. In neither of their cases was the route to conviction straightforward. Plaine appeared before the Assistants at New Haven in 1646, accused of having "committed sodomy with two persons in England" and of having "corrupted a great part of the youth of Guilford [New Haven Colony] by masturbations, which he had committed, and provoked others to the like above a hundred times." Despite this impressive record, the governor refused to condemn Plaine until he had sought the advice of magistrates and ministers in Massachusetts. Only when his consultants declared that Plaine "ought to die" did the court sentence him accordingly. In 1655, the New Haven General Court found John Knight guilty only of "a sodomitical attempt" on a teenaged boy, but the Assistants eventually decided that Knight's clear intention to commit sodomy, in conjunction with other "defiling ways" and his having been found guilty by a previous court of sexually abusing a neighbor's child, justified the death sentence.[59]

Magistrates and ministers viewed sodomy as a sacrilegious and disorderly act but not as an expression of desire or sexual identity. Yet some men did have an ongoing sexual interest in members of the same sex that was recognized as such by their neighbors, even though the proclivity that they identified was not acknowledged in official pronouncements.[60] Surviving court depositions show that popular perceptions of sodomy were by no means always consistent with official teachings. Whereas ministers sought to understand sodomy as it related to other sins such as sloth and disobedience, townspeople and villagers saw it as a distinct phenomenon. And whereas magistrates focused on the act of penetration, deponents in sodomy prosecutions seem to have found intent equally significant. New Englanders were, furthermore, remarkably slow to act against offenders. The evidence suggests that there was no consensus within local communities as to how (or whether) to respond to sodomy.

New Englanders were sometimes well informed about sodomitical behavior in their midst and the attempts of those who were so inclined to establish local networks. John Allexander of Plymouth Colony, tried in 1637 for "lude behaviour and uncleane carriage" with Thomas Roberts, was found by the court "to have beene formerly notoriously guilty that way." He had apparently sought "to allure others thereunto."[61] Five years later, in 1642, when Edward Michell and Edward Preston appeared before the same colony's court for "lude practises tending to sodomye," Preston was also accused of "pressing" a third man, John Keene, to join them. Keene had refused and reported the incident. The court ordered him "to stand by" while Michell and Preston were whipped. Although Keene had "resisted the temptation, & used meanes to discover it," the judges suspected that "in some thing he was faulty," presumably in having given Preston reason to think that he might be amenable.[62] Magistrates may have feared that Allexander, Preston, and others like them might experience little difficulty in convincing their neighbors and acquaintances to make the transition from what Shepard called "heart sodomy" to actual sodomy. Allexander's notoriety presumably originated with men who did not welcome his overtures and who sought to warn others against him, but Roberts may not have been the only man to accede. Indeed, these two cases may well have resulted from attempts to extend, rather than to create, a sodomitical network in Plymouth Colony.

The depositions presented at Nicholas Sension's trial in 1677 documented one Connecticut man's prolonged quest for sexual partners among his fellow townsmen. Sension had approached a number of men repeatedly, but the young fellow on whom he fixed his attentions most assiduously was Nathaniel Pond, a servant in the Sension household. Pond had complained to his brother Isaac about his master's "grossly lascivious carriages toward him, who did often in an unseemly manner make attempts tending to sodomy." Several witnesses claimed to have seen Sension attempt sodomy with Pond, mostly in the sleeping quarters at Sension's house, where the master seems to have prowled at night, a sexual predator among his servants.[63] Sension's interest in Pond does not appear to have been purely physical. In conversation with neighbor Joshua Holcombe, he spoke of the "fond affections which he had toward" Nathaniel.[64] Pond's feelings about the relationship were clearly ambivalent. On the one hand, he resented his master's attempts to sodomize him and complained about them to his brother. On the other, when Sension responded to a local investigation of his behavior by offering to release Pond from his indenture, the young man refused, claiming that "he was loathe [sic] to leave him who had the trouble of his education in his minority." Nathaniel, who referred to his master as "Uncle Sension," may well have felt a loyalty and affection toward the man that Sension misinterpreted as an invitation to physical intimacy.[65]

Nathaniel Pond was not the only male servant with whom Sension tried to have sex. Most of the men he approached were, like Pond, in their teens or early twenties. Sension appears to have been interested in penetrating men whose age and status placed them in a position subordinate to himself; his sexual impulses were articulated in the context of power relations. This fits well with a study by Alan Bray, who argues that sex between men in Renaissance England expressed the "prevailing distribution" of economic and social power.[66] For most sodomy prosecutions in early

New England, there survives only a brief record of the charge and outcome; in some cases, we do not even know the names of those involved, let alone their age or status relative to each other. But the social context that emerges from the unusually informative transcripts for Sension's trial does at least suggest that for men attracted to members of the same sex in New England as elsewhere in early modern English culture, intercourse, hierarchy, and power were closely intertwined.

Although his interest in sodomizing men was bound up with the expression of social power, Sension characterized his many sexual overtures as a distinct realm of activity. When neighbor William Phelps berated Sension for attempting to seduce various young men, Sension admitted that he had "long" practiced "this trade."[67] It is not clear from Phelps's deposition whether he or Sension introduced the word "trade" into their conversation; indeed, Phelps may have used it retroactively. But the application of the term to Sension's "sodomitical actings," by whomever, is significant in that "trade" implied a specific calling or way of life. Use of that term to describe Sension's behavior indicates a sense of its significance, distinctiveness, and permanence in his life. "Trade" as a signifier went well beyond the act-oriented view of sodomy propounded by official discourse. It fitted Sension's own experience much better than did authorized categories. Phelps's deposition, then, provides a rare glimpse of ordinary people creating their own sexual taxonomy, their own discourse.

Yet even if Sension originated or participated in that creative process, doing so did not enable him to discard religious values that condemned the acts in which he wanted to engage. Testimony at his trial revealed that he had been tormented by his attraction to men. John Enno deposed that one night he saw Sension slip into bed with one of his servants, masturbate against him, and then go into the adjoining room, where Enno "heard Sension pray God to turn him from this sin he had so long lived in."[68] Not all of those who engaged in sodomy were disturbed by religious sanctions. William Plaine challenged the very system of values that condemned sodomy. When questioned about "the lawfulness of such a filthy practice," Plaine "did insinuate seeds of atheism, questioning whether there were a God." Such insinuations underscored the spiritual threat posed by Plaine and doubtless contributed to the court's decision to execute him.[69]

Sension was concerned about his fate in this world as well as the next and realized the legal dangers that faced him. He described his affection for Pond as "foolish," and Enno, who had witnessed several incriminating incidents, told the court that Sension had begged him "to say nothing of these things."[70] Far from being brazen about his attempts at sex with the young men who slept in his house, he was clearly scared and did his best to dissimulate when caught in the act. Samuel Wilson testified that one night in 1671 he "lay back to back" with Nathaniel Pond when Sension came to the bed and started to fondle Pond's "breech," whereupon Wilson "turned about." Sension immediately pulled his hand "out of the bed and said he had come for some tobacco."[71] But neither private warnings from local court members and the fear of more formal proceedings against him, nor repeated rejection, nor spiritual misgivings could deflect Sension from his "trade."

Sension's predilections were apparently well known. Whether or not he found willing partners in and around Windsor, Sension had a reputation for being sexually aggressive that made at least some of his neighbors and acquaintances nervous of him. When Thomas Barber, another man's servant, found he was expected to sleep with Sension "in a trundel bed" during a stay in Hartford, he was "unwilling and afraid" to do so "because of some reports he had heard formerly concerning him." Barber overcame his apprehension, partly because he was reluctant to make "disturbance in a strange house" and partly because members of the General Court "lay in the chamber" and so "he hoped no hurt would come of it." But not long after Barber got into bed, Sension "strove to turn [Barber's] back parts upwards and attempted with his yard to enter his body." Barber now found himself "in a great strait," on the one hand "fearing to disturb the courtiers in the other bed" and on the other "fearing he should be wronged." The anxious servant "turned his elbow back to Sension's belly with several blows which caused him to desist for that time." Barber "slept in fear all night, and in [the] morning told his master . . . that he would lie no more with Goodman Sension."[72]

Sension's persistence, despite his notoriety and the danger in which that placed him, may have been encouraged by the live-and-let-live attitude adopted by the elders of Windsor. After investigating his sexual aggression toward Pond, town elders insisted only that Sension shorten the young man's indenture by one year and pay him forty shillings "for his abuse."[73] The primary concern seems to have been to compensate Pond, not to punish Sension. It is striking that community leaders allowed Pond to stay in the Sension household and, in general, that Sension was able to pursue his "trade" for over three decades before being brought to trial. There were those in and near Windsor who had long condemned Sension's interest in men and feared that others might be seduced into similar behavior. It was,

. William Phelps claimed, the "hazard" of Sension "infecting the rising generation" that drove him to initiate the first informal inquiry into Sension's "actings."[74] Barber was not the only young man who was displeased by his attentions. When Sension got into bed with Daniel Saxton and tried to mount him, Saxton "thrust him off" and declared, "You'll never leave this devilish sin till you are hanged."[75] Saxton left his master before his apprenticeship was completed and told several acquaintances that he did so because of Sension's attempt to have sex with him. Yet the community as a whole seems to have been remarkably tolerant of Sension's behavior.

Issues of power may have figured in Sension's impunity as well as in his choice of partners. The status accorded him as one of the wealthiest householders in town probably shielded him to some degree. Reluctance to tear the fabric of community life by taking formal action against an established citizen and employer may also have counterbalanced disapproval of his sexual proclivities. Sension's popularity among his neighbors and acquaintances may have helped protect him. The court depositions are remarkable for their lack of hostility to the accused, save in regard to his sexual behavior. Sension's evident attraction to men did not undermine the general esteem in which he was held. Thomas Barber, whom Sension had tried to sodomize in Hartford, declared that he was "much beholden" to the accused for "entertainment in his house" and "therefore [was] much troubled that he should be any instrument to testify against him in the least measure."[76] Similar feelings on the part of other Windsor citizens may have long delayed legal proceedings against him.

Why then the community's change of heart in the late 1670s? The key event seems to have been the death of Nathaniel Pond in 1675, after which Sension's approaches to other young men became more frequent. This would have provided his enemies with ammunition to secure the support, however grudging, of formerly loyal neighbors such as Barber.[77] There is no evidence from the preceding decades to suggest that any of Sension's neighbors actually condoned his behavior, but neither does it appear that many people in Windsor, apart from the targets of Sension's lust, cared sufficiently about his sexual tastes to advocate a strong community response. Legal prosecution became possible only when the social disruption brought about by Sension's advances seemed to outweigh his worth as a citizen.

There are remarkable parallels between the Sension case and a superficially quite different situation that developed in another Connecticut community in the mid-eighteenth century. Stephen Gorton, minister at the Baptist church in New London, was suspended from his position in 1756 for "unchaste behaviour with his fellow men when in bed with them."[78] Like Sension, Gorton was a married man who had apparently exhibited his attraction to men "in many instances through a number of years."[79] In 1726, he had appeared before the New London county court for "hav[ing] lasciviously behaved himself towards sundry men, endeavouring to commit sodomy with them."[80] The charge had been dismissed for lack of evidence, but in 1757 the General Meeting of Baptist Churches judged that his "offensive and unchaste behaviour, frequently repeated for a long space of time," indicated "an inward disposition . . . towards the actual commission of a sin of so black and dark a dye." The meeting did not explain what it meant by "inward disposition" but went on to recommend that Gorton absent himself from the Lord's Supper for "several months at least" to "give thereby the most effectual evidence" of his "true humiliation" and reformation.[81] The assumption that Gorton could overcome his proclivities suggests that the meeting viewed his "crime" in terms consistent with earlier religious formulations, as an expression of inner corruption that afflicted everyone but that sinners could defeat with Christ's support. Yet although the phrase was not being used to denote a permanent or specifically sexual orientation, it did depict Gorton's depravity as expressing itself in a particular and consistent form. The plain facts of Gorton's sexual history prompted the meeting to recognize attraction to men as an ongoing facet of his life. The official judgment against him was a diplomatic and subtle response to the situation: it used language in ways that did not actually breach the parameters of authorized discourse but pushed standard categories to their very limits in accommodating local impressions of Gorton's behavior.

Like Sension, Gorton managed to survive more or less unscathed, despite his sexual reputation. Gorton's notorious interest in men caused such discomfort that "many" members left the church "on that account." According to his opponents in 1756, the church had "been broken thereby."[82] Yet once Gorton acknowledged and confessed his sins, the remaining members voted by a two-thirds majority to restore him to the pastorate.[83] Almost three quarters (71.4 percent) of the voting women favored Gorton's restoration, whereas only half (52.2 percent) of the men did so. This vote suggests that Gorton's reputation and behavior made his male parishioners particularly nervous, possibly because they felt threatened by his sexual tastes.[84]

How can we explain the congregation's apparent inaction during the three decades between 1726 and 1756 and then its willingness to reinstate him? Gorton's clerical office is unlikely to have afforded him much protection, considering the frequency with which New Englanders challenged unsatisfactory ministers. It seems more plausible that elders had berated Gorton informally and were hoping that he would mend his ways without their having to initiate formal proceedings. Throughout the colonial period, New England communities preferred to handle problematic behavior through informal channels; they resorted to ecclesiastical discipline or the legal system only when private exhortation failed. Although most of the surviving information about sodomitical activity comes from court records, townspeople and villagers did not see such behavior primarily as a legal problem.[85]

The likelihood that members who disapproved of Gorton's inclinations were interested primarily in reclaiming rather than punishing or dismissing him is strengthened by the church's treatment of Gorton, even after it was driven to formal proceedings against him. Gorton was not the only man accused of "unchaste behaviour" with others of the same sex to benefit from faith in the possibility of spiritual renewal. Ebenezer Knight, a member of the First Church at Marblehead, Massachusetts, suspended from communion in 1732 for his "long series of uncleanness with mankind," was restored to full membership after spending six years in Boston and convincing the membership that he had seen the error of his ways. Why the church finally took action against Knight is unclear, but his expressions of repentance and the assuaging effect of an extended absence brought about his reacceptance into the church community.[86]

There is another possible explanation for the New London congregation's behavior. While some of the church members disapproved of Gorton's behavior and so either sought his spiritual reclamation or lobbied for his removal, others may have been less perturbed by his activities, as long as they did not become a public embarrassment. Most of the correspondence relating to the dispute between pastor and congregation addressed not Gorton's exploits, but the fact that "rumour, offense, and reproach" arising from them had now reached "distant parts and different churches." Indeed, the most striking aspect of local hostility toward Gorton is that church members seem to have been more concerned with rumors having "spread abroad in the world" than with Gorton's actual behavior.[87] Gorton's flock resorted to disciplinary proceedings against him only when the spread of scandal made action imperative. The church members who left the congregation may well have done so rather than stay to fight for his dismissal because they realized that their brethren were either inclined to mercy or did not see Gorton's "unchaste" acts as a serious issue in its own right. If so, their hunch was borne out by the events of 1756.

The impunity with which men such as Gorton pursued their sexual inclinations suggests an attitude on the part of their neighbors that was far removed from the spirit of official pronouncements on the subject. We should not downplay too much the effectiveness of such pronouncements: they may well have deterred individuals from experimenting with sodomy and doubtless incited condemnation of those who committed it. Others may have neglected to act against sodomitical behavior because they were slow to recognize or label it as such, especially when the proscribed behavior took place in the context of established relationships such as that between master and servant. Just as sexually predatory behavior toward a female servant might not always be perceived as a distinct issue of assault because it seemed to fall within the parameters of a master's prerogative, so sexual advances made by a master toward a male servant could also be understood in terms of the power dynamic between the two individuals; there was no compelling need to treat sexual aggression in this context as distinct from the broader relationship or to label it explicitly as sodomy. Those unable or unwilling to do so may well have been disturbed by what they saw but were unable to respond because the behavior was undefined.[88]

New Englanders who did identify and condemn sodomy often may have been deterred by the rigorous demands of the legal system from taking formal action against offenders. Just as colonists waited to prosecute suspect witches until they had accumulated enough evidence to mount a credible prosecution, so when dealing with men like Sension hostile neighbors and acquaintances may have delayed for similar reasons.[89] Informal measures by local magistrates or church elders constituted an attractive alternative to the expensive and often intractable legal system. Moreover, addressing the situation through nonjuridical channels was less direful than invoking capital law and so would have appealed to those who wanted to proceed against offenders but did not want to endanger the lives of those involved. If the local standing of the offender was also an element, as in the Sension case, an informal investigation would provide a more discreet way of addressing the situation. And finally, just as a cunning person's social value as a healer might offset suspicions of "*maleficium*" and protect her for many years from prosecution as a witch, so too the positive attributes of men such as Sension might counterbalance disapproval of their sexual propensities. Risking the loss of a good neighbor and the disruption of social and economic relations in the local community might well have struck the practical minded as too high a price to pay for the expunging of the unclean.[90]

We cannot assume that a majority of New Englanders took their leaders' strictures against sodomy all that seriously. Roger Thompson's claim that official condemnation of sodomy translated into an equally intense "public hostility" seems unwarranted by the evidence.[91] Some incidents relating to sodomy may never have reached court or church records because local communities handled such matters informally; others may have gone unreported because too few people were upset for prosecution to be worthwhile. In the Sension and Gorton cases, formal action was taken only when illicit behavior became socially disruptive or threatened to damage the community's reputation. It seems plausible that lay responses to sodomy ranged from outright condemnation to a live-and-let-live attitude that did not go so far as to condone such behavior but that did enable peaceful cohabitation, especially if the individual concerned was an otherwise valued member of the local community. The weight of opinion does not appear to have rested with those actively hostile toward sodomy.[92]

During the years between Nicholas Sension's trial and the proceedings against Stephen Gorton, the metropolis of London provided the setting for a transformation in the relationship among sodomy, social identity, and gender. By the early eighteenth century, there had emerged in London a distinct and visible sodomitical subculture. Men who were attracted to their own sex could meet others with similar tastes in recognized gathering places such as particular taverns, parks, and public latrines. They adopted a distinctive semiotics of slang, gesture, and dress. They became "mollies," in contemporary parlance. In "molly houses" scattered across London it was customary to adopt effeminate behavior; some mollies cross-dressed. One visitor to a molly house in the Old Bailey observed "men calling one another 'my dear' and hugging, kissing, and tickling each other as if they were a mixture of wanton males and females, and assuming effeminate voices and airs." Many were dressed as women, "completely rigged in gowns, petticoats, headclot'ıs, fine laced shoes, furbelowed scarves, and masks."[93]

Unlike the word "sodomy," which had been used to describe specific acts, "molly" denoted a more broadly conceived identity that included not only sexual attraction to other men but also clearly delineated patterns of self-presentation, even of personality. Whereas theologians in England and New England had argued that everyone was susceptible to sodomitical impulses, molly referred to a specific cadre within the metropolitan population. In focusing on persons instead of acts and in its application to a particular group instead of fallen humanity, in general, the molly represented a major shift in the classification of sexual attraction between men away from "sodomy" and toward what thinkers in the late nineteenth century would term "homosexuality." But neither the rise of a distinctive subculture nor the conflation of sodomy and effeminacy that it embodied was discernible in English communities outside the metropolis. In smaller towns and villages, men who wanted to have sex with other men continued to rely on more tenuous networks and what Bray terms "socially diffused" encounters,[94] a pattern apparently true of early American communities. Surviving evidence from colonial cities gives no signs of a subculture such as London offered. Nor did attacks on cross-dressing in the colonies imply that the wearing of female clothes was related to sodomitical behavior; effeminacy and sodomy were separate categories in early America.[95]

Recent scholarship on the reconfiguration of sexuality and gender in eighteenth-century London and other major European cities shows that modern notions of sexual identity began to develop long before they became crystallized in the taxonomy that now dominates sexual discourse.[96] The New England evidence suggests that making a clear-cut distinction between premodern conceptions of sodomy as an *act* and the modern construction of a homosexual *identity* is problematic not only for eighteenth-century urban culture but also for early modern popular attitudes in the provinces and colonies. To argue that New Englanders identified a distinct sodomitical sexuality would be to stretch the evidence far beyond the bounds of credibility. But exposure to the recurrent impulses of men like Nicholas Sension does seem to have led neighbors and acquaintances to treat sodomy as a specific and persistent impulse; it became in their minds a habitual course of action that characterized some men throughout their lives.[97]

The boundaries between official and popular attitudes should not be overdrawn. In the judgment against Gorton, we see an ecclesiastical body adapting authorized categories so as to incorporate social observation, mediating between doctrinal formulations and reports of actual behavior.[98] Some people doubtless used official categories to interpret what they saw going on around them. Yet the surviving evidence suggests that other men and women identified in certain individuals an ongoing predilection for members of the same sex. The latter response, which falls somewhere between the paradigms focused on act and identity, was quite different from the authorized view of sodomy. That difference was more than a function of rhetoric or occasion: it evinced distinct interpretive responses to sex, one determined by a theological system, the other more empirical.

The long-term survival of apparently incorrigible offenders suggests that many New Englanders either did not condemn sodomy as readily as their leaders or else took the view that acting against such behavior was less important than maintaining the social integrity and reputation of their communities. People who felt compelled to do something may often have preferred private exhortation to public confrontation, partly because of the difficulties inherent in legal prosecution and partly because informal channels were more discreet. But others seem to have felt no compulsion to do anything, in some cases perhaps because they did not identify the behavior as specifically sodomitical and in others because they did not particularly care. Difficult though it was to secure a conviction for sodomy in a New England court, the greater challenge for those who favored legal action was persuading their neighbors to join them in pressing charges, even against "notorious" individuals like John Allexander. Thus, the citizens of Windsor allowed Nicholas Sension to avoid prosecution for over thirty years and to live as a respected member of his community, despite his "sodomitical actings." And thus the Baptist congregation in eighteenth-century New London would delay for several decades before acting against even a pastor, who was known for his sodomitical "disposition."

### NOTES

Editor's note: From "'The Cry of Sodom': Discourse, Intercourse, and Desire in Colonial New England," by Richard Godbeer, *The William and Mary Quarterly*, 3rd Series, Vol. 52, No. 2, April 1995. © 1995 Omohundro Institute of Early American History and Culture. Reprinted by permission.

1. For the transcripts from Sension's trial see "Crimes and Misdemeanours," Connecticut Archives, 1st ser. (1662/3–1789), vol. I, nos. 85–102, Connecticut State Library, Hartford, and Norbert B. Lacy, ed., "Records of the Court of Assistants of Connecticut, 1665–1701" (M.A. thesis, Yale University, 1937), 67–68. Jonathan Ned Katz discusses this case in *Gay/Lesbian Almanac: A New Documentary* (New York, 1983), 111–18. See also Linda Auwers Bissell, "Family, Friends, and Neighbors: Social Interaction in Seventeenth-Century Windsor, Connecticut" (Ph.D. diss., Brandeis

University, 1973), 123–28. Limited biographical information is contained in Henry Reed Stiles, *The History and Genealogies of Ancient Windsor, Connecticut,* . . . 1635–1891, 2 vols. rev. ed. (Hartford, 1891–1892). Sension's date and place of birth are unknown. His wife was admitted to church communion in January 1649, but Sension himself does not appear to have been a church member.

2. "Crimes and Misdemeanours," Conn. Arch., I, nos. 87a, 88a.

3. Ibid., no. 101. See also ibid., no. 88a.

4. William Phelps had prompted town elders to reprimand Sension in the late 1640s after discovering that Sension had made advances to his brothers and other young men in the neighborhood. Twenty years later, Isaac Pond initiated a second investigation after his brother Nathaniel, a servant in the Sension household, complained to Isaac about his master's attempts to sodomize him.

5. "Crimes and Misdemeanours," Conn. Arch., I, no. 93.

6. This essay is indebted to the pioneering work of Katz in *Gay American History: Lesbians and Gay Men in the U.S.A.* (New York, 1976) and *Gay/Lesbian Almanac*; Roger Thompson, "Attitudes Towards Homosexuality in the Seventeenth-Century New England Colonies," *Journal of American Studies,* 23 (1989), 27–40; Robert F. Oaks, " 'Things Fearful to Name': Sodomy and Buggery in Seventeenth-Century New England," *Journal of Social History,* 12 (1978), 268–81, and "Defining Sodomy in Seventeenth-Century Massachusetts," in Salvatore J. Licata and Robert P. Petersen, eds. *Historical Perspectives on Homosexuality* (New York, 1981), 79–83; Louis Crompton, "Homosexuals and the Death Penalty in Colonial America," *Journal of Homosexuality,* I (1976), 277–93; and David Joseph Hibler, "Sexual Rhetoric in Seventeenth-Century American Literature" (Ph.D. diss., University of Notre Dame, 1970), esp. 61–68. See also John Putnam Demos, *Entertaining Satan: Witchcraft and the Culture of Early New England* (New York, 1982), 50–51.

7. This very influential view of sexuality as rooted in culture instead of nature was developed by Michel Foucault in *The History of Sexuality,* vol. I: *An Introduction,* trans. Robert Hurley (New York, 1988).

8. John H. Gagnon and William Simon develop the concept of sexual "scripts" in *Sexual Conduct: The Social Sources of Human Sexuality* (Chicago, 1973), esp. 1–26, and "Sexual Scripts," *Society,* 22, No. I (1984), 53–60. These scripts coordinate both the conventions of interpersonal encounters and the ways in which individuals interpret their feelings and behavior. Gagnon and Simon identify different "levels" of scripting, from "cultural scenarios" shared by all members of a given culture to "intrapsychic scripts" that express an individual's most private and idiosyncratic desires.

The relationship between cultural constructs and sexual attraction has given rise to a complex debate among social scientists and, more recently, historians; see Diane Richardson, "The Dilemma of Essentiality in Homosexual Theory," *Journal of Homosexuality,* 9, Nos. 2–3 (1983–1984), 79–90; Gregory A. Sprague, "Male Homosexuality in Western Culture: The Dilemma of Identity and Subculture in Historical Research," ibid., 10, Nos. 3–4 (1984), 29–43; Editors' Introduction, in Martin Bauml Duberman, Martha Vicinus, and George Chauncey, Jr., eds., *Hidden from History: Reclaiming the Gay and Lesbian Past* (New York, 1989); Stephen O. Murray, "Homosexual Acts and Selves in Early Modern Europe," in Kent Gerard and Gert Hekma, eds., *The Pursuit of Sodomy: Male Homosexuality in Renaissance and Enlightenment Europe* (New York, 1989), 467; David M. Halperin, *One Hundred Years of Homosexuality: And Other Essays on Greek Love* (New York, 1990); and Edward Stein, ed., *Forms of Desire: Sexual Orientation and the Social Constructionist Controversy* (New York, 1990).

9. As Bruce R. Smith points out, for the 16th and 17th centuries "sexuality was not, as it is for us, the starting place for anyone's self-definition"; Smith, *Homosexual Desire in Shakespeare's England: A Cultural Poetics* (Chicago, 1991), 10–11. See also Robert A. Padgug, "Sexual Matters: On Conceptualizing Sexuality in History," *Radical History Review*, 20 (1979), 16. The application of 20th-century sexual categories such as "homosexual" to earlier cultures can be extremely misleading. Smith makes a useful distinction between "homo*sexuality*" as "specific to our own culture and to our own moment in history" and "homo*sexual behavior*" as "a cross-cultural, transhistorical phenomenon"; Smith, *Homosexual Desire in Shakespeare's England*, 12, but "homosexual" carries so many connotations for the 20th-century reader that I prefer to avoid it, along with the term "gay."

10. Katz's introduction to pt. I of *Gay/Lesbian Almanac*, 29–35, implies that colonists in general viewed sodomy through an officially approved interpretive lens. But scholars of early modern England and Europe have suggested recently that a sharp distinction between premodern and modern notions of sex may be less useful for understanding social experience and the attitudes of ordinary people than for discussion of theological and legal discourse; see note 96 below.

11. See especially Thompson, "Attitudes Towards Homosexuality in the Seventeenth-Century New England Colonies."

12. Foucault, *History of Sexuality*, I, 11.

13. See, for example, Samuel Willard, *A Compleat Body of Divinity* (Boston, 1726), 674, and John Cotton, *A Meet Help* (Boston, 1699), 16.

14. See James T. Johnson, "The Covenant Idea and the Puritan View of Marriage," *Journal of the History of Ideas*, 32 (1971), esp. 108–10.

15. Willard, *Compleat Body of Divinity*, 609. Marital sex was not without its dangers. Husband and wife must take care lest their physical relationship distract them from their love for Christ. The act of generation was, moreover, tainted by its association with the curse placed on Adam and Eve, so that intercourse and the children that resulted from it were marked by the legacy of original sin. For two very different impressions of Puritan attitudes toward sex see Edmund S. Morgan, "The Puritans and Sex," *New England Quarterly*, 15 (1942), 591–607, and Kathleen Verduin, " 'Our Cursed Natures': Sexuality and the Puritan Conscience," ibid., 56 (1983), 220–37. See also Michael Zuckerman, "Pilgrims in the Wilderness:

Community, Modernity, and the Maypole at Merry Mount," ibid., 50 (1977), esp. 264–67.

16. Samuel Danforth, *The Cry of Sodom Enquired Into* (Cambridge, Mass., 1674), 6. Frequent use of "uncleanness" to describe unauthorized sexual acts, in court records and sermons, derived from this conception of the body as a temple that must be kept undefiled, "a house for the soul to dwell and act in"; Jonathan Mitchel, "Continuation of Sermons on the Body of Divinity," 209, Feb. 7, 1657, Massachusetts Historical Society, Boston. See also Cotton Mather, *The Pure Nazarite* (Boston, 1723), 17.

17. Danforth, *Cry of Sodom*, 3–5.

18. Willard, *Compleat Body of Divinity*, 681–82.

19. See, for example, William Bradford, *Of Plymouth Plantation, 1620–1647*, ed. Samuel Eliot Morison (New York, 1952), 316. For an intriguing commentary on Bradford's discussion of illicit sex that draws on recent "queer theory" see Jonathan Goldberg. *Sodometries: Renaissance Texts, Modern Sexualities* (Stanford, 1992), 223–46. Mitchel distinguished between "wantonness and unnatural pollutions," terms equivalent to Danforth's "fornication" and "going after strange flesh," in "Continuation of Sermons Concerning Man's Misery," June 21, 1654, MHS.

20. Cotton, "An Abstract of the Laws of New-England as they are now established" (1641), *Massachusetts Historical Society Collections*, 1st Ser., 5 (1798), 183; Shepard, *The Sincere Convert: Discovering the Small Number of True Believers . . .* (Cambridge, Mass., 1664), 67; Chauncy, "Opinions of Three Ministers on Unnatural Vice" (1642), in Bradford, *Of Plymouth Plantation*, ed. Morison, 411; Whiting, *Abraham's Humble Intercession for Sodom* (Cambridge, Mass., 1666), 46.

21. It also "might be committed with more secrecy and less suspicion," presumably because the parties involved did not have to worry about exposure through pregnancy; Rayner, "Opinions of Three Ministers," 405.

22. Chauncy, ibid., 410.

23. Mather, *An Holy Rebuke to the Unclean Spirit* (Boston, 1693), 44; *The Sailor's Companion and Counsellor* (Boston, 1709), viii. See also the denunciations by Ralph Partridge in "Opinions of Three Ministers," 407, by Mitchel in "Continuation of Sermons Concerning Man's Misery," Aug. 15, 1655, and by Increase Mather in *Solemn Advice to Young Men* (Boston, 1695), 37. The main biblical prohibitions and precedents that provided the bases for clerical teaching on this subject were Gen. 19:1–29; Lev. 18:22, 20:13; Deut. 23:17; Judg. 19:22–23; I Kings 15:12; II Kings 23:1; Rom. 1:26–27; I Cor. 6:9–10; I Tim. 1:10. Thompson discusses "the conventional revulsion against homosexuals" in early modern England and New England in "Attitudes Towards Homosexuality in the Seventeenth-Century New England Colonies," esp. 31–34.

24. Bradford, *Of Plymouth Plantation*, ed. Morison. 316. See also John Rainolds, *Th'overthrow Of Stage-Plays . . .* (Middleburgh, 1599), 10, 32.

25. Shepard, *Sincere Convert*, 42. See also Danforth, *Cry of Sodom*, 11. This general propensity toward at least "heart sodomy" included the ministers themselves. Michael Wigglesworth, for example, admitted to "filthy lust . . . flowing from [his] affection to [his] pupils"; Wigglesworth, "Diary," *Colonial Society of Massachusetts Publications*, 35 (1946), 350. For a detailed discussion of Wigglesworth's struggle with his filthy lust see Katz, *Gay/Lesbian Almanac*, 94–100.

26. Cotton Mather, *A Christian At His Calling* (Boston, 1701), 43.

27. Mitchel, "Continuation of Sermons Concerning Man's Misery," Feb. 1, 1653.

28. Willard, *Useful Instructions of a Professing People in Times of Great Security and Degeneracy . . .* (Cambridge, Mass., 1673), 12. The importance of Sodom as an inspiration to collective discipline is discussed in Michael Warner, "New English Sodom," *American Literature*, 64 (1992), 19–47.

29. Danforth, *Cry of Sodom*, 6, 18–19. Cotton Mather and Danforth both used a developmental framework to portray sodomy and bestiality as the culmination of a career in sin, both sexual and nonsexual; Mather, *Holy Rebuke*, 42–44; Danforth, *Cry of Sodom*, 8–9. See also *The Life and Death of John Atherton, Lord Bishop of Waterford and Lysmore* (London, 1641), and Guillaume de Salluste Du Bartas, *The Divine Weeks and Works of Guillaume de Salluste Sieur du Bartas*, trans. Joshua Sylvester, ed. S. Snyder (Oxford, 1979), 518, 522.

Commentators on both sides of the Atlantic associated sodomy with disorder and linked it to other sins that inverted the "natural" state of things or challenged authority. See Alan Bray, *Homosexuality in Renaissance England* (London, 1982), 25–26. Thus, Danforth saw fit to emphasize Benjamin Goad's disobedience to his parents and his sabbath breaking as part of his slide into "sodomitical wickedness" and bestiality. Edward Coke included the crime in a trio with sorcery and heresy, both of which embodied treason against God; Danforth, *Cry of Sodom*, 8–9; Coke, *The Twelfth Part of the Reports . . .* (London, 1656), 36.

30. Foucault, *History of Sexuality*, I, 101.

31. There was no identifiable change in clerical attitudes toward sodomy during the 17th century, and ministers' views on the subject were remarkably consistent with each other. Rayner's comment that sodomy's nonreproductive character made it a less serious offense against "family and posterity" than "some other capital sins of uncleanness" was an unusual concession, albeit overshadowed by standard denunciations elsewhere in his Opinion: "Opinions of Three Ministers," 405.

32. Across the Atlantic, sodomy referred sometimes to sex between men and sometimes to anal sex. As Arthur N. Gilbert points out, this dual meaning ("relational" vs. "behavioral") gave rise to "endless confusion"; Gilbert, "Conceptions of Homosexuality and Sodomy in Western History," *J. Homosexuality*, 6 (1980–1981), esp. 62–63.

33. Rayner pointed out that "there was not the like reason and degree of sinning against family and posterity in this sin as in some other capital sins of

uncleanness." From this perspective, sodomy's nonprocreative nature made it less threatening than adultery or rape, either of which could intrude illegitimate offspring into a family's line of inheritance; "Opinions of Three Ministers," 405.

34. The English statutes of 1533 and 1563 used "buggery" to denote both sodomy and bestiality, thus conflating the two principal categories of "unnatural" sex, whereas the New England legal codes treated the two crimes separately. "Buggery" was mostly used in New England to denote bestiality, although it did occasionally refer to sex between men. Sodomy and bestiality were apparently becoming more distinct in English legal minds during the 17th century; see Gregory W. Bredbeck, *Sodomy and Interpretation: Marlowe to Milton* (Ithaca, 1991), 19–20.

35. The Plymouth code of 1636 merely listed capital crimes; Nathaniel B. Shurtleff and David Pulsifer, eds., *Records of the Colony of New Plymouth in New England,* 12 vols. (Boston, 1855–1861), XI, 12, whereas the much fuller General Laws of 1671 incorporated the Levitical injunction; *The Book of the General Laws of the Inhabitants of the Jurisdiction of New-Plimouth* . . . (Cambridge, Mass., 1672), 4. The original Massachusetts law of 1641, "The Capital Laws of New England," *Col. Soc. Mass. Publications,* 17 (1913–1914), 117, was amended to exempt from the death sentence parties who were either "forced" or under age 14 in the 1647 version, *The Book of the General Lawes and Libertyes Concerning the Inhabitants of the Massachusets* (Cambridge, Mass. 1648), 5–6. The Connecticut law of 1642, later incorporated into the code of 1650, copied the 1641 Massachusetts law; J. Hammond Trumbull, ed., *The Public Records of the Colony of Connecticut . . .* vol. I (Hartford, 1850), 77, 515. It was amended in 1672 along lines similar (force or under age 15) to the Massachusetts revision of 1647; *The Book of the General Laws for the People within the Jurisdiction of Connecticut . . .* (Cambridge, Mass., 1673), 9. For the New Hampshire law of 1680, see "Cappitall Lawes" in John D. Cushing, ed., *Acts and Laws of New Hampshire, 1680–1726* (Wilmington, Del., 1978), 205. The sodomy laws remained unchanged under the Dominion. Nor were there immediate changes under the 1691 charter, although Massachusetts adopted a new law in 1697 that combined biblical language with legal phraseology taken from the English statutes of 1533 and 1563; *Acts and Laws of His Majesties Province of the Massachusetts Bay . . .* (Boston, 1699), 114. New Hampshire followed suit in 1718; *Acts and Laws of New Hampshire . . .* , ed. Cushing, 141.

36. "Proceedings of the First General Assembly," in Cushing, ed., *The Earliest Acts and Laws of the Colony of Rhode Island and Providence Plantations, 1647–1719* (Wilmington, Del., 1977), 25–26. See also the slightly modified law of 1663, ibid., 64. Unlike the Leviticus-inspired laws, this formulation alludes to the "affection" and "lusts" that apparently drove men to commit sodomy. Puritan writers regularly used these words in describing the impulses, sexual and nonsexual, that innate depravity aroused. Even when used in a specifically sexual context, as in Chauncy's reference to the "unnatural lusts of men with men. or woman with

woman," such language did not signify a distinct sexual agency or subjectivity underlying the acts; "Opinions of Three Ministers," 411.

37. Cotton, "Abstract of the Laws of New-England," 183.

38. *New-Haven's Settling in New-England. And Some Laws for Government. . . .* (London, 1656), 19. The law gave no clue as to how sex between women was to be defined or proven.

39. Ibid., 19. Why New Haven rejected a simple restatement of biblical injunction in favor of a lengthy, unusually explicit, and broadly conceived formulation is a mystery. If this sodomy law had been the first to appear in New England, it might be tempting to argue for a narrowing definition of the crime as years passed. Yet other northern colonies had already adopted laws that specified sex between men as their purview. New Haven's code was thus anomalous, not part of a trend. The General Court may have hoped that a far-reaching definition of the crime would facilitate legal process in dealing with sex offenders, reacting against the restrictive format used elsewhere. If so, no other colony followed New Haven's example. The New Haven law remained in effect for only 10 years since the colony united with Connecticut in 1665 and thereafter came under Connecticut's legal code.

40. George Francis Dow, ed., *Records and Files of the Quarterly Courts of Essex County,* vol. I: *1636–1656* (Salem, Mass., 1911), 44.

41. Shurtleff and Pulsifer, eds., *Plym. Col. Recs.,* II, 137.

42. The legal system's focus on male sex was driven not only by a generally phallocentric discourse but also by a preoccupation with the effects of illicit reproduction on lines of inheritance or (in case of bastardy) the public purse and further by the practical difficulty of defining and proving nonphallic sexual acts. For discussion of theological and legal perspectives on sex between women in premodern western society see Louis Crompton, "The Myth of Lesbian Impunity: Capital Laws from 1270 to 1791," in Licata and Peterson, eds., *Historical Perspectives on Homosexuality,* 11–25, and Judith C. Brown, "Lesbian Sexuality in Medieval and Early Modern Europe," in Duberman et al., eds., *Hidden from History,* 67–75.

43. John Winthrop describes this case in his *History of New England from 1630 to 1649,* ed. James Savage, 2 vols. (Boston, 1825–1826), II, 45–48.

44. Ibid., 48. The court was also uncertain whether Dorcas had been a willing party. In a rape case that would be a central issue, whereas if the sexual acts performed by Daniel Fairfield, Jenkin Davis, and John Hudson were categorized as sodomy, they could be judged as capital regardless of consent.

45. Ibid.; Shurtleff, ed., *Records of the Governor and Company of Massachusetts Bay in New England,* 5 vols. (Boston, 1853–1854), II, 12–13. On the same day, the General Court amended the law against rape so as to enable use of the death penalty in future cases of child molestation; ibid., II, 21–22.

46. Winthrop, *Journal* (Hartford, 1790), 229. No case of anal sex between a

man and a woman is known to have come before a New England court, in New Haven or elsewhere, although it seems possible that magistrates would have considered such an act "against nature" and so at least related to sodomy.

47. Coke held that there must be "*penetratio,* that is, *res in re* (one thing inside another)," although he added that "the least penetration maketh it carnal knowledge"; Coke, *The Third Part of the Institutes of the Laws of England: Concerning . . . Criminal Cases . . .* (London, 1644), 58–59. Yet this restrictive view of the crime was rejected in the Westminster trial of Mervyn Touchet, Lord Audley, second earl of Castlehaven, who was accused of "abetting a rape upon his countess" and "committing sodomy with his servants." The attorney general argued that the law of 1563 did not actually require that penetration had taken place: it described the crime "in general terms, and *ubi lex non distinguit, ibi non distinguendum* (where the law does not distinguish, no distinction should be made)." The lord chief justice followed the same line of reasoning, insisting that the law made "no distinction" between ejaculation without penetration and penetration itself. See Caroline Bingham, "Seventeenth-Century Attitudes toward Deviant Sex," *Journal of Interdisciplinary History,* 1 (1970–1971), 447–72, quotations on 448, 456, 459.

48. Winthrop, *History of New England,* II, 47.

49. "Opinions of Three Ministers," 404–13.

50. Bradford, *Of Plymouth Plantation,* 319.

51. The inconsistencies appear to have been ad hoc; they do not form any clear pattern of changing attitudes within the magistracy over time. But the surviving records are often so laconic or vague that it is not possible to tell what criteria were being used. In the case of William Plaine, for example, it is unclear whether his conviction was based on his having committed sodomy "with two persons in England" or his encouraging young people in Guilford, New Haven Colony, to masturbate, or both; Winthrop, *History of New England,* II, 265.

52. Drawing on the responses of Rayner, Chauncy, and Partridge, Hibler suggests that the "tendency" among New England theologians was to believe "that a full act of sodomy was constituted merely in the emission of seed, even if penetration did not take place"; Hibler, "Sexual Rhetoric in Seventeenth-Century American Literature," 62–63. Yet the accounts by Winthrop and Bradford indicate that most of those consulted in 1642 tended toward the more restrictive view.

53. See, for example, Shurtleff and Pulsifer, eds., *Plym. Col. Recs.,* II, 35.

54. In 1637, a Plymouth court found John Allexander and Thomas Roberts "guilty of lude behaviour and unclean carriage one with another, by often spendinge their seed one upon another." The emission of seed established beyond doubt their unclean carriage, but there was no evidence to support a charge of outright sodomy. Caution is in order here since the record does not specify whether the ejaculations in question resulted from autoerotic or mutual stimulation. The latter may have been treated as closer to sodomy than the former; ibid., I, 64. The officials who presided over the trial concerning Dorcas Humfry in 1642

seem to have assumed that the ability to ejaculate was at least relevant. When Humfry claimed not only that three men had "abused" her but also that two of her own brothers had "used such dalliance with her," the magistrates decided that the boys in question were too young to be capable of "semination" and so left them to "private correction"; Winthrop, *History of New England*, II, 46.

55. As Foucault put it, because sodomy was "a category of forbidden acts, their perpetrator was nothing more than the juridical subject of them"; Foucault, *History of Sexuality*, I, 43.

56. Coton Mather's reference to "Sodomites on board" is the only exception to this that I have found; Mather, *Sailor's Companion*, 39. Ministers did mention "Sodomites" as in the citizens of Sodom. See, for example, Danforth, *Cry of Sodom*, 1.

57. Shurtleff and Pulsifer, eds., *Plym. Col. Recs.*, II, 35.

58. Ibid., 28.

59. Winthrop, *History of New England*, II, 265; "Early General Records of the Colony of New Haven," vol. IB, 89–91, Conn. St. Lib. For three cases of sodomy heard by eighteenth-century Massachusetts courts, see Thomas Foster, "Sex and the Eighteenth-Century Man: Anglo-American Discourses of Sex and Manliness in Massachusetts, 1690–1765" (Ph.D. dissertation, Johns Hopkins University, 2002), 157–60.

60. It is not possible to tell whether any of those who engaged in sodomy (or acts "tending to sodomy") were gender exclusive in their sexual tastes, but some were clearly not. Edward Michell of Plymouth Colony had apparently engaged in lewd carriages with Lydia Hatch as well as lewd and sodomitical practices with Edward Preston; Shurtleff and Pulsifer, eds., *Plym. Col. Recs.*, II, 35–36. Teage Joanes, also of Plymouth Colony, was presented in 1649 on charges of sodomy with an unnamed individual and other unclean carriages with Sara Norman, who herself appeared in court that same year for lewd behavior with Mary Hammon; ibid., II, 137, 146–48. The laconic court records give no clue as to whether these assorted offenders were aware of each other's activities. See also the 1655 case of John Knight, who was charged with having assaulted both Peter Vincon and Mary Clarke, in "Early General Records of the Colony of New Haven." vol. IB, 89–91.

61. Shurtleff and Pulsifer, eds., *Plym. Col. Recs.*, I, 64.

62. Ibid., II, 35–36.

63. Fortunately for Sension, only one deponent at his trial claimed actually to have seen him engage in intercourse with Pond. Daniel Saxton, another of Sension's servants, told the court that he saw his master get into bed with Pond "and make the bed shake," which led Saxton to believe that Sension had indeed "committed the sin of sodomy"; "Crimes and Misdemeanours," Conn. Arch., I, nos. 93, 95b. But Sension denied having sodomized anyone, and, since Pond himself had died in Metacomet's Rebellion, the court lacked the two witnesses required by law for a capital conviction.

64. Ibid., no. 95b.

65. Ibid., no. 89. Katz has suggested that since Sension's marriage was childless, the servant may also have been motivated by hopes of an inheritance, in *Gay/Lesbian Almanac*, 114.

66. Bray, *Homosexuality in Renaissance England*, 49–51, 56. Bruce Smith identifies the myth of "Master and Minion" as an important component in the cultural poetics of same-sex desire in the English Renaissance. That particular mythic configuration "reinforced the hierarchical relationships in which Renaissance readers defined themselves as individuals, as members of society, and as partners in love"; Smith, *Homosexual Desire in Shakespeare's England*, 193.

67. Sension "acknowledged he took [it] up at the school where he was educated"; "Crimes and Misdemeanours," Conn. Arch., I, no. 98b.

68. Ibid., nos. 96a, 96b.

69. Winthrop, *History of New England*, II, 265. Bray discusses Christopher Marlowe's controversial views on sodomy and religion in *Homosexuality in Renaissance England*, 63–66.

70. "Crimes and Misdemeanours," Conn. Arch., I, nos. 88a, 95b.

71. Ibid., no. 91.

72. Ibid., no. 99.

73. Ibid., no. 89.

74. Ibid., no. 98.

75. Ibid., nos. 87a, 88b, 93.

76. Ibid., no. 99.

77. Ibid., no. 92. In 1677, Sension himself sued Saxton for defaming him by "charging of him with a notorious crime." The timing of the suit relative to Sension's trial is unclear from the surviving transcripts. It is possible that Sension precipitated the charges against himself by bringing the suit and so provoking a series of depositions defending Saxton and incriminating Sension. But it seems unlikely that Sension would have taken such a risk, especially given his sense of his own endangerment as reported in some of the depositions.

78. New London [Conn.] congregation to General Meeting of Baptist Churches, Sept. 11, 1756, Backus Papers, box 7, Andover-Newton Theological School, Newton Centre, Mass. I am much indebted to Susan Juster, who kindly shared her transcripts of the correspondence between the General Meeting of Baptist Churches, the church at New London, and Gorton. Juster discusses the controversy over Gorton's behavior in *Disorderly Women: Sexual Politics and Evangelicalism in Revolutionary New England* (Ithaca, 1994), 90–92.

79. General Meeting of Baptist Churches to Stephen Gorton, Sept. 13, 1756, Backus Papers, box 7.

80. New London County Court Records, loose files, June Term, 1726, Conn. St. Lib. Since neither the court record nor the church correspondence from 1756 revealed the identity of the men with whom Gorton tried to have sex, the distribu-

tion of social power between those involved cannot be reconstructed, although Gorton's position as a household head is suggestive.

81. General Meeting of Baptist Churches to Stephen Gorton, Sept. 10, 1757, Backus Papers, box 7.

82. New London congregation to General Meeting of Baptist Churches, Sept. 11, 1756.

83. Thirty-seven members (12 men and 25 women) supported Gorton's restoration; 16 (9 men and 7 women) agreed that he should be restored to church membership but opposed his resumption of pastoral responsibilities; only 5 (2 men and 3 women) voted against his restoration to membership or the pastorate; vote of New London congregation re receiving Stephen Gorton as minister again, June 8, 1757, Backus Papers, box 7.

84. Gorton's restoration to the pastorate might have been less decisive were it not for the preponderance of women in the church membership. He might also have had more difficulty holding on to his position had the disciplinary hearing taken place in the 17th century. As Cornelia Hughes Dayton has noted, New England clergymen were apparently better able to weather accusations of fornication by the early 18th century. It does seem remarkable, nonetheless, that Gorton could survive notoriety for "unchaste behavior with his fellow men"; Dayton, "Taking the Trade: Abortion and Gender Relations in an Eighteenth-Century New England Village," *William and Mary Quarterly,* 3d Ser., 48 (1991), 39 n. 72.

85. Any number of local incidents and controversies involving sodomy may have escaped record because of New Englanders' preference for noninstitutional forms of social control. Laurel Thatcher Ulrich argues convincingly that "courts seldom prosecuted sexual deviance because informal mechanisms of control were so powerful"; Ulrich, *A Midwife's Tale: The Life of Martha Ballard, Based on Her Diary, 1785–1812* (New York, 1990), 149. The paucity of legal cases in the 18th century does not necessarily represent a decline in either sodomitical activity or popular concern about such behavior. As courts took less and less interest in the enforcement of moral values, incidents of illicit sexual behavior were addressed through informal action within local communities and within the families concerned; Dayton, "Turning Points and the Relevance of Colonial Legal History," *William and Mary Quarterly,* 3d Ser., 50 (1993), 12–13.

86. "Marblehead First Church Records, 1688–1800," Old North Church, Marblehead, Mass. I am grateful to Christine Leigh Heyrman for sharing this citation. There is no evidence to indicate whether Knight or Gorton did mend their ways.

87. New London congregation to General Meeting of Baptist Churches, Sept. 11, 1756; General Meeting of Baptist Churches to Stephen Gorton, Sept, 13, 1756.

88. See Bray, *Homosexuality in Renaissance England,* 69, 76.

89. Ibid., 69. A witness in the English case of George Dowdeney (an innkeeper from Hatch Beauchamp, Somerset) came forward only when "he heard diverse others charge him with facts of the same kind"; Somerset Record Office/Q/SR/40.

This case is discussed in G. R. Quaife, *Wanton Wenches and Wayward Wives* (New Brunswick, NJ, 1979), 175–77, and Bray, *Homosexuality in Renaissance England*, 70, 74, 76, 128–29.

90. According to Thompson, "the evidence suggests that homosexual behavior was virtually unknown in everyday life"; Thompson, "Attitudes Towards Homosexuality in Seventeenth-Century New England," 34. But the tendency of locals to act against such behavior either informally or not at all supports Oaks's contention that "there was undoubtedly much more homosexual activity than the court records indicate"; Oaks, " 'Things Fearful to Name,' " 271. As the Rev. John Rayner pointed out in 1642, it was more likely that those who engaged in sodomy would escape detection than when a man and a woman fornicated, since there was no threat of pregnancy (see note 21 above). This further strengthens Oaks's case.

91. Thompson, "Attitudes Towards Homosexuality in Seventeenth-Century New England," quotations on 31, 34.

92. Popular attitudes toward sodomitical behavior in early modern England do not seem to have been particularly disapproving. As B. R. Burg argues, although sodomy was not "an accepted form of conduct," it had "little inherent capacity to evoke passionate detestation." There were very few prosecutions for sodomy in part because the law could not be enforced without local cooperation; Burg, *Sodomy and the Pirate Tradition: English Sea Rovers in the Seventeenth-Century Caribbean* (New York, 1984), 40; Bray, *Homosexuality in Renaissance England*, 70–71.

93. *Select Trials for Murders, Robberies, Rape, Sodomy, Coining, Frauds, and Other Offences at the Sessions-House in the Old Bailey*, 3 vols. (London, 1742), II, 257–58. For discussion of molly houses in 18th-century London, the subculture that developed around them, and the reconfiguration of sexual and gender identity in the late 17th and early 18th centuries, see Randolph Trumbach, "London's Sodomites: Homosexual Behavior and Western Culture in the 18th Century," *Journal of Social History*, 2 (1977–1978), 1–33; Mary McIntosh, "The Homosexual Role," in Kenneth Plummer, ed., *The Making of the Modern Homosexual* (Totowa, NJ, 1981), 30–49; and Bray, *Homosexuality in Renaissance England*, chap. 4. Trumbach, McIntosh, and Bray disagree over exactly when the subculture emerged, but it was clearly in place by the early 18th century. For discussion of similar developments in other major European cities, see Stephen Murray and Kent Gerard, "Renaissance Sodomite Subcultures?" in *Among Men, Among Women* (Amsterdam, 1983), 183–96; Trumbach, "Sodomitical Subcultures, Sodomitical Roles, and the Gender Revolution in the Eighteenth Century: The Recent Historiography," *Eighteenth-Century Life*, 9, No. 3 (1985), 109–21; and Gerard and Hekma, eds., *Pursuit of Sodomy*, passim.

94. Bray, *Homosexuality in Renaissance England*, 92.

95. Thompson argues that Puritan hostility to sodomy was a defensive response to "the presence of gender role confusion and sexual insecurity within an

aggressively masculine environment"; Thompson, "Attitudes Towards Homosexuality in Seventeenth-Century New England," 34. This assumes, inter alia, a connection between effeminacy and sodomy that did not exist in early American culture. None of the depositions given in the 1629 trial of Thomas/Thomasina Hall in Virginia for cross-dressing made any mention of sodomitical behavior on Hall's part; H. R. McIlwaine, ed., *Minutes of the Council and General Court of Colonial Virginia,* 2d ed. (Richmond, 1979), 194–95. Nor did any of those who accused Lord Cornbury, royal governor of New York and New Jersey (1701–1708), of appearing in public dressed as a woman attempt to besmirch his reputation further by suggesting that he was interested sexually in other men; Katz, *Gay/Lesbian Almanac,* 125–27. Nor did English colonial documents make any connection between "effeminacy" and sodomy among Native Americans; ibid., 50.

96. Bray, for example, questions the radicalism of developments in the late 19th century in *Homosexuality in Renaissance England,* 134–37. See also Murray, "Homosexual Acts and Selves in Early Modern Europe," and Joseph Cady, " 'Masculine Love,' Renaissance Writing, and the 'New Invention' of Homosexuality," in Claude J. Summers, ed., *Homosexuality in Renaissance and Enlightenment England: Literary Representations in Historical Context* (New York, 1992), 9–40.

97. The English case of George Dowdeney resembles that of Sension in that locals described many attempts by the accused during at least the previous 14 years to seduce men and youths in the vicinity, presenting Dowdeney's interest in members of the same sex as an ongoing "course" (analogous to Sension's "trade").

98. This is reminiscent of the mediations between clerical and lay concerns captured brilliantly in David D. Hall, *Worlds of Wonder, Days of Judgment: Popular Religious Belief in Early New England* (New York, 1989).

# Chapter 5

# Border Crossings

## The Queer Erotics of Quakerism in
## Seventeenth-Century New England

### Anne G. Myles

One of the more arresting stories circulated in the English pamphlet literature attacking the emerging Quaker movement of the 1650s concerned a
Quaker who purportedly committed an act of bestiality: "What doe you
think of the Quaker that acted that most abominable, unnameable sin
with a Mare? What doe you think of it, was it not from his light within?"
asked Christopher Fowler and Simon Ford, the tract's authors.[1] In linking
such an act of perversion with the reliance upon the "light within" that
was the most distinguishing and radical feature of Quaker belief, the authors relied on the long-established Western association between religious
difference and sexual deviance.[2] This association, while it often leads to
the targeting of same-sex sexuality, operates much more broadly as a kind
of "heterophobia," a tendency to link the threats posed by otherness of all
kinds. Yet while it is easy to see the strategic uses of such rhetoric in cultivating fear and prejudice toward individuals or groups who pose any
threat to established belief or structure, Fowler and Ford's language was
not merely rhetorical; rather, it reflected an early modern world in which
it would not necessarily have occurred to anyone to isolate sexuality from
other categories of order and disorder, of spiritual motive and outward
manifestation.

The connection between religious and sexual order was even more integral within early New England, for Puritanism's vision of a godly society
rested on marital and familial metaphors. As one commentator aptly sum-
marizes it, "The regulation of sexual expression was an integral, even essential part of the Puritan commonwealths; sex explicitly became the car-

rier of social meaning. The marital and reproductive, familial and patriarchal order of the Puritan settlements was thought to replicate in small the larger order of the commonwealths. These, in turn, dramatized the covenantal bonds of marital love between God and His people."[3] Such an ideological foundation meant that religious, social, and sexual dissidence could scarcely be distinguished from one another. To falsify the plan of God's covenant love, by ignoring or departing from orthodox faith and one's appropriate place within the social and familial hierarchy, suggested that one either already had, or likely very soon would, transgress sexually as well. Within this context, same-sex behavior did not draw unique attention as a form of sexual aberration; rather, any departure from marital heterosexuality represented a threat to the colony's symbolic integrity.[4]

While the marital metaphor implicit in the covenant helps explain New Englanders' policing of deviant sexual behavior, it does not tell the whole story about the complex relationship between spirituality and sexuality with Puritanism. Expanding the study of sexuality beyond recorded evidence of literal genital behavior, a range of scholars have considered how sexual metaphors permeate the devotional rhetoric of early modern Protestantism, and explored how religious communities are shaped by discourses and forms of affect that cannot be clearly distinguished from the erotic. In many cases, such spiritual and social erotics complicate and/or transgress traditional gender distinctions and heteronormative assumptions about sexuality. A number of studies of Puritan spirituality have observed how frequently the male devotional subject occupies a feminized position in relation to God—a male God toward whom he expresses desire to be penetrated or possessed. This potential for evoking an apparent spiritual homoeroticism holds true even within what might seem the resistant context of New England Puritanism, although there is less agreement about how to interpret such formations or Puritans' responses to them.[5] However we construe these spiritual erotics, they take on added resonance when one considers them in light of the centrality of (male) homosocial bonds to early modern English society, to the Anglo-American Puritan spiritual network, and to the very symbolism of the religious and social covenant.[6] Indeed, Michael Warner has found these dimensions at play in one of the founding documents of the New England way, John Winthrop's "A Modell of Christian Charity." Warner points out how Winthrop invokes the idea of "*simile simili gaudet*, or like will [i.e., is drawn] to like" as the foundation of the Puritan covenant. This concept of Christian love is based in sameness rather than in hierarchy, a love that Winthrop illustrates through the same sex Biblical relationships of David and Jonathan and Ruth and Naomi—and one his personal letters suggest he experienced in his own life through intense emotional bonds with other men.[7] In Warner's reading there is no clear dividing line between, on the one hand, the theologically and socially central discourses of same-sex friendship and Protestant religious fellowship, and, on the other, the explicitly sexual and forbidden realm known as sodomy. Far from being simply the covenant's abjected "other," then, a desire predicated on sameness—hence in a symbolic and etymological sense *homoerotic*—is as integral within Puritanism as the hierarchical model of the patriarchal family. Seen from this perspective, official denunciation of acts of sodomy takes on a somewhat different connotation: it can be interpreted as reflecting an anxious displacement of tensions *within* orthodoxy, an attempt to maintain a clear boundary between a "sanctioned homoeroticism" and what are regarded as disruptive, antisocial forms of same-sex expression.[8]

It is thus not a simple matter to demarcate a clear object of analysis in studying same-sex or alternative sexuality in early New England. But the very uncertainty of prying apart the ambiguities of spiritual erotics from more explicit manifestations of sexuality suggests that we can and must be flexible in seeking to trace what we might call the conceptual space of same-sex sexuality in the period. Such flexibility is even more essential if we seek to give equal attention to desire circulating among women or to erotics that are discursively gendered female, a terrain that has been rendered largely invisible by the masculine connotations of sodomy in both historical practice and contemporary scholarship.[9] In this essay I want to explore the notion that even where we have no explicit evidence about sexual behavior to work with, the domain of the sexual "other" may be mapped indirectly by looking at the points where spiritual and social erotics threaten to break from containment, where religious and social dissidence comes to express, to encode, or to be constructed by outsiders as some form of nonnormative erotic desire. Jonathan Goldberg has argued compellingly that the discourse of sodomy offers us a way to go beyond the obvious, seeking "the sites of sexual possibilities, the syntax of desires not readily named" within the early modern period; I would suggest that the discourse of religious conflict contains a similar potential for uncovering aspects of the sexual that lie at least partially outside available conceptual categories, yet are brought into prominence by their perceived threat to the social order.[10]

My context for mapping this symbolic space of erotic otherness is the

Quaker "invasion" of New England in 1656–1661. As numerous scholars have delineated, this extended crisis, with origins stretching back to the Antinomian controversy of the 1630s and repercussions extending to the witchcraft crisis of the 1690s, represented to Puritan authorities a grave threat to every form of order in the church and commonwealth, including religious and political institutions, the family, and class relations. The Puritans' conflict with the Quakers has been a natural locus for studying the problem of deviance in New England, for if orthodox Puritans saw in the Quaker movement a nightmarish eruption of every desire that was radically and transgressively other, Quakerism at the same time represented an extreme point on the Puritan continuum.[11] Although the Quaker movement was not especially associated with literal same-sex practices, it suggested an extreme rejection of hierarchy in favor of a radical spiritual and social erotics of sameness, of like drawn to like. It was, in a sense, Puritanism's own erotic potential that had come back to haunt New England's saints, its radical implications unleashed and on view in a way they had never been before. And as the conflict reached its first crisis with the execution of four Friends in 1659–1661, the Quakers appropriated and mirrored back another feature of the Protestant inheritance: the affective power of martyrdom to propagate religious community through erotically inflected performances of joyful sacrifice and the narrative and epistolary accounts that quickly found their way into print circulation.

### "Most Beastly, Shameful, and Horrid": The Quaker Movement as Sexual Threat

On both sides of the Atlantic, the Quaker movement, which came to prominence in Interregnum England and within a few years had sent emissaries to most parts of the known world, appeared to its opponents as the culmination of heresies extending back throughout the history of Christianity.[12] Quakers themselves, although they were articulating a theology in many ways radically new, saw themselves, conversely, as renewing the apostolic age after 1,600 years of apostasy. The movement was rooted in the idea of the key revelation George Fox recorded in his *Journal*, that "Christ has come to teach his people himself."[13] Quakers used a wide range of metaphors such as the Light, the Word, and the Seed to speak of the presence of Christ within, that would show anyone who chose to follow it the truth and enable them to live righteous, even sinless earthly lives. Knowledge gained from the "inward teacher" was congruent with the message of the Scriptures, but did not depend on their mediation, or that of ministers or religious institutions, and it was available and saving to all who sought it. People gained the authority to preach from the clarity with which they perceived and the fidelity with which they lived out God's inward teaching, regardless of their gender, age, rank, or educational level.[14]

These beliefs had radical consequences for worship and social order. Quaker worship, based on unstructured "waiting upon the Lord," was in this early period typically ecstatic, dramatic, and profoundly corporealized, and the preaching of men and women was often permeated with sexual and maternal imagery.[15] Women were prominent as preachers and prophets, and the movement was strongly egalitarian, seeking to do away with traditional distinctions of gender roles and rank. And women and men alike felt called in the early years to engage in dramatic symbolic acts of spiritual testimony, such as interrupting church services and, most famously, "going naked as a sign." And Friends of the first generation did nothing to moderate their radical self-presentation; as Barry Reay writes, "Extravagant behaviour and perfectionist claims became the badge of divine approbation, symbolically setting the Quakers apart from the ungodly."[16] For opponents, all of these practices seemed at best highly offensive, likely seditious, and potentially even demonically possessed. While the movement rapidly gained a large following in England, it equally quickly evoked widespread hostility at both elite and popular levels.[17] This hostility was expressed in the outpouring of anti-Quaker tracts published in the 1650s, countering the even more massive body of publications put out by the Quakers themselves.

The prominence of allusions to Quaker perversion in 1650s anti-Quaker literature reveals how sexuality functioned as a nexus in conceptualizing the dangers posed by the movement. The earliest examples of such accusations come from England, where many feared that the period's widespread sectarian radicalism would cause the country to be completely overcome by "tumults, madnesses, disorders, and Anarchicall licentiousnesse[.]"[18] A particularly lurid report of sexual deviance appeared in 1655, in John Gilpin's *The Quakers Shaken*. It recounts the aforementioned "horrid buggery committed by . . . a Quaker, with a Mare" on a public common.[19] The incident was turned into a popular song published as a broadside and it circulated through several other tracts, including the 1660 heresiography *Hell Broke Loose*. The song's author used the incident to mock both the Quakers' theology and their radical egalitarianism:

'Twas meer impulse of Spirit
Though he used the weapon carnal,
Filly Foal quoth he
My bride thou shalt be:
Now how this is lawfull, learn all.

For if no respect of persons
Be due 'mongst the sons of Adam,
In a large extent
Then may it be meant
That a Mare's as good as a Madam.[20]

This discourse of buggery that is woven throughout anti-Quaker writings of the 1650s is also connected to the persistent association between the Quakers and the Catholics, particularly the Jesuits: "Now Alas what hope / Of converting the Pope / When a Quaker turns *Italian*[?]" runs the song's refrain. Numerous early tracts insist that the Jesuits or other Catholic agents were the designing force between the new religious movement, and buggery was seen as a characteristically "Romish" vice.[21] Such purported behavior signified more than spiritual evil; it elicited fears of a profound threat to national security. In Reay's words, it appeared to opponents that "Rome was out to destroy Protestant England by any means at its disposal, even through the agency of sectarianism."[22]

Sexualized imagery of Quakers was not limited to the masculine realm of buggery; sexual accusations were also directed against Quaker women, who were most conspicuous in their gender deviance. Phyllis Mack comments tellingly, "In assuming the personae of Biblical prophets, Quaker women seemed to be denying the reality of all outward cultural constraints. They denied class and status differences by refusing to use the verbal or body language of deference; they denied gender differences by insisting that they preached as disembodied spirits 'in the light,' not as women. Indeed, if Quaker women prophets could be said to resemble any cultural archetype, it was that of the aggressive, male Old Testament hero."[23] The deep unease evoked by such transgression is revealed when Fowler and Ford ask the Quakers rhetorically:

Whether your *Prophetesses* that come to declare in public Assemblies, and some of them sometimes naked, do not break the Lawes of Nature, and civility[?] Whether such immodest practices, be not too great evidences against many of them, that they are so far from *Religion*, that they have much corrupted the principles of *common honesty*? And whether such brazen-faced impudency in such, be not in the language of Scripture, an *Whores forehead*?[24]

"Common honesty" here denotes chastity, reflecting the nearly universal belief that Quaker women, prone to engage shamelessly in radical public acts, must surely be sexually corrupt. And while no categories are cited here other than that of the "whore"—a broad label for any woman whose sexuality exceeds the bounds of propriety—the claim that such women broke the laws of nature is particularly suggestive of censures against "unnatural" sexual behavior. As Roger Thompson has noted in a New England context, the terms in which women Quakers' behavior was frequently described—"most beastly shameful and horrid and against the light of nature and common dictates of modesty"—echo language commonly used in the context of sodomy and buggery.[25]

The importance of female-gendered sexual deviance in Quakerism cannot be overemphasized, because it was such a prominent category in fears about Quakerism. The idea that female Quakers might, in fact, be witches was prominent in New England from the arrival of the first missionaries to the Salem crisis of 1692. The association between Quakers and witches is, in fact, a prime locus in most of seventeenth-century New England for conceptualizing extreme kinds of female sexual deviance. While Valerie Traub and other literary scholars have described the representations of "lesbian" desire that proliferate in the English Renaissance, these appear to remain metropolitan formations that do not make a measurable appearance in seventeenth-century New England discourse; conversely, the criminal/execution narrative ultimately becomes an important New England genre for representing female (hetero)sexual deviance, but it emerges only later in the century—hence, the heretic/witch nexus, which fills a discursive space about deviant women that is not otherwise clearly occupied.[26]

But it is important to recognize that the association of Quakerism with feminine-gendered deviance is not limited to images of women: even Quaker men were, in a sense, symbolically female. For one thing, the feminine gender of the soul within Puritan devotion was a feminization of the body within Quaker worship, the elevation of what Michele Tarter calls "corporeal prophecy" that led the first generation of Friends to "radically [honor] the feminized body as the very opening to God."[27] In a social context, too, by relinquishing their patriarchal authority and allowing women equal status as prophets, indeed encouraging and supporting them in their bold public acts and voices, Quaker men were symbolically feminized within the scheme of hierarchical order. If, as Elizabeth Dillon has argued, gender in early New England was fundamentally conceptualized as a hierarchical position rather than a trait based in sexed physical bodies, it could be said that *all* Friends in the early, egalitarian movement were of the same gender; by erasing the traditional borders between male and female roles, they had all become implicitly female.[28] In this sense, one could claim that for their opponents all Quaker relations, even those between men and women, were same-gender ones, circulating energy among unruly feminized subjects. Based as it was on the bond of "like to like" and the spiritual eradication of distinctions ("no respect of persons"—a notion that the mare-buggering ballad satirically extends to suggest eradication of not just rank and gender but even species distinctions), the movement's energies were quite literally homoerotic, but in a symbolically feminine way rather than masculine way. Indeed, Tarter points out that one of the fears about Quakerism was that even spectators exposed to its meetings for worship ran the risk of "becom[ing] the very essence of what they beheld —in a word, feminized."[29]

It is important, however, not to lose sight of the association between feminine deviance and actual same-sex bonds between women, as this connection had a particular historical resonance in New England. The Quaker invasion called up real and perceived links to the Antinomian crisis of the 1630s, in particular through the relationship between Anne Hutchinson and Mary Dyer, who in 1660 became the only woman ever executed as a Quaker.[30] This female connection provides a window into some of the most deeply rooted linkages of religious, political, and gender disorder that underlay Massachusetts' response to this later challenge. Numerous scholars have detailed the ways in which Anne Hutchinson represented a threat to the order of the family and state in 1630s Massachusetts. Speaking in large gatherings, challenging the authority of ministers, she paid no heed to the proper behavior of her gender. In Hugh Peter's famous accusation during her 1638 church trial, she had "stept out of [her] place, [and had] rather bine a Husband than a Wife and a preacher than a Hearer; and a Magistrate than a Subject."[31] This disregard for the fundamental hierarchies, combined with the devaluation of marriage examiners felt was implied by her apparent embrace of the "mortalist heresy," suggested that she had "set an open Doore to all Epicurisme and Libertinisme."[32] In his final condemnation, John Cotton warned Hutchinson that her beliefs would lead to "that filthie Sinne of the Comunitie of Woemen and all promiscuous and filthie cominge together of men and Woemen without distinction or relation of Marriage . . . and soe more dayngerous Evells and filthie Unclenes and other sines will followe than you doe now Imagine or conceave."[33] Cotton's words here suggest that he is thinking of something worse than "free love," bad as that was—something that his circumlocution hints may connect to sexual acts he cannot bring himself to name. Mary Beth Norton draws out the striking ambiguity of Cotton's phrase "the community of women" when she observes of this passage, "If men and women came together 'without Distinction,' that pointed to the likelihood of same-sex relationships, which were particularly 'filthie.'"[34]

Mary Dyer's entry into the public record came about in 1637 through a dramatic performance of same-sex loyalty on behalf of Hutchinson, her midwife and friend. As John Winthrop recounted it, "that very day Mistris *Hutchinson* was cast out of the Church for her monstrous errors, and notorious falsehood . . . being commanded to depart the Assembly, Mistris *Dyer* accompanied her, which a stranger observing, asked another what woman that was, and the other answered, it was the woman who had the Monster."[35] That comment led to questioning of Hutchinson along with the Boston midwife Jane Hawkins, and ultimately to exhumation of the grotesquely deformed body of a stillborn "woman childe."[36]

Hutchinson's failure to report the birth and burial of the stillborn infant and Dyer's departure from the church together signified the dangerous power of allegiances growing from the separated female "closet" of the birthing-chamber.[37] To mother a monster and to be oneself a monstrous woman are inseparable notions here, underlined by the birth of Hutchinson's own "monster" a year later. The narrative that arose from these events, which links this pair of women under twinned notions of spiritual and biological abnormality, offers perhaps the nearest thing we have in seventeenth-century New England to the conceptualization of a specifically female kind of queerness. While no directly sexual accusations were leveled at the Hutchinson-Dyer bond, that bond nonetheless mapped out a space of intimate female deviance that posed a destabilizing threat to patriarchal power. If Dyer's departure was not an erotic act, it was a dramatic assertion of female loyalty played out on a public stage, a kind of literalized performance of the bond between Ruth and Naomi ("whither thou goest, I will go," Ruth 1:16). The ideology of same-sex connection, carefully contained in most orthodox discourse as the privileged realm of implicitly male saints, is here revealed as something to which women and dissenters can also, dangerously, lay claim. In the 1650s, returning from England to the colonies as a convinced Friend, Dyer would continue to enact radical demonstrations of allegiance in visiting imprisoned Friends of both sexes, repeatedly entering the Massachusetts in the face of mounting anti-Quaker laws until she was eventually hanged.

In both Old and New England, same-sex or otherwise transgressive allegiances were a highly visible feature of Quakerism. Friends who felt called forth as missionaries or prophets typically traveled in same-sex or at any rate nonmarital pairs, highlighting the degree to which what Barry Levy calls their spiritual tribalism had taken precedence over the stability of traditional family bonds.[38] Female missionary partners, who as Christine Trevett has pointed out modeled themselves on women partners in early Christianity, were very common and attracted heightened attention for their conspicuous flouting of gender norms.[39] The most famous example is the missionary pair of Katherine Evans and Sarah Chevers, who were imprisoned in Malta together and, though each was married, identified as "Yoak-Mates" to the point where they spoke of their partnership in marital language: "*The Lord hath joined us together, and wo be to them that should part us.*"[40] Similarly, the very first Quakers to arrive in New England in July 1656 were traveling companions Ann Austin and Mary Fisher, who were stripped and examined for witches' marks and imprisoned in isolation together for five weeks before being banished and sent to Barbados.[41]

Even aside from the prominence of such pairings, the itinerancy of Quaker prophets was itself seen as a sexually threatening phenomenon: the uncontrolled freedom of such wanderings suggested the practice of free love, and overturned the stability of family life that was integral to maintaining an orderly society.[42] Puritan Thomas Weld wrote, "It is a *sinfull neglect* of their families and callings which we speak against . . . we say that *they do sinfully neglect their Callings*, thats apparent in their constant wanderings up and downe"; Quaker Humphrey Norton confirmed that in New England "they did openly accuse us of uncleanness . . . in going men and women together, running away from our Parents, wives, and children."[43] While transatlantic in practice, itinerancy took on added symbolic resonance in the colonies, since Friends' travels moved them not simply from town to town but from colony to colony.[44] In crossing with impunity over political borders, Friends impinged upon all the religious and moral boundaries those borders both symbolized and were designed to police.

The charge that Quakers neglected their families did not rest wholly upon their itinerancy. It was fueled by the belief that some had chosen to renounce marital sexuality outright. The heresiographer Thomas Underhill, for example, asserts such practices to be a Quaker principle:

> And for subjecting the flesh to the *intellect,* [the Quakers say] we must live in *contemplation, lay by all Offices* in the Commonwealth, and own *no fleshly Relations* as they call them. . . . That none should own the Relation of *Husband,* or *Wife,* nor love each other, as so related.

> That we should endeavour to be perfect; and therfore to forbear all *carnall acts of Generation,* as being of *sin,* and of the *Devil*; and therefore *Husband* and *Wife* should *part asunder,* or *abstain.*[45]

Such a passage makes clear the ideological connection between questioning marital heterosexuality and threatening the state. Besides the prospect of what would happen if a significant sector of the population became convinced to disown "the Relation of a *Magistrate,* or of a *Master* . . . a *Father,* or *Mother, Son,* or *Daughter,*" opposition to marriage—in particular when combined with the image of missionary circulation—also carried an implicit challenge to national and religious boundaries, evoking again the recurrent fear of Catholic/monastic plots. There was for opponents no contradiction between images of the libertine and the ascetic Quaker; the sins were essentially interchangeable, as both represented a departure from normal, proper sexual practice.[46]

While accusations about Quakers rejecting marital relations may have been largely scandal-mongering in England, in New England an indeterminate number of Friends did in fact embrace the idea that their new faith demanded a change in their sexual lives. In a letter to the "mother of Quakerism" Margaret Fell, Joseph Nicholson reported anxiously on several Salem, Massachusetts Friends who "said they would not joyn with us because my wife was with child . . . one of them a man hath refused to lye with his wife and two of them women have refused to lye with their husbands as the rest of friends say[,] which thinge I doe believe is true."[47] He added a few months later that "it went for a comon report att Boston [that] ther men run way from ther wifs and wifs from ther husband and that the quakers would have no children."[48] Friends identified in his letters as believers in celibacy included some of the prominent sufferers in New England, and several of them asserted that William Robinson and Marmaduke Stephenson, who would gain fame as the first two Quaker martyrs, held the tenet as well. "I doe believe it will hurt the truth," lamented Nicholson of this dissident strand, which had apparently gained a notoreity wider than the scope of its actual practice.[49] Did he simply fear the propagation of an incorrect version of Quaker tenets, one with likely political consequences? Or was he also worried that the practice of celibacy, which he knew from his own experience to have a powerful lure, might threaten to give rise to a version of Quakerism too openly constituted in opposition to the conventional order of desire?[50] The celibacy faction brought into plain view the extent to which the Quaker movement, even when it did not embrace this extreme "error," supplanted the primacy of familial affections with passions of another nature. Leo Damrosch writes, "To be a Quaker was to redefine former connections, even affectionate ones. . . . From this firmness might spring joy, but it was a joy that would henceforth diminish or exclude other kinds of relationships."[51] While the literal perversions anti-Quaker pamphleteers dwelt on were largely fantasy, there is truth in anti-Quaker tracts' sexualized rhetoric about the movement's dangerous allure, for it drew people into a community that involved them in a new and oppositional mode of spiritual erotics.

## *"Then Feel Me Present": The Erotics of New England Quaker Martyrdom*

The Quakers who came to New England in the 1650s were not, of course, literally persecuted as sexual offenders. But the Reverend John Norton's *The Heart of New England Rent,* Puritan orthodoxy's official written response to the Quaker threat, stresses their offenses "unto Religion, the Churches of Christ, and the State" by emphasizing their opposition to the foundations of order, which Norton describes as "a divine disposal[,] of superiour and inferiour relations": "Neither nature, nor society, whether humane or Christian, not not so much as a family can stand without order," Norton writes. He casts Quakerism as an example of "heresie turbulent," with the secret design of "mak[ing] the power, honours, and possessions of the Godly . . . to become a lawful prize and plunder to the ravening lusts of their Proselytes."[52] Insofar as Quakerism is cast as a lustful force committed to subverting proper hierarchical distinctions and the institutions informed by them, I would contend that it signified for Norton and the orthodoxy he speaks for a domain analogous to what contemporary theory calls the "queer." The Quaker movement signified not so much acts of unacceptable sexual behavior as a massive rejection of a vast range of gender relations, institutional allegiances, and ideological commitments that, along with properly contained marital sexuality, constituted the "regime of the normal" in Puritan society.[53]

The rising tide of persecution can thus be seen as arising from a kind of "queer panic" on the part of New England orthodoxy, as officials attempted through a series of ever more stringent laws and ever more somatized punishments—whippings, brandings, ear-croppings—to stem the waves of Friends who kept entering the colonies, driven onward by communal and spiritual energies that registered as both tremendously dangerous and, at the human level, bizarrely intransigent. The Quakers seemed almost encouraged by persecution: they perversely refused to stay banished, and gloried in their sufferings as evidence of their faithfulness—and as further occasion to prophetically declaim against the bloodiness of their opponents. The climax of the rising action of persecution in the 1650s was the hanging on October 27, 1659 of William Robinson and Marmaduke Stephenson, with Mary Dyer led along with them to the scaffold but reprieved at the last minute (she would return from her latest banishment some months later to be herself hanged at last). Ironically, at the point of their most extreme attempt to rid themselves of these most persistent border-crossers and turn their deviance into a monitory public spectacle, Puritan officials had to confront a quite different spectacle, that of their own spiritual and literary inheritance being mirrored back to them, as Friends proved themselves adept participants in not only the erotics of prophetic and ecstatic community but also in the performance and memorializing of martyrdom.[54]

A Quaker account of Robinson's and Stephenson's hanging and Dyer's trip to the scaffold first appeared in a letter written from Plymouth jail by Peter Pearson, and in 1660, Edward Burrough published *A Declaration of the Great and Sad Persecution and Martyrdom*, which reprinted this account and included his narrative of Dyer's 1660 execution as well. Pearson's rendering of the two men's deaths emphasizes their calmness, unity, and prophetic conviction:

> So they walked along in pure retired Chearfulness to the Place of Execution, triumphing in the strength of the Lamb, over all the wrath of man, and fury of the Beast, in the pure retired Heavenly Dominion of the Invisible God. And when they came to the Ladders-foot, they took their leave of each other; and William Robinson stept up the Ladder, and spake to the People,

saying, *This is the day of your Visitation, wherein the Lord hath visited you;*
*This is the Day the Lord is Risen in his Might Power to be Avenged on all his*
*Adversaries.* . . . So the Executioner being about to turn him off the Ladder,
he said, *I Suffer for Christ, in whom I live, and for whom I die.*

An account of Stephenson's final moments comes next, concluding with
the summation, "Thus the faithful Witnesses sealed their Testimony for
the Lord against the Dragon's Power, and blessedly departed with Praises
in their mouths, entering joyfully with their Beloved into Everlasting
Rest."[55] Though such a passage is entirely consistent with Quaker self-
representation, there is relatively little within it, outside the prophetic denunciation of adversaries, that is distinctive to the movement. Although
Friends typically compared themselves explicitly to Biblical precedents
rather than to the Marian martyrs of a century earlier memorialized by
John Foxe, the patterns of Protestant (and for that matter Catholic) martyrdom were deeply ingrained in the English-speaking world. Studies by
John Knott and others have established the ideological centrality of discourses of joyful and heroic suffering in the Foxian literature of martyrdom, as well as the importance of communal experience as a "locus of the
sacred."[56]

Some scholars have also drawn attention to the erotic dimensions that
emerge within martyr narratives, and the fact that they frequently operate
in homoerotic terms.[57] While sometimes martyrdom's physical suffering
can be represented in terms of what scholar James Truman cites as "the
image of the raped man, invoking the abject erotics of sodomy," there is
another dimension as well, concerned with the bonds of friendship among
martyrs and based on what Truman calls "a balanced and symmetrical exchange of desire."[58] Truman links this second dimension to the energies of
an "apostolic homosocial intimacy" that occupies the ambiguous terrain
of resembling sodomy while never being discursively identified with it.[59]
Such dynamics, which visible in the Quaker accounts as well, are clearly
congruent with the nonhierarchical, like-to-like love that is a defining feature of Quaker community. George Bishop's influential revision and expansion of already-circulating accounts of suffering and martyrdom in
*New England Judged* (1661) heightens the erotic element while it metaphorically invokes a different image for intimacy, that of marriage. He
writes, "So being come to the Place of Execution, hand in hand, all Three
of them, as to a Wedding Day, with great chearfulness of heart [they took]
Leave of each other with the dear Embraces of one anothers Love in the

Love of the Lord[.]"[60] Yet it is important to note there is nothing conventionally heteroerotic or hierarchical in this passage. Even though Bishop's statement can be contained within the acceptable devotional image of feminized martyrs sharing joy at their imminent union with Christ, it is hard for the reader to escape the image presented of a decidedly queer three-way ecstasy, in effect a kind of communal marriage, more or less randomly involving two men and a woman. As I read it, the passage's wedding reference emphasizes the quality of eroticized intimacy, an intimacy that remains thoroughly invested in the distinctive dynamic of Quaker "same-gender" relations, which draws Friends together irrespective of biological sex distinctions and normal divisions of age and rank.[61]

Such obliteration of difference is echoed and intensified in the Quaker version of another standard feature of Protestant martyrology, the reprinting of letters from martyrs to other members of the community. William Robinson's and Marmaduke Stephenson's letters to "the Lord's People" play a prominent role in the latter's *A Call from Death to Life* and are reprinted in later texts, and their ecstatic and erotic inflection is hard to miss: "Oh, my beloved ones, what shall I say unto you, who drink with me at the living fountain, where we are nourished and brought up, as twins in the womb, at the breasts of consolation, where I do embrace you in the bond of peace, which will never be broken?" wrote Marmaduke Stephenson shortly before his execution.[62] Likewise, William Robinson wrote:

> I am swallowed up with love, and in it I dwell with the holy seed [i.e., Friends], to which the blessing of love is given from God. . . . Ye children of the living God, feel me when you are waiting in [the life and love of God], when your hearts and minds are gathered into it, when in the strength of it you are travelling, feel me, when it runs from the fountain into your vessel, when it issues gently, like new wine, into your bosoms, when the strength and power of it you feel, when you are overcome with the strength of love, which is God, then feel me present in the fountain of love, wherein are many mansions.[63]

In letters such as this, all divisions have been overcome; the martyr, alive or dead, has become the lover of the entire community. The erotic rhetoric seems to have transcended gender entirely in its mingling of penetration and permeation; the flowing fountain of love cited in both men's writings seems at once fluidly feminized and malely emissive. Robinson's effusion of love seems to transcend the very boundary of death, in his "feel me" projected toward an unending future. Theologically, although such writing exemplifies the Quaker community as the site of the individual Friend's passionate allegiance, it extends beyond that, drawing on a final dimension of Quaker sameness: the obliteration of distinctions between God and the community. Rosemary Moore explains that "[Quakers'] sense of their unity with God, or with Christ, extended to a strong sense of unity with each other. . . . This was not just a vague sense of undefined spiritual unity; body and spirit together were one with Christ."[64] The issue came up explicitly in confrontations in New England: "That Christ's body is divided from his members, we do not believe," maintained Quaker John Rous and others under interrogation by Governor John Endecott.[65] There is, then, as Carla Pestana points out, no distinction between Friends expressing desire for or ecstatic unity with God and desire for members of the community.[66] In such devotional/communal expression spiritual and social erotics are no longer simply related but literally merged, in an apotheosis of border-crossing.[67]

Such a configuration was, of course, anathema to New England Puritan orthodoxy. The performances and narratives of the New England martyrs took up motifs that were a treasured part of their own Protestant heritage and recast them in a way that seemed to throw to the wind all the necessary distinctions between self and other, male and female, human and divine. To top it off, the burgeoning movement displayed the power of a radical religious community to multiply and perpetuate itself through the power of spiritual and social erotics alone. During the same period of the Quaker "invasion," Puritan orthodoxy was experiencing a crisis around the issue of reproduction: few members of the current generation were finding in themselves the grace that would permit them to become church members, and the church was not succeeding in reproducing its numbers through procreation in the families of the saints. This was the crisis that would lead to the much-contested adoption of the Half-Way Covenant in 1662, a measure designed to ensure that church and family would remain closely linked. Yet Quakerism was spreading rapidly; in a sense, it did not matter if "the Quakers would have no children," because some New Englanders were being drawn to the movement even when they witnessed Friends being jailed, whipped, branded, and banished. Cast in terms of issues of sexuality and reproduction, the Covenant helped ensure that marital heterosexuality would be able to compete in reproductive power with the social erotics endemic to dissident communities.[68]

Finally, Quaker community manifested its affinitive and generative capacity in practical terms through an extremely active, effective transatlantic publication network, which assured that accounts of New England sufferings were quickly passed on, shared, adapted, and circulated in print —an outcome essential both to strengthening the affective bonds among Friends and to capitalizing on the spiritual and political potency of martyrdom.[69] Quaker accounts spawned other accounts, even when the original authors were in prison, dead, or symbolically silenced (as in the case of Humphrey Norton, who for punishment had a key bound across his tongue)—a "seductive and poisonous" wave of texts that could in turn recruit more believers.[70] In the realm of print culture, as in other dimensions of Quaker community, the erotics of sameness is in evidence. Almost all of the tracts of New England sufferings, irrespective of whichever Friend is named as author, are composed of letters and reports and versions of earlier texts by different writers through a process of transmission that is presented as a testament to the "intire nearness" among sufferers.[71] Indeed, in an even more radical blurring of distinctions, at points in some texts it can be difficult to determine who the "I" that narrates a particular section is.[72] And while certain individuals' dramatic experiences receive sustained attention, the narratives of Quaker sufferings focus on association and on shared and collective experiences; not until considerably later, in Joseph Besse's *The Sufferings of the People called Quakers* (1753), do we get an orderliness of presentation that begins to approach that of Foxe. While the carelessness of hasty composition and the metaphorically fluid, self-consciously prophetic elements of Quaker style are two sources of these characteristics in the narratives of Quaker sufferings, their loose, overlapping structure also analogizes the distinctive features of Quakerism as an erotic order, grounded simultaneously in communal bonds and the transcendence of difference.[73]

### "You Will Own Yourself a Quaker, Will You Not?": Religious Identification and Sexual Identities

In summation, while the model of queer erotics implied by Quakerism has much in common with the homoerotic dimensions that some scholars have found latent (and at key moments, such as scenes of martyrdom, more nearly emergent) in early modern Protestantism, its radical border-crossing means it cannot be wholly contained within that model. Both this element of difference and the simple fact that the Quaker movement exposed tensions within the Puritan inheritance and the distance New England had come from that inheritance do much to explain the conflicts that arose in the 1650s. Yet the broader question remains: what, if anything, can looking at a religious movement tell us about sexuality in early America? Certainly, whether such an examination is even a valid undertaking will remain for some highly debatable. But one thing this study might suggest is another way in which we might complicate what remains of the much-contested Foucauldian paradigm distinguishing early modern sexual acts from modern sexual identities. One kind of challenge to this model has come from the evidence Richard Godbeer and other contributors to this volume have found of sexual practices and discourses that do not seem to fit Foucault's historical schema. But I would contend that another, less direct yet still suggestive way is to examine the range of possibilities for individual and communal identity formation that were available to people in the early modern period: in particular, what resources did people have for consciously forming an identity that meant they would be identified by dominant elements of society as "other"—other in the encompassing way that we associate with rhetorics of sexual deviance? Whether or not early Quakers could have imagined their community as in any sense an erotic one—and almost certainly they would have vigorously rejected such a notion—becoming a Quaker (or for that matter a member of any radical religious group) meant choosing to know oneself as part of a marginalized, persecuted community and to act on the basis of allegiance to relationships within that community, relationships that would henceforth take precedence over the normative loyalties to family and state. This is not, it seems to me, so very different from the consciousness that marks gay identity in the post-Stonewall era. The dynamics of being "convinced" as a Quaker in the seventeenth-century and those of coming to identify as a gay, lesbian, or otherwise queer person in the present have a great many similarities: whether or not they involve dramatic public declarations, both are markedly performative identities, enacted through such overt means as dress, behavior, and speech as well as more subtle ones, both involve identification with larger communities and their perceived origins, and both require the subject to own his or her own agency and desire— to say, in effect, "yes I am" in the face of the actual or potential persecution initiated by such hostile interrogations as "you will own yourself a Quaker, will you not?"[74] Seventeenth-century Quakers, in short, knew what it meant to "come out." What this suggests to me is that while people in the 1600s might not have been able to think about same-sex sexuality in this apparently modern way, they were perfectly capable of thinking about *themselves* in this way. In other words, the conceptual equipment for imagining something akin to a queer identity/community was already in place. Do dissident religious communities—and their martyrs—come to offer something of an imaginative precedent for members of same-sex networks as they begin to emerge more recognizably in slightly later periods? This seems to me a potentially illuminating historical avenue to explore.

Whether or not it is ever possible to find evidence of actual historical connections, considering the structural and emotional analogies between radical religious movements and same-sex communities, dramatically expands the possibilities for a queer vision of the early American past, a past where otherwise there seems little to affirm. In her study of an earlier dissident religious movement, literary scholar Carolyn Dinshaw embraces what she calls "a queer historical impulse, an impulse toward making connections across time between, on the one hand, lives, texts, and other cultural phenomena left out of sexual categories back then and, on the other, those left out of current sexual categories now. Such an impulse extends the resources for self- and community building into even the distant past."[75] As a lesbian early Americanist, the possibility of finding such connections feels sustaining and vital for me, as does exploring ways to conceive of historical forms of same-sex affect and eroticism that do not rely on the masculinist framework of sodomy. It is important as well to recognize that religion's historical role has not universally been that of a force of social and erotic control; religious communities have equally been contexts for the expression of transgressive allegiances and forms of affect. Perhaps the history of alternative sexuality in early America might be usefully reconceived as the history of such radical loves and the politics they have engendered—which would inevitably be a story, too, of martyr figures and their legacies in collective memory, both within and beyond the communities in which they were rooted.[76]

NOTES

1. Christopher Fowler and Simon Ford, *A Sober Answer to an Angry Epistle: directed to all the publick teachers in this nation* (London, 1656), 75. Quaker responses to these tracts contended that the individual concerned, one Hugh Bisbrowne, was not really a Friend, and assert that "all such beasts and beastly tricks and works of the flesh, we abhor and deny. . . ." See Gervase Benson, *An Answer to John Gilpin's*

*Book* (London, 1655), 6, also George Fox, *The Great Mistery of the Great Whore Unfolded* (London, 1659), 298.

2. For one account of the origin of these associations, see R. I. Moore, *The Formation of a Persecuting Society* (Cambridge, MA: Blackwell, 1987), esp. 91–94. Studies dealing with associations between sex/gender deviance and heresy (among other "disorders") in the medieval period are discussed in Carolyn Dinshaw, *Getting Medieval: Sexualities and Communities, Pre- and Postmodern* (Durham: Duke University Press, 1999), 209–10 n. 10. For a discussion of attitudes in an early modern English context, see David S. Lovejoy, *Religious Enthusiasm in the New World: Heresy to Revolution* (Cambridge, MA: Harvard University Press, 1989), chap. 2.

3. Ed Ingebretsen, "Wigglesworth, Mather, Starr: Witch-Hunts and General Wickedness in Public." In *The Puritan Origins of American Sex: Religion, Sexuality, and National Identity in American Literature,* ed. Tracy Fessenden, Nicholas F. Radel, and Magdalena J. Zaborowska (New York: Routledge, 2001), 23. For a comprehensive recent treatment of Puritan attitudes toward sexuality, see Richard Godbeer, *Sexual Revolution in Early America* (Baltimore: Johns Hopkins University Press, 2002), chaps. 1–3; see also Thomas A. Foster, "Deficient Husbands: Manhood, Sexual Incapacity, and Male Marital Sexuality in Seventeenth-Century New England," *William & Mary Quarterly* 3d ser., 56.4 (1999): 723–745. A classic study of marital and family ideology is Edmund S. Morgan, *The Puritan Family: Religion and Domestic Relations in Seventeenth-Century New England* (New York: Harper and Row, 1985 [orig. pub. 1942]); see also his "The Puritans and Sex," *New England Quarterly* 25 (1942): 591–607. The family as a foundation for notions of order and hierarchy in early New England is considered extensively in Mary Beth Norton, *Founding Mothers and Fathers: Gendered Power and the Forming of American Society* (New York: Vintage Books, 1996).

4. Studies that provide a foundation for understanding attitudes toward sexual deviance in seventeenth-century New England include Robert F. Oaks, " 'Things Fearful to Name': Sodomy and Buggery in Seventeenth-Century New England," *Journal of Social History* 12.2 (1978): 268–282; Jonathan Ned Katz, "Introduction: The Age of Sodomitical Sin," in his *Gay/Lesbian Almanac* (New York: Harper and Row, 1983), 31–65; Kathleen Verduin, " 'Our Cursed Natures': Sexuality and the Puritan Conscience," *New England Quarterly* 56 (1983): 220–237; John Canup, "The Cry of Sodom Enquired Into," *Proceedings of the American Antiquarian Society* 98 (1988): 113–34; Roger Thompson, "Attitudes Towards Homosexuality in Seventeenth-Century New England Colonies," *Journal of American Studies* 23.1 (1989): 27–40; Michael Warner, "New English Sodom," in Jonathan Goldberg, ed., *Queering the Renaissance* (Durham: Duke University Press, 1994), 330–358; Richard Godbeer, " 'The Cry of Sodom': Discourse, Intercourse, and Desire in Colonial New England," in this volume; Godbeer, *Sexual Revolution,* chap. 3.

5. Elizabeth Maddock Dillon comments on a range of contemporary scholarship that addresses the metaphors of the feminized convert in Puritan spiritual

rhetoric and how this imagery relates to broader Puritan notions of gender and sexuality in "Nursing Fathers and Brides of Christ," in Janet Moore Lindman and Michele Lise Tarter, eds., *A Centre of Wonders: The Body in Early America* (Ithaca: Cornell University Press, 2001), 129–143; see esp. 140 n. 5. For an astute discussion of Puritan spiritual erotics see Richard Godbeer, " 'Love Raptures': Marital, Romantic, and Erotic Images of Jesus Christ in Puritan New England, 1670–1730," *New England Quarterly* 68 (1995): 355–384. The homoerotic dimensions of early modern Protestant devotional writing are explored in Richard Rambuss, *Closet Devotions* (Durham: Duke University Press, 1998), while in "Romance of the Spirit: Female Sexuality and Religious Desire in Early Modern England," *ELH* 69.2 (2002): 413–438, Sharon Achinstein extends Rambuss's interest in "devotion as a form of desire" to dissenting and Quaker writers within a feminine devotional tradition.

6. On the blurred line between male friendship and sodomy, see Alan Bray, *Homosexuality in Renaissance England* (1982; reprint New York: Columbia University Press, 1995) and Bray, "Homosexuality and the Signs of Male Friendship in England," in *Queering the Renaissance*, 40–61; Jeffrey Masten, *Textual Intercourse: Collaboration, Authorship, and Sexualities in Renaissance Drama* (Cambridge: Cambridge University Press, 1997), and the articles in *The Work of Friendship: In Memoriam Alan Bray*, ed. Jody Greene, a special issue of *GLQ: A Journal of Lesbian and Gay Studies* 10.3 (2004). For another discussion of the intersection between community and sodomy in a New England context, see also Jonathan Goldberg, *Sodometries: Renaissance Texts, Modern Sexualities* (Stanford: Stanford University Press, 1992), chap. 7. On the centrality of male friendship networks to Puritan orthodoxy, see Francis J. Bremer, *Congregational Communion: Clerical Friendship in the Anglo-American Puritan Community, 1610–1692* (Boston: Northeastern University Press, 1994).

7. Warner, "New English Sodom," esp. 339–345.

8. James Truman, "John Foxe and the Desires of Reformation Martyrology," *ELH* 70.1 (2003): 49. Godbeer ("The Cry of Sodom") makes the point that while sodomy was uniformly denounced by colonial ministers and legal codes, actual juridical practice and communal attitudes appear to have been more ambivalent.

9. Although in theory sodomy applied to same-sex activity between women—indeed, it could refer to any nonprocreative sex—the term was in practice almost always applied to men. The Massachusetts Body of Liberties did not apply the sodomy law to women, as had been proposed in John Cotton's original legal code; women were included only in New Haven's 1656 code. See Godbeer, "The Cry of Sodom," in this volume, and Mary Beth Norton, 349. The male focus has been perpetuated within contemporary scholarship on sodomy in early modern culture; studies include Gregory W. Bredbeck, *Sodomy and Interpretation: Marlowe to Milton* (Ithaca: Cornell University Press, 1991); Jonathan Goldberg, *Sodometries*; Cameron McFarlane, *The Sodomite in Fiction and Satire, 1660–1750* (New York:

Columbia University Press, 1997), and, with a specifically New England focus, Walter Hughes, "'Meat Out of the Eater': Panic and Desire in American Puritan Poetry," in Joseph A. Boone and Michael Cadden, eds., *Engendering Men: The Question of Male Feminist Criticism* (New York: Routledge, 1990); Warner, "New English Sodom"; and Nicholas F. Radel, "A Sodom Within: Historicizing Puritan Homoerotics in the Diary of Michael Wigglesworth," in Fessenden, Radel, and Zaborowska, 41–55. Recently, there has been an increasing body of work on early modern lesbianism; see Harriette Andreadis, *Sappho in Early Modern England: Female Same-Sex Literary Erotics, 1550–1774* (Chicago: University of Chicago Press, 2001) and Valerie Traub, *The Renaissance of Lesbianism in Early Modern England* (New York: Cambridge University Press, 2002). In "Romance of the Spirit: Female Sexuality and Religious Desire in Early Modern England," Sharon Achinstein focuses Rambuss's interest in "devotion as a form of desire" on the writers within a feminine devotional tradition. Virtually no work has extended this discussion to seventeenth-century New England, although some work has been done on New Spain. Jodi Schorb and Amanda Powell chaired the first workshop on early American lesbian studies at the "Beyond Colonial Studies: An InterAmerican Encounter" conference in November 2004. See also Anne G. Myles, "From Monster to Martyr: Re-Presenting Mary Dyer," *Early American Literature* 36.1 (1999): 17–18.

10. Goldberg, *Sodometries,* 22. Goldberg expands insightfully on the intrinsic connection between the discursive appearance of sodomy and threats to social order: "Thus, although sodomy is, as a sexual act, anything that threatens alliance— any sexual act, that is, that does not promote the aim of married procreative sex[—]and while sodomy involves therefore acts that men might perform with men, women with women (a possibility rarely envisioned), men and women with each other, and anyone with a goat, a pig, or a horse, these acts—or accusations of their performance—emerge into visibility only when those who are said to have done them also can be called traitors, heretics, or the like, at the very least, disturbers of the social order that alliance—marriage arrangements—maintained" (19). He points out that sodomy accusations in seventeenth-century New England "are ways of policing emerging social and class relations" (24).

11. On Quakerism as deviance, see Kai T. Erikson, *Wayward Puritans: Studies in the Sociology of Deviance* (New York: John Wiley, 1966), and, with a historical rather than sociological orientation, Carla Gardina Pestana, "The City upon a Hill under Siege: The Puritan Perception of the Quaker Threat to Massachusetts Bay, 1656–1661, *The New England Quarterly* 56.3 (1983): 323–353. Other studies focused on New England's response to the Quaker "invasion" include Lovejoy, chap. 6, Jonathan M. Chu, *Neighbors, Friends, or Madmen: The Puritan Adjustment to Quakerism in Seventeenth-Century Massachusetts Bay* (Westport, CT: Greenwood Press, 1985); Philip F. Gura, *A Glimpse of Sion's Glory: Puritan Radicalism in New England, 1620–1660* (Middletown, CT: Wesleyan University Press, 1984). Historical accounts from a markedly pro-Quaker perspective include Richard Hallowell, *The*

*Quaker Invasion of Massachusetts* (Boston, 1887) and Rufus Jones, *The Quakers in the American Colonies* (New York: W.W. Norton, 1966). A more recent historical study is Arthur Worrall, *Quakers in the Colonial Northeast* (Hanover, NH: University Press of New England, 1980).

12. In the central anti-Quaker tract to emerge from New England, *The Heart of New-England Rent* (London, 1660), the Reverend John Norton emphasizes the Quakers as "but the opening of that vast and horrid sink" of former heresies, in particular "the Doctrine of the Enthusiasts in Germany, and Libertines in the Low-Countreys," 2. Conversely, in the English heresiography *Hell Broke Loose: or an History of the Quakers Both Old and New* (London, 1660), Thomas Underhill retroactively turns all past heretics into "Quakers."

13. *The Journal of George Fox,* ed. Nigel Smith (New York: Penguin Classics, 1999). Versions of this formulation appear at many points throughout the text.

14. Major studies of Quaker origins, focusing variously on theological, social, and/or historical dimensions, include William C. Braithwaite, *The Beginnings of Quakerism* (London: Macmillan, 1923); Hugh Barbour, *The Quakers in Puritan England* (New Haven: Yale University Press, 1964); Richard T. Vann, *The Social Development of English Quakerism, 1655–1755* (Cambridge: Harvard University Press, 1969); Barry Reay, *The Quakers and the English Revolution* (London: Temple Smith, 1985); Douglas Gwyn, *Apocalypse of the Word: The Life and Message of George Fox* (Richmond, IN: Friends United Press, 1986); Richard Bailey, *New Light on George Fox and Early Quakerism: The Making and Unmaking of a God* (San Francisco: Mellen Research University Press, 1992); Larry Ingle, *First Among Friends: George Fox and the Creation of Quakerism* (New York: Oxford University Press, 1994); and Rosemary Moore, *The Light in their Consciences: Early Quakers in Britain, 1646–1666* (University Park: Penn State University Press, 2000). There have recently been an outpouring of studies devoted to early Quaker women; the most influential has been Phyllis Mack's broad but substantially Quaker-focused study, *Visionary Women: Ecstatic Prophecy in Seventeenth-Century England* (Berkeley: University of California Press, 1992); see also Christine Trevett, *Women and Quakerism in the Seventeenth Century* (York, England: Sessions, 1991), and Bonnelyn Kunze, *Margaret Fell and the Rise of Quakerism* (Stanford: Stanford University Press, 1993).

15. See Michele Lise Tarter, "Quaking in the Light: The Politics of Quaker Women's Corporeal Prophecy in the Seventeenth-Century Transatlantic World," in *A Centre of Wonders,* 145–162.

16. Reay, 35–36.

17. For an analysis of the sources of elite and popular hostility, see Reay, chap. 3 and 4.

18. Anonymous, *The Querers and Quakers Cause, at the second hearing* (London, 1653), 37. Such a vision of the Quaker movement was given great impetus in 1656 by the public "fall" of James Nayler, a leader nearly equal with George Fox,

when he entered Bristol in a complex christological performance surrounded by passionate female admirers. For a sustained interpretation of the Nayler incident and its contexts, see Leo Damrosch, *The Sorrows of the Quaker Jesus: James Nayler and the Puritan Crackdown on the Free Spirit* (Cambridge: Harvard University Press, 1996).

19. John Gilpin, *The Quakers Shaken* (London, 1655), title page. An earlier version of the tract, published in 1653, does not contain this material.

20. *A Relation of a Quaker, That to the Shame of his Profession, Attempted to Bugger a Mare near Colchester* (London, 1659), n.p. The song has been attributed to Sir John Denham. It is reprinted as "News from Colchester" along with a second song on the same incident, "The Four-Legg'd Quaker," in *The Rump, or Collection of Songs and Ballads, made upon those who would be a Parliament* (London, 1660). I am unclear, however, whether these songs refer to the same act as that related by Gilpin; although it seems unlikely there would be two separate incidents, the songs were written at least four years after Gilpin's account and name the man involved "Ralph Green." It is possible they conflated the earlier Hugh Bisbrowne incident with a 1659 Colchester event in which "a *Man-Quaker* went stark naked all through the Market" (Underhill, 3). I have not come across other references to either name.

21. For a vivid English view of "Romish" debauchery, see Philanax Misopapas [pseud.], *Rome's Rarities, or the Pope's Cabinet Unlock'd, and Exposed to View* (London, 1680), esp. 154–156. Tracts associating Quakers and Jesuits are numerous: see, for example, D. Lupton, *The Quacking Mountebanck, or the Jesuite turned Quaker* (London, 1655); William Prynne, *Some Popish Errors Unadvisedly Embraced* (London, 1658); and William Brownssword, *The Quaker-Jesuite, or, Popery in Quakerisme* (London, 1659). Reay comments that while the accusation of being "Jesuits in disguise" has been leveled at most sects, it was used with special frequency against Quakers (59); on the New England context, see Thompson, 33. On anti-Catholic rhetoric and imagery in Protestant England, see Frances Dolan, *Whores of Babylon: Catholicism, Gender, and Seventeenth-Century Print Culture* (Notre Dame: University of Notre Dame Press, 2005).

22. Reay, 60. Memories of the Jesuit mission to England in 1581, which led to the arrest and execution of Edmund Campion and others perceived as "invaders" on behalf of Rome, certainly contributed to this paranoia. For an English Protestant defense of the state's actions, see William Cecil, *The Execution of Justice in England* (London, 1584).

23. Mack, 133–134.

24. *A Sober Answer,* 30.

25. Thompson, 38. The text he cites is John Wilson, *Seasonable Watch-Word* (Boston, 1677), iii.

26. On the association between Quakers and witchcraft, see Pestana, "The City upon a Hill under Siege," 337–338; Reay, 68–69; Carol F. Karlsen, *The Devil in the*

*Shape of a Woman: Witchcraft in Colonial New England* (New York: W.W. Norton, 1987), esp. 122–125; and Christine Leigh Heyrman, "Spectres of Subversion, Societies of Friends: Dissent and the Devil in Provincial Essex County, Massachusetts," in *Saints and Revolutionaries: Essays on Early American History,* ed. David D. Hall, John M. Murrin, and Thad W. Tate (New York: W.W. Norton, 1984), 38–74. For a broader consideration of Puritans' belief in women's proclivity toward sexual sin and diabolic possession, see Elizabeth Reis, *Damned Women: Sinners and Witches in Puritan New England* (Ithaca: Cornell University Press, 1997), esp. chap. 3. On female sexuality in the Puritan execution narrative, see Jodi Schorb, "Uncleanliness is Next to Godliness: Sexuality, Salvation, and the Early American Women's Execution Narrative," in Fessenden, Radel, and Zaborowska, 72–92.

27. Tarter, 148, 149.

28. Dillon, 144–145. Godbeer makes a similar point about gender for Puritans being attached to roles rather than bodies in *Sexual Revolution,* 79.

29. Tarter, 151. On Quaker belief in "unity of the genders," see Rebecca Larson, *Daughters of Light: Quaker Women Preaching and Prophesying in the Colonies and Abroad, 1700–1775* (Chapel Hill: University of North Carolina Press, 1999), 20–23. See also Mack, esp. chap. 2.

30. Katherine Marbury Scott, Anne Hutchinson's sister, also became a Quaker and experienced persecution in New England, a point that was not lost on early Friends; see Humphrey Norton, *New England's Ensigne* (London, 1659), 98–99.

31. David Hall, ed. *The Antinomian Controversy, 1636–1638: A Documentary History* (Durham: Duke University Press, 1990), 382–383. Discussions of the Antinomian Controversy that focus substantially on gender issues include Ben Barker-Benfield, "Anne Hutchinson and the Puritan Attitude Toward Women," *Feminist Studies* 1.2 (1972): 65–96; Lyle Koehler, "The Case of the Female Jezebels: Anne Hutchinson and Female Agitation During the Years of the Antinomian Turmoil," *William & Mary Quarterly,* 3d ser., 31.1 (1974): 55–78; Amy Schrager Lang, *Prophetic Woman: Anne Hutchinson and the Problem of Dissent in the Literature of New England* (Berkeley: University of California Press, 1987); Lad Tobin, "A Radically Different Voice: Gender and Language in the Trials of Anne Hutchinson," *Canadian Review of American Studies* 25.3 (1990): 253–70; Marilyn J. Westerkamp, "Anne Hutchinson, Sectarian Mysticism, and the Puritan Order," *Church History* 59 (1990): 482–96, Westerkamp, "Engendering Puritan Religious Culture in Old and New England," *Pennsylvania History* 64 (1997): 105–22, and Mary Beth Norton, chap. 8.

32. Hall, 372.

33. Ibid.

34. Mary Beth Norton, 393. Norton insists that the phrase "without distinction" refers in context to the distinction between sexes; see 476 n.73. For a contemporary accusation that Quakers practiced "community of women," see *The Quacking Mountebanck,* 16.

35. Hall, 281–282. Another account of the birth and its discovery is given in John Winthrop, *The History of New England, 1630–1649*, ed. James Kendall Hosmer (New York, 1908), 266–269.

36. Ibid., 267.

37. The birthing room as an all-female sphere in which patriarchal authority is temporarily suspended is discussed by Mary Beth Norton, 222–225 (she also discusses how this affects the revelation of Mary Dyer's "monster"), and by Bryce Traister, "Anne Hutchinson's 'Monstrous Birth' and the Feminization of Antinomianism," *Canadian Review of American Studies* 27.2 (1997): 133–158. Traister comments that "While reproduction perpetuated (ideally) patriarchal social order, the moment of birth in fact suspended patriarchal authority," 141. I draw from Traister (135) the notion of the "closeting" of the birth. On the other hand, if closeting implies the hiding of shameful things, in the seventeenth century the "closet" or private room was also the literal and symbolic space for cultivating spiritual subjectivity and its accompanying erotics: see chap. 3, "The Prayer Closet," in Rambuss. Both of these dimensions are relevant to the Hutchinson-Dyer connection. See also Anne Jacobson Schutte, "'Such Monstrous Births': A Neglected Aspect of the Antinomian Controversy," *Renaissance Quarterly* 38.1 (1985): 85–106.

38. "[George Fox's] vision [was] that holy spiritual tribalism was to be the burgeoning religion's social form. In his view, Quakers were to be a great spiritual tribe, the "Royal Household of God." Barry Levy, *Quakers and the American Family: British Settlement in the Delaware Valley* (New York: Oxford University Press, 1988), 53. Another study of the family in Quakerism (focused, like Levy's, on a slightly later period) is J. William Frost, *The Quaker Family in Colonial America* (New York: St. Martin's Press, 1973).

39. Christine Trevett, *Quaker Women Prophets in England and Wales, 1650–1700* (Lewiston: Edwin Mellen Press, 2000), chap. 2. Trevett draws on Mary Rose D'Angelo's suggestion that these partnerships "can be seen as a sexual as well as a social choice," 78. See D'Angelo, "Women Partners in the New Testament," *Journal of Feminist Studies in Religion* 6 (1990): 65–86.

40. *A Short Relation of some of the Cruel Sufferings (For the Truths sake) of Katherine Evans and Sarah Chevers* (London, 1662), excerpted in Mary Garman et al., *Hidden in Plain Sight: Quaker Women's Writings, 1650–1700* (Wallingford, PA: Pendle Hill Publications, 1996), 205, 182.

41. On this incident see Pestana, "The City upon a Hill Under Siege," 323–324, and Karlsen, 122–123; for a fuller discussion of Fisher's life, see Mack, 168–70. Mack discusses the motives of women traveling partners (208–210), commenting that for early Quaker prophets "it was their collective identity that mattered most" (208). For discussion of itinerant female Quaker ministers in a slightly later period, see Larson.

42. On the Puritan perception of Quaker itinerancy as a threat to the family, see Pestana, "The City upon a Hill Under Siege," 345–52. Timothy D. Hall discusses

the perceived "menace of itinerancy" in an eighteenth-century colonial context in *Contested Boundaries: Itinerancy and the Reshaping of the Colonial American Religious World* (Durham: Duke University Press, 1994), chap. 2; on issues of the family and gender roles, see esp. 57–58.

43. Thomas Weld, *A Further Discovery of that Generation of Men called Quakers* (Gateside, 1654), 14; Humphrey Norton, 12.

44. A letter by the missionary John Rous, for example, recounts within the space of a few pages the travels of a group of male Friends from Barbados to Rhode Island to Boston to Plymouth to Sandwich and several other towns, and then to Connecticut, back to Rhode Island, to Plymouth again, to Rhode Island, then Boston, and so on. In Francis Howgill, *The Popish Inquisition* (London, 1659), 16–18.

45. Ibid., 16.

46. On English Protestant views of virginity and celibacy, see Theodora Jankowski, *Pure Resistance: Queer Virginity in Early Modern English Drama* (Philadelphia: University of Pennsylvania Press, 2000), chap. 3. Although Jankowski focuses on (female) virginity rather than rejection of sexuality within marriage, I find much relevance in her argument that not having sex can be considered a form of queerness, 8–10.

47. Joseph Nicholson to Margaret Fell, May 3, 1660. Swarthmoor Manuscripts (Friends House Library, London), I: 107.

48. Joseph Nicholson to Margaret Fell, July 10, 1660. Ibid., I: 108.

49. Ibid.

50. Nicholson's anxious (and rather gossipy) reporting on Quaker asceticism reflects his own prior struggles with it: "that spirit did vex mee much after I came from London . . . and many times did much over power mee when I could not know what it was . . . often times it did much [cool] my afection towardes my wife and alsoe towards my children . . . if the lord had not upheald me in the thinge I had been [overthrown] by it . . . as my wife knows right well." Ibid., I:107. Mabel Brailsford contends that the celibacy scandal "was in a fair way . . . to achieve by internal schism and family discord what persecution and martyrdom had failed to accomplish." *Quaker Women, 1650–1690* (London, 1915), 147. For other discussions of the New England celibacy issue, see Pestana, "The City upon a Hill Under Siege," 349; Levy, 72; Reay, 36; Mack, 182. For an insightful broader discussion of the strands of sexuality and asexuality in early Quakerism, see Damrosch, chap. 3, esp. 125–126.

51. Damrosch, 58–59.

52. John Norton, 40, 41, 71, 53.

53. The idea of "queer's" opposition to "regimes of the normal" comes from Michael Warner, "Introduction," in Warner, ed., *Fear of a Queer Planet: Queer Politics and Social Theory* (Minneapolis: University of Minnesota Press, 1993), xxvi. For an account of the political and theoretical emergence of "queer" in the early

1990s, see Lisa Duggan, "Making It Perfectly Queer," *Socialist Review* 22.1 (1992): 11–31. See also Annamarie Jagose, *Queer Theory: An Introduction* (New York: New York University Press, 1996) and Tamsin Spargo, *Foucault and Queer Theory* (New York: Totem Books, 1999).

54. On the importance of the scaffold in both sexual and religious "dramas of scandal and exposure," see Ingebretsen, 24.

55. Burrough, 24. Burrough's account of Mary Dyer's martyrdom is discussed at length in Myles, 6–13.

56. John Knott, "John Foxe and the Joy of Suffering," *Sixteenth-Century Journal* 27.3 (1996): 728. The classic study of the *Acts and Monuments* is William Haller, *Foxe's Book of Martyrs and the Elect Nation* (London: Jonathan Cape, 1963). For differing assessments of the ways and extent to which early Quaker martyrology was influenced by Foxe see John Knott, *Discourses of Martyrdom in English Literature, 1563–1694* (New York: Cambridge University Press, 1993), esp. 223; Rosemary Moore, 161–162; and Carla Pestana, "Martyred by the Saints: Quaker Executions in Seventeenth-Century Massachusetts," in Allan Greer and Jodi Bilinkoff, eds., *Colonial Saints: Discovering the Holy in the Americas, 1500–1800* (New York: Routledge, 2003), 179–180. Major studies of early modern martyrdom include Brad S. Gregory, *Salvation at Stake: Christian Martyrdom in Early Modern Europe* (Cambridge: Harvard University Press, 1999); John Coffey, *Persecution and Toleration in Protestant England, 1558–1689* (London: Longman, 2000); Sarah Covington, *The Trail of Martyrdom: Persecution and Resistance in Sixteenth-Century England* (Notre Dame: University of Notre Dame Press, 2003); and with a focus on English literary representations, Knott's *Discourses of Martyrdom* and Susannah Brietz Monta, *Martyrdom and Literature in Early Modern England* (New York: Cambridge University Press, 2005).

57. While the fact that Foxe and other martyr accounts include scenes that can be construed as eroticized is fairly widely recognized, the most extensive exploration of this dimension is in Truman, and, for Quakers, Pestana, "Martyred by the Saints."

58. Truman, 37, 48.

59. Ibid., 55.

60. Bishop, 93.

61. Dyer was considerably older than Robinson and Stephenson; going to the scaffold she was taunted in a sexualized way by the marshal, who asked " 'whether she was not ashamed to walk hand in hand between two young men?' " (Bishop, 109). Dyer, referred to as "Mistress," and Robinson, a member of the merchant class, were higher-ranking than Stephenson, a farmer.

62. Marmaduke Stephenson, *A Call from Death to Life, Out of the Dark wayes and Worships of the World* (London, 1660), 37.

63. Ibid., 40.

64. Rosemary Moore, 78. Moore speaks of early letters among Friends—which

later came to be a source of anxiety and were censored—"in which the recipient is addressed in the language of popular devotion as Christ would be." She comments on an erotically inflected letter from Quaker Richard Farnsworth to George Fox that "an unexpressed sexuality probably lay at the root of [it]" (78).

65. Howgill, 19. As one anti-Quaker writer saw it, "these men either cannot or will not distinguish between the Body of *Christ,* which is glorified in the Heavens, and the *Church* of *Christ,* which is his Mysticall Body upon Earth." Jeremiah Ives, *The Quakers Quaking* (London, 1656), 41. In polemical responses to such accusations, Friends generally insisted that they did indeed recognize this distinction, but in practice there was clearly much slippage. For further discussion of this issue, see Damrosch, 94 ff.

66. Pestana, "Martyred by the Saints," 177.

67. This intense rhetoric of sameness uniting spiritual to social erotics is distinctive to early Quakerism, and suggests a very different emphasis than that which Richard Rambuss finds in other Protestant devotional writing, where intense, frequently same-sex bonds between believers are vectored through the person and body of Jesus. As a result, the spiritual erotics of Quaker devotion did not foster only the private interiority that Rambuss outlines, grounded in the model of the individual worshipper in the "prayer closet," but also, and more profoundly, an identity with and allegiance to the group (see *Closet Devotions* chap. 3, also Rambuss, "Pleasure and Devotion: The Body of Jesus and Seventeenth-Century Religious Lyric," in *Queering the Renaissance,* 253–279).

68. Historical connections between support for the Half-Way Covenant and for a hard line on dealing with the Quakers and the Baptists (and, conversely, opposition toward both measures) are discussed in Stephen Foster, *The Long Argument: English Puritanism and the Shaping of New England Culture, 1570–1700* (Chapel Hill: University of North Carolina Press, 1991), 198 and 355 n. 64. Foster discusses what he sees as the relative failure of the Quakers to make converts in New England (190–91). While this observation may be true in statistical terms, the movement as a whole grew mightily between 1652 and 1662, and the New England ministry would likely have been more influenced by this spread and the movement's implied potential than by actual numbers to date locally.

69. On Quaker publication practices, see Kate Peters, *Print Culture and the Early Quakers* (New York: Cambridge University Press, 2005).

70. *New England's Ensigne,* 6; the incident with the key is on 50–52. Norton's punishment is discussed in Jane Kamensky's *Governing the Tongue: The Politics of Speech in Early New England* (New York: Oxford University Press, 1997), 125–26.

71. *New England's Ensigne,* 18. Norton addresses the reader about this intimacy as he begins to quote from "the substance taken out of [Robert Hodghouse's] own true relation given out under his hand." While the narrative lists Humphrey Norton as its author, its title page states that it was "Written at Sea, by *us* whom the Wicked in scorn call Quakers" (italics mine); its text includes the text of colonial

laws, the relation of Robert Hodghouse, a section written by Christopher Holder and John Copeland, Norton's own story, a section about Norton's experiences in New Haven, etc. Most other texts are similarly structured.

72. One conspicuous example of this confusion occurs in the section titled "New Havens proceedings against Humphrey Norton and others," in *New England's Ensigne*. Although Norton is the volume's author, it gradually becomes evident that the narrative voice of this section in fact is that of Norton's close associate John Rous.

73. On the characteristics of Quaker literary expression see Jackson Cope, "Seventeenth-Century Quaker Style," *PMLA* 71 (1956): 724–54; Nigel S. Smith, *Perfection Proclaimed: Language and Literature in English Radical Religion, 1640–1660* (Oxford: Clarendon Press, 1989); and the essays collected in Thomas N. Corns and David Lowenstein, eds., *The Emergence of Quaker Writing: Dissenting Literature in Seventeenth-Century England* (London: Frank Cass, 1995).

74. Burrough, 28. Eve Kosofsky Sedgwick has written that a person's calling him- or herself "queer" (as opposed to what pass as the more objective identity categories "lesbian" or "gay") depends "upon a person's undertaking particular, performative acts of experimental self-perception and filiation"—acts that I believe also apply to identifying as a member of a nondominant religious community. *Tendencies* (Durham: Duke University Press, 1993), 9.

75. Dinshaw, 1. All of Dinshaw's Introduction is useful for developing the notion of what it might mean to practice a "queer history" in the context of studying past religious cultures. See also *The Queer Issue: New Visions of America's Gay and Lesbian Past*, ed. Jeffrey Escoffier, Regina Kunzel, and Molly McGarry, special issue of *Radical History Review* 62 (1995), and Lisa Duggan, "The Discipline Problem: Queer Theory Meets Lesbian and Gay History," *GLQ: A Journal of Lesbian and Gay Studies* 2 (1995): 179–91. For a contemporary first-person exploration of the resonances between religious and homoerotic affections and an argument about religious ecstasy as an essential model for erotic transgression, see Michael Warner, "Tongues Untied: Memoirs of a Pentecostal Boyhood," in *The Material Queer: A Lesbigay Cultural Studies Reader*, ed. Donald Morton (Boulder: Westview Press, 1996), 39–45.

76. On the changing political and communal uses of the New England Quaker martyrs, see Carla Pestana, "The Quaker Executions as Myth and History," *The Journal of American History* 80 (1993): 441–469.

# Chapter 6

# Hermaphrodites and "Same-Sex" Sex in Early America

## *Elizabeth Reis*

Individuals born with ambiguous genitals (then called hermaphrodites, now intersexed) provoked a particular unease in early America. The biblical story of Adam and Eve established and authorized a rigid binary system of appropriate sex. Despite the occasional occurrence of ambiguous and contradictory genital markers in the extrabiblical world, it was mandatory, God's will, for every human in a well-regulated society to be, and to stay, either male or female, and as we shall see, to have sex with the suitable gender. The early modern definition of a hermaphrodite was simple in theory, but much more complicated when medical men confronted actual bodies. A hermaphrodite was defined as an individual with a perfect set of both male and female genital organs, capable of having sex and reproducing as both male and female. Medical authorities assumed that hermaphrodites would use their male organs when having sex with women and their female organs when having sex with men. However, no person examined fit this definition, and so medical men came to insist that hermaphrodites, as they had been defined, did not exist.

Even if perfect hermaphrodites did not exist according to medical authorities, the idea of *one* body exhibiting *two* sexes, able to couple with either sex, raised a host of anxieties about gender and sex. This was, in part, because observers believed that these people would be able to have sexual intercourse with either sex. This essay explores colonial attitudes toward hermaphrodites insofar as ambiguous bodies raised the question of same-sex sexual behavior. Though there was equal concern with men possibly having sex with other men, hermaphrodites were frequently considered really women during the colonial period and into the nineteenth century, able to have sex with men, but with clitorises so long that these women were also thought capable of penetrating other women in same-sex liaisons. We will see how these fears determined medical and legal practice during this period.

## Sex and Gender Ambiguity in Early America

In early America, doctors lacked the social status and the medical knowledge they would acquire in the nineteenth century, and lay-people typically managed illness and disease without professional help. Because most people tended to their own health needs, extensive official medical records are not available for this era. Consequently, historians are left with a comparative dearth of such sources. Later, in the nineteenth century, as doctors professionalized, they wrote journal articles about various conditions their patients presented, including atypical genital anatomies, and so, since the early 1800s, historians have had rich medical material to interpret. Some American midwives and doctors read European medical manuals, and their understanding of various conditions was no doubt influenced by a European intellectual tradition going back centuries. The handful of early American authors who wrote their own medical books cited these European writers in agreement or disagreement. Early American readers, we know, also looked at European and British treatises; in fact, some of these books, such as Jane Sharp's *The Midwives Book: or the Whole Art of Midwifery Discovered* and Nicholas Culpeper's *The Compleat Practice of Physick,* became quite popular in the colonies. Fortunately, medical treatises are not the only available sources for historians to mine. In New England, at least, sermonic literature exists, which reflected the religious interpretation of illness and disability, and throughout the colonies legal records sometimes contained references to what we now recognize as intersex conditions. In addition, newspapers and literary sources can sometimes offer clues as to how colonists understood hermaphrodites in an era before hermaphroditism was considered a medical condition requiring treatment.

Records of divorce proceedings for impotency are a rich source for historians, combining both legal and medical interpretations of intercourse and marriage. Charges of impotency provoked physical examination of the impugned husbands. Some of these colonial cases revealed what we might today consider intersex conditions, exposing not only the husband's failure to perform sexually, but also his physical anomaly. In June 1686, for example, Dorathy Clarke of Plymouth, Massachusetts, petitioned the court for a divorce stating her husband, Nathaniel Clarke, "hath not performed the duty of a husband to me." In this case, Dorathy alleged that her husband was "misformed" and that he was "always unable to perform the act of generation." She requested a divorce because their "lives are very uncomfortable in the sight of God." Dorathy's husband, Nathaniel, denied the charges of "infirmity of body," and so the court ordered that "his body be viewed by some persons skilfull and judicious." The court chose three male physicians to inspect Nathaniel's body and give their judgment at the next court date. The findings of these physicians are not clear, but one month later the court decided that Dorathy would not be granted the divorce she requested.[1]

Impotency, particularly if thought to be caused by a "misformed" penis, was regarded as a potential indicator of a hermaphroditic condition. Body searches were not uncommon in such cases. The three doctors who searched Nathaniel Clarke may have been looking for an unusually small penis that might have hindered sexual intercourse or a malformation known as hypospadias, where the urethral opening was on the underside rather than the tip of the penis. These conditions were recognized and, according to colonial law, would have been reason enough for a divorce, since presumably the conditions existed before the marriage contract was made. As the divorce was not granted, Nathaniel Clarke must have displayed some lesser (and acceptable) physical anomaly and have been thought capable of coitus even with his condition, or alternatively, he was judged to have had fully normal genitalia.

In 1662, a Massachusetts court heard a similar case, though in this instance, the husband admitted his impotency. Mary White sought a divorce from her husband, Elias White, because he "cannot performe the duty or office of a husband to hir." The court "perused the evidence" and did not see sufficient cause to separate the couple. Instead, the court advised them to work harder at their marriage. The husband appended a note to the court documents attesting to the truth of his wife's charges. He explained that when he first married he thought himself "sufficient: otherwise I neuer would have entered into that estate." Later he came to discover that he was "Infirmous not able to performe that office of marriage," though he could not determine the cause. Two men questioned White and his wife about the husband's sexual performance. When White lay with his wife, they asked, was "there any motion in him or no?" He answered that sometimes, after lying together four or five hours, there was, but "when he turned to hir It was gonn againe." Mary White asked her husband "whither or no he had euer made vse of hir," and he answered "no."[2] Here, too, the court ruled against the divorce, perhaps because White agreed that at the time when he got married, he considered himself "sufficient." In other words, his infirmity became known only after the couple had been married for several years. As there was no fraud in the initial contact, a divorce on these grounds would not have been warranted.[3]

Women with congenital malformations of the genital organs could also be ruled unable to copulate. And they too were subjected to physical scrutiny by doctors and midwives in order to see if such conformation was causing their sexual problems. Early nineteenth-century doctors in America combed the published records of European doctors, searching for cases that would help them diagnose the sheer variety of genital malformation and its effects. American medical treatises include many examples of seventeenth and eighteenth-century cases of European women seeking medical (and often legal) attention because their marriages could not be consummated. Theodric Beck described a Parisian woman who married in 1722 at age twenty-five, but had not achieved intercourse for six years because, she said, "she could find none of the sexual organs, and that their place was occupied by a solid body." A surgeon was called in to evaluate, and he made an incision in the mass, which he thought would alleviate her condition, but to no avail. Twenty years later, in 1742, the husband sought to annul the marriage. As in the cases noted above, the woman's body was open to scrutiny. Two doctors found an "aperture of two or three inches" left from the previous surgeon's efforts, but they agreed that "either through fear or the prudence of the surgeon," the mass had not been entirely removed. Nonetheless, the court refused the annulment, on the grounds that the woman's situation was operable. Despite the failed earlier attempt, the court insisted that a "cure" was possible.[4]

The people in the aforementioned cases may have had intersex conditions that prevented sexual relations for one or both partners, but the term "hermaphrodite" was not raised or implied in court, perhaps because the litigants lived their lives uncomplicatedly as either men or women.[5] The first explicit case of ambiguous sex found in early American legal records is that of Thomas/Thomasina Hall, who was apprehended in Virginia and came before the court in 1629 for "dressing in women's apparel."[6] Hall's indefinite gender performance matched the subject's bodily conformation, and various people in the town took it upon themselves to physically inspect Hall's genitals and render a verdict as to whether Hall was a man or a woman. One man, in fact, cried out to Hall, "thou hast beene reported to bee a woman and now thou art proved to bee a man, I will see what thou carriest." The deposition then describes the ensuing violation of Hall: "Whereuppon the said Rodes laid hands upon the said Hall, and this examiner did soe likewise, and they threw the said Hall on his backe, and then this examiner felt the said Hall and pulled out his members whereby it appeared that hee was a Perfect man."[7] Hall was commanded to "lye on his backe" and show his genitals many times during his ordeal. Hall was searched by both male and female investigators; one time two men even came in his room while he slept to sneak a look. Perhaps Hall resisted and it was not recorded, or perhaps close scrutiny of bodies was tolerated because such intimate inspection was not unusual. Searches of suspected "witches" occurred throughout the colonies as well, with examiners looking for the devil's mark or a teat whereby the devil's familiar could suck from the witch's body.[8]

Individuals born with ambiguous genitals, even if they weren't pronounced perfect hermaphrodites, with two perfect sets of genitals, worried authorities. Eighteenth-century medical manuals emphasized the legal regulations that applied to hermaphrodites, including laws of marriage, which derived from Jewish Talmudic law and ancient Latin canon and civil law.[9] For example, James Parsons, despite arguing in his 1741 English treatise, *A Mechanical and Critical Enquiry into the Nature of Hermaphrodites,* that human hermaphrodites did not exist, listed each possible legal question, from whether a hermaphrodite should be given a male or female name at birth to whether or not a hermaphrodite should be allowed to marry or divorce. Parsons' answers to these questions required that hermaphrodites or their parents make a permanent choice of sex. Unlike later medical practitioners, Parsons was willing to entrust this vital decision to the individual most concerned. He states, "predominancy of sex . . . ought to be regarded; but if the Sexes seem equal, the Choice is left to the Hermaphrodite."[10] Parsons would not have approved of Hall's movements back and forth across the gender divide, and he emphasized choosing one sex.

Although Parsons detailed the legalities relevant to persons with ambiguous genitals and advised such individuals and their parents on their correct course of conduct, most of his book denies the existence of human hermaphrodites. He defined a hermaphrodite as "an Animal, in which the two Sexes, Male and Female, ought to appear to be each distinct and perfect, as well with regard to the Structure proper to either, as to the Power of exercising the necessary Offices and Functions of those Parts."[11] Lower forms of animal life, earthworms, snails, and some reptiles, may display perfect hermaphrodism—entire male and female sexual organs, each with normally functioning sexual and reproductive capability—but not humans. Parsons was right. Humans, unlike hermaphroditic earthworms, are not able to reproduce as either sex. Eliminating hermaphrodism as a human phenomenon, however, justified medical and lay people in their insistence on the rigor of two mutually exclusive sexual categories, discrete categories into which not all bodies were easily sorted.

Apparently, Hall's body was one that could not be easily classified, and Hall's life reflected that ambiguity. Hall told his history to the court. In England, "she" had been baptized Thomasine and lived with her parents until the age of twelve in their house near Newcastle upon Tyne. She spent the next ten years at her aunt's house in London. After her brother became a soldier, Hall dared to cut her hair, wear men's clothes, and join the army. "He" served an unspecified time in the military and then resumed life as Thomasine. According to the court's deposition, "hee changed himselfe into woemans apparel and made bone lace and did other worke with his needle." Not content to remain a woman, Hall decided to adopt a new persona and emigrated to Virginia as a male indentured servant. Once again Hall donned masculine garb. In Virginia, despite his status as a bound laborer, s/he exercised a predilection for crossing back and forth between genders.[12]

When asked "wether hee were man or woeman," Hall answered, "both man and woeman." Hall's own description of his/her genitals suggests that Hall was a hermaphrodite. S/he explained that s/he had features of both sexes and added that s/he "had not the use of the mans parte," though s/he also said there "was a peece of fleshe growing at the . . . belly as bigg as the top of his little finger [an] inch longe." Those who viewed his/her body were uncertain as to which sex Hall belonged, for when a group of female examiners saw this piece of flesh and asked if "that were all hee had," s/he answered, "I have a peece of an hole."[13]

Had the court been able to decide which of Hall's sexual characteristics were predominant, it might have required him/her to assume and maintain this preferred sex. Such a solution would have been consistent with scripture-based laws as interpreted by Talmudic commentaries and consonant with early modern European customs. Instead, the court acknowledged Hall's own self-description as a person embodying both sexes. It decreed that henceforth s/he be required to wear a paradoxical costume consisting of "mans apparel, only his head to be attired in a Coyfe and Crosscloth with an Apron before him."[14] The court did not wish to endorse and promote uncertainty but chose this sanction, I believe, to preclude future acts of deception, to mark the offender, to warn others against similar abomination, and to greatly reduce the possibility of Hall's sexual coupling. The court's ruling made it impossible for Hall to seduce the unwary of either sex, should s/he attempt to do so, and to then have coitus with the "wrong" sex. This was not a tolerant and understanding ruling, permitting Hall to switch between male and female roles as circumstances allowed and opportunities afforded. It prevented any sexual autonomy and ability to blend in with the populace. Hall would have to live the rest of his/her days as a public freak and laughing-stock, an ambiguously gendered being, at once male and female.

There was no category of intersex into which the dual-sexed Hall could be fit; there were men and there were women. Hall therefore embodied an impermissible category of gender. Hall might have favored a laissez-faire approach to sexual expression, but the authorities insisted on precise rules of gender display that would reflect and announce his/her equivocal condition. The court's judgment, mandating the simultaneous performance of both genders, rose from the impossibility of clear classification. Ironically, its solution confounded social conventions; individuals did not normally go about in both male and female attire. Though the court might have been less concerned with imposing a punitive solution than with protecting unaware townspeople from sexual congress with the wrong sex, its legal decision was devastating to Hall's dignity. By this humiliating sentence, Hall was marked as a creature of indeterminate sex, a ludicrously dressed object of disgust perhaps, or of amusement, or of pity.[15] Hall could no longer switch between living as a man or as a woman, nor live solely as either a man or a woman. Under this sentence, Hall could live only as a public spectacle of no specific sex. Unfortunately for historians, Hall drops from public records after the court's decision. We can only hope that s/he worked off the indenture, changed name and location, eschewed the farcical costume, and resumed life as whichever sex s/he preferred.

Hall would not be the last person in early America to move back and forth between genders. Conventional masculinity and femininity in the colonial period were rigidly defined yet nonetheless transgressed, and it may be the case that the indistinct nature of these people's genitals prompted their exchange between the genders. Although sources are limited, some newspaper evidence depicts, as historian Alfred Young has aptly written, "a hidden world of plebeian deception and disguise."[16] *The Pennsylvania Gazette* published a story in 1764 of a woman, Deborah Lewis, who had "constantly appeared in the female Dress," and was always assumed to be a woman. She "suddenly threw off that Garb, and assumed the Habit of a Man." As if to certify that she was truly a man, and that hers was not merely a case of cross-dressing, the paper included that she was "on the Point of Marrying a Widow Woman."[17] In 1770, *The Pennsylvania Gazette* printed another article presumably about the same Deborah Lewis, suggesting that the Lewis story had become something of an urban legend.[18] The second piece provided details of Deborah's infancy, when supposedly as a baby she bore "a similarity to both Sexes." Apparently there was some discussion at her birth as to what apparel the baby should wear. It was decided that she be dressed as a female, and she was baptized as such. She "passed for a Woman" for twenty-three years. As an adult, Deborah Lewis lived with a woman who became pregnant and declared Deborah the father. The paper reported that they got married and that Deborah added the man's name, Francis, calling himself Deborah Francis Lewis. According to an entry in a book of genealogies, an obituary from 1823 recorded the death of one Francis Lewis who for thirty-two years "dressed as a woman and was supposed to be such. Afterwards he assumed male apparel, married and raised a family."[19]

Was Deborah Lewis a woman who lived as a man, a man who lived as a woman, or an intersexed person whose ambiguous genitals allowed him/her to do what seemed appropriate and natural at different points in life? Without more substantive sources, it is impossible to determine. What will become clear below is that concerns over gender-crossing often attended anxiety surrounding same-sex sexuality. The medical and legal conversation about hermaphrodites, in particular, was often conflated with discussion of same-sex sexuality, especially among women, for as I said earlier, hermaphrodites were thought to be actually women with long clitorises, capable of and interested in sexual penetration.

### Sexual Ambiguity and Same-Sex Intimacy

In 1696, Massachusetts adopted a law specifically against cross-dressing, perhaps to thwart same-sex intimacy. The Bible, of course, deplores mingling of any sort; one cannot wear linen mixed with wool; one cannot yoke an ox and a donkey together, or sow a field with two kinds of seed. Yet no law was framed in Massachusetts to prevent these other biblically proscribed minglings. Nor were there laws requiring colonists to eat only kosher food, also biblically decreed. Troubled by gender masquerading, colonial lawmakers believed that cross-dressing, like homosexuality, belonged in a category of more serious offenses. As the Middlesex County Court contended in 1692, while charging a woman named Mary Henly with wearing men's clothes, these offenses were those "seeming to confound the course of nature."[20]

In Haverhill, Massachusetts in 1652, Joseph Davis was convicted of "putting on woemen's apparell and goeinge about from house to house in the nighte." Twenty-five years later, in 1677, Dorothy Hoyt, a woman of Hampton, New Hampshire was convicted of "putting on man's apparel."[21] Not surprisingly, English colonists adamantly opposed cross-dressing of any sort, based on the biblical injunction against either sex wearing the clothes of the other (Deut. 22:5). Even outside of Puritan New England, colonists lived in a world dominated by Christian belief. Women and men had their respective places in the divine scheme, and crossing from one category to the other, to perform what Susan Juster calls "social hermaphroditism," violated providential order.[22]

Unlike similar laws against homosexuality, which typically punished men but not women (women having sexual intercourse with other women is not biblically interdicted), laws against cross-dressing punished women and men equally.[23] None of these statutes mentioned sexuality directly, thus making it difficult for modern readers to judge if the threat to the patriarchal order was deemed social or sexual. In other words, did authorities arrest and convict people for cross-dressing because these offenders publicly violated conventional gender roles and biblical law, or was there something left unsaid in this prosecution, namely, the fear of same-sex intimacy that might follow from the cross-dressers' deception and seduction of unaware partners? Though no court case I have found specifically linked cross-dressing to homosexuality, it might have been less fraught for judges to punish cross-dressing than to inquire too intimately into sexual matters that were considered heinously unnatural.

In the case of Thomas/Thomasina Hall, Hall's physical sex needed to be established so that the sexual behavior could be understood and, if necessary, punished accordingly. In answer to why "he" dressed as a woman, Hall had responded rather obliquely, "I goe in woemans apparel to get a bitt for my Catt." Historian Mary Beth Norton has suggested that Hall's response may have been a reference to prostitution. Echoing the French phrase, "pour avoir une bite pour mon chat" ("to get a penis for my cunt"), Hall, an indentured servant, might have dressed as a woman for financial reasons.[24] As a female prostitute, perhaps Hall could find male sexual partners and supplement "her" meager resources.

But further investigation into Hall's transgression of "wearing women's clothes" revealed more serious issues. The ambiguously gendered servant was rumored to have had sexual relations with a woman, "greate Besse." If Hall was *really* a man, his crime would have been fornication, a common offense in seventeenth-century Virginia. If Hall was "really" a woman, however, the sexual relationship with great Besse might be considered an unnatural act, or it might have been dismissed as being of no consequence, for typically only same-sex liaisons between two men were condemned. Norton says that a clear determination of Hall's anomalous sex would have been required by the court to determine the nature and severity of the crime: was Hall a man or a woman? Was the "piece of flesh" that Hall mentioned an enlarged clitoris by which Hall could penetrate other women? Hall's master and other onlookers were interested in Hall's case. These parties were quoted by the court as pursuing the matter so that "hee might be punished for his abuse."[25] The bystanders seem more exercised by their image of Hall's erotic adaptability than by the possibility of ordinary fornication, and they highlight the anxiety over same-sex liaisons raised by the potential fluidity of gender in the early modern period. In the end, the court's punishment of dual embodiment effectively protected uninformed townspeople from sexual congress with the wrong sex, as well as prevented Hall from engaging in same-sex sex.

Though no one's modesty was respected in bodily searches, women's bodies were subject to even more scrutiny than men's because the clitoris played such an important role in the early modern understanding of hermaphrodites. All of the examples Parsons had provided in his 1741 treatise on hermaphrodites were, he argued, truly women with enlarged clitorises or (less frequently) men with small penises, which hid in bodily folds and were often accompanied by undescended testicles. Not content with confirming examples from his own practice, his book discusses each case of human "double Nature" that he had encountered in medical literature from the early Greeks onward, proving the descriptions therein mistaken.[26] Parsons joined a long tradition of doctors examining hermaphrodites; since the fourteenth century medical men had been interested in the subject and had proffered various theories about such occurrences. Some insisted that hermaphrodites were possible; others, like Parsons, believed that Hermaphroditus, the figure from Greek mythology whose male body was merged by the gods with the female body of the nymph Salmacis, found no counterparts in the mortal human world. Holders of the latter opinion maintained that it was folly to imagine the actual existence of what they regarded as purely mythical beings.[27]

The classification of normal humans as mythical hermaphrodites, according to Parsons, was due to ignorance of human anatomy, particularly of female anatomy. The clitoris, he said, was so little known, so unrecognized as a female organ, it was no wonder that "at the first sight of a large Clitoris, divers odd Conjectures should arise."[28] But medical authors were not completely ignorant of the clitoris. Nicholas Culpeper, herbalist, astrologer, and English translator and coauthor of the 1655 manual, *The Compleat Practice of Physick,* had compared the clitoris to the penis: "[It] suffers erection and falling as that doth; this is that which causeth Lust in women, and gives delight in Copulation, for without this a woman neither desires Copulation, or hath pleasure in it, or conceives by it."[29] Henry Bracken, author of a 1737 British midwifery manual, also wrote of the clitoral role in sexual pleasure: "The Clitoris, or Penis, of the Woman is erected, which, by its Fullness of Nerves, and exquisite Sense, affords unspeakable Delight."[30]

Most early midwifery manuals found in America, though, offered scant mention of the clitoris and even less mention of its function. In Dr. Alexander Hamilton's 1790 textbook, *Outlines of the Theory and Practice of Midwifery,* for example, the organ is mentioned in only two of the book's 307 pages. Similarly, William Smellie's 1786 text, *An Abridgement of the Practice of Midwifery,* only notes the clitoris, in a list of female anatomical parts. William Cheselden briefly alludes to it in two pages of his 350-page book on human anatomy, and barely hints at its significance, explaining in one sentence that it "is a small spongy body, bearing some analogy to the penis in men, but has no urethra."[31] In an 1802 midwifery manual, Thomas Denman wrote, "The clitoris is little concerned in the practice of midwifery, on account of its size and situation."[32]

Though the organ itself was usually ignored or deemed insignificant, clitorises of pronounced size provoked comment and concern. According to Parsons, oversized clitorises were particularly common among African women and could lead to "two Evils: the hindering [of] the Coitus, and Womens abuse of them with each other."[33] Sixteenth-century French medical writers had anticipated Parsons in his latter concern. They suggested that women with large clitorises could give sexual pleasure to other women. One such doctor described the clitoris in 1597 as "that part with which imprudent and lustful women, aroused by a more than brutal passion, abuse one another with vigorous rubbings, when they are called confricatrices."[34]

Even Jane Sharp, who did not hesitate to describe the clitoris's function and form in great detail, linked an enlarged clitoris to both hermaphrodites and to women having sex with other women. "Some think," she said, "that hermaphrodites are only women that have their Clitoris greater, and hanging out more than others have, and so shew like a Mans Yard."[35] Implying that an enlarged clitoris could be used for penetration in same-sex relations, she continued, "Commonly it is but a small sprout, lying close hid under the Wings, and not easily felt, yet sometimes it grows so long that it hangs forth at the slit like a Yard, and will swell and stand stiff if it be provoked, and some lewd women have endeavoured to use it as men do theirs."[36]

Occasionally, writers conflated medical discourse on hermaphrodites with quasi-pornographic tales of women with large clitorises (or other penis substitutes) having sex with each other.[37] One book in particular, *A Treatise on Hermaphrodites,* published in England in 1718, sandwiched several salacious stories of women using their large clitorises for penetrative sex with female partners in an ostensibly scientific account of hermaphrodites. The author, Giles Jacob, introduced the book by explaining the five types of hermaphrodites, a schema he derived from Nicholas Venette's *Conjugal Love; or the Pleasures of the Marital Bed Considered in Several Lectures on Human Generation.*[38] The first two types looked like men, Jacob explained, though their genitalia included "a pretty deep slit between the Seat and the Cod." Both categories were capable of generation. The third type, by contrast, had "no visible privy Parts of Man, only a slit." But these hermaphrodites become men during puberty "through the coming forth of the privy parts . . . in an Instant, and are as valiant in the Adventures of Love as other Males." Jacob cautioned that because these "men" could look very much like women at first, young gentlemen should not be too hasty in their marriages; one could never know if "in a vigorous Consummation with a very youthful Partner, the imaginary Female should at once appear an Hermaphrodite."[39] The fifth kind "have neither the Use of the one or the other Sex, and have their privy Parts confus'd."

These hermaphrodites have the "temper" of both men and women, and their whole constitution is so "inter-mix'd" that it is impossible to say which sex predominates.

Jacob devoted most of his discussion to the type he found most intriguing: the fourth category: "Women who have the Clitoris bigger and longer than others." Jacob knew the function of the clitoris under usual circumstances. He compared it to the penis and agreed with his contemporaries that "without this Part, the fair Sex would neither desire the Embraces of the Males, nor have any Pleasure in them, or Conceive by them." But, just as other European authors had warned, a large clitoris could be problematic, at the very least interfering with heterosexual copulation. "Sometimes the Clitoris will grow out of the body two or three inches" because of the "over much Heat of the Privities," he explained, and this gets in the way of satisfactory intercourse. Though the female's own pleasure may be enhanced by clitoral enlargement, its increased size would prevent a man from "knowing his Wife."[40]

Here the stories of hermaphrodites and lesbians merged.[41] Unable to copulate effectively with men, "robust and lustful" women, "well furnish'd in these Parts," might turn to the "unnatural Pleasures" of sex with women. The middle section of Jacob's book turned to the story of two "masculine-females" of the noble class, Marguereta and Barbarissa, from Italy and France, respectively. Jacob described these two women as "very near equal to the largest siz'd Male" in their faces, shoulders, hands, and feet. Only their hips and breasts were small. A servant spying on their "amorous adventure," observed Marguereta naked and saw "something hang down from her body of a reddish colour, and which was very unusual." Later in the narrative, the focus shifts to the partner, Barbarissa, who was having trouble with the "erection of her female Member," but ultimately succeeded in penetration. With such an obvious emphasis on their large clitorises, it is no small wonder that Jacob conceded that both were "suspected to be Hermaphrodites."[42]

As the debate over hermaphrodites' existence continued, the clitoris remained a significant marker. Medical writers commented on its dimensions, increasingly linking its magnitude to homosexual activity between women. In 1807, for example, Dr. William Handy of New York believed that he had seen an actual hermaphrodite. Cognizant of the common understanding of hermaphrodites, he had always assumed that "an animal, uniting the sexes distinctly, had no existence in nature." And so when presented with the "opportunity of visiting and examining so rare a phenomenon" in Lisbon, he eagerly accepted. Like other medical observers, Handy had supposed that the term "hermaphrodite" was reserved for those women "in whom the clitoris was found to be of an uncommon size." But Handy pushed the association even further, suggesting that the clitoris sometimes grew to unnatural proportions *because of* "the morbid effect of frequent lascivious unnatural excitement, as we learn to have occurred in the case of two Nuns at Rome."[43] Not only were hermaphrodites really women with large clitorises, but also apparently the clitoris in some women grew unusually large as a result of sex with other women. Hermaphrodites, large clitorises, and sex between women were bound together in Handy's account.

According to historian Sander Gilman, Europeans believed that sexual irregularities, especially large clitorises, were particularly common among women in Africa, India, and the Caribbean.[44] Indeed, Ambrose Pare, the sixteen-century French surgeon, had written about the clitoral excision of female diviners of Fez, in North Africa, and subsequent European and American authors continued to project genital and sexual anomalies onto the bodies of women of other races and from other continents. In her section on enlarged clitorises, Jane Sharp pointed out that "In the Indies, and Egypt they are frequent," and in fact she claimed to have never heard of the problem in England. If there were any women afflicted with what Sharp called a "counterfeit Yard," she was sure they would "do what they can for shame to keep it close."[45] Similarly, James Parsons linked the exoticized body of an Angolan woman to his study of hermaphrodites. He wrote that upon the arrival in England of this unnamed African woman, considered by many to be a man, he decided to undertake his entire project on hermaphrodites, to prove that she was really a woman with a large clitoris, and that hermaphrodites did not exist in humans.[46] Ultimately, Parsons supported clitoral excision. In Asiatic and African countries, he said, "the Women have them most commonly very long," and knowing the trouble they can bring, the people "wisely cut or burn them off while Girls are young."[47]

Clitoral excision would come to be a common, though contested, cure for all sorts of female conditions, including incessant masturbation, nymphomania, syphilis, and hysteria.[48] Genital surgery for "hermaphroditism" would also become medically accepted, including, but not limited to, clitoral removal. Perhaps because seventeenth- and eighteenth-century medical men believed that hermaphrodites were simply women with distended clitorises, it stood to reason that their solution for this incipiently dangerous "abnormality" would be its straightforward removal.

Genital surgery for hermaphroditism became more and more common in the late nineteenth and early twentieth centuries, when the paradigm of sexual inversion emerged as a scientific explanation for homosexuality. Doctors wanted sexual desire to match genitalia. The early cases of interventionist surgery were connected to the patients' perceived sexual needs as determined by the doctor in attendance. By the turn of the century, hermaphrodites became potential homosexuals or "inverts"; if some bodies could look both male and female, then would these patients be attracted to the wrong sex? Though the possibility of hermaphrodites being physically intimate with both sexes had long been a concern for physicians, now American doctors began to evaluate their patients' sexual inclinations in order to ensure surgically that potential sexual intercourse would be between two differently sexed bodies.

James Parsons, as we have seen, was unusually forward-thinking to allow patients to choose their own sex (and, though he did not say it, their own sexual partners). When later doctors made the choice, they prioritized heterosexuality, to some patients' life-long grief. If an indeterminately sexed patient, even one who seemed predominantly male, expressed sexual interest in men, for example, doctors advocated surgical intervention to make that person's genitals appear female. After a sorry history of well-meant but tragic surgical transformations, contemporary intersex activists have begun to campaign for surgical restraint, advocating that intersexed bodies be left alone until they have passed puberty, when individuals can decide for themselves what, if any, surgery is desirable.

Those with ambiguous genitalia escaped debilitating surgery in early America, yet even before "hermaphroditism" became a medical condition inevitably necessitating medical intervention, early medical and legal authorities had opinions on how people with atypical genitalia should be regarded. When sexual performance, law suits, illness, or chance brought their condition to the court's attention, their sexual lives were no less scrutinized and publicized than their physical conformation. Their sex lives were regulated to the best of the court's ability and, often relegated, with optimum early American propriety, to heterosexual marriage.

Courts were not only concerned lest the physically dubious enjoy sex with both men and women, they were also suspicious that sexual duality could lead to sexual duplicity—an innocent individual might be seduced into sex with a same-sex partner. And they were no less anxious lest the ambiguously sexed eschew deception and copulate, frankly and openly, with their own sex. Though the one true sex of a person like Thomas/ Thomasina Hall was, in early American eyes, known only to God, that sentencing, in which, as we have seen, Hall was required to live as neither man nor woman but as a public burlesque of both, was a legal effort to stifle the possibility of any sexual expression. For even if the court imposed a sexual identity upon him/her, or if Hall were willing to choose one sex in perpetuity, what if the court's choice or the defendant's choice were wrong? What if the court, in puzzlement, fostered a same-sex alliance or if Hall, in perverted desire, were able to choose a same-sex mate? Intersex bodies were a source of anxiety about same-sex sexuality, for if God created no such creature as a true hermaphrodite, then persons with indeterminate genitalia indeed had a certain sex, though man might not be able to discern it. As time passed, medical (and therefore, legal) authorities became more and more certain of their ability to distinguish a person's actual sex or to surgically impose a sexual conformation that would suit their own prejudices against same-sex unions. To uncover the hidden history of intersex, is to expose both early American and later attitudes toward sexual normality and difference. In studying early social response to the challenge of ambiguous genitalia and comparing it to contemporary perspectives, we broaden our understanding of the shifting tensions over gender difference and same-sex sexuality.

NOTES

1. Nathaniel Shurtleff, ed., *Records of the Colony of New Plymouth in New England. Court Orders:* VI (1678–1691) (Boston: William White, 1856), 191–92.

2. John F. Cronin, ed., *Records of the Court of Assistants of the Colony of the Massachusetts Bay, 1630–1692* (Boston: Published by the County of Suffolk, 1928), 131–32.

3. On New England divorce, see Cornelia Dayton, *Women Before the Bar: Gender, Law, & Society in Connecticut, 1639–1789* (Chapel Hill: University of North Carolina Press, 1995), esp. 105–56. A law passed in Philadelphia in 1815 stated "that if either party, at the time of the contract, was and still is naturally impotent, or incapable of procreation, it shall and may be lawful for the innocent and injured person to obtain a divorce." See John Purdon, Esq., ed., *A Digest of the Laws of*

*Pennsylvania from the Year One Thousand Seven Hundred to the Twenty-First Day of May, One Thousand Eight Hundred and Sixty-One* (Philadelphia: Kay & Brother, 1862), 345.

4. Theodric Romeyn Beck and John B. Beck, *Elements of Medical Jurisprudence* (Philadelphia, 1838), 104–5.

5. Contemporary medical experts estimate that one out of every two thousand babies is born with indeterminate genitalia. There are a range of intersex conditions, some of which appear at puberty or go undetected until much later, and so the incidence of intersex may even be greater. See the Intersex Society of North America website for comprehensive resources: http://www.isna.org (December 13, 2005).

6. For two interpretations of Hall's life, see Mary Beth Norton, *Founding Mothers and Fathers: Gendered Power and the Forming of American Society* (New York: Alfred A. Knopf, 1996), 183–97, and Kathleen Brown, " 'Changed . . . into the fashion of man': The Politics of Sexual Difference in a Seventeenth-Century Anglo-American Settlement," *Journal of the History of Sexuality* 6 (1995), 171–93. The case is also discussed in Alden Vaughan, "The Sad Case of Thomas(ine) Hall," *Virginia Magazine of History and Biography* 86 (1978), 146–48, and Jonathan Ned Katz, *Gay/Lesbian Almanac: A New Documentary* (New York: HarperCollins, 1983), 71–72.

7. H. R. McIlwaine, ed., *Minutes of the Council and General Court of Colonial Virginia, 1622–1632, 1670–1676* (Richmond, Va.: The Colonial Press/Everett Waddey Co., 1924), 194–95. Quotation on 194. H. R. McIlwaine, ed., *Minutes of the Council and General Court of Colonial Virginia, 1622–1632,* 194.

8. See Elizabeth Reis, *Damned Women: Sinners and Witches in Puritan New England* (Ithaca: Cornell University Press, 1997), 112–16.

9. On Jewish law regarding hermaphrodites, see Rabbi Alfred Cohen, "Tumtum and Androgynous," *Journal of Halacha & Contemporary Society* 38 (Fall 1999), 62–85; "Tumtum" refers to those whose sex is indeterminate; "androgynous" refers red to those whose organs have both male and female characteristics. See also Sally Gross, "Intersexuality and Scripture," *Theology and Sexuality* 11 (1999), 65–74.

10. James Parsons, *A Mechanical and Critical Enquiry into the Nature of Hermaphrodites* (London, 1741), 1–2.

11. Parsons, *A Mechanical and Critical Inquiry,* xxxiv.

12. I will use male pronouns when discussing Thomas Hall's life as a man and female pronouns when Hall lived as a woman. When the sources are unclear, I will use neutral language.

13. H. R. McIlwaine, ed., *Minutes of the Council and General Court of Colonial Virginia, 1622–1632,* 195.

14. Ibid., 195.

15. Mary Beth Norton argues as well that the verdict was unprecedented, and

that Hall was probably lonely and "perhaps the target of insults or assaults." See Norton, *Founding Mothers and Fathers*, 196.

16. Alfred F. Young, *Masquerade: The Life and Times of Deborah Sampson, Continental Soldier* (New York: Alfred A. Knopf, 2004), 9.

17. *The Pennsylvania Gazette*, August 9, 1764.

18. The first account had said Lewis was thirty-two years old in 1764; the information from the 1770 story would make her seventeen years old in 1764.

19. My thanks to Al Young for sharing some of his findings on Lewis with me. One of Young's assistants, Paul Uek, tracked down Lewis's genealogical information. If Lewis was born in 1747 (as the 1770 story suggested) and died in 1823 (per the obituary), he lived almost half of his life as a woman. See Charles Edward Banks, M.D., *The History of Martha's Vineyard, Dukes County Massachusetts in Three Volumes* (Edgartown: Dukes County Historical Society, 1966), 3:235.

20. Records of the Middlesex County Court, 1691/1692, vols. 1689–1699, n.p., as cited in Lawrence W. Towner, "The Indentures of Boston's Poor Apprentices: 1734–1805," *Transactions*, Colonial Society of Massachusetts, 43 (1956–1963), 417–468.

21. Otis Hammond, ed., *New Hampshire Court Records*, 1640–1692, New Hampshire State Papers Series, 40 (1943), 96; George F. Dow, ed., *Records and Files of the Quarterly Courts of Essex County, Massachusetts* (Salem, Mass., 1911–1921), VI, 341. As cited in Mary Beth Norton, "Communal Definitions of Gendered Identity in Seventeenth-Century English America," in Ronald Hoffman, Mechal Sobel, and Fredrika J. Teute, eds., *Through a Glass Darkly: Reflections on Personal Identity in Early America* (Chapel Hill: University of North Carolina Press, 1997), 53.

22. Susan Juster, "'Neither male nor female': Jemima Wilkinson and the Politics of Gender in Post-Revolutionary America," in Robert Blair St. George, ed., *Possible Pasts: Becoming Colonial in Early America* (Ithaca: Cornell University Press, 2000), 357–379.

23. The 1656 New Haven statute was an exception; it read: "If any man lyeth with mankind, as a man lyeth with a woman, both of them have committed abomination, they both shall surely be put to death. Lev. 20:13. And if any woman change the natural use, into that which is against nature, as Rom. 1:26 she shall be liable to the same sentence, and punishment." See *New Haven's Settling in New England and Some Lawes for Government* (London: printed by M.S. for Livewell Chapman, 1656), in J. Hammond Trumbull, ed., *The True-Blue Laws of Connecticut and New Haven* (Hartford: American Publishing Company, 1876), 198–201.

24. Norton, *Founding Mothers and Fathers*, 193.

25. H. R. McIlwaine, ed., *Minutes of the Council and General Court of Colonial Virginia, 1622–1632*, 195.

26. His skepticism notwithstanding, Parsons's book is invaluable for the brief vignettes of those "mistakenly" called hermaphrodites. Because Parsons was convinced that hermaphrodites were really "normal" men or women, he urged readers to recognize and avoid past injustices: "Thus it often fared with our reputed

Hermaphrodites, who have been banished, tormented, abused, and employed in such Offices as were in themselves severe; cut off from the common Privileges and Freedoms enjoyed by the Publick wheresoever they have been; yea, and put to Death in an inhuman and pitiless Manner" (lii).

27. On the role of medical men in ascertaining the cause of marital problems such as impotency that might have been due to intersex conditions, see Michael R. McVaugh, *Medicine Before the Plague: Practioners and their Patients in the Crown of Aragon, 1285–1345* (Cambridge: Cambridge University Press, 1993), 200–207.

28. Parsons, *A Mechanical and Critical Enquiry into the Nature of Hermaphrodites*, 9. On the "rediscovery" of the clitoris in sixteenth-century Europe, see Katharine Park, "The Rediscovery of the Clitoris," in David Hillman and Carla Mazzio, eds., *The Body in Parts: Fantasies of Corporeality in Early Modern Europe* (New York: Routledge, 1997), 171–193.

29. Nicholas Culpeper, *The Compleat Practice of Physick* (London, 1655), 503. On the relationship between conception and orgasm for women, see Thomas Foster, "Deficient Husbands: Manhood, Sexual Incapacity, and Male Marital Sexuality in Seventeenth-Century New England," *William and Mary Quarterly,* 3d Series 56: 4 (October 1999), 723–44. Angus McLaren argues that though linking conception and female orgasm lingered into the eighteenth century in England, the notion was relegated to popular culture status as newer ideas of scientific embryology emerged. See McLaren, *Reproductive Rituals: The Perception of Fertility in England from the Sixteenth Century to the Nineteenth Century* (London: Methuen, 1984), 22.

30. Henry Bracken, *The Midwife's Companion; or, a Treatise of Midwifery: Wherein the Whole Art is Explained* (London, 1737), 10.

31. See Alexander Hamilton, *Outlines of the Theory and Practice of Midwifery* (Philadelphia: Thomas Dobson, 1790), 44–45; William Smellie, *An Abridgement of the Practice of Midwifery* (Boston: John Norman, 1786), 7, 24; William Cheselden, *The Anatomy of the Human Body* (Boston: Manning and Loring, 1795), 272–73. See also Benjamin Bell, *A System of Surgery* (Worcester, Mass.: Isaiah Thomas, 1791), 367; Andrew Fyfe, *A Compendious System of Anatomy. In Six Parts* (Philadelphia: Thomas Dobson, 1790), 76.

32. Thomas Denman, *An Introduction to the Practice of Midwifery* (New York: Printed by James Oram, for William Falconer and Evert Duyckinck, 1802), 34.

33. Parsons, *A Mechanical and Critical Enquiry into the Nature of Hermaphrodites*, 10.

34. As quoted in Park, "The Rediscovery of the Clitoris," 178.

35. Sharp, *The Midwives Book,* 40. Like Culpeper, Sharp highlighted the clitoris's significance: "[T]he Clitoris will stand and fall as the yard doth, and makes women lustfull and take delight in Copulation, and were it not for this they would have no desire nor delight, nor would they ever conceive" (39).

36. Sharp, *The Midwives Book,* 40.

37. Giles Jacob, *A Treatise of Hermaphrodites* (London: E. Curll, 1718), 41–2.

38. Nicholas Venette, *Conjugal Love; or the Pleasures of the Marital Bed Considered in Several Lectures on Human Generation* (London, 1750). According to Thomas Laqueur, the 1750 edition was the twentieth edition, and there were at least eight French editions before Venette's death in 1698. See Laqueur, *Making Sex: Body and Gender from the Greeks to Freud* (Cambridge: Harvard University Press, 1990), 245, n.5.

39. Jacob, *A Treatise of Hermaphrodites*, 6–8. Stories of women suddenly becoming men had been circulating since at least the sixteenth century. Michel de Montaigne recounted, "Passing through Vitry-le-Francois, I might have seen a man whom the bishop of Soissons had named Germain at confirmation, but whom all the inhabitants of that place had seen and known as a girl named Marie until the age of twenty-two. He was now heavily bearded, and old, and not married. Straining himself in some ways in jumping, he says, his masculine organs came forth; and among the girls there a song is still current by which they warn each other not to take big strides for fear of becoming boys, like Marie Germain." See Michel de Montaigne, *The Complete Essays of Montaigne,* trans. Donald M. Frame (Stanford: Stanford University Press, 1958), 69.

40. Jacob, *A Treatise of Hermaphrodites*, 16.

41. The term 'lesbian' was not used until the late nineteenth century, and so I use it here as merely a shorthand indicating sexual relations between women.

42. Jacob, *A Treatise of Hermaphrodites*, 19.

43. Dr. William Handy, "Account of an Hermaphrodite," *The Medical Repository of Original Essays and Intelligence* 12(May-July 1808), 86–87. Later medical observers disagreed with Handy's assessment of this case. Handy thought this person had a penis, but considered her predominantly female; others believed the supposed penis to be "of a cliteroid nature," and agreed that she was primarily female. See also, Beck, *Elements of Medical Jurisprudence*, 122.

44. Sander L. Gilman, *Difference and Pathology: Stereotypes of Sexuality, Race, and Madness* (Ithaca: Cornell University Press, 1985), esp. 76–108.

45. Sharp, *The Midwives Book,* 40.

46. Parsons, *A Mechanical and Critical Enquiry into the Nature of Hermaphrodites,* liv.

47. Ibid., 10–11.

48. Carol Groneman, *Nymphomania: A History* (New York: W.W. Norton, 2000). See, for example, Pierre Lefort, M.D, "A Case of Excision of the Clitoris and Lubia Pudendorum," *The Medical Repository of Original Essays and Intelligence* 19 (1818), 84–87; Anon., "Extirpation of the Clitoris," *The American Medical Review* 2:1 (Sept. 1825), 188.

# Chapter 7

# Mapping an Atlantic Sexual Culture
## Homoeroticism in Eighteenth-Century Philadelphia

## Clare A. Lyons

At the end of the eighteenth century, Ann Alweye, a male transvestite, lived with John Crawford in a relationship presumed to be sexual. Half a century earlier, Mary Hamilton had fled England for the New World after her conviction for "pretending herself a Man" and living as husband to Mary Price. Both Alweye and Hamilton were members of the greater Philadelphia community during the second half of the eighteenth century, and both lived out their lives unmolested by the larger society around them. They are unusual because their lives enter into the record of eighteenth-century sexual practice. They are part of a small group of individuals who embraced homoerotic desire and who are documented in an otherwise profoundly silent historical record. Is it possible to recover the meanings of homoeroticism (ideas about homoerotic sexual practice and desire as well as physical behavior) for eighteenth-century urban British North Americans despite this documentary silence?[1]

One way to read these silences and interpret the fragmentary evidence of homoerotic sexual practice for the eighteenth century is to examine the dynamics of cultural exchange in the larger Atlantic world and explore the sexual cultures that many urban Americans had contact with. A comparative cultural analysis will help develop a history of homoeroticism that conceptualizes the port cities as part of an Atlantic cultural web, that follows the movement of bodies and texts through these cultural waterways, that draws on our knowledge of the pivotal transformations in English and western European conceptualizations of homoeroticism in the eighteenth century, and that analyzes the links in popular culture between colonial ports and European metropolitan centers during a century that saw both Europeans and colonial British North Americans become intrigued by literary representations of homoerotic desire.

To develop this line of analysis fully one would need to trace the entire eighteenth-century Atlantic seafaring web. Here I concentrate on one particularly dense strand to explore the links between Philadelphia, the largest English colonial city after midcentury, and England and western Europe. Philadelphia's maritime economy, communication network with England, and highly developed print culture make it an ideal place to explore the dynamics of cultural exchange of ideas about sexuality. It can serve as a test case for this conceptual and methodological framework. Philadelphia shared conditions with other colonial port cities and also had particular characteristics that influenced the reception of ideas from Europe about same-sex intimacy. Thus, studying Philadelphia in an Atlantic context will also add to our understanding of regional sexual cultures that developed in British North America.

Historians of early America interested in understanding the beliefs and practices associated with homoerotics have faced a difficult task because of scant documentation. There are few court cases to generate testimony, and no evidentiary trail of children conceived in same-sex sexual relations to expose sexual behavior. To date we know the most about Puritan New England. Richard Godbeer in chapter 4 has demonstrated that the official legal and religious condemnation of sodomy as an abhorrent act may not accurately reflect what ordinary colonists in New England thought about sodomy and those who practiced it. By examining the lives of Nicolas Sension and Stephen Gorton, Godbeer demonstrates that colonists sometimes recognized and tolerated the ongoing or habitual homoerotic predilection of well-placed men in their communities. Godbeer suggests that in Sension and Gorton one can see the beginnings of a recognized sexual subjectivity. In New England, official condemnation existed side-by-side with a toleration of men who practiced sodomy, unless their behavior disrupted the social hierarchy or threatened the community's reputation.[2]

Discourses of sexuality and the development of sexual subjectivities were certainly conditioned by the particular cultural influences of each locale. Puritans condemned sodomy and influenced the decisions to invoke the laws against it when communities brought criminal charges against individuals. Trials for sodomy were not frequent in colonial New England, and the mid-Atlantic region, Philadelphia in particular, produced even fewer trials for alleged same-sex intimacy.[3] There were no prosecutions of sodomy in the Philadelphia courts from 1750 to 1800 (and no evidence of criminal sodomy in the surviving court records for the first half of the century) and only one instance of lesbian-like cohabitation documented in the court records. Religious leaders in Philadelphia did not, as did those in New England, invoke the specter of Sodom and Gomorrah for moral instruction.

Some Philadelphia seafarers and immigrants could have experienced the sexual underworlds of the Atlantic port cities firsthand, and many Philadelphians shared a fascination with fictional creations of the homoerotic with their eighteenth-century English and European counterparts. Thus, we must read the legal lack of interest in prosecuting homoerotic practice against the evidence of cultural interest in the inventions of new homoerotic categories in England and western Europe. What we will find is that new constructions of sexuality traveled across the Atlantic with colonists and seamen and in cargoes of books, pamphlets, and newspapers. When these ideas landed in Philadelphia, they were understood in distinct ways.

Philadelphia in the second half of the eighteenth century was the most cosmopolitan city in British North America and simultaneously a colonial outpost of the expanding British empire. It was an important commercial, intellectual, and cultural center.[4] Philadelphia was an extraordinarily culturally diverse city where the English majority lived side-by-side with Scots, Welsh, German, Scots-Irish, African, Afro-Caribbean, and a smattering of French, Spanish, and Portuguese. The city's people maintained their links to many strands of European culture through ongoing immigration and an expanding maritime economy.[5] Hundreds of European ships sailed into its docks each year, making it the largest shipping center of the region. These ships brought more than commerce. They brought seamen familiar with the contemporary sexual issues and sexual cultures of their home ports. The seasonal influx of mariners brought men from London, Paris, Lisbon, Amsterdam, and the Caribbean who would stay in the city for a fortnight or longer. The transatlantic maritime economy that brought thousands of European seamen to Philadelphia each year also took the city's men to the commercial centers of Europe and the Caribbean. As many as 20 percent of the city's free adult males and many of its African-American slaves were part of a transatlantic community of seafarers who called Philadelphia their home port.[6] Many of these Philadelphian mariners would have dropped anchor in London, Lisbon, Kingston, and the islands of the French West Indies.[7]

Beliefs about homoeroticism had been fundamentally transformed in the European societies Philadelphia's mariners and immigrants would have encountered. The understandings of same-sex sexual practices shifted dramatically from the seventeenth century to the early decades of the eighteenth. In London, Paris, The Hague, and Amsterdam, new cultural and legal meanings of sodomy emerged. In many regions the onset of legal prosecutions of sodomy, targeting urban men of the moderate classes in the early eighteenth century, articulated a new form of deviancy, suggesting new cultural meanings of same-sex intimacy and revealing sodomitical sexual subcultures in many of Europe's cities.[8]

The cultural understandings of same-sex intimacy in English society probably had the greatest impact on eighteenth-century Philadelphians and are worth examining in some detail. Painted in its broadest strokes, the sexual landscape of seventeenth-century England had tolerated sexual intimacy between men, despite its legal status as a capital offense. James I's interest in male sexual partners at the beginning of the century and a well-established cadre of aristocratic men who practiced male sodomy during the Restoration suggest that the dearth of prosecutions for sodomy was in part due to court and aristocratic interest in this sexual practice. These men were understood as aristocratic libertine rakes. They indulged their passions in a wide range of sexual practices, taking women as well as men to their beds. They were understood as ultramasculine men. In their sexual practices they demonstrated the patriarchal and aristocratic power to command the sexual service of women and lesser men. As such, their erotic exchange with younger men of lower economic standing did not compromise their masculinity but instead bolstered it. This aristocratic rake came under fire by the early decades of the eighteenth century. Simultaneously, cultural and legal attention began to focus on a new homoerotic type, the pejorative effeminate sodomite, who was expected to desire only men. These men were represented as the antithesis of masculinity in popular print and became the target of social-sexual reform, resulting in waves of criminal prosecutions for sodomy in the first half of the eighteenth century.[9] The sodomite, or "molly," as he was known in contemporary parlance, had breached the boundaries of eighteenth-century masculinity and been expelled from the ranks of manhood.[10]

Police activity to arrest men who practiced sodomy provides historians with evidence of the sexual underworlds inhabited by the sodomite.[11] In London, Paris, and Amsterdam, sodomites were the targets of periodic waves of arrest. In London, these began in 1708–1709, returned in 1726–1727, and continued sporadically through midcentury. In Paris, the mid-1720s and mid-1730s were especially dangerous, but arrests by under-cover vice agents in the public gardens were an ever-present threat. In Amsterdam, 1730 marked the beginning of a series of arrest cycles when the confession of an unlucky man caught in the act snowballed into mass indictments. Those convicted of sodomy were executed. The more typical outcome, however, was a prison term for the lesser crime of attempted sodomy or seduction. In the Dutch Republic, hundreds fled and were convicted in absentia and suffered exile, and in Paris some of those convicted were deported to the French West Indies, to Martinique, Guadeloupe, Sainte-Domingue, or Mississippi, where Philadelphia seamen may have encountered them. For the men of England and the Dutch Republic, this was a radical shift from the legal laissez faire treatment of sodomy during the seventeenth century.[12]

This police activity reveals communities of men who shared an underworld subculture in many early eighteenth-century European cities. They had established meeting places in specific taverns and "molly houses" that catered to cross-dressing men and their male partners and identifiable cruising areas in public gardens, streets, and boulevards, along canals and under bridges, and in particular public toilets and pissoirs. In each city men had created a coded language of speech and gesture to facilitate recognition and safeguard themselves from detection by the unknowing and potentially hostile populace.

Evidence from London, Paris, and Amsterdam suggests that many of these men also lived public lives in marriages to women and that their relationships generally were not confined to the seventeenth-century pattern of older, elite men with younger, lower-status men. Men of all class backgrounds, paired in any number of combinations, participated in the sodomitical sexual underworld. In London, sodomites developed a sophisticated subculture centered in the city's molly houses. Patrons often assumed female names and garb and performed parodies of heterosexual marriage ceremonies and childbirth. Some men also engaged in transvestite prostitution on the London streets in the company of female prostitutes.[13]

Recent works on English conceptualizations of homoerotic intimacy suggest that attempts to fit the sodomite into the modern category of the homosexual are misguided. The English had several categories for understanding same-sex intimacy, none of them equivalent in meaning to later constructions of homosexuality. During the eighteenth century, sexual aspects of the self were just beginning to be considered important or legitimate components of an individual's subjectivity, and a person's sexual nature (as distinct from gender) would not be elevated to core status of identity until the following century. A man's sexual interest in other men was certainly part of the eighteenth-century understanding of the sodomite, but this was not equivalent to the pathologized innate sexual inclination of the nineteenth-century homosexual. An oppositional heterosexual-homosexual construction of same-sex intimacy cannot accommodate the complex configurations of gender, sexual desire, and power relations that constituted the various ways the eighteenth-century English made sense of same-sex male desire.[14]

The sodomite was the most publicized of four recognized forms that same-sex intimacy could take. The libertine rake and the effeminate fop each embodied the potential for same-sex sexual relations but from opposite positions of gender performance. The rake's virile masculinity led him to initiate sexual relations that demonstrated his dominance over women and lesser men. The fop was sexually suspect because his excessive effeminacy marked him as vulnerable to taking on female attributes, including a subordinate role in sexual relations, that might lead him to succumb to sodomitical activities.[15] Heroic friendship was the most legitimate form of male same-sex intimacy recognized in eighteenth-century English culture. Deep emotional relationships between men of the emerging middle classes became a marker of one's class standing and character. The class standing of men whose friendships included sexual intimacy shielded them from public scrutiny and cast their relationships in a positive light. The sodomite, who was typically a member of the urban artisan or working classes, enjoyed no such class privilege. The sexual behavior of both the sodomite and the erotic heroic friend produced a new form of deviancy because it discarded hierarchal power relations as the basis for homoerotic sex and replaced it with consensual same-sex intimacy between men of similar status. To this sexual (and class) deviancy the sodomite added the transgression of gender deviancy in his effeminacy. The sodomite was thus a sexual deviant and a gender deviant and, as a man of the laboring classes, bore the brunt of public criticism and recrimination for his triple threat.[16]

In general, prosecution of homoerotic relationships and the prominence of one deviant homoerotic social type—the sodomite—were confined to men. In England, women who loved women were variously understood as hermaphrodites whose anatomy and unusually large clitoris led them to act the part of men with female lovers or, in other instances, as women whose deviant personal inclination directed their sexual love of women. Both notions remained current throughout the eighteenth century, although the interpretation of women loving women as a deviant choice did gain ground on the biological mandate by the middle decades of the century. While a fascination with fictional accounts of female homoeroticism is evident in literary texts, it was not until the last decades of the century that commentators began to remark on it in their private writings and courts began to prosecute sexual love between women.[17]

In England and the cities of western Europe, the construction of the sodomite had been transformed in both fact and fiction. Information about these sexual worlds and the social types of the libertine rake, effeminate fop, and the sodomite was disseminated through popular print during the late seventeenth and eighteenth centuries. Popular works of fiction presented an imagined homoerotic world that often denigrated people practicing same-sex intimacy and also presented the opportunity for a voyeuristic erotic gaze by the reader. The underworld of the sodomite was publicized through sensational true-crime literature that chronicled the activities in it and in newspaper accounts of sodomy trials. From midcentury to the century's end, Philadelphians imported and sold the whole range of homoerotic texts available in Europe.[18] In July 1754, for instance, Tench Francis advertised and sold books from each of the following genres in his Front Street store: classical Greek and Roman texts with homoerotic content, Restoration satire employing homoerotic sex and politics, French erotica depicting pairs of women making love and the *chroniques scandeleuses* of the French aristocracy, English novels with homoerotic and prostitute adventure narratives, and trial reports of criminal prosecutions for sodomy.

The books available for sale in Philadelphia varied with each shipment from London, but Francis's July shipment is representative of imports after midcentury. It included Ovid's *Art of Love,* with its homoerotic scenes; John Oldham's satirical condemnation of the sodomite in *Upon the Author of the Play Call'd Sodom;* English translations of French novels depicting love-making between women, such as L'Estrange's translation of *Lettres Portugaises traduites en francois (Portuguese Love Letters); The Secret Memoirs of the Duke and Dutchess of Orleans,* recounting the sodomitical practices of Louis XIV's brother the duc de Orleans; and the quintessential eighteenth-century English homoerotic novel *Roderick Random* by Tobias Smollett.[19]

*Roderick Random,* with its homoerotic characters Lord Strutwell and Captain Whiffle, was one of the most popular English novels in mid- to late eighteenth-century Philadelphia. Advertisements for it appeared nineteen times in the city's newspaper, the *Pennsylvania Gazette,* between 1748 and 1778; ten different booksellers included it in their lists of books "just arrived from London and for sale." It was also advertised in the book catalogues issued by the city's booksellers, owned by the city's new lending libraries, and reprinted in a Philadelphia edition in 1794.[20] Strutwell and Whiffle have been interpreted as representing the effeminate evil associated with the sodomite, as the site of male-male desire, and as the embodiment of a new affectional system of love between men.[21] It is difficult at this late remove to know how *Roderick Random* was read by midcentury Philadelphians. What we can know is that Lord Strutwell's attempted seduction of Roderick Random, initiated by Strutwell's discussion of sodomy among the ancients and his assertion of "the exquisite pleasure" of "this inclination," and the detailed description of the archetypal effeminate sodomitical fop Captain Whiffle, clothed in pink and red satin with his coat "cut . . . backward," bejeweled, powdered, and perfumed, equipped with "an amber-headed cane" that "hung dangling" from his wrist, were available to them for their own imaginings.[22]

It seems that a wide range of literate Philadelphians undertook this literary imaginary journey. *Roderick Random*'s purchase price put it within reach of Philadelphia's merchants and master craftsmen who could afford to spend the 9–12 shillings for the two-volume set to accompany Roderick on his travels.[23] But the desire for novel reading in Philadelphia stretched beyond those who could afford to purchase the latest novels from London. These men and women borrowed novels like *Roderick Random* from Thomas Bradford's circulating library, opened in 1769, and from the city's three subscription libraries.[24]

The availability of circulating libraries in the city, a dramatic increase in the importation of books after midcentury, and a rising reading literacy rate made access to popular print material possible for a broad spectrum of Philadelphians.[25] City dwellers from many walks of life sought out books and desired to participate in the growing print world around them. Innkeepers, sea captains, shoemakers, tanners, bricklayers, and laborers of limited resources like John Dorsey, whose tax burden was abated owing to his poverty, each borrowed and read the latest books.[26] Women, too, availed themselves of Bradford's lending library, composing more than 40 percent of his patrons.[27] Midcentury Philadelphia readers were a diverse lot, but they all shared a thirst for novels, intrigues, tall tales, travel adventures, and sensational occurrences.[28]

*Roderick Random* was one of their favorites. It was among the novels most frequently checked out of Bradford's library. Those who borrowed the book were representative of the library's readers. They ranged from James Wood, a wealthy boatbuilder who owned his own home, and Miss Oliphant, presumably the daughter of the well-to-do schoolmaster William Oliphant, to John Whinney, a grocer of middling class status, and down to Frederick Stuben, Thomas Hughs, Christin Willit, and Soloman Holden, all men without the resources to pay taxes in 1772, the year they paid their 6 pence to read *Roderick Random.*[29] In Philadelphia, *Roderick Random*, like most eighteenth-century imprints, was available to literate readers from all but the poorest classes.

The century's most explicit male homoerotic encounter appeared in John Cleland's *Memoirs of a Woman of Pleasure*, first published in 1748–1749. Philadelphia's booksellers were more cautious in their advertisement of *Memoirs*, but short oblique references to it appear in newspapers and catalogues of books for sale during the 1760s.[30] Again, we cannot know how Philadelphia readers reacted when they encountered Fanny Hill curiously spying on two men making love through the partition in their shared room or how they felt when Fanny narrates this graphic description of consensual erotic sodomy. This book, however, was overtly intended for erotic fantasy of the reader and encouraged its readers' erotic participation in the behaviors Fanny witnesses.

The best source of information about the sodomitical subculture of eighteenth-century London is *Select Trials at . . . the Old Bailey.* Published as court proceedings, the salacious details of seduction, sexual assault, and sodomitical intrigue assumed a more legitimate air than the erotic novels of the era. The volumes included appropriate condemnatory introductions, yet the accounts of sodomy prosecutions were clearly intended to satisfy a voyeuristic gaze into sexual experience. Philadelphia's readers eagerly took a look. The city's booksellers imported and advertised *Select Trials* during the 1740s, 1750s, 1760s, and 1780s. It appeared in booksellers' catalogues and was owned by the lending libraries. People did not avoid acknowledging ownership of the book, advertising for its return from tardy borrowers.[31]

From *Select Trials* Philadelphians learned a great deal about the social type of the sodomite and the sodomitical subculture of eighteenth-century London.[32] They learned that some men sought out relationships with younger men, resembling the seventeenth-century age-asymmetrical norm, and that men also paired off with equal age partners; they learned that the social geography of sodomitical intimacy included public walks, houses of worship, molly and bawdy houses, and public latrines and necessary houses. Most important, they learned of the clandestine ways men made connections with one another and how the larger society depicted and responded to them.

*Select Trials* depicted how men like John Dicks approached other men and moved from casual conversation to homoerotic intimacy. John Meeson, who provided the evidence against Dicks in his 1722 trial, recalled for the court that he was standing in St. Martin's Church yard:

> The Prisoner came up to me, and, clapping me on the Shoulder, said, *Honest Dyer! how fares it?* and then fell he a talking with me about the Coffins that were dug up, and lay in the Church yard, and afterwards asked me to go to the Alehouse to take a Pot.

Meeson reputedly first refused, but on Dicks's repeated entreaties agreed to accompany him drinking. Meeson continued:

> When he had made me almost fuddled [drunk], he buss'd me, put his Hand into my Breeches, and took my Hand and put it into his Breeches. From the Alehouse he took me to a Cellar in the *Strand*, where we had one Pint of Beer, and, I having some Goods to carry into *White-hart-yawl*, in *Fleet-street*, I told him I must go thither, and if he'd stay for me, I would come to him again.

Meeson did not rebuff Dicks's initial genital groping and agreed to reunite with him after his errands. When Meeson returned to the cellar, he "found him waiting. But, that Place not being private enough, we went to another Alehouse in *Chancery-lane* where he treated me with hot Ale and Gin; and from thence he carried me to the *Golden-ball*, in *Bond's stables*, near *Fetter-lane*, where we drank more Ale and Geneva, 'till I was so drunk and sick that I vomited, and lay down to sleep." When Meeson awoke, his "Breeches were down," and Dicks had had his way with him. Meeson was unable to provide the court with evidence of sodomy, but a couple sharing their tavern room, separated by a partition, testified to the intimate details. They had heard Dicks's love-talk calling Meeson "*Dear,*" "his *Jewel,*" and "his *precious little Rogue*" and "saw the Prisoner in the very Act of Sodomy, making several Motions with his Body, and then I saw him withdraw his Yard from the Boy's Fundament." The observer's female partner then "cry'd out, *I can look no longer,—I am ready to swoon—He'll ruin the Boy!*" and they rushed in to prevent a second act.[33] The narrative presents the excitement this scene elicited for the male-female couple who were watching and scripted for readers an erotic response.

Each of the cases in *Select Trials* gave important details of the sodomitical sexual terrain. Philadelphians heard from Thomas Newton, an informant during the 1726 crackdown, who explained how men identified each other by publicly exposing their genitals in the act of public urination, knowledge he used to entrap William Brown for the police.[34] They read of the legal persecution in 1726 of sodomitical men and the descriptions of the molly subculture presented in court by the undercover agents who infiltrated the city's molly houses. They learned details about "Mother" Margaret Clap's molly house that sheltered "40 to 50 Men making Love to one another, as they call'd it." Dancing and kissing, the men would make "Curtsies, and mimick the Voices of Women," then go out as couples to another room "to be married," as they called it, and of Thomas Wright's flat where he "kept Rooms for the entertainment of the Molly-Culls," where one could find "a Company of Men fiddling, and dancing, and singing bawdy Songs, kissing, and using their Hands in a very unseemly Manner."[35]

Philadelphians who read *Select Trials* or the fashionable imported British newspapers and magazines encountered prosecutions for attempted sodomitical seduction. They read of trumped-up sodomy charges used as blackmail, of botched pickups, where young men responded to propositions by entrapping the sodomite, and of seductions where seemingly reputable men, needing a night's lodging, turned on their host to attempt a sodomitical liaison.[36] In each of these cases the slander or innocent solicitation took a criminal turn. Men reacted by invoking the law. The social reconstruction of the sodomite as the antithesis of manhood led to a fear of being labeled a sodomite. This in turn gave rise to an increase in prosecutions for attempted sodomy as men worked to maintain their claim to full manhood status by actively policing their sexual reputations.

Some of the Philadelphians who spent time in England during the middle decades of the century would have noticed these social and cultural changes. Mariners who lived much of their lives in the homosocial shipboard environments may have been particularly good observers of homoerotic behavior and keen listeners to tales of sodomy.[37] Sailors spent much of their time on shore in the neighborhoods, streets, taverns, and boardinghouses that catered to both prostitutes and mollys. Philadelphia sailors who disembarked in London during the summer of 1764 probably heard the gossip circulating about John Gill, known as "Mrs. Beasly," who was arrested wearing female clothes while having sex with a man in a coach. Fall arrivals may have heard of the police raids on prostitutes that revealed two cross-dressing men among the "women" hawking their wares.[38] Immigrants from England and Philadelphians who visited England in these years may well have encountered the cheap pamphlets published following the sodomy trials of men such as Charles Bradbury, Richard Branson, and William Sheppard during the 1750s and 1760s.[39]

Philadelphians also learned of English homoerotic "crime" and intrigue through their local newspapers. Philadelphia's weekly newspapers were well established by the late 1720s and 1730s, reaching a wide audience by subscription, daily sales, and recycled reading in taverns, coffeehouses, and homes.[40] Philadelphia's newspaper readers periodically encountered news stories of sodomites and cross-dressing women copied from the London papers. They first learned of the 1726 crackdown on London molly houses by reading about it in the *American Weekly Mercury*. Margaret Clap's conviction for "Keeping a Disorderly House in Chick-Lane, for the Entertainment of Sodomites" qualified as intriguing news of metropolitan events for provincial readers.[41] So did a humorous tale printed in the spring of 1739, in which the *American Weekly Mercury* entertained its readers with a salacious news story, reprinted from the *Gentlemen's Magazine*, about English sodomites engaged in secret intrigues and amours.

Two Fellows being taken up at Bristol on Suspicion of committing a Robery on the Highway, on Examination they were found to be Sodomites lately come from London; among their Papers was a list with their proper Names and effeminate Titles, and a Letter to an old Offender, dated that Day, and directed

To Tho. E———rds, *Esq*; at Frampton.

Dear Friend and Loving Sister,

   We thank you for all past Favours, especially for the last at your House. We got home safe that Night, and are now bound to *London*. We would willingly see you before we go, and caress one the other, We are two of us, you shall have your Choice; two clean, wholesome, smooth-faced Fellows, well dress'd, of either of whom you shall have your Will. Pray appoint the Day, because we will be at home. Our Lodgings are at ——— in St. *James's Church-yard.* We beg you to bring some Money with you (as being Church-warden it will be nothing out of your Way) to bear our Charges to *London.* You need not be afraid to send an answer by the Bearer, because he can neither read nor write. So I remain,

> *Your once adopted and Loving Spouse,*
> Thomas Rogers, *alias* Mary Fly.[42]

This story was full of references to the sodomite subculture of England. The two "sodomites" who made themselves available to an aristocratic gentleman had assumed women's names and used the affectionate terms of "loving sister" and "loving spouse." They were described in attractive, if slightly effeminate, terms as "clean, wholesome, smooth-faced Fellows." They arranged clandestine meetings using coded messages. Full appreciation of this story required some knowledge of the new social type of the sodomite in English culture. The story also explained to the uninitiated the secret workings of this amorous underworld. Well-read Philadelphians encountered similar descriptions of homoerotic sexuality in imported copies of British newspapers and magazines available in Philadelphia throughout the century. Joseph Addison's readily available *Spectator,* for example, periodically railed against London masquerades for providing anonymous cover for same-sex assignations, while simultaneously publicizing these sexual practices.[43]

Philadelphians at both ends of the social spectrum, therefore, had exposure to the transformations in masculinity and sexuality underway in England. Many had witnessed the transformations of the English views of sodomites through a shared print culture. They almost certainly heard stories of arrests and caricatures of the sodomite by word of mouth from those mariners, immigrants, and elite travelers who had close contact with London. Thus, they had knowledge of the English and European relationship to the sodomite and could have adopted a similar response to homoerotic behavior in their own city. But they did not. They made no raids on taverns that allowed male intimacy, nor did they turn in men who made unwelcome advances. There is little evidence that they policed sodomy at all. The only mention of sodomy in all the city's courts from 1700 to 1800 concerned one Philip Bower, whose case was dismissed as "ignoramus" when the grand jury failed to indict him in 1784. Court records are incomplete for the first half of the century, but the absence of reports in the city's newspapers of criminal prosecutions for sodomy suggests that there were no sodomy trials during the eighteenth century.[44]

Pennsylvania authorities clearly condemned sodomy, just as they did incest, bigamy, and bestiality. But Pennsylvania statutes never incorporated inflammatory language characterizing sodomy as a particularly unnatural or abominable sin as New England colonial authorities did.[45] Rejecting the English statutory requirement of the death penalty, which Quakers reserved for murder, Pennsylvania statutes of 1700 and 1705 made sodomy punishable by imprisonment for life at hard labor initiated with public whipping. Sodomy became a capital offense in 1718 when the crown required Pennsylvania to follow English law. After the Revolution, Pennsylvania quickly revised its legal code and abolished capital punishment for sodomy in 1786, making the act a misdemeanor with a maximum sentence of ten years.[46] By the end of the century, the manual published for constables and justices of the peace included cautions to treat accusations of sodomy with care. "Sodomy," constables were told, was "so easily charged, and the negative so difficult to be proved, that the accusation should be clearly made out: for, if false, it deserves a punishment inferior only to that of the crime itself."[47]

Eighteenth-century legal prosecutions were a direct reflection of public sentiment. Prosecution for all sex crimes relied on private individuals to initiate and sustain prosecutions. Unlike the modern system of state-sponsored policing, investigation, and trial, Philadelphians had to take the initiative to bring people to court and sustain the prosecution by producing willing witnesses to prove their case. The lack of criminal prosecution for sodomy was owing in part to an overall lack of policing of nonmarital sexual behavior. Fornication, for instance, was never prosecuted during the 1790s, but we have ample evidence of it in the illegitimate children who resulted. Charges of adultery and bigamy did come before the courts, but these crimes, which would have resembled cases of consensual sodomy, only entered into the criminal courts because they were initiated and sustained by the wronged spouse.[48] Active involvement of a wronged party and a willingness to expose a husband, friend, or neighbor as a sodomite was necessary for prosecution. Neither materialized in eighteenth-century Philadelphia. Whatever same-sex intimacy may have gone on in the back rooms of taverns or in the shared beds of cramped homes was free of aggressive policing, just as heterosexual nonmarital sex generally was.

Philadelphians were not charging each other with attempted sodomy, nor were they, apparently, blackmailing each other with exposure as sodomites. As we have seen, those who read trial reports, such as *Select Trials,* or the short true-crime pamphlet literature were familiar enough with these scenarios. Philadelphians had been informed in their newspapers of their own small role in the most notorious English sodomy blackmail case of the eighteenth century. Walter Patterson, one of the conspirators who plotted to blackmail Lord Edward Walpole, reportedly left Philadelphia in spring 1753. Patterson had escaped Bridewell jail and eventually made his way to Philadelphia, "where he resided unknown and unsuspected for some Months." Apparently, Patterson believed he would receive safe haven in the city or that he could at least blend into the port town. The *Pennsylvania Gazette* warned readers about the "smooth" and "insinuating" Patterson, who had been convicted "in a horrid Conspiracy to charge the Lord Walpole with a detestable Crime (not to be named among Christians) in order to extort Money."[49] There is no evidence of blackmail for sodomy in eighteenth-century Philadelphia. When in 1818 a youth and his parents attempted such a scheme, backed up with charges of attempted sodomy, the court confined its inquiry strictly to the specific alleged assault, choosing not to explore evidence of the accused man's potential sodomitical character and allowed the trial to proceed only so he could clear his name.[50] In this, their first sodomy blackmail trial, the Philadelphia courts demonstrated their desire to discourage this sort of case in their jurisdiction. The contours of the case suggest that the archetypal sodomy seduction scenario was well known, as it was replicated here for the court.

It appears Philadelphians did little to document the nature of homoerotic experience. It is significant, however, that the evidence we do have of individuals who took on gender performances and sexual behaviors that deviated from heteroeroticism comes to us almost accidentally. We learn of these individuals, not because they were the focus of a sensational trial, but rather by casual comment in documents about other issues. We know of Ann Alweye, the transvestite who lived with John Crawford, only because of Crawford's testimony when he was charged with adultery. Crawford's defense rested on his claim that one of the women with whom he was suspected of adultery was a man. He testified before the Court of Quarter Sessions "that he [Crawford] could have come prepared to prove that Ann Alweye (or the person so called) was not a *Woman.* He prayed the Court therefore to direct the Jury to acquit him."[51] Were Crawford and Alweye long-term lovers? Adultery could mean a casual affair, but it was more typically used in the early national period to describe an extended substitution of the primary spouse.[52] Was Alweye a molly in the style of contemporary London or a sodomite fleeing persecution in Europe? The evidence gives us no answers. But it does tell us that Alweye lived his life unmolested by Philadelphia society at the end of the eighteenth century.

A few notations in the Prisoners for Trial Docket suggest the presence of men in search of other men.[53] The docket, which recorded initial arrests, contains a few cases describing men who had caused a nuisance by publicly exposing their genitals. Public urination was a common eighteenth-century practice and not enough to cause notice. These men had done something more, or were thought to have done so by those who took offense.[54] John Place, for example, was charged in 1806 with "public indecency in exposing himself naked on the highway." Was Place engaging in the coded public ritual to make contact with a potential partner, as men in London, Amsterdam, and Paris did? Could this have been what was going on when Thomas Mullen "pulled down his pantaloons" in "the State House yard"?[55] Again, we will never know. Such snippets of information catch actions that seem to replicate sodomitical behavior of contemporary Europe. Yet these men were treated no differently from those picked up drunk in the streets or who were too loud and disruptive for their neighbors' ears, suggesting that, unlike their European counterparts, Philadelphians chose not to associate such behaviors with gender and sexual deviancy. Nor were mid- to late eighteenth-century Philadelphians particularly troubled or impressed by their cross-dressing neighbors. When Daniel Sweeny was arrested for "being a Nuisance," the docket records that his nuisance was created, at least in part, by "dressing in woman's clothes." Sweeny, however much nuisance his cross-dressing created, was released four days later with no further legal action.[56]

Maybe the effeminate or transvestite sodomites were simply not there. Perhaps the emergence of identifiable sodomitical subcultures in England and western Europe remained confined to the eastern shores of the Atlantic Ocean. Given the nature of the transatlantic commerce and culture, this seems unlikely. But here, at last, Philadelphians give us some guidance. It appears they saw the effeminate fop and the sodomite as staple characters of the post-revolutionary city. In 1784, an eighty-page pamphlet was published in the city, entitled *The Philadelphiad; or, New Pictures of the City, interspersed with a candid review and display of some first-rate Modern* CHARACTERS *of both sexes.* This is one of the few surviving locally produced descriptions of the social terrain of the city written by one of its residents. It was a humorous look at many of the key people and institutions of the city. Personages such as Benjamin Rush and Dr. William

Shippen and key institutions like the Courthouse, the New Jail, Bell's Bookstore, a Bagnio (a house of prostitution), the London Coffee House, and the Lunatic Asylum were lampooned in its pages. The *Philadelphiad* also presented key social types and characters of the city. It offered humorous descriptions of Quakers, an Irish Beauty, the Country Clown, the Emigrant, a Whore, and "The Fop," immediately followed by an anecdotal tale, "Misfortunes of a Fop."[57]

In these two pieces, the Fop is described as a standard personage of the city, as important to a description of the social terrain as the Irish Emigrant, the Quaker, and the Whore. The opening lines of "The Fop" place him on the city's streets:

> At ev'ry corner and in ev'ry street / Some gaudy useless animal we meet, / Resembling men in nothing but their shape, / Their truest lineage is the friskful ape: / . . . / Observe the thing its gaudy pinions spread, / Pride in its eye with sense inverted head.

This is a description of the sexually suspect effeminate fop. The references to "animal" and "friskful ape" were meant to associate the fop with the "bestial" nature of the sodomite, and the claim that he "resembles men in nothing but their shape" and the use of the term "inverted head" suggests his utterly unmanly status.[58]

Those familiar with the English comic and salacious literature of the day would have understood the references to the fop with sodomitical potential. His physical description, from his scarlet coat and kidskin gloves to his Paris cane, is reminiscent of Captain Whiffle from *Roderick Random*:

> His dogskin shoes (for calf would hurt his toes) / His knees adorn'd with party colour'd bows, / His monst'rous buckles, just the Paris mode. / Their use unknown, except his feet to load, / Or when he walks with nicely picking tread, / Perhaps the[y] serve for ballast to his head; / His scarlet coat, that ev'ry one may see, / Mark and observe and know the fool is he, / With buttons garnish'd, sparkling in a row / On sleeves and breasts and skirts to make a show, / His waistcoat too with tinsel shining o'er / . . . / Now to complete the figure nice and vain, / Send quick to Paris and procure a cane, / With head of ivory and gold inlaid, / A pinchbeck ferril by some artist made, / A spangled tassel to put round his wrist, / Green kidskin gloves to guard his lilly fist.[59]

For those who failed to recognize the sodomitical potential of "the Fop," the *Philadelphiad* next presents the sodomite in unequivocal terms in "The Misfortunes of a Fop." Staged as a dialogue between "Tom Tug," a Philadelphia sailor, and "Jack Tinsel," just off the ship from England, the piece begins with a description that suggests that Tinsel is a molly and a "bugger":

> Tom Tug a tar, with toddy half-seas over, / Espi'd Jack Tinsel just arrived from Dover, / Zounds, Dick, says he, observe the sail a-head, / Full rigg'd by Jove, with all his canvass spread, / Tho' damn his eyes, the bouger's not from France— / Come, lend a hand, we'll learn him how to dance. / . . . / His green silk breeches grafted blue behind, / With all his trapings of a piece with these, / Behind a fright, before designed to please.

"Bouger" is a synonym for "bugger," and the allusion to France derives from the century-long English association of sodomy with European origins. Later references to "the Pope" and "the Saints" recall the association of sodomy with licentious Catholics, also a staple of English caricatures. The description of Tinsel's breeches is designed to show that Tinsel brings attention to his arse, and the phrase "Behind a fright, before designed to please" suggests the various uses of his anatomy.[60]

Tom Tug identifies Tinsel as a molly by his description of Tinsel as "the sail a-head, full rigg'd by Jove, with all his canvass spread." Molly was an adaptation of the slang term for prostitute applied to effeminate sodomites in early eighteenth-century England. In Philadelphia, prostitutes had been identified and described in popular print as women lavishly dressed "like full spreading Sails" during the 1760s.[61] "Full rigg'd" "with all his canvass spread" was meant to identify Tinsel as a molly and demonstrates that some Philadelphians were familiar with the transformations in meaning associated with the term. In the *Philadelphiad,* the language used in past local lore to depict a "cruising" prostitute has been applied to Jack Tinsel, the "cruising" molly. The political twist in "The Misfortunes of a Fop" is the substitution of the English molly for the usual depiction of a Frenchman or an Italian as a sodomite. It is thus simultaneously a political attack on the English in post-revolutionary Philadelphia and a locally produced depiction of the European-style sodomite operating in Philadelphian society. Tom Tug is provoked by the sight of Tinsel to instigate a fight. He taunts Tinsel, makes him cry, but ultimately lets him off with a warning to mend his ways, concluding that "*Tom* thought *Jack* had punishment complete, / To be the scoff and scandal of the street."[62]

And what of women's homoerotic experiences in eighteenth-century Philadelphia? In England, some women used textual representations to help them fashion a homoerotic identity for themselves. Yorkshire gentlewoman Anne Lister sought out classical texts for their descriptions of Sappho and used these as a measure of her sense of herself. Lister's secret diary shows that she fashioned her identity through a dialectical process between textual representations of women who loved women and her understanding of her same-sex desire. Books themselves were represented in novels as important sources for sexual instruction.[63] If there were women in Philadelphia interested in searching out models of female same-sex love and sexual desire, the texts Lister used were available.

Women loving women were presented in a broad range of genres from medical texts, stories of female husbands, and romantic friendships to erotic novels and tales of secret lesbian cabals.[64] Again, Philadelphia booksellers imported and sold texts from all of these genres. Medical books, like Robert James's *Medicinal Dictionary* describing "tribades," whose sexual relations with other women made them "fonder of associating themselves with Women than Men," and Dr. Tissot's famous *Onania*, which describes sex between women as "*clitorical*" "pollution" known since the time of Sappho of Lesbos and "frequently practiced at present," were available in Philadelphia.[65] Sappho, the seventh-century B.C. Greek poet, and her sexual love of women were known to early modern readers of classical texts. The most candid of these were sold in Philadelphia.[66]

Philadelphians imported and read the only known eighteenth-century imprint of love-making between women written by a woman, *Secret Memoirs and Manners of Several persons of quality of both Sexes, from the New Atlantis* by Delariviere Manley. Manley suggested that there exists a new breed of women who "have all of happiness in themselves." These women prefer not to marry but satisfy all their needs in the company of women. They create a "new Cabal," a kind of secret society of women who embrace exclusive homoerotic desire. While the members are allowed marriages of convenience with men, they must reserve their erotic passion exclusively for other women. This secret society consisted of pairs of women, depicting the broad range of eighteenth-century characterizations of female homoeroticism. Some were women who slipped from romantic friendship to sexual intimacy, others aggressively sought out casual sex with prostitutes, and at least one was a mannish female who took on male gender attributes.[67] In midcentury London, those in aristocratic circles gossiped about women who seemed to be overly fond of their favorite lady friends, and in Philadelphia at least some readers borrowed or bought the *Secret Memoirs . . . from the New Atlantis* and read of women who courted other women.

Novel-reading Philadelphians encountered the possibility of female homoerotic seduction and desire in several mainstream novels of the day. Samuel Richardson's *Pamela,* for example, places the heroine in the path of the amorous Mrs. Jewkes, whose kisses Pamela must fend off. The encounter is a side plot, but it is presented as a pursuit any young woman might encounter.[68] *Pamela,* like *Roderick Random,* was a consistent seller in Philadelphia during the second half of the eighteenth century. People of means purchased it, and many others, usually women, borrowed it from Bradford's circulating library.[69]

English translations of French erotic texts also circulated. Infrequent advertisements for Nicolas Chorior's *School of Women, Venus in the Cloister* by Jean Barrin, and *School for Lovers* appear in the *Pennsylvania Gazette* at midcentury.[70] These were, by eighteenth-century standards, pornographic novels. In addition to graphic descriptions of male-female intercourse and group sex, these novels all begin their stories with the sexual initiation of a young woman by a more experienced older woman. Depicted here are the imaginary sexual encounters between women. In *Venus in the Cloister,* Sister Angelica teaches the novice Agnes by example, kissing and fondling her and initiating their passionate mutual masturbation. Tullia, in *School of Women,* likewise brings her cousin Octavia to orgasm in the second instructional dialogue, entitled "Tribadicon."[71] Perhaps this is why the Frenchman Moreau de St. Méry, living in Philadelphia in the 1790s, assumed that Philadelphia sleeping arrangements of older servant girls bedding with the householders' younger daughters was evidence of homoerotic sexual practice among the city's young women.[72]

Sometimes the connections between English sexual culture and colonial North America were even more direct, as the transatlantic history of Mary/Charles Hamilton demonstrates. In July 1752, a letter appeared in the *Pennsylvania Gazette* sent from Chester, just outside of Philadelphia. It recounted the story of "Charles" Hamilton, an itinerant doctor who was discovered to be a cross-dressing woman. The story she told on discovery was that she had been "brought up to the business of a Doctor and Surgeon, under one Doctor *Green,* a noted Mountebank in *England.*" She had set sail for Philadelphia in the fall of 1751, been "cast away" on the shore of North Carolina, and had made her way north toward Philadelphia selling medicines and treating patients along the way. What had occurred in Chester to raise suspicion about her gender is not articulated. The letter simply states "it being suspected that the Doctor was a Woman in Mens Cloaths, was taken up, examined, and found to be a Woman; and confessed she had used that Disguise for several Years."[73]

This is a remarkable case. This woman's assumed name and her mode of operation are identical to the English female husband Mary Hamilton recorded in Henry Fielding's fictionalized account of her life in *The Female Husband,* published in 1746, the year of her discovery and prosecution in England. Outside Philadelphia, four and a half years after Mary Hamilton completed her six-month jail term for fraud in marrying a reputedly unsuspecting wife, appeared a woman with the same assumed name and personal history.[74] Could this have been Mary Hamilton, sexual outlaw, moving to the empire's colonial outpost? Philadelphia was one of the most genteel and cosmopolitan frontiers the British empire had to offer a woman at midcentury. Or was this someone else, someone who had assumed Hamilton's mode of operation and personal history as a means of communicating her identity to those in the know?

The surviving evidence suggests that she was indeed Mary Hamilton, continuing her life as Dr. Charles Hamilton. Several key identifying pieces of information in the story she told Chester officials did not appear in the Fielding 6-pence pamphlet or in the small newspaper reportage the case generated at the time. The story she related, therefore, was unlikely to be generally known. Fielding's pamphlet gives her the assumed name of George Hamilton, but her actual assumed name was Charles Hamilton, as she attested to in her deposition in court. These court documents are also the only known sources in which "Doctor Green, a noted Mountebank" is presented.[75] While Fielding's account of a cross-dressing doctor probably circulated in midcentury Pennsylvania and may have caused suspicion of Dr. Charles Hamilton in Chester, the particular biographical details of Mary Hamilton's court testimony were not available for imitation. We know of only one Mary/Charles Hamilton, one persecuted sexual outlaw, who sought a fresh start at the edge of empire. Her story suggests that the ideas transmitted in texts and that produced a literal paper trail for historians' sleuthing were not the only, or even perhaps the most powerful, means of cultural transmission of eighteenth-century homoerotic notions and practices.

Chester County authorities arrested Hamilton as a safeguard against any frauds this imposter may have committed. As they said, "She is detained in Prison here, till we see whether any Body appears against her, if not she will be discharged." With a willing partner, the female husband might operate unmolested. She had committed no crime in her cross-dressing guise, and only if a woman chose to protest against her would her sexual and gender transgression be policed.[76]

Perhaps this is what happened in the only documented Philadelphia case of female cohabitation. A terse entry in the Prisoners for Trial Docket notes: "Ann Hannah, August 17, 1792, Charged on Oath of Margaret Marshall with Harboring and Cohabiting with the said Margaret." Hannah was released the same day. This entry reads exactly like the cases of male-female illegal cohabitation, except that the cohabitation is between women, and Marshall herself brought the charges. Typically, complaints of illegal cohabitation were lodged against a man or woman who had brought a married partner into his or her home, and the wronged spouse was always the complainant. These cases were rarely pursued after the initial arrest.[77] But here the cohabiting woman herself brought the case to the authorities. One wonders on what basis Marshall believed herself wronged by Hannah's harboring and cohabiting with her. It may be that Hannah lived with Marshall as a man, and Marshall was outraged when the guise was discovered. Or it may be that Marshall went to the constable in a fit of anger over an unrelated issue and swore out an ordinary low-level charge. We, unfortunately, cannot know. What we do learn from these examples is that nonconforming homoerotic women, like their male counterparts, were dealt with no more harshly than more conventional individuals.[78]

Philadelphians, therefore, were well informed about the eighteenth-century European homoerotic social types, including the new sodomite, and they, too, were interested in the erotics of same-sex relations. But they did not identify homoerotic behavior as a special category of deviance in need of aggressive policing. In comparison to authorities in London, Paris, The Hague, and Amsterdam, who actively persecuted sodomites, Philadelphians were relatively tolerant of those who embraced homoerotic practices. In Philadelphia the meanings of homoeroticism had not solidified around a set of attributes delineating a social type as it had in Europe creating a new deviant actor in the sodomite. In eighteenth-century Philadelphia, homoerotic desire and behavior remained malleable categories open to multiple meanings and interpretations.

Philadelphians had demonstrated their cultural interest in homoerotic themes in literature and lowbrow popular print material. They brought this culture into their society on their own terms. They read bawdy tales and even caricatured homoerotic social types in British ways, but they did not find the discourse of sodomy particularly potent in their own cultural production. Unlike their Boston neighbors, Philadelphians produced no pamphlets like Samuel Danforth's *Cry of Sodom* or Josiah Smith's *Burning of Sodom*.[79] As historian Thomas Foster demonstrates, New England ministers used the biblical story of the fall of Sodom and Gomorrah to encourage spiritual vigilance and to mark sodomy in particular as unnatural, a sin.[80] In contrast to New Englanders, Philadelphians did not attach particular symbolic meaning to sodomy in religious literature published in the city. They also chose not to incorporate the tales of the sodomite in their own production of true-crime pamphlets that proliferated in the first thirty years after the American Revolution. Nor were homoerotic character traits or desires part of the litany of the behaviors crime pamphlets articulated as the path to villainy.[81] While Philadelphians were interested in an erotic view into same-sex intimacy, they did not embrace it as an important category of deviancy.[82]

The sexual culture of mid- to late eighteenth-century Philadelphia left open the space for a wide array of cultural meanings of homoerotics. For many Philadelphians, homoerotic experience was probably confined to reading about it. If these individuals read erotic texts in the ways their authors intended, they experienced homoerotic sexual behavior as one of many available erotic possibilities, as voyeuristic readers, to enhance their sexual imaginations. From the earliest sodomy trial pamphlets on Lord Audley, the earl of Castlehaven, to Fanny Hill, the narratives structured observers into the texts. While these texts did not advocate adopting these sexual practices, they did actively suggest that watching them had erotic benefits. Even the newspaper reportage of supposed sexual outlaws like Mary Hamilton invited readers to take an imaginary erotic journey. Describing Hamilton's marriage the *Pennsylvania Journal* encouraged readers to imagine *how* she convincingly acted the part of husband in the marriage bed. The account explained that Hamilton had married and "bedded" Mary Price "and lived as man and wife for a quarter of a Year, during which time, *she thought the Prisoner a Man, owing to the Prisoner's vile and deceitful Practices.*"[83] Because the sexual culture had not encapsulated homoerotic sexual behavior in a distinct deviant social type or sexual identity, it may have remained one among many erotic sexual possibilities if only in the imagination throughout the eighteenth century.

For those participating more directly in homoerotic experiences, understandings of homoerotic sexuality were probably conditioned by class status. Men in the top social strata were probably allowed their sexual dalliances with men just as they were with women.[84] Class prerogatives would probably have shielded them from being associated with the sodomite. But by the 1770s, men of the elite and upper middle classes may have understood homoeroticism in the framework of acute sensibility. Sensibility stressed the importance of deep authentic emotional feeling and highlighted the importance of emotional expression in primary relationships. Many Philadelphians of the middle and upper strata, like their English counterparts, had come to value the capacity for sentiment in the individual. For these men the cult of sensibility infused their relationships with other men with emotional importance and intimacy. Sexual expression between men in this context could be understood as an expression of the purest of loves.

The best example of this type of relationship in Philadelphia was that between John Fishbourne Mifflin and James Gibson, documented in the journals kept by both men. Mifflin and Gibson developed an intense, emotionally intimate relationship in the 1780s that Mifflin saw through the lens of sentiment. He valued Gibson as the primary relationship in his life during those years. The two wrote letters filled with emotional self-disclosure, gave each other personal gifts conveying their special intimacy, anticipated secluded private moments, slept together when they visited each other, and dreamed of one another. Were they sexually intimate? We do not know. But if they were, they would probably have interpreted their sexual relationship in the context of acute sensibility, as a physical expression of a pure sincere love and affection for one another.[85] Those around them may have understood their intimacy as heroic friendship because of the refined emotional quality of their relationship.

Men from Philadelphia's middling and lower classes, the artisans, shopkeepers, craftsmen, and laborers, may have interpreted homoerotic sexual expression in any number of ways. Both the older aristocratic rake and the newer sodomite were available as interpretive models for individuals who experienced sexual desire for members of their own sex. The sodomite, in particular, had been associated in English society with urban men from just these social classes. But these possibilities were not the only ones. In this period before the heterosexual-homosexual dyad took hold of the sexual imaginations of Philadelphians, the sexual culture still held the space for individual creations and understandings. Male cross-dressing, for instance, could suggest the effeminacy of the sodomite or it could be a guise used by a man to obtain access to an unsuspecting woman's bed.[86] Distinct sexual categories with prescribed sexual scripts had not solidified in the popular imagination. In this world, the Ann Alweyes and Mary Hamiltons may have had greater flexibility to fashion themselves and interpret their relationships.

Why did Philadelphians take such a different path from their English relatives? Why did they not conceptualize homoeroticism as a distinct deviant sexual category and develop an active and aggressive fear of the sodomite during the eighteenth century? Why was late colonial and early national Philadelphia different? I would like to suggest three interrelated possibilities. First, the character of Philadelphia as a colonial outpost of empire and a vibrant port city founded by Quakers mediated against the formation of a single, easily enforced moral code. The city teemed with ethnic, racial, and religious diversity. It accommodated a constant influx and outflow of individuals. Quaker commitment to freedom of conscience as the basis of faith emphasized the individual's choice in moral decisions, and the city's Quaker leadership did not adopt an activist stance toward policing morality beyond the church's own membership. Philadelphia had developed neither the moral mandate to initiate aggressive policing of homoerotic behavior nor the state policing mechanisms to enforce any prohibitions.

Second, perhaps the choice not to police homoerotic sexuality was a way of not integrating the social type of the sodomite into colonial and early national society. Legal ignorance of homoerotic practices kept the sodomite "unknown" to the recognized public culture of the city. The sodomite in print was of European origin, often an Englishman like John Dicks or "Jack Tinsel." By turning a blind eye, public officials denied the sodomite recognition and provided a way of keeping colonial distance from British vice.

Finally, I suggest that Philadelphians had different concerns about gender, class, and masculinity and their relationship to the organization of power than did the English during the eighteenth century. Both societies were concerned with constructing forms of masculinity that would structure social position and guide social relations. In England, the onset of persecution of the sodomite in the early eighteenth century has been attributed to struggles to establish social position in an era of great social, political, and economic transformation. Some scholars see the attacks on the sodomite as part of the larger class struggle for the consolidation of power by the middle class. Others argue that a crisis in masculinity was precipitated by changes in gender relations between men and women. Still others explain that the fear of effeminacy was a product of the construction of gendered masculinity, as society moved from a hierarchy based on social status to one primarily ordered around gender binary opposites of male and female. Each of these interpretations presents the persecution of eighteenth-century sodomites as a tool to create and maintain divisions among men.[87]

Unlike the English who were engaged in a process of defining men out of full manhood status based on effeminacy and sexual inclinations, Philadelphians, by the last third of the eighteenth century, were engaged in just the opposite sort of social construction. The political imperatives of the Revolution and early nation formation required building a shared sense of identity to bind white men of diverse interests and backgrounds together. In Philadelphia the timing of the influx of new English ideas about the sodomite corresponded with these developments and mediated against adopting the English pejorative model. Texts depicting English notions of homoeroticism became widely available in the 1760s and 1770s as imports of printed matter increased, literacy spread, and libraries opened their doors to a broader reading public. It was in just these years that patriots drawn from the elite and middling ranks took on the project of creating and reinforcing a shared sense of identity and interest.[88] An inclusive model of manhood available to all white men became an important tool for building male unity. In revolutionary Philadelphia, the economic and political activism of the artisans and laboring classes demonstrated to political elites the potential the emergent working class had for developing a distinct class-based political interest and reinforced the importance of minimizing cultural symbols of male class divisions.[89] The creation of the white male republican citizen was the most obvious manifestation of this process. But beneath this development, and more fundamental to a shared masculinity, was sexuality. Sexuality bound white men together in their shared access to male sexual prerogatives and separated them from men of color without eliminating hierarchical differences based on social status or economic class. It provided a common ground to conceptualize their essential sameness, in contrast to women and African-American men, and minimized the symbolic importance of recognizing class-based differences among them. In early national Philadelphia, white men of all classes experienced increased opportunities to engage in nonmarital sexual behaviors with diminishing social repercussions and decreased personal responsibility.[90] Revolutionary and early national Philadelphians became more manly, not by circumscribing sexual behavior, but by expanding access to sexual privilege to white men of all classes. The shared masculinity constructed by Philadelphians in the revolutionary and early national periods was not one built on the negative referent of the sodomite, but one based on enhancing the prerogatives of white manhood in contrast to black men and at the expense of women.[91]

## NOTES

Editor's note: From "Mapping an Atlantic Sexual Culture: Homoeroticism in Eighteenth-Century Philadelphia," by Clare A. Lyons, *The William and Mary Quarterly*, Third Series, Vol. 60, No. 1, January 2003. © 2003 Omohundro Institute of Early American History and Culture. Reprinted by permission.

I would like to thank Cornelia Dayton, John D'Emilio, Patricia Cline Cohen, Robyn Muncy, Elsa Barkley Brown, Daryle Williams, and Steve Berg for their insightful comments on earlier versions of this article and Tom Foster for all his work to make this volume possible.

1. *Pennsylvania Journal*, Mar. 10, 1747. I purposely use "homoerotic" to refer to same-sex erotic desire and practice rather than "homosexual," the nineteenth-century coinage, to avoid evoking modern understandings of homosexuality and to invite an open-ended inquiry into the mental conceptualizations of same-sex intimacy entertained by eighteenth-century Euroamericans.

2. See Thomas A. Foster, "Antimasonic Satire, Sodomy, and Eighteenth-Century Masculinity in the *Boston Evening-Post*," *William and Mary Quarterly* 60 (2003): 171–84; Foster, "Locating Sodomy in Eighteenth-Century Massachusetts," paper presented at the MCEAS/OIEAHC Conference on Sexuality in Early America, Philadelphia, June 2001; and Richard Godbeer, " 'The Cry of Sodom': Discourse, Intercourse, and Desire in Colonial New England," *William and Mary Quarterly*, 3d Ser., 52 (1995), 259–84. See also Roger Thompson, "Attitudes Towards Homosexuality in the Seventeenth-Century New England Colonies," *Journal of American Studies*, 23 (1989), 27–40; Robert F. Oaks " 'Things Fearful to Name': Sodomy and Buggery in Seventeenth-Century New England," *Journal of Social History*, 12 (1978), 268–81, and "Defining Sodomy in Seventeenth-Century Massachusetts," *Journal of Homosexuality*, 6 (1980–1981), 79–83; and Colin L. Talley, "Gender and Male Same-Sex Erotic Behavior in British North America in the Seventeenth Century," *Journal of the History of Sexuality*, 6 (1996), 385–408. For Virginia, see Oaks, "Perceptions of Homosexuality by Justices of the Peace in Colonial Virginia," *Journal of Homosexuality*, 5 (1979–1980), 35–41. On bestiality, see John M. Murrin, " 'Things Fearful to Name': Bestiality in Early America," *Pennsylvania History*, Supplement: Explorations in Early American Culture, 65 (1998), 8–43.

3. Foster, "Locating Sodomy," documents 15 cases of sodomy throughout New

England during the 17th century and three prosecutions in Massachusetts during the first half of the 18th century, and Godbeer, " 'Cry of Sodom,' " explores two Connecticut prosecutions for sodomy, one in the 17th and one in the 18th century.

4. Philadelphia's population of 12,000 at midcentury had grown to 42,000 by 1790; Billy G. Smith, *The "Lower Sort": Philadelphia's Laboring People, 1750–1800* (Ithaca, 1990), 206.

5. Until the mid-1760s, virtually all of Philadelphia's demographic growth depended on immigration. The majority of the city's population had been born abroad. The city continued to depend on immigration for much of its growth for the remainder of the century; Susan E. Klepp, "Demography in Early Philadelphia, 1690–1860," in Klepp, ed., "The Demographic History of the Philadelphia Region, 1600–1860," *Proceedings of the American Philosophical Society*, 133 (1989), 85–111.

6. Smith, *"Lower Sort,"* 214; W. Jeffrey Bolster, *Black Jacks: African American Seamen in the Age of Sail* (Cambridge, 1997), table 1, 236.

7. More than 50% of the ships entering Philadelphia between midcentury and the American Revolution arrived from transatlantic commercial ports in Britain, southern Europe, and the Caribbean. During the Seven Years' War and the Revolution, ca. 40% of the ships remained part of the transatlantic trade; Smith, *"Lower Sort,"* 72–73. Most of England's industrial output was exported from London in the years before the American Revolution; Thomas M. Doerflinger, *A Vigorous Spirit of Enterprise: Merchants and Economic Development in Revolutionary Philadelphia* (Chapel Hill, 1986), 70–77.

8. There is a growing body of literature on early modern homoeroticism in Europe. The following synthesis is drawn from Mary McIntosh, "The Homosexual Role," *Social Problems*, 16, No. 2 (1968), 182–92; Alan Bray, *Homosexuality in Renaissance England* (London, 1982); Bray and Michel Rey, "The Body of the Friend: Continuity and Change in Masculine Friendship in the Seventeenth Century," in Tim Hitchcock and Michele Cohen, eds., *English Masculinities, 1660–1800* (London, 1999), 65–84; the works of Randolph Trumbach, esp. "London's Sodomites: Homosexual Behavior and Western Culture in the Eighteenth Century," *Journal of Social History*, 11 (1977), 1–33; "Sodomitical Subcultures, Sodomitical Roles, and the Gender Revolution of the Eighteenth Century: The Recent Historiography," in Robert Purks Maccubbin, ed., *'Tis Nature's Fault: Unauthorized Sexuality During the Enlightenment* (New York, 1987), 109–21; "Sodomy Transformed: Aristocratic Libertinage, Public Reputation, and the Gender Revolution of the Eighteenth Century," *Journal of Homosexuality*, 19 (1990), 105–24; and "Sex, Gender, and Sexual Identity in Modern Culture: Male Sodomy and Female Prostitution in Enlightenment London," ibid., 2 (1991), 186–203; Michael S. Kimmel, "From Lord and Master to Cuckold and Fop: Masculinity in Seventeenth-Century England," *University of Dayton Review*, 18 (1986–1987), 93–109; Kimmel, " 'Greedy Kisses' and 'Melting Extasy': Notes on the Homosexual World of Early Eighteenth-Century England in *Love Letters Between a certain late Nobleman and the famous Mr. Wilson*," *Journal*

*of Homosexuality,* 19 (1990), 1–10; G. S. Rousseau, "The Pursuit of Homosexuality in the Eighteenth Century: 'Utterly Confused Category' and/or Rich Repository?" *Eighteenth Century Life,* 9 (1985), 132–68; George E. Haggarty, *Men in Love: Masculinity and Sexuality in the Eighteenth Century* (New York, 1999); Michel Rey, "Parisian Homosexuals Create a Lifestyle, 1700–1750: The Police Archives," trans. Robert A. Day and Robert Welch, in Maccubbin, ed., *'Tis Nature's Fault,* 179–91; Rey, "Police and Sodomy in Eighteenth-Century Paris: From Sin to Disorder," in Kent Gerard and Gert Hekma, eds., *The Pursuit of Sodomy: Male Homosexuality in Renaissance and Enlightenment Europe* (New York, 1989), 129–46; Theo van der Meer, "The Persecutions of Sodomites in Eighteenth-Century Amsterdam: Changing Perceptions of Sodomy," ibid., 263–310; and L. J. Boon, "Those Damned Sodomites: Public Images of Sodomy in Eighteenth-Century Netherlands," ibid., 237–48.

9. In addition to those cited in note 8 above see Rousseau, "An Introduction to the *Love-Letters:* Circumstances of Publication, Context, and Cultural Commentary," *Journal of Homosexuality,* 19 (1990), 47–92, and David F. Greenberg, "The Social-Sexual Milieu of the *Love-Letters,*" ibid., 93–103.

10. Some literary scholars see a more gradual shift and a persistence of 17th-century meanings in representations of the sodomite into the mid-18th century; Cameron McFarlane, *The Sodomite in Fiction and Satire, 1660–1750* (New York, 1997).

11. Our knowledge of homoerotic sexual practices among men below the aristocratic elite in the 17th century is limited. It was the onset of policing of homoerotic practices among urban men in the early to mid-18th century that generated the evidence we have for the 18th century.

12. Trumbach, "London's Sodomites"; Rey, "Police and Sodomy"; Rey, "Parisian Homosexuals"; van der Meer, "Persecutions of Sodomites."

13. Rey, "Parisian Homosexuals"; Bray, *Homosexuality*; Trumbach, "London's Sodomites" and "Sodomitical Subcultures"; van der Meer, "Persecutions of Sodomites." Craig Patterson, "The Rage of Caliban: Eighteenth-Century Molly Houses and the Twentieth-Century Search for Sexual Identity," in Thomas DiPiero and Pat Gill, eds., *Illicit Sex: Identity Politics in Early Modern Culture* (Athens, Ga., 1997), 256–69, and McFarlane, *Sodomite in Fiction and Satire,* have questioned the veracity of the descriptive accounts of urban molly houses written in popular imprints. They question whether the texts can be read as evidence of an emergent sexual identity and as evidence of a subculture. For my purposes here, the debate over the interior sexual identity of the sodomite is less important than the cultural production of a new character in the sodomite and his legal prosecution by the authorities. What these accounts do provide is evidence of the public understandings of the sodomite and the discursive importance he took on in 18th-century representations of homoeroticism. The English did invent a new social type of the sodomite in print and prosecuted men of the urban laboring classes under this

rubric. The extent to which men labeled as sodomites understood themselves to have a particular sexual identity may be impossible to determine.

14. Haggarty, *Men in Love*; David M. Halperin, "How to Do the History of Male Homosexuality," *GLQ: A Journal of Lesbian and Gay Studies*, 6 (2000), 87–124; Bray and Rey, "Body of the Friend." Trumbach takes a different position, arguing that the recognizable social type of the sodomite represented the invention of a third gender and precipitated the creation of the heterosexual-homosexual dyad in 18th-century England.

15. The sexual inclinations of the effeminate fop has generated a debate among historians. His primary transgression was to be too womanly, to seek out the company of women and to emulate their behavior. Sometimes his interest is portrayed as a means to attain sexual intimacy with women; at other times it suggests the desire to be like women in their sexual inclinations, meaning to be subordinated by men in sexual relations and to be penetrated by men. Haggarty, *Men in Love*, makes a compelling argument that from an 18th-century perspective the effeminate fop would have been expected to have sexual interest in both men and women. He was a character who wanted to emulate the libertine rake but failed due to his excessive effeminacy. Haggarty points out that it would be misguided to dismiss the effeminate fop's potential for sodomy because sexual interest in both men and women was part of the libertine ethos. For an interpretation of the heteroerotic sexual desire of the fop see Trumbach, "Birth of the Queen: Sodomy and the Emergence of Gender Equality in Modern Culture, 1660–1750" in Martin Bauml Duberman et al., eds., *Hidden from History: Reclaiming the Gay and Lesbian Past* (New York, 1989), 129–40.

16. I have relied heavily on Haggarty, *Men in Love*, and Halperin, "How to Do the History of Male Homosexuality," to present this typology of 18th-century same-sex relationships.

17. Emma Donoghue, *Passions between Women: British Lesbian Culture, 1668–1801* (London, 1993); Trumbach, "London's Sapphists: From Three Sexes to Four Genders in the Making of Modern Culture," in Julia Epstein and Kristina Straub, eds., *Body Guards: The Cultural Politics of Gender Ambiguity* (New York, 1991), 112–41; Eve Kosofsky Sedgwick, *Epistemology of the Closet* (Berkeley, 1990), and "Privilege of Unknowing," *Genders*, 1 (1988), 102–24; Judith C. Brown, "Lesbian Sexuality in Medieval and Early Modern Europe," in Martin Bauml Duberman et al., eds., *Hidden from History: Reclaiming the Gay and Lesbian Past* (New York, 1989), 67–75.

18. This analysis of print culture in mid- to late 18th-century Philadelphia is based on research of books for sale advertised in the city's newspapers and almanacs, listed in booksellers' catalogues, and books held in the city's libraries. The *Pennsylvania Gazette* was searched exhaustively for specific texts, and booksellers' advertisements were taken from the other midcentury Philadelphia newspapers, the *American Weekly Mercury*, the *Pennsylvania Journal*, the *Pennsylvania Packet*, and the *Pennsylvania Chronicle*.

19. *Pa. Gaz.*, July 18, 1754.

20. *Pamela*, by comparison, appeared in 14 advertisements placed by 8 book-sellers, and Fielding's *Tom Jones* was listed for sale 26 times during this same era. See *Pa. Gaz.*, 1730–1800; *Father Abraham's Almanac for 1760*, "Books for sale by the Publisher" (Philadelphia, 1759); *A Catalogue of Books . . . W. Bradford* (Philadelphia, 1760); *Catalogue of Books Belonging to the Association Library Company of Philadelphia* (Philadelphia, 1765); *Just Published and now Selling, at Bell's Bookstore . . . A Catalogue of . . . Books* (Philadelphia, 1783); *Catalogue of Books . . . and other Goods at Moreau de St. Mery, & Co's. Store* (Philadelphia, 1795); *Bradford's Catalogue of Books . . . for 1796* (Philadelphia, 1796) ; *A Catalogue of all the Books, printed in the United States . . .* (Boston, 1804); *The charter, Laws, and catalogue of books, of the Library Company of Philadelphia* (Philadelphia, 1765); *A Catalogue of books, belonging to the Association Library Company of Philadelphia . . .* (Philadelphia, 1765); Thomas Bradford, Day Book of Bradford's Circulating Library, 1771–1772, Historical Society of Pennsylvania (HSP). Robert B. Winans, "Bibliography and the Cultural Historian: Notes on the Eighteenth-Century Novel," in William L. Joyce et al., eds., *Printing and Society in Early America* (Worcester, 1983), 177–80, found that *Roderick Random* was the sixth most popular novel in British North America, 1750–1800, based on its prominence in American book catalogues. Edwin Wolf, *The Book Culture of a Colonial American City: Philadelphia Books, Bookmen, and Booksellers* (Oxford, 1988), 189–97, also identified *Roderick Random* as a popular 18th-century text.

21. Rousseau, "Pursuit of Homosexuality," 132–68; Steven Bruhm, "Roderick Random's Closet," *English Studies in Canada*, 19 (1993), 401–15; McFarlane, *Sodomite in Fiction and Satire*, 23–24, 108–44; Haggarty, *Men in Love*, chap. 2; Robert Adams Day, "Sex, Scatology, Smollett," in Paul-Gabriel Bouce, ed., *Sexuality in Eighteenth-Century Britain* (Manchester, Eng., 1982), 225–43.

22. Smollett, *Roderick Random* (London, 1748), 194–95, 307–10.

23. *Roderick Random* sold for 9s., 10s., and 12s. in the early 1770s; $2.00 in 1783; and, when printed in Philadelphia by Mathew Carey in 1794, $1.75 for fine paper and $1.50 for coarse paper. See Robert Aitken, Waste Book, Dec. 23, 1772, July 12, 1775, HSP; *Robert Bell's Sale Catalogue . . .* (Philadelphia, 1773); Robert Bell, *Just Published and Now Selling* (Philadelphia, 1783); Carey, *Catalogue of Books, Pamphlets, Maps, and Prints, published by Mathew Carey* (Philadelphia, 1795); Wolf, *Book Culture*, 197. The price of *Roderick Random* was comparable to other imported English imprints of the day, which in the early 1770s generally cost 5–12s. for a two-volume set depending on the size and quality of the text. These books were luxury purchases for master craftsmen and difficult for journeymen or apprentices. Prices based on William Bradford and Thomas Bradford, Invoice Book for 1767–1769, HSP. For typical income and expenses for Philadelphia's laborers see Smith, "*Lower Sort*," 117–21.

24. Bradford's library provided popular books cheaply for a broad audience.

The weekly lending rate was 6d., the price of a pair of stockings; Bradford, Day Book of Bradford's Circulating Library, 1771–1772, HSP; *Pa. Journal*, Oct. 26, 1769, and Jan. 13, 1772. In the 1760s, the Library Company of Philadelphia charged non-members 4d.–8d. per week for the use of books from its extensive holdings; *The Charter . . . Library Company of Philadelphia* (Philadelphia, 1765).

25. Philadelphia had four lending libraries before the American Revolution. Scholars estimate that more than 50% of women and as many as 75–90% of men could read by 1776; Cathy N. Davidson, *Revolution and the Word: The Rise of the Novel in America* (New York, 1986), 55–61; James N. Green, "The Middle Colonies, 1720–1790," in Hugh Amory and David D. Hall, eds., *A History of the Book in America, vol. 1: The Colonial Book in the Atlantic World* (New York, 2000), 247–313; Stephen Botein, "The Anglo-American Book Trade before 1776: Personnel and Strategies," in Joyce et al., *Printing and Society*, 80–81.

26. Men like Dorsey appeared on the tax rolls but were rated at £ 0 because of their limited resources. More than half the male readers who patronized Bradford's circulating library in 1771–1772 did not appear on the 1772 tax list and in the first Philadelphia city directory in 1785. Many of them were probably of middling or lower economic status. Had they been sons of established families one would expect them to have grown into their adult professional status over a decade later. Some may also have been men who had left Philadelphia; *Macpherson's Directory, for the City and Suburbs of Philadelphia* (Philadelphia, 1785); Francis White, *The Philadelphia Directory* (Philadelphia, 1785). This analysis of Philadelphia readers is based on a six-week random sample of Bradford's Day Book, which runs from Dec. 1771 through Dec. 1772.

27. More than half the women patrons are named without the title "Mrs.," signifying their youth and probable single status. Only a few female patrons can be identified. Some were wives of middling or elite men who were also library patrons. Others were unmarried daughters of well-established families. At least one was a well-off woman of independent means who headed her own household.

28. These genres dominated Bradford's library shelves, outnumbering works of history, philosophy, and science.

29. Readers were located on the 1772 Philadelphia tax list.

30. *Memoirs of a Woman of Pleasure* was advertised as "Memoirs of," "Ditto Fanny," or simply "Fanny in 2 vols." Cleland did publish an expurgated version entitled *Memoirs of Fanny Hill* in one volume in 1750. The original *Memoirs of a Woman of Pleasure the Life of Fanny Hill* was twice as long and was published in two volumes. The short title references giving "Fanny" and " 2 vols" were meant to indicate the availability of the longer, explicitly erotic version. For advertisement in Philadelphia see *Pa. Gaz.*, June 28, 1764, Rivington and Brown; *Pa. Journal*, Jan. 8, 1756, William Bradford (this ad ran weekly from Jan. through May 1756 and again from Sept. 1756 through Jan. 1757); Bradford, *Catalogue of Books* (for 1760), and *Father Abraham's Almanac for 1760*, "Books for sale by the Publisher." *Memoirs*

*of a Woman of Pleasure* was also apparently printed in Philadelphia in 1806. See John Tate to Mathew Carey, July 8, 1806, HSP. Tate complained that Carey's type had been used to print "The Memoirs of a Woman of Pleasure, Other Wise Called Hannah Hill and the Abomible plates are Ingraved in this city."

31. *Select Trials at the Sessions-House in the Old Bailey. . . .* 4 vols. (London, 1742), advertised by David Hall in *Pa. Gaz.,* Oct. 12, Dec. 19, 1749, Dec. 10, 1751; by Dunlap in *Pa. Gaz.,* Dec. 29, 1763; and by Carey in *Pa. Gaz.,* May 14, 1788; *Father Abraham's Almanac for 1760*; and *A Catalogue of Books, Sold by Rivington and Brown* (Philadelphia, 1762); *Catalogues . . . Library Company of Philadelphia* (Philadelphia, 1765), and the *Catalogue Association Library Company* (Philadelphia, 1765). Advertisements requesting its return to an individual: *Pa. Gaz.,* Mar. 7–14, 1738; as overdue to the Library Company in *Pa. Gaz.,* Oct. 23, 1766; *Pa. Packet,* Apr. 29, 1784, and *Pa. Gaz.,* Feb. 4, 1789; and by the Association Library, *Pa. Gaz.,* Oct. 23, 1766. It was added to the Library Company's holdings sometime between 1757 and 1765.

32. Newspaper accounts of arrests for sodomy and its counterpart, blackmail, appeared periodically in London papers throughout the century. These papers were available in city taverns and coffeehouses that catered to the mercantile classes. The London Coffee House, for instance, regularly stocked and advertised the latest London papers. Philadelphians could also subscribe to London periodicals through the General Post Office in London, according to *Pa. Gaz.,* Feb. 19, June 10, 1756, Sept. 3, 1767, Oct. 6, 1778.

33. Dicks was convicted of an attempt to commit sodomy, sentenced to stand in the pillory—for public humiliation—serve two years' imprisonment, and pay a fine. Meeson, who displayed his interest in Dicks, at least to a point, was not indicted; *Select Trials,* 1:158–60. The similarity between this description and Cleland's subsequent fictional sodomite encounter in *Memoirs of a Woman of Pleasure* is obvious.

34. *Select Trials,* 3:39–40.

35. Trial of Gabriel Lawrence, 1726, ibid., 2:362–64; trial of William Griffin, 1726, ibid., 365–66; trial of Margaret Clap, 1726, ibid., 3:37–38; trial of Thomas Wright, 2:367–69. For descriptions of other molly houses see trial of George Whitle, 1726, ibid., 369–72, and trial of George Kedger, 1726, ibid., 366–67.

36. Trial of George Duffus, 1721, ibid., 1:105–08; trial of Thomas Rodin, 1722, ibid., 280–82; trial of Charles Banner, 1723, ibid., 329–30.

37. Maritime scholars disagree about the extent of homoerotic sexuality in 18th-century shipboard communities of men. See B. R. Burg, *Sodomy and the Perception of Evil: English Sea Rovers in the Seventeenth-Century Caribbean* (New York, 1983); Hans Turley, *Rum, Sodomy, and the Lash: Piracy, Sexuality, and Masculine Identity* (New York, 1999); Marcus Rediker, *Between the Devil and the Deep Blue Sea: Merchant Seamen, Pirates, and the Anglo-American Maritime World, 1700–1750* (Cambridge, 1987); Bolster, *Black Jacks*; Margaret S. Creighton and Lisa

Norling, eds., *Iron Men, Wooden Women: Gender and Seafaring in the Atlantic World, 1700–1920* (Baltimore, 1996).

38. *London Chronicle,* July 17–19, 1764; *London Evening Post,* July 17–19, 1764, for John Gill. *London Chronicle,* Sept. 11–13, 1764, for the arrests of transvestite male prostitutes. Trumbach discusses these events in "Sodomy Transformed," 116–17.

39. *The Tryal of Charles Bradbury* (London, 1755); *The Trial of Richard Branson* (London, 1760); *Some Particulars relating to the life of William Dillon Sheppard* (Bristol, 1761). Because Philadelphia booksellers rarely advertised pamphlets by title we cannot know if these pamphlets were among those imported and sold in midcentury Philadelphia. Booksellers' ads made general claims such as "the latest and most entertaining . . . plays . . . pamphlets." See *Pa. Journal,* Oct. 22, 1761, and *Pa. Packet,* Dec. 5, 1778, Oct. 26, 1782.

40. The *American Weekly Mercury* was begun in 1719, and the *Pa. Gaz.* followed in 1728; Charles E. Clark, *The Public Prints: The Newspaper in Anglo-American Culture, 1665–1740* (Oxford, 1994). Naomi Tadmor, "'In the even my wife read to me': Women, Reading and Household Life in the Eighteenth Century," in James Raven et al., eds., *The Practice and Representation of Reading in England* (Cambridge, 1996), 162–74.

41. *American Weekly Mercury,* Oct. 6–13, 1726. The paper reported that Clap was sentenced to stand in the pillory, pay a fine, and be imprisoned for two years; Thomas Brown and Benjamin Mackintosh were convicted of "Sodomitical Practices," each sentenced to stand in the pillory, pay a small fine, and be imprisoned for a year's term; and a woman known as "George Kelf," who "for about 17 Years hath gone in Men's Apparel," was fined for adopting a male identity. On Sept. 17, 1730, the paper reported the conviction and execution of 45 men for sodomy in Amsterdam, and on Oct. 8, 1730, of 7 at The Hague. The *Pa. Journal,* Feb. 13, 1753, reported news from Lisbon of an "Auto de Fe" that included the conviction of a Portugese man from Brazil for sodomy. He was sentenced to "be whipt and banish'd ten years."

42. *American Weekly Mercury,* Apr. 12–19, 1739.

43. Terry Castle, *Masquerade and Civilization: The Carnivalesque in Eighteenth-Century English Culture and Fiction* (Stanford, 1986). The *Spectator* was available for sale by most Philadelphia booksellers from the 1750s to the end of the century and was among the holdings at the city's lending libraries. William Bradford advertised it in multiple advertisements in 1754, 1755, 1756, 1759, 1760, as did his son Thomas in 1769; J. Rivington advertised it when he entered into the Philadelphia book trade in the early 1760s, as did John Sparhawk in the 1770s; Roger Bell advertised it in the 1770s, and William Prichard stocked it among his books when he entered the book trade and lending library business in the 1780s. See, for example, *Pa. Journal,* Mar. 28, 1751, Dec. 12, 1754, May 8, Sept. 11, 1755, Jan. 8, July 29, 1756, June 7, 1759, July 17, 1760, Nov. 5, 1761, June 3, 1762, Nov. 30, 1769; and *Pa. Packet,* Dec. 2, 1771, Oct. 26, 1782.

44. There is no evidence of criminal sodomy for the first half of the 18th century in the court records. See Ancient Records of Philadelphia and Grand Jury Presentments, Wallace Collection, HSP, and record no. 3093, Miscellaneous Court Papers, HSP. Court records from midcentury on are Mayors Court Docket; Prisoners for Trial Docket; Vagrancy Dockets; Court of Quarter Session Docket; Court of Oyer and Terminer Docket and File Papers. There is a total of 10 years, from the period 1750–1800, for which no Oyer and Terminer file papers or dockets survive. It is possible that some trials went unreported in the city's newspapers; it is unlikely that there would have been executions that went unreported or that there could have been numerous trials for sodomy in Philadelphia without notice in the public papers or any mention of the events in the journals and diaries kept by its citizens.

No men were executed for sodomy in Philadelphia, and it is doubtful that any were executed in the rest of the colony. Murrin, "Bestiality in Early America," following the lead of Negley K. Teeters, "Public Executions in Pennsylvania, 1682-1834, with Annotated Lists of Persons Executed; and of Delays, Pardons, and Reprieves of Persons Sentenced to Death in Pennsylvania, 1682–1834," *Journal of the Lancaster County Historical Society,* 64 (1960), 148–63, incorrectly reports that Thomas White was hanged for sodomy in 1748. White was hanged in "Newcastle," in 1748, for buggery with a mare. See *Pa. Journal,* Nov. 3, 1748. Bestiality was policed more stringently in Pennsylvania than sodomy in the 18th century. Bestiality was probably the crime John Ross was hanged for in western Pennsylvania, in Westmoreland County, in 1786. His offense appears as only "buggery" in the record.

My research into Philadelphia church disciplinary records uncovered no sodomy accusations. All extant records from Philadelphia's Presbyterian churches were examined for the 18th century for evidence of disciplinary action for instances of homoerotic sexual behavior. Newspapers were examined for reports of criminal prosecution or punishment for sodomy. Philadelphia newspapers did generally report local court news and judicial executions, but report no sodomy trials or convictions. For a full list of church records and Philadelphia diaries see Clare A. Lyons, *Sex Among the Rabble: An Intimate History of Gender and Power in the Age of Revolution, Philadelphia 1730–1830* (Chapel Hill, 2006).

45. Foster, "Locating Sodomy," examines the use of the language of Massachusetts sodomy statutes.

46. *Pennsylvania Statutes at Large* (Harrisburg, Pa., 1896), 2:3–14 (1700), 178–83 (1705), 3:199–202 (1718), 12:280–81 (1786). Sodomy was classified with incest and bestiality in the 1700 statute and received the same punishment as bigamy in the 1700 and 1705 statutes. Capital punishment was rescinded for robbery, burglary, and sodomy in 1786. A second round of reforms removed capital punishment for all crimes except first degree murder. This development was part of penal reforms in Pennsylvania in response to Enlightenment notions of human perfectibility fol-

lowing the Revolution. See Michael Meranze, *Laboratories of Virtue. Punishment, Revolution, and Authority in Philadelphia, 1760–1835* (Chapel Hill, 1996), 79, 168.

47. William Graydon, *The Justices and Constables Assistant* (Harrisburg, Pa., 1805), 357.

48. Lyons, *Sex Among the Rabble,* 196–98.

49. *Pa. Gaz.,* Apr. 5, 1753. The pamphlet, *The Whole Proceedings on the wicked Conspiracy carried on against the Hon. Edward Walpole* (London, 1751), describing this case may have been read by Philadelphians. Pamphlets were rarely advertised by title.

50. Case of John Elliot, Oyer and Terminer, Jan. 13, 1818.

51. William Meredith, Appearance Dockets, Quarter Sessions, Philadelphia County, June 1802, Meredith Family Papers, HSP. This was attorney Meredith's personal court docket book. See also Prisoners for Trial Docket, June 2, 1802, where the case is noted as "discharged."

52. Lyons, *Sex Among the Rabble,* 203–04, 270–76.

53. The Prisoners for Trial Docket was the log used to record all those brought in for arrest. People were logged in even when they were only held long enough to explore whether there was a reason to keep them longer. Hundreds of Philadelphians were arrested in this way each year, usually for annoying behavior in the city's streets. Most of those recorded in the Prisoners for Trial Docket were dismissed without further prosecution. Some were fined or posted bond for good behavior, and many were simply released outright.

54. These cases distinguish themselves because they do not mention that the man in question exposed himself to women, a fact that was recorded in many other exposure cases. In each of these cases the male complainant was a private person, not a member of the watch or a constable.

55. Case of John Place, June 4, 1806; case of Thomas Mullen, Sept. 10, 1822, in Prisoners for Trial Docket, Philadelphia. See also cases of: Thomas Patterson, Sept. 30, 1811; Philip Reinheart, July 13, 1812; Hanson Waters, Aug. 28 1823; and Jeremiah Dunkin, May 25, 1825, ibid.

56. Case of Daniel Sweeny, July 5, 1814, ibid.

57. *The Philadelphiad* (Philadelphia, 1784), 34–38.

58. Ibid., 34.

59. Ibid., 35.

60. Ibid., 38.

61. "A New Song About Miss Ketty" (broadside) (Philadelphia, 1765).

62. *Philadelphiad,* 34–38. Advertisements and commentary about the *Philadelphiad* appeared in *Pa. Journal,* Sept. 29, Oct. 2, 6, 13, 16, 1784, and in *Pa. Packet,* Dec. 14, 1784. Vol. 2, which contained the caricatures of the fop, was published in Dec. 1784 and sold for $0.25.

63. Anna Clark, "Anne Lister's Construction of Lesbian Identity," in Kim M. Phillips and Barry Reay, eds., *Sexualities in History: A Reader* (New York, 2002),

247–70; Helena Whitbread, ed., *I Know My Own Heart: The Diaries of Anne Lister, 1791–1840* (London, 1988); Donoghue, *Passions between Women*. For an exploration of English interpretations of a late 18th-century female couple see Susan S. Lanser, "Befriending the Body: Female Intimacies as Class Acts," *Eighteenth-Century Studies*, 32 (1998–1999), 179–98.

64. Donoghue, *Passions between Women*.

65. James, *Medicinal Dictionary* (London, 1745), vol. 3, quoted in Donoghue, *Passions between Women*, 50. James, *Medicinal Dictionary*, advertised by David Hall in *Pa. Gaz.*, Sept. 22, 1748, Aug. 3, Aug. 17, 1749; and by William Prichard in *Pa. Journal*, Dec. 18, 1782. [S.A.D.] Tissot, M.D., *Onania* (London 1766), 45–47, advertised in Robert Bell's Sale Catalogue of a collection of new and old books (Philadelphia, 1773). See also John Quincy, *Lexicon Physico Medicum or, a New Physical Dictionary* (London, 1719), advertised in the *Pa. Gaz.*, Dec. 10, 1751, by David Hall; in Bell, *Catalogue* (Philadelphia, 1773); and in *Pa. Chronicle*, Aug. 13–20, 1770, by John Sparhawk.

66. Alexander Pope's translation of Ovid's 15th epistle, known as "Sappho to Phaon," presents Sappho declaring "No more the Lesbian dames my passion move, Once the dear objects of my guilty love." "Sappho to Phaon" was advertised by James Rivington, *A Catalogue of Books* (Philadelphia, 1762). The earliest 18th-century translation of Sappho's own poetry acknowledges her love of women in the introduction; *Sappho Odes*, trans., with a life by A. Phillips, in *The Works of Anacreon and Sappho* (London, 1713). This may have been the edition imported by William Bradford in 1769, listed simply as "Anacreon and Sappho" in Bradford, "Invoice of books received from London, May 20 1769, " Invoice Book, 1767–1769, HSP.

67. *Secret Memoirs . . . from the New Atlantis*, advertised by Dunlap in *Pa. Gaz.*, May 18–25, 1738; ibid., Mar. 19, 1761, David Hall; ibid., Nov. 18, 25, Dec. 2, 1762; Rivington, *A Catalogue of Books* (Philadelphia, 1762); Bell, *Catalogue*. The 4 -vol. set was priced at 12s. *Secret Memoirs . . . from the New Atlantis*, originally published in 1709, was extremely popular in England. It was repeatedly reprinted through mid-century. It was initially repressed when Manley and her printer were briefly imprisoned for libel; Donoghue, *Passions between Women*, 232–36; Trumbach, "London's Sapphists," 126.

68. Donoghue, *Passions between Women*, 184–90. Other novels with female homoerotic desire that were particularly popular in Philadelphia were baron de Montesquieu's *Persian Letters* and Swift's *Gulliver's Travels*.

69. Advertisements in the *Pa. Gaz.* for *Pamela* appeared 14 times, placed by 8 booksellers, in the 30 years before the Revolution. Bradford stocked at least three copies of *Pamela* in his lending library; Bradford, Day Book.

70. *School of Women*, advertised in *Pa. Gaz.*, July 18, 1754, by Tench Francis. *Cloister* was advertised in *Pa. Gaz.*, May 10, 1765, by Rivington and Brown. *School for Lovers* (this may be Edmund Curll, *The School of Venus, or The Lady's Miscel-*

*lany* [1688, 1739], attributed to Michel Millot and Jean l'Ange), advertised in *Pa. Gaz.*, Sept. 30, 1762, by Rivington and Brown. Thompson, *Unfit for Modest Ears. A Study of Pornographic, Obscene and Bawdy Works Written or Published in England in the Second Half of the Seventeenth Century* (Totowa, N.J., 1979), 29–34, 151–55; Peter Wagner, *Eros Revived: Erotica of the Enlightenment in England and America* (London, 1988), 204, 227–31.

71. "Tribadicon" is derived from tribade, which meant one who rubs. It was commonly used to refer to women who engaged in sex with other women in 18th-century texts.

72. "I am going to say something that is almost unbelievable. These women, without real love and without passions, give themselves up at an early age to the enjoyment of themselves; and they are not at all strangers to being willing to seek unnatural pleasures with persons of their own sex. Among common people, at a tavern-keeper's, for example, or at a small shop-keeper's, the daughter of the house, when no longer a child, sleeps with the servant. That is to say, from her eighth to her tenth year she may have shared the bed of fifty or sixty creatures of whom nothing is known except their names. They may be dirty, unhealthy, subject to a communicable disease of more or less seriousness and the possessors of habits that could be disastrous to young persons"; Moreau de St. Méry, in Kenneth Roberts and Anna M. Roberts, eds. and trans., *Moreau de St. Méry's American Journey* (Garden City, N.Y., 1947), 286.

73. *Pa. Gaz.*, July 16, 1752.

74. The court proceedings reveal that Hamilton had been turned in to the authorities by her wife for posing as a man in marriage. In the Fielding pamphlet, the duped wife's relatives turn in the female husband Hamilton over the initial objections of the unsuspecting wife.

75. Newspaper reports about Mary Hamilton appeared in the *Bath Journal*, Sept. 22, 29, Nov. 3, 1746 (the Nov. report was reprinted in *Daily Advertiser*, Nov. 7, 1746, *St. James Evening Post*, Nov. 8, 1746 , and *Ipswich Journal*, Nov. 15, 1746). The *Pa. Journal* printed a brief account of Hamilton on Mar. 10, 1747. A slightly abridged version of the Nov. news of her conviction, it omitted all reference to a male name and did not identify her as a doctor or as Charles Hamilton, but focused on her relationship with other women. Fielding's pamphlet, *The Female Husband. or, the Surprising History of Mrs. Mary, alias Mr. George Hamilton*, published in London, Nov. 12, 1746, sold out quickly. We do not know how widely this pamphlet circulated in Pennsylvania. English court documents of the case are printed verbatim in Sheridan Baker, "Henry Fielding's *The Female Husband*: Fact and Fiction," *PMLA*, 74 (1959), 213–24. For interpretations of *The Female Husband*, see Baker, "Henry Fielding," and Castle, "Matters Not Fit to be Mentioned: Fielding's *The Female Husband*," *ELH*, 49 (1982), 602–22.

76. There is no follow-up newspaper account of Hamilton's case in the *Pa. Gaz.* or the *Pa. Journal*. It would have been typical reporting to bring the story

back to the newspaper pages if a victimized sexual partner had come forward, or if Hamilton had received any punishment. Unfortunately, the Chester county court records that might confirm this do not exist. The *Pa. Gaz.*, Jan. 12, 1764 , does refer to a Charles Hamilton for stealing a horse from Horsham Township, Philadelphia County. The description of "a Person who called himself Charles Hamilton . . . a small built person," who "pretends to be a Doctor," may be Mary/Charles Hamilton in Philadelphia County.

77. Prisoners for Trial Docket, 1790–1799.

78. This was also true for the two cross-dressing women arrested in Philadelphia. In 1797, Rosanna Stokes was "charged with being apprehended in the night disguised in Men's Clothes in the company with a Sailor." She was arrested under the vagrancy laws, kept in prison at hard labor for three months, and then released. She was probably engaged in sex commerce when arrested, because her treatment by the officials mimics that dealt out to prostitutes in the 1790s. Maryan Connelly (alias Hazel, or Hazellet) was arrested in 1801 for "dressing herself in mens cloths [and] running through the streets thereby rasing a great mob." Connelly persisted in her cross-dressing ways and was arrested two years later for "being dressed in a full suit of men's cloaths and in that situation she was found Rioting in the street." In both instances she was jailed for two months; Prisoners for Trial Docket, Sept. 7, 1797, Oct. 4, 1801, July 28, 1803.

79. Danforth, *The Cry of Sodom* . . . (Cambridge, Mass., 1674); Smith, *The Burning of Sodom* . . . (Boston, 1741).

80. Foster, "Locating Sodomy."

81. Crime pamphlets printed in Philadelphia focused exclusively on vice between men and women; Lyons, *Sex Among the Rabble*, 100, 369–372, 369n.21.

82. Domestically produced crime pamphlets were printed and sold by the same men who were actively involved in providing salacious English and French texts.

83. *Pa. Journal*, Mar. 10, 1747 (emphasis added).

84. For Philadelphia, see Lyons, *Sex Among the Rabble*. For sexual privilege of elite men elsewhere in 18th-century British North America see Kathleen M. Brown, *Good Wives, Nasty Wenches, and Anxious Patriarchs: Gender, Race, and Power in Colonial Virginia* (Chapel Hill, 1996); Sharon Block, "Lines of Color, Sex, and Service: Comparative Sexual Coercion in Early America," in Martha Hodes, ed., *Sex, Love, Race: Crossing Boundaries in North American History* (New York, 1999), 141–63; and Kirsten Fischer, *Suspect Relations: Sex, Race, and Resistance in Colonial North Carolina* (Ithaca, 2002).

85. Caleb Crain, "Leander, Lorenzo, and Castalio: An Early American Romance," *Early American Literature*, 33 (1998), 638; Journal of Leander [Mifflin], James Gibson Collection, HSP; Journal of Lorenzo [Gibson], ibid.

86. For an example of a man using female guise for sexual access to women see "Singular impostor," reprinted from a London paper in *Pa. Gaz.*, Nov. 11, 1789.

87. Bray, *Homosexuality in Renaissance England*; Maccubbin, ed., *'Tis Nature's Fault*; Trumbach, *Sex and the Gender Revolution, vol. 1: Heterosexuality and the Third Gender in Enlightenment London* (Chicago, 1998 ), "Sodomitical Subcultures," "Sex, Gender, and Sexual Identities," and "Birth of the Queen"; Kimmel, "'Greedy Kisses'"; Haggarty *Men in Love*; and Hitchcock and Cohen, *English Masculinities.*

88. Susan Juster, *Disorderly Women: Sexual Politics and Evangelicalism in Revolutionary New England* (Ithaca, 1994 ), presents one example of the heightened importance of masculinity as a unifying factor for men in the 1770s in her study of New England evangelicalism. Karin Wulf, *Not All Wives: Women of Colonial Philadelphia* (Ithaca, 2000), demonstrates the masculinization of Philadelphia's political culture and the eclipse of political participation of single women of property by the creation of the male republican polity.

89. Eric Foner, *Tom Paine and Revolutionary America* (New York, 1976); Gary B. Nash, *The Urban Crucible: The Northern Seaports and the Origins of the American Revolution* (Cambridge, Mass., 1979); Steven Rosswurm, *Arms, Country, and Class: The Philadelphia Militia and "Lower Sort" during the American Revolution, 1775–1783* (New Brunswick, N.J., 1987); Ronald Schultz, *The Republic of Labor: Philadelphia Artisans and the Politics of Class, 1720–1830* (New York, 1993).

90. Expanding male sexual privilege is evident in changes in the regulation of bastardy and treatment of male responsibility for out-of-wedlock children and in the changing treatment of sex commerce and adultery in early national Philadelphia. See Lyons, *Sex Among the Rabble,* on bastardy and sex commerce. Marybeth Hamilton Arnold, "'The Life of a Citizen in the Hands of a Woman': Sexual Assault in New York City, 1790 to 1820," in Kathy Peiss et al., eds., *Passion and Power: Sexuality in History* (Philadelphia, 1989), 35–56, also finds evidence of enhanced male sexual privilege that cut across class lines in early national New York. See her treatment of rape and the republican citizen.

91. For scholarship that supports this interpretation of the centrality of womanhood in the construction of the republican state also see Ruth H. Bloch, "The Gendered Meanings of Virtue in Revolutionary America," *Signs,* 13 (1987), 37–58; Joan R. Gunderson, "Independence, Citizenship, and the American Revolution," ibid., 59–77; James Jasinski, "The Feminization of Liberty, Domesticated Virtue, and the Reconstruction of Power and Authority in Early American Political Discourse," *Quarterly Journal of Speech,* 79 (1993), 146–64; and Carroll Smith-Rosenberg, "Dis-Covering the Subject in the 'Great Constitutional Discussion,' 1786–1789," *Journal of American History,* 79 (1992), 841–73.

# Part III

# Romantic Bonds in the Early Republic

*Chapter 8*

# An Excerpt from *Surpassing the Love of Men*

## Lillian Faderman

By the mid-eighteenth century, romantic friendship was a recognized institution in America too. In the eyes of an observer such as Moreau de St. Méry, who had just recently left Revolutionary France for America and must have been familiar with the accusations of lesbianism against Marie Antoinette, the women of her court, and most of the French actresses of the day, women's effusive display of affection for each other seemed sexual. Saint Méry, who recorded his observations of his 1793–1798 journey, was shocked by the "unlimited liberty" which American young ladies seemed to enjoy, and by their ostensible lack of passion toward men. The combination of their independence, heterosexual passionlessness, and intimacy with each other could have meant only one thing to a Frenchman in the 1790s: that "they are not at all strangers to being willing to seek unnatural pleasures with persons of their own sex."[1] It is as doubtful that great masses of middle- and upper-class young ladies gave themselves up to homosexual sex as it is that they gave themselves up to heterosexual sex before marriage. But the fiction of the period corroborates that St. Méry saw American women behaving openly as though they were in love with each other.

Charles Brockden Brown, the first professional American novelist, shows a particular interest in such love relationships. His early untitled fragment about the romantic friendship between Sophia and Jessica[2] demonstrates what Americans considered to be within the realm of the "natural" in female same-sex love, in contrast to St. Méry's observation about the "unnatural." In this fragment, Sophia and Jessica, both in their early twenties, exchange letters asserting their love:

> I want you so much. I long for you. Nay, I cannot do without you; so, at all
> events, you must come . . . You shall dine, sup, and sleep with me alone. I
> will have you all to myself. (SOPHIA TO JESSICA)

> What I feel for you I have not felt since I was sixteen, yet it cannot you know
> be love. Yet is there such a difference brought about by mere sex—my
> Sophia's qualities are such as I would doat upon in man. Just the same
> would win my whole heart; where then is the difference? On my word,
> Sophia, I see none. (JESSICA TO SOPHIA)

Jessica seems to have been destined to see a difference, since there is some
suggestion that the love between the two women in this unfinished work
was to be, as Brantome said about sex between women, an apprenticeship
to heterosexuality.[3] Because Jessica has learned to respond to the person
of Sophia, she has been prepared to respond to a man. Upon meeting
Colden, to whom she is powerfully attracted, she writes her friend, "Such
eyes, Sophia! They often made me think of yours." While not enough of
the fragment is finished so that we can be sure of what Brown actually intended to do with the heterosexual relationship (the man's name—Colden
—is certainly inauspicious), there are enough clues to suggest that he
thought to make it a central aspect of the novel.

Of course, both women, typical of romantic friends, vow never to
marry. They assure each other of the exclusivity and superiority of their
love and swear that they could never love men as they love each other:

> Truly, truly, thou art an admirable creature, Jessy, and I love thee, that I do.
> A friend! Till this age, and till I knew thee, I never had a friend, and shall
> never have another, of either sex; for surely the world contains not such an-
> other creature as thou: at least in the form of *man*. Single, then, Jessy, shall I
> ever be.

They talk about living together in sweet retirement in the country, an ideal
of romantic friendship which we saw in *Millenium Hall* and will see more
of in the story of Eleanor Butler and Sarah Ponsonby.

Their attachment is by no means simply ethereal. They claim to "have
fallen in love with" each other, and speak often of the physical as well as
the moral perfections of the other. There is a definite sensuous element in
their love. Jessica, for example, refers to one of her most joyous experiences of their conversational intimacies—which took place in a bed:

You honoured me once, you know, with your company for one night. How delighted was I . . . Shall I ever forget that night! We talked till past three; and such unbosoming of all your feelings, and all your pleasures and cares, and what you called your foibles; spots in the sunny brightness of your character. Ever since that night I have been a new creature; to be locked in your arms; to share your pillow with you, gave new force, new existence to the love which before united us; often shall we pass such nights when thou and I are safe together at Wortleyfield [where they plan to "retire"].

The height of bliss for these two romantic friends is to share secrets and to open their souls to each other, to "speak our love" as Katherine Philips wrote a century earlier. That is best done, however, "locked [in each other's] arms," in the dark on a bed. But since decent women of the eighteenth century could admit to no sexual desires, and decent men would not attribute such desires to them, the sensual aspect of their relationship goes no further in fiction, as it probably would not in life.

A male's relationship with another male was more likely suspected to have the worm in it. Even Brown, who viewed love between women with such indulgence, appears to have had quite different ideas about love between men.[4] In another fragment, "Memoirs of Stephen Calvert,"[5] a character describes the "depravity" of a man whose "associates were wholly of his own sex," and speaks of being "frozen with horror" at witnessing him with other men. What Brown intended finally to do with his homosexual male character is not known, but it is certain that he never regarded love between women in the same manner nor permitted any of his characters to express such distaste toward it.

Brown's novel *Ormond: or the Secret Witness* (1798), for which the Jessica fragment may have been a false start, presents a complete full-length treatment of love between women. Robert Hare has suggested that Brown was influenced in his portrayal of the love relationship between Constantia and Sophie by Rousseau's depiction of Julie and Claire's love in *La nouvelle Heloise* and by William Godwin's description of Mary Wollstonecraft's "ruling passion" for Fanny Blood in his *Memoir* of her.[6] But it was not necessary for Brown to turn to literature to discover romantic friendship between women; he needed only to look around him.[7]

The American ideals of romantic friendship were no different from the English according to *Ormond*. The important intimacy in the lives of Brown's two heroines is with each other, despite the fact that one of them is married. Men are treated with suspicion or barely treated at all. The women's fondest dream is to be together. A sensual aspect in their relationship is hinted at, but their great joy is in mere proximity and in "speaking their love."

The narrator of *Ormond* is Sophie Courtland, who had been raised with Constantia and who now tells Constantia's story. The two had been separated for four years while Sophie traveled in Europe after inheriting a good deal of money. During that time Constantia's once-wealthy father lost all his money and his health and Constantia became his supporter and comforter. With his death she finds herself quite alone, with the exception of the company of two women to whom she is briefly attracted before she discovers their faults. Constantia has also been attracted to and then quickly repelled by a type of gothic villain with supernatural powers—Ormond. Meanwhile, Sophie has married, but she returns alone to America to find Constantia and take her back to Europe. After a blissful reunion between the two women, Constantia goes to make a sentimental farewell to her childhood home. She again encounters Ormond, who locks her in a room and threatens to rape her. She vows to kill herself first, but when he retorts, "Living or dead, the prize that I have in view shall be mine," she kills him. Sophie arrives and releases her friend from the room. The two women go off to England together.

Constantia is not without some heterosexual feeling. At some point she is aroused by Ormond and upset by her discovery of "a passion deeper and less curable than she suspected." But nevertheless she cures it quickly, since she believes him to be an unsavory character. She knows that he has seduced and abandoned at least one young woman, and therefore she decides that "every dictate of discretion and duty" enjoins her to have nothing to do with him. Her passion for Ormond is somewhat of an anomaly in her life, since she had had little interest in men earlier and had even decided that she would prefer not to marry. Brown, himself a feminist,[8] attributes feminist arguments to her in this regard:

> Now she was at least mistress of the product of her own labour. Her tasks were toilsome, but the profits, though slender, were sure, and she administered her little property in what manner she pleased. Marriage would annihilate this power. Henceforth she would be bereft even of her personal freedom. So far from possessing property, she herself would become the property of another. . . . Homely liberty was better than splendid servitude.

She rejects not only Ormond, who may or may not have been willing to engage in a relationship as orthodox as marriage, but also an unnamed young man who courted her in the days of her father's prosperity and a character by the name of Balfour.

While she is generally suspicious of men, Constantia feels sympathy for and attraction to women. When she first sees Martinette in a music shop, she is haunted by her beauty and demeanor, which make a "powerful impression" on her. She has fantasies of their friendship and intimacy; "her heart sighed" for such a relationship, and she becomes "daily more enamoured" of Martinette. Helena, the young woman whom Ormond has seduced and abandoned, Constantia loves "with uncommon warmth." Her longing for Sophie, from whom she is separated for the first part of the novel, is characterized as being "pregnant with such agonizing tenderness, such heart-breaking sighs, and a flow of such bitter yet delicious tears, that it were not easily decided whether the pleasure or the pain surmounted."

Sophie has married a young man, Courtland, during her stay in Europe. While her affection for her friend Constantia is depicted in terms that twentieth-century popular novelists might use to describe that of a lover, her affection for her husband is portrayed in terms that today would be considered appropriate for a friend: We are told that there is between Sophie and Courtland "a conformity of tastes and views," and this gives rise to "tenderness," as compared with the passion between the two women. It would perhaps have been considered unseemly to depict such fiery intensity between a woman and a man, but detailed descriptions of the greatest passions between a woman and a woman were apparently not thought so. In any case, Brown makes absolutely no suggestion that passion existed between the husband and wife.

Although she is married, Sophie returns alone to America to look for Constantia. She claims that she would like to spend her life with Courtland in England, where her maternal family lives, but first it is "indispensable" to be reunited with Constantia and bring her to England too. "If this could not be accomplished," Sophie says, "it was my inflexible purpose to live and die with her." At the conclusion of the novel, the two women go together to England, where Courtland is waiting; and presumably they will be a *ménage à trois*. However, Constantia decides not to sell her childhood home because she hopes "that some future event will allow her to return to this favourite spot without forfeiture of [Sophie's] society." It is not clear what that event might be, but she seems to want to preserve inviolate

the place where the two women were once happy together without inter-
ference from other parties.

The relationship between Constantia and Sophie has nothing in common with "friendship" in a contemporary sense. The two women are totally involved with each other. As an initial sign of the intensity of their
love, Brown depicts Constantia fainting for joy when, after their long separation, she hears Sophie's familiar voice singing in an adjoining room (cf.
Maria's fainting in *Euphemia* when she hears that her beloved friend has
returned from America). When, prior to this reunion, Sophie thinks that
Constantia has died in the plague, "all hope of happiness" in this world
disappears, and she desires only "to join my friend" in death, where they
will never be separated. Once the two women are finally reunited, their ecstasy is overwhelming, as Sophie reports:

> The appetite for sleep and for food were confounded and lost amidst the
> impetuosities of a master passion. To look and to talk to each other afforded
> enchanting occupation for every moment. I would not part from her side,
> but ate and slept, walked and mused and read, with my arm locked in hers,
> and with her breath fanning my cheek. . . . O precious inebriation of the
> heart! O pre-eminent love! What pleasure of reason or of sense can stand in
> competition with those attendant upon thee? . . . Henceforth, the stream of
> our existence was to mix; we were to act and to think in common; casual
> witnesses and written testimony should become superfluous. Eyes and ears
> were to be eternally employed upon the conduct of each other; death, when
> it should come, was not to be deplored, because it was an unavoidable and
> brief privation to her that should survive.

Although the love between the two women is intoxicating and all-con-
suming, Brown does not suggest that it is genital, anymore than do other
eighteenth-century authors who deal with romantic friendships. In fact,
Sophie seems specifically to discount the genital possibilities of their passion by saying that nothing occurred during their nights in bed together
that was "incompatible with purity and rectitude." But Sophie clearly considers herself, as does Ormond her rival, to be Constantia's lover in all
other ways. For example, Ormond complains to Constantia that he knows
she was about to write him "that thy affections and person were due to another." When Sophie contemplates a union between Constantia and Ormond, she remarks, "I could not but harbour aversion to a scheme which

should tend to sever me from Constantia, or to give me a competitor in her affections."

Perhaps it is an indication of the relative independence of the eighteenth-century American woman that the heroine of this novel, unlike her English counterpart, is permitted to reject all her suitors and remain unmarried to the end of the book with no husband in sight—or perhaps the conclusion merely reflects the feminist convictions of the author that women should have such freedom. The love relationship between the two women goes beyond what Brown hints at in his earlier fragment about Jessica and Sophia, in which Jessica appears to be developing a strong heterosexual interest as the work breaks off. In *Ormond* the female-female love, despite the title of the work, is the central and most powerful relationship in the book, and it provides the happy ending.[9]

Helen Williams's novel, *Anecdotes of a Convent* (1771), shows how far romantic friendships could go without being thought questionable, that is, sexual. A subplot concerns Louisa, a lovely young woman who has just returned from a French convent where she had been sent to be educated. She is in a deep depression. Julia, one of the epistolary narrators, tells us that Louisa's "sorrows flow from the loss of a female friend." When at dinner Louisa's father inquires after Miss Merton as the friend "whom you was so wrapt up in at the convent," Louisa "turns pale and sinks off her chair." Julia learns after this scene that Louisa stayed at the convent two years longer than her parents had intended her to "because she could not be brought to leave the nunnery whilst her friend remained in it."

Julia, who finds Louisa's sorrows only somewhat excessive, comforts her as she lies in bed crying and sighing, and finally she learns Louisa's story. The first day at the convent Louisa met Fanny Merton: "I raised my eyes on her," Louisa says, "and felt as if my soul at that instant had darted through my breast into hers, there to take up its residence forever." Fanny returns her affection. She is an active young woman whose attention could be fixed by nothing but Louisa and books, "both of which were her passions . . . [and] tender only to me, the business of her life was to oblige me." When another attractive, lively girl comes to the convent, Louisa fears that she will be a rival for Fanny's affections, "and I looked on her, for that reason, with some degree of coldness," but Fanny remains faithful. Louisa is completely enthralled by her relationship. When she is taken to Paris she can enjoy nothing of the diversions; in the midst of the loveliness and grandeur, "I sighed in my heart for the hour which was to restore me to my friend Miss Merton." As the years go by, the intensity of her affection becomes greater still. The two wish only to be together every minute. When Louisa's father calls her home, "I trembled at the apprehension of being separated from my friend," and she convinces him she must stay at the convent longer.

When the Father Confessor attempts to get Louisa to convert to Catholicism, he uses the argument he believes will reach her the deepest: "Should you not be very sorry, after this life, to go to a place where your friend Miss Merton [who is Catholic] can never come. . . . You must *both* be of the same religion my Dear, or you can never meet in another world." Louisa, who misses his Catholic chauvinist meaning, nevertheless responds, "No place can be a heaven to me where she is not." When it appears that Fanny will be called home, Louisa reports, "I could not sleep, and I would not eat, so that in a few days I look'd like the picture of death, and had hardly the strength to crawl about the house."

All of this behavior is considered within the limits of appropriateness to passionate friendship. It is only after Fanny embraces her "violently," stifling her with kisses, that the reader is supposed to suspect that here is not the usual passionate friendship. Finally, it is learned that Frances Merton is really Francis Merton, who had been at birth placed in a convent by his Catholic mother, who did not want to honor the agreement with her Protestant husband that he would raise a boy child as a non-Catholic. In the reverse of Ovid's story of Iphis, at Francis's birth his mother told her husband that the boy was a girl. Francis, never having been informed of the difference between male and female, also believed himself to be a girl.

Once he discovers his sex, he can ask Louisa to marry him. But it is significant that their love is viewed as unchanged, except for the possibility of its permanence now. Francis asks, "Will you not love me as well as you did when you were ignorant of my sex? Yes, I know you will—you must—my heart is not alter'd by the change, why then should that of my beloved Louisa's?" The only distinctions, then, that are made between romantic friendship and heterosexual love in this eighteenth-century novel are that the latter is manifested by "violent" embraces and kisses, and that no one can separate the heterosexual lovers. These are also the major distinctions in most other novels of the period that deal with both romantic friendship and heterosexual love.

NOTES

Editor's note: This chapter is excerpted from Lillian Faderman's groundbreaking 1981 book, *Surpassing the Love of Men*, pp. 109–117. Copyright © 1981 by Lillian Faderman. Reprinted by permission of HarperCollins Publishers.

1. *Moreau de St. Méry's American Journey, 1793–1798,* trans. and ed. Kenneth Roberts and Anna M. Roberts (Garden City: NY: Doubleday, 1947), pp. 285–86.

2. *The Life of Charles Brockden Brown, Together with Selections from the Rarest of His Printed Works, from His Original Letters, and from His Manuscripts Before Unpublished,* ed. William Dunlap (Philadelphia: James P. Parke, 1815), Vol. I, pp. 107–69.

3. Brantome, *Lives of Fair and Gallant Ladies* (first complete edition, 1665), trans. A. R. Allinson (New York: Liveright, 1933), p. 131.

4. He shared the views of his countrymen. Male homosexuality had been punishable by death in the colonies. In 1777, Thomas Jefferson pleaded for "liberalizing" Virginia law, making sodomy punishable by castration, in Jonathan Katz, *Gay American History* (New York: Thomas Crowell, 1976), p. 24.

5. *The Life of Charles Brockden Brown,* Vol. II.

6. Constantia's reunion with Sophia is described in terms of "the impetuosities of a master passion," Robert Rigby Hare, "Charles Brockden Brown's *Ormond:* The Influence of Rousseau, Godwin, and Mary Wollstonecraft," Ph.D. dissertation, University of Maryland, 1967.

7. The notion seems hard for many twentieth-century critics to accept since contemporary women are more guarded in their expressions of affection toward other women. Since modern scholars have so little chance to witness actual romantic friendships, they generally assume that it is a literary convention with strictly literary models or that the author was making some subtle remark about his characters' "abnormality." See Ernest Marchaud, introduction to *Ormand* (New York: American Book Co., 1937), p. xxxii, who calls the relationship between the two girls in Brown's novel, "almost unnatural"; and Harry R. Warfel, *Charles Brockden Brown: American Gothic Novelist* (Gainesville: University of Florida Press, 1949), p. 132, who suggests it is an "abnormal relationship." Donald A. Ringe, *Charles Brockden Brown* (New York: Twayne Publishers, 1966), pp. 60–61, attempts to explain the girls' closeness by the fact that they "were reared together," which would "understandably bind them to one another," but still finds something uncomfortably Sapphic about it and concludes that "at best, the relationship is not one to increase the stature of Constantia as the heroine of the novel." Those twentieth-century critics who see Constantia as the ideal woman often have a difficult time when they attempt to reconcile her perfection with her passion for another woman; thus, they tend to ignore the intense love relationship which is central to the novel, or they defensively assert, as David Lee Clark does, that there is no evidence that Constantia is a "victim of homosexuality" and drop the subject at that.

One of the most blatant examples of a critic's inability to distinguish between his own expectations and those of a reader from another century is found in Leslie Fiedler, *Love and Death in the American Novel* (1952; revised edition New York: Stein and Day, 1966). Fiedler states that Brown's contemporaries did not like the novel because they did not know what to make "of such a perverse reversal of the expected terms of affection" and that while they could have understood and responded to love between the Pure Maiden and her brutal Seducer, they could not have been sympathetic to love "between the Maiden and an old girl friend." But if reading audiences were so confused and upset by the depiction of romantic friendship, the theme would not have appeared so frequently in the most commercially intended novels. Nor is there any reason to believe that *Ormond* was as unsuccessful as Fiedler implies: the first edition sold out completely in England within the first year and a second edition was brought out almost immediately (1800). A short time later it was translated into German and published in Leipzig (1802). While *Ormond* did not go into a second printing in America, neither did any of Brown's other novels.

8. See, for example, Brown's *Alcuin,* a dialogue about the rights of woman; David Lee Clark, "Brockden Brown and the Rights of Women," *University of Texas Bulletin,* No. 2212 (March 22, 1922); and Augusta Genevieve Violette, "Economic Feminism in American Literature Prior to 1848," *University of Maine Studies,* Second Series, No. 2 (Orono, 1925).

9. Twentieth-century critics, however, have not been so satisfied with this ending. Robert Hare, "Charles Brockden Brown's *Ormond,*" pp. 216–18, for example, protests, "If, as Brown seems to say, the sum of all Constantia's virtues leads to spinsterhood, the confrontation seems hardly worthwhile. . . . She certainly deserves better than spinsterhood."

*Chapter 9*

# Leander, Lorenzo, and Castalio
## *An Early American Romance*

## *Caleb Crain*

On 1 August 1786, a Princeton undergraduate wrote of his twenty-seven-year-old friend, "after recitation [I] went to Leander—he gave me a hair ribbon and I promised to sleep with him to night" (Lorenzo 58). More than two centuries later, it is hard to read this sort of diary entry without either exaggerating or pooh-poohing its hint of sex. In the late eighteenth century, male friends often shared a bed, and many gentlemen were fastidious about their personal appearance. However, the entry does show a man flattering a boy's vanity, in a relationship where the two are easy and familiar with each other's bodies.

Gay love as we know it is modern, and as Thoreau wrote, "the *past* cannot be *presented*" (155). However, close examination in context of the language men used in early America to describe and convey their feelings may reduce the anachronism of our understanding. Such an examination may also cast light on the peculiar ambition of classic American literature to represent the nation's spirit as male-male love, according to a metaphoric logic that in D. H. Lawrence's opinion climaxed with the Whitmanian equation of "The last merging. The last Democracy. The last love. The love of comrades" (178). Two diaries I have examined, of John Fishbourne Mifflin (1759–1813) and James Gibson (1769–1856), offer a uniquely detailed and extensive chronicle of passion between men in early America. Under the cognomens of Leander and Lorenzo, Mifflin and Gibson wrote for each other and about each other. Two volumes (546 pages) of Mifflin's diary survive, and one volume (100 pages) of Gibson's. Read in conjunction

Reprinted from *Early American Literature*, vol. 33. A more detailed version of this essay appears in *American Sympathy: Men, Friendship, and Literature in the New Nation* by Caleb Crain (New Haven: Yale University Press, 2001).

with the family correspondence of a third young man, Isaac Norris III (known as Castalio), these diaries tell a story of affection between American men at a crucial moment: at the acme of the culture of sentiment and sensibility, when individuals first considered following the unruly impulse of sympathy as far as it would go. The men's writings also sensitively register the period's changing ideal of literary beauty: the diaries begin as marks of refinement, like fancy ribbons gentlemen might add to their coiffures, but they gradually break into gestures—exposures of the self that attempt to let out something unexpected.

Where the Second Bank of the United States now stands, on Chestnut Street between Fourth and Fifth streets in Philadelphia, one block east of Independence Hall, the Norris family once grew a famously elegant garden. Charles Norris had built his house on the western edge of the city, but Philadelphia grew outward to meet the Norrises: by the 1780s, their home enviably combined rural proportions with urban location. The Quaker matron Ann Warder recorded in her diary on 18 October 1786 that the Norrises "have a noble house and beautiful garden, which are rare in this city" (Cadbury 54).

The Norris garden was a mix of beauty and science typical of the eighteenth century. They, or the Swiss gardener they employed for twenty-five years, raised pineapples in their hothouse and medicinal herbs in their herbarium. Just outside the window of the back parlor, a palisade of scarlet honeysuckle, sweetbriar, and roses enclosed a terrace shaded by catalpas. Further down grew willows, the first trees of the species ever brought to the region, a gift from Benjamin Franklin. To reach the garden proper, one descended a flight of stone steps into a neoclassical design of "square parterres and beds, regularly intersected by graveled and grass walks and alleys." Espaliers of fine grapes led to a rustic-style cottage that lodged one of the women whom the Norrises were always too tactful to call a servant. The garden was a kind of jewel. The balance and order of its design, the attention to previously unknown species, and the fastidious upkeep of the grounds spoke of the Norrises' "taste and industry" (Logan, *Norris House* 3–11).

On Saturday, 20 May 1786, John Fishbourne Mifflin rambled through the Norris garden alone, a frequent habit. At about 127 pounds, he was a slight figure. He carried a cane, which as a twenty-seven year old he did not quite need. He was very nearsighted. His powdered hair was gathered at the rear into a fashionable queue. He was the sort of man that children threw snowballs at-finicky about his appearance, mildly pompous in his manners, and too delicate to do much harm if he caught the offender. His father had been a successful merchant; he was a lawyer with a trust fund. He spent most of his days either sipping tea with Philadelphia ladies or trying to collect rent from his own or his half-brother's tenants.[1]

On this visit, as on most of his visits to the Norris garden, Mifflin headed to the pear grove. It was his favorite spot, "the scene of friendship," he called it in his diary (Leander 1: 3). "Dear delightful spot," he wrote, "it sheds a charming influence over my spirits" (1: 47). As Richard Bushman has noted, an eighteenth-century genteel garden was meant to be "an extension of the parlor, a place where polite people walked and conversed" (130). It was intended as a backdrop for highly staged, decorous socializing; if the garden was sufficiently scientific, it could provide a topic of conversation as well. Mifflin, however, did not visit the Norris garden's pear grove to show off his knowledge of botany or to court women. (Or rather, not exclusively for these reasons: on another day he would gather hyacinths to catch the interest of young Mary Rhoads who lived next door [2: 211].) He sat in the pear grove because "it always brings Lorenzo [James Gibson] affectionately to my mind" (1: 8). He came to meditate on a young friend and on the pleasures of friendship.

An alluring new fashion in selfhood had caught Mifflin's imagination: sympathy. His pining in the garden defied the rules of politeness, which would have disapproved of the imprudence of missing an absent friend when other companions could be found. And it had even less to do with republican virtue, the starchy ethic that politeness had displaced. Like politeness, sympathy looked toward others; like virtue, it came from deep inside the self. Sympathy thus trumped both virtue's solipsism and politeness's superficiality. But unlike either virtue or politeness, sympathy seemed free. Friendships inspired by it seemed cut loose from the financial duties and political allegiances that had constrained traditional relationships. Sympathy fascinated Mifflin, who studied its vicissitudes as if it were a caught animal he had untethered as an experiment.[2]

Mifflin's reveries in the Norris pear grove are among the earliest entries in his diary. They are a strange mix of emptiness and superfluity: an actorless stage cluttered with props. He was trying to take hold of someone who was not there; he was trying to produce an absence and then preserve it. In order not to lose his bittersweet longing for his friend, Mifflin attempted to write it down. Precious emotions had come over him in surplus, and he wanted to invest the excess back into the scene that had produced it.

Well read in British literature, Mifflin turned to a fragmented novelistic style to bank his feelings against time's usury. In Richardson's novels, time had flowed fitfully, released in discrete, intermittent quanta. This stop-and-go pace had begun as a side-effect of epistolary form, but writers were discovering in it new emotional possibilities. Sterne exploded the sequence of his scenes with ekphrastic commentary to see if the fragments could be made to cohere into a new emotional sense. The power of sympathy and the structure of plot had squared off evenly in Richardson, but sentimentalists would increasingly side with the power against the structure. They prefer to hover over what Wordsworth would later call "spots of time" (428). They wanted their emotions to accumulate. Since time and plot would only squander feelings, the sentimentalists described special scenes where a gap in time collapsed into a place, where "feeling comes in aid / Of feeling," never dissipated by result (Wordsworth 432). Mifflin's pear-grove tableau thus marks him as a sophisticated belletrist, up-to-date on literary techniques evolving across the Atlantic and quick to adopt recent innovations as he constructs for himself an *aide-sentiment*.

Mifflin first met his young friend Gibson at 6 P.M. on 14 March 1785; he set down an account of the event in his diary two years afterward, as one of his "happy anniversaries." On that early spring night, Mifflin joined an audience of nearly eight hundred to hear a blind philosopher named Moyes visiting from Europe.[3]

> We happened to meet on the front row of the gallery at one of Dr. Moyes's lectures—It was on electricity—the gallery was crowded & I was indebted to my new friend for a seat—His gentle manners & modest politeness made me feel an immediate attachment to him—when the lecture was over we returned home together—& at parting made an appointment to meet at the next lecture. (Leander 2: 213)

Fifteen years old, James Gibson was an earnest and quiet Princeton undergraduate. While Mifflin probably attended Moyes's lecture because electricity was a voguish topic, Gibson would have gone because he took his education seriously. Mifflin wrote that Gibson was "a handsome lad" but not prepossessing (1: 13). To borrow Mifflin's condescending turn of phrase, "My little friend is not a prominent or striking character, but of that amiable kind for which your esteem increases with your acquaintance" (1: 184). He weighed about five pounds less than Mifflin, but people matured more slowly in those days, and Gibson would have continued to grow for another decade (later that year, he would write to his mother asking for "another pair of breeches as I have but too [*sic*] and they are both too short at the knees"). Like Mifflin, Gibson had a "taste for old fashioned queues," sometimes with a wig extension, but one does not get the impression he was quite as dapper as his older friend. For one thing, he did not have as much money to spend on his appearance. Although he employed a hairdresser named Barlowe, Gibson had to bargain to be able to afford his services. Gibson's father, mayor of Philadelphia in 1771 and 1772, had died three years earlier, after losing most of his capital in a series of financial misfortunes. Gibson's family was genteel but no longer wealthy. They lived in an "obscure and humble residence" that Gibson's sisters, who would soon be looking for husbands, looked upon with "Mortification." This house stood at Chestnut Street above Fourth Street, the same block as the Norris House.[4]

Gibson's family must have made a considerable sacrifice in order to send him to Princeton; he appears to have tried hard to deserve it.[5] In his diaries, he is diligent to the point of overwork, parsing out his hours with strict economy. Mifflin reports hearing that he was at the top of his class, although it's impossible to know if this was fact or flattery (Leander 1: 136). To relax, Gibson played battledores (badminton) and pitched quoits (horseshoes). His only rebellion against the numbing regime of rote memorization was an occasional dry comment, like this the night before an exam: "Euclid is wished into non existence by many" (Lorenzo 90).

When Mifflin wrote that Gibson had "a prudence beyond his years," he might have been putting a nice spin on Gibson's adolescent awkwardness (1: 85). Whenever the college boys roughhoused, it was always Gibson who got injured. His roommate John Rhea Smith, who also kept a diary, was rowdier and more lackadaisical in his studies, much more adept at provoking and then charming away the frowns of their tutor Gilbert Snowden. "After dinner scuffle with Reed, Furman & Gibson in the entry," Smith recorded on 10 January 1786. "Enter the Room & lock the door on Gibson who bursts it open & falls—Gilbert sees him & enters the room immediately after—[. . .] he reproves it as imprudent & very wrong but at the same time scar[c]ely keeps from laughter." In a free-for-all slicing competition for pie on 12 June, Smith "came off not very successfully though I had better fate than poor James my roommate who lost unfortunately part of his thumb in the fray." On 1 August, Gibson was "walking out in the campus when one of the Lads flung a stone and struck me on the Leg" (Lorenzo 59). Gibson was liked and accepted by his classmates—

he was a member of the Cliosophic Society, a debating club, where his secret name was Decius—but the string of accidents suggests he was not entirely at ease with them.

The klutzy and dutiful Gibson would have been an unlikely match for
the sociable and dandyish Mifflin, but Mifflin was always on the lookout
for a new friend. It was a habit, not a coincidence, for John Mifflin to
strike up a new acquaintance in a public place. Consider, for instance, the
adventure recorded in Mifflin's diary for 30 January 1787. Mifflin had gone
to the theater alone. "I had no body near me that I knew to talk to which is
very requisite to enjoy a play." Fortunately, Mifflin soon picked out from
among the masses a "young gentleman [. . . who] was very genteelly
dressed & seemed to be much in my own situation without any person he
cared for near him—I touched him on the shoulder with my cane & made
room for him between myself & a jolly looking dame of vulgar deport-
ment." Since the young gentleman's previous benchmates had been crowd-
ing him and drinking grog, he was grateful for Mifflin's offer. "Upon the
whole his getting next to me was an event 'to be wished'—for by us both
—he was very clever & appeared to be in his teens—I found he was a Mr
Coxe" (2:141–43). Together the two formed an island of cool gentility
among the rabble. They ratified each other's delicacy, sharing severe criti-
cisms of the performance that the other audience members were too lost
in riotous enjoyment to appreciate. In the absence of Mr. Coxe, no one
would have witnessed the insult to Mifflin's critical faculties inflicted by
the evening's pantomime sequence, which involved an elephant. Mifflin's
meeting with Coxe is so similar to his first meeting with Gibson as almost
to amount to a technique. Good manners gave sensitive young men a code
by which to recognize each other.

Cognomens were another important element in this code. As David S.
Shields has noted in his pioneering study *Civil Tongues & Polite Letters in
British America,* cognomens were "fixed personae" that helped to define a
space of cultural play. They "aestheticized conversation by distancing it
from the mundane talk of familiars" (263–64). When Gibson joined the
Cliosophic Society, he was given the cognomen Decius. The renaming sig-
naled that as a member, he would act to some extent as a new person. The
new name also marked out an aspect of Gibson's self as the club's domain,
a part of his identity that the Cliosophists but no one else knew how to
summon. In a similar way, when Gibson took the name Lorenzo, he sur-
rendered a hold on his self to another group, much more rarefied and
flexible and powerful than any undergraduate fraternity: the society of

well-educated, well-connected Philadelphia Quaker gentry. The Norrises, Logans, Wisters, Pembertons, Dickinsons, Fishers, and their friends and relatives prided themselves on their spirit as well as their station. Every young man and woman in their circle had a cognomen; the alias certified membership in a playful, intimate group with literary taste. Deborah Norris Logan was Ardelia; Sarah Wister was Laura (Derounian). Sally Fisher was Amelia; George Logan was Altamont; Richard Wistar was Horatio (Sweeney; Logan to Fisher). When Joshua Fisher courted Hannah Pemberton, he addressed his love letters to Cleora and signed them as Philander. The names represented one's social persona, like a marker in a board game. The Cliosophic Society swore Decius to secrecy; if Gibson disclosed that identity, he would betray his fellows.[6] But Gibson did not need to hide Lorenzo; he needed to reveal him, selectively.

Mifflin's nom de plume was Leander. In Greek myth, Leander swam the Hellespont every night to reach his beloved Hero, until one stormy night the torch she lit to guide him blew out, and he drowned. Mifflin was known as Leander to the Norris circle as early as November 1779, long before he met Gibson (Sweeney 196).

Lorenzo might have been named after the lover in *The Merchant of Venice*, but more likely for the reckless youth of Edward Young's *Night Thoughts*. Mifflin's diary quotes *Night Thoughts*'s most famous line: "Procrastination is the thief of time" (Leander 1: 223). If Mifflin chose the name, he probably chose it not so much because Gibson resembled the character Lorenzo—who is giddy, indolent, and in need of reformation—as because the poem addressed Lorenzo the way Mifflin wanted to address Gibson. "Thou say'st I preach, LORENZO!" Young wrote; "'Tis confess'd" (29). The narrator's tone, sometimes hectoring, sometimes doting, always pleased with his own advice, is very much the tone Mifflin adopted. Mifflin wanted to be Gibson's patron; he wanted to provide and help. Concerned about Gibson's public speaking, the older man wrote orations for him to deliver at his debating club (Leander 2: 15–18,100). As graduation approached, Mifflin used his connections to find Gibson a job as an apprentice in Mordecai Lewis's counting house (2: 119). Mifflin did not want Gibson to become a lawyer, Mifflin's own career choice, because he felt lawyers were "a rapacious set of cormorants feasting & fattening upon the miseries & misfortunes of their fellow citizens," and he knew Gibson was too kindhearted to "brook such an ungracious ungenerous inurbane line of life, the prosperity of which depends on the wretchedness of thousands" (2: 57–58). There is something disingenuous about Mifflin's asking

Gibson to be a purer sentimentalist than he ever was, and Gibson must have seen through some of the posturing, because he eventually would become a lawyer despite Mifflin's mentorship.

Although Mifflin and Gibson met on 14 March 1785, Gibson did not begin his diary until 6 February 1786. Mifflin began his even later, on 22 May 1786. Surprisingly, the idea of keeping a diary probably came from Gibson's Princeton roommate, Smith, who started his on 1 January 1786. Not introspective, Smith might have decided to keep a journal to figure out why his days accomplished so little. His journal aspires to be evidence of his good intentions to study longer and harder, but his resolve almost always fails, and the entries instead record the pranks and socializing that distracted him. In the typical entry, Smith sleeps late, tries to memorize a geometry lesson or write a composition until he admits that "my attention [is] diverted from study," arrives at recitation unprepared, gets caught in some collegiate misdemeanor, stays up late talking with his friends, and goes to bed realizing he forgot to exercise (Smith, 2 January 1786; Woodward 46: 273). It's a sociable diary. There are many friends and no cognomens, and Smith chronicles the politicking of the Cliosophic Society in detail.

When Gibson started his diary, he modeled it on Smith's. The layout of Gibson's pages is nearly identical to Smith's: the day of the week and date, without the month, appear flush left, and the entry follows immediately in a smaller script. In the beginning, Gibson also followed Smith in using his journal as more of a memorandum book than an aid to self-reflection. Since Gibson was a straight arrow where Smith was a troublemaker, in Gibson's case the plain-style reporting sounds fairly banal:

> 5 o'clock had a tooth-ach which prevented my studying much, but left me at 8 o'clock, When I eat a hearty breakfast. Half after, had some cakes sent from Dr. Smiths, which being a rarity I liked very well at 10 went to recitation, recited 6 propositions of the fifth Book beginning at the second. (Lorenzo I)

Like Smith, Gibson used no cognomens, at least not in his early entries. On 8 March 1786, he prosaically referred to his friend as "Mr. Mifflin" (22).

The first entry in Mifflin's diary opens in a tone almost as perfunctory and mechanical:

> Went with Lorenzo to wait on Dr Rush—not at home—talked with the ladies awhile and then withdrew—In the afternoon on business—very absent

—Went twice out of my way—Drank tea with Mrs. G.—took leave of my dear Lorenzo—God bless him. (Leander 1: 1)

Princeton separated Gibson from Mifflin. The merchant-lawyer had brought Gibson with him on several trips—in October 1785 to Lancaster (M. Norris to Isaac, 28 October 1785), and in April 1786 to Nottingham (Leander 2: 87)—but still regretted that they could not spend more time together. He could to some extent compensate by visiting the boy's mother, "Mrs. G.," to gossip about James, but he still felt lonely. Mifflin later wrote that his journal "began by the desire of Lorenzo" (1: 195); Gibson must have suggested it to Mifflin as a way to ease the pain of parting when he left for school on 12 May 1786.

Mifflin's first entry is colorless, but the words "very absent" hint at what will break out of the dry journalizing. The observation might mean that the debtors Mifflin was dunning were not to be found, but more likely it describes Mifflin's state of mind. Gibson would not have thought to notice such a thing, but Mifflin can't help it. He lost his way twice, because he was paying no more attention to his course than Laurence Sterne did when he wandered into Paris without a passport, in his distraction forgetting that England and France were at war. Mifflin's sympathies were drifting away from him, tugging him along, engaged by the person whose name begins and ends the entry—Lorenzo.

Mifflin never calls Gibson by his proper name. From page one Gibson is Lorenzo. In Mifflin's diary, Dr. Benjamin Rush appears undisguised, as do other respectable adult figures, including Benjamin Franklin, Hugh Brackenridge, Thomas Paine, and James Madison. But grown-ups who are Mifflin's intimates get abbreviations, and young men and women who provoke Mifflin's sentiments have fanciful aliases. The widow Mary Parker Norris, proprietor of the Norris House and its garden, appears as Mrs. N.; her three sons are called Castalio (Isaac, the oldest), Josephus (Joseph Parker), and Carolus (Charles, the youngest). Deborah Norris had been Ardelia when she was single and writing to her girlfriends, but she had married George Logan in 1781 and in Mifflin's diary appears as Mrs. L. James Gibson is Lorenzo, of course; his mother is Mrs. G.; and his younger brother John is Johannes or Jean. In the Rhoads family, who also lived on the Norrises' block, the widowed mother Sarah is Mrs. R.; her daughters Elizabeth and Mary are Eliza and Maria; and her twelve-year-old son Samuel is Ascanius. There are also a young woman known as Leonora, a deceased friend known as Eugenius, and a young man with the epithet "the young squire," none of whom I have been able to identify.[7]

The early pages of Mifflin's diary are restless with the knowledge that the diary is not an adequate substitute for the young man for whom it is written. "Not in very high spirits," Mifflin writes on day two. "In the morning rambled in the garden—missed my friend" (1: 1). Gradually Mifflin's heartsickness takes on a texture, and the absence of Lorenzo, dwelled upon, becomes an uneasy presence.

> Read Biography & travels to pass away the time—not in a reading humour —After dinner in the figits—did not know what to do with myself—scribbled to Nort[h]ampton—walked about—tumbled over different books— dull dismal weather still continues—hope Lorenzo has a fire and takes bark—wish he or Castalio were here—such days lag heavily without a Friend. (1: 7)

"How I want a confidant," Mifflin writes (1: 7). Left alone, Mifflin seems agitated and overwhelmed by his own sentiments. Freud might have explained Mifflin's complaint as the depredations of unbound libido, erring without an object. Mifflin might have explained the remedy he wanted by quoting Cicero to Atticus: "There are many things to worry and vex me, but once I have you here to listen I feel I can pour them all away in a single walk and talk" (Cicero 49).

Lacking an immediate auditor, Mifflin at first told his stories with abortive brevity. "Vexed at the insolence of *some people*," he writes in an early entry, declining to specify who offended or what the offense might have been (1: 2). On another day, "Heard something in the evening which put me in spirits-a proposal of a friend which met my entire approbation," again left unexplained (1: 6). Mifflin's early diary is full of the unsaid, but Mifflin himself gives the key to the puzzles: "pland something [. . .] which I will tell Lorenzo when I see him" (1: 7). The ellipses were meant to provoke Gibson's curiosity. When they met again, the two would read each other's diaries together; to spark conversation, the text was left deliberately incomplete. "This morning we examined the first volume of my journal," Mifflin wrote during one such reunion, "& I explained to him certain blanks & other things which he did not understand" (2: 7–8).

But one of the lessons a diary teaches is the stunning amount that one forgets. Mifflin might have discovered the hard way that he could no longer remember the anecdotes behind some of his earliest telegraphic en-

tries, because after about a month, Mifflin struggles to get down the outline of the stories he wants to tell. Then he starts to add detail. The diary
gets richer. For example: "A visit from the 'Private Secretary'—has grown
monstrous fat and lusty—alias *pinguid* (a newfashioned word) & think he
bids fair to be big enough for an alderman" (1: 25). His vanity piqued, Mifflin has also started to fret about whether or not his diary is amusing. He
spices up his vocabulary (*cozily* is another "new word," 2: 129) and rounds
his stories out.

By contrast, Gibson elaborates his narrative rarely in its first two
months. Even when he passes on "a rumour that the Devile was seen in
college wrapt up in a white sheet," his only follow-up is a laconic "I did
not see him" (Lorenzo 4). April and May are missing, probably misplaced
in one of Mifflin and Gibson's exchanges of diary installments by mail.
But when the diary picks up again in June (Lorenzo 25), something has
happened: Gibson is calling Mifflin "Leander." He has started to use the
abbreviation "N.B." at the end of his entries to introduce an entertaining
detail that somehow got left out of the day's narrative—a writerly tic of
Mifflin's. And he has a new refrain:

> expected a letter from Leander though[t] of him (25)
> wished to hear from Leander and his journal (26)
> wished to hear from Leander and read his journal—intend to devote to
> morrow in writing to him—a fine Day—at five used exercise—thouthght
> of Leander (26)

Gibson misses Mifflin with the same plodding mechanical repetition
that he does his chores, memorizes Euclid, and eats three square meals a
day. Nonetheless it's a new element. Gibson is now studying and rehearsing sentiment with the same oxlike effort he applied to geometry. His textbook is Mifflin's journal; reading Mifflin's plaintive, lonely entries must
have embarrassed Gibson into imitation. The boy's progress exemplifies
an aphorism Mifflin once quoted at a tea party: "a sentiment of Rochefou-
cault's 'that people would never be *in love* if they had never heard of such a
thing'" (Leander 2: 122). Mifflin saw to it that Gibson heard of love, and
taught him how to pine about it expressively.

But who taught Mifflin? Mifflin read widely, and friendship seems to
have been one of his favorite topoi· he quotes Pope and Akenside on the
subject (1: 15, 169; 2: 180). He was practiced in journal-writing (he had
kept one as a boy) and in friendships (several young men had preceded

Gibson). But Mifflin's most instructive apprenticeship may not have been to books or to other men, but to a woman.

Mifflin was neither the only nor the first person to frequent the Norris pear grove in a sentimental mood. In 1780, Deborah Norris had set an ode to friendship in a "sylvan scene" resembling it (Delia, "Again the sun"). According to Shields, the garden as "an experimental haven for the heart" was at the time as conventional in genteel American women's poetry as neoclassical cognomens were (130). Shortly after her brother Isaac Norris III left for Europe in 1783, Deborah visited the spot before writing to tell him how much she missed him. "The House looks gloomy. I sat half an hour the other day under the pear tree in ye garden indulging a kind of pleasing Melancholy. I do not love to see things going to decay, and yet it raises ideas that soothe my mind" (Logan to Norris, 7 August [1783?]). In the same letter, Deborah referred approvingly to Isaac's friend "Leander," who had stayed behind in Pennsylvania.

In their youth, John Mifflin and Deborah Norris had been close. She had called him "an agreeable friend of mine," despite the "poor opinion of platonic sentiments" other people held, carefully signaling that he was not a suitor (letter to Sally Fisher, n.d., Sweeney 215). In 1779, Mifflin had pestered Deborah about the letters she and her girlfriends were exchanging, until she was charmed into betraying their intimacies. "Thee will laugh it my folly," Deborah wrote to Sarah Wister,

> indeed it is what thee can't avoid doing when I tell thee, that I have been prevailed upon to read part of this letter to J. Mifflin. I read (to divert too close an attention excuse me Sally) an extract of thine, he liked the style it was sprightly and interesting, he praised it had never been so happy before as to see any of thy productions see it, he did not, he sat at a respectful distance and I culld out the prettiest part of what thee wrote. (2 August 1779, Derounian 513)

He also asked Deborah to show him Sally Fisher's letters, but in that case Deborah claimed to her friend that "I did not satisfy his curiosity—Shall I do it, my dear!" (Sweeney 197).

Years later, when a cluster of young belles cornered Mifflin at a tea party and asked whether he kept a journal, he tried to be vague about the details. "I acknowledged I kept a sort of a register of new ideas opinion & sentiments—& some incidents—but particularly travelling adventures Miss R. seemed very desirous to know how it was conducted—(I thought with a view of regulating her own)" (Leander 2: 208). In his sniffy reticence, Mifflin was conveniently forgetting how many of his sentimental habits he had learned by snooping on women, and on Deborah Norris Logan in particular.

In her groundbreaking essay, "The Female World of Love and Ritual," Carroll Smith-Rosenberg discovered in early America an emotionally intense community of female friendship "in which men made but a shadowy appearance" (53). The story of Mifflin and Gibson suggests that that world had a male complement. But the interaction between Mifflin and Deborah Norris Logan also suggests that the border between the two worlds may have been more porous than Smith-Rosenberg estimated.[8]

Smith-Rosenberg also established that female friendships, far from being stigmatized, amounted to a cultural norm in antebellum America. Because research on male friendships is scantier, it is unclear whether John Mifflin's chronic friendliness was a rule or an exception, but the obstacle to interpretation here is not a scarcity of material but an overabundance. "As rational equalitarian friendship was neither habitual [. . .] nor dangerously passionate," Jay Fliegelman has observed, "it was hailed in numerous eighteenth-century volumes as the ideal relationship" (41). Friendship was everywhere during the period; it coats every surface men exposed to each other with cottony, saccharine rhetoric (Ditz).

It was not unusual in the eighteenth century for a man to keep a journal expressly for another man. Boswell hoped that his London journal would "be of use to my worthy friend Johnston, . . . while he laments my personal absence," and mailed it to him in installments (40). Nor was it unheard of for gentlemen to exchange the word *love*. In 1779, Alexander Hamilton wrote to John Laurens that he wished it were in his power "to convince you that I love you. I shall only tell you that 'till you bade us Adieu, I hardly knew the value you had taught my heart to set upon you. [. . .] You should not have taken advantage of my sensibility to steal into my affections without my consent." Daniel Webster proposed bachelor marriage to James Hervey Bingham in 1804, vowing that "Yes, James, I must come; we will yoke together again; your little bed is just wide enough; we will practise at the same bar, and be as friendly a pair of single fellows as ever cracked a nut."[9] In both cases, although the affection seems genuine, the tone is somewhat arch. Hamilton and Webster are addressing the language of courtship to a male friend; they relish the misapplication, but the extravagance of their conceits signals that they know, and their readers know, it is a misapplication. In both Webster's and Hamilton's correspondence, vows of friendship were accompanied by political news, delivered with a touch of melodrama, and by in-depth analysis of their personal careers—the same distinctive mix to be found in Cicero's letters to Atticus. To some extent the young men were striking a pose: the passionate young hero of the republic.

Mifflin records his social milieu in such detail that if he were shunned as deviant, his diary would betray it. I could find no evidence that polite society considered Mifflin's behavior to be outside its norms. Mifflin's friendship with Gibson was no secret. Gibson had to ask his Princeton professors for permission to spend the night with Mifflin when he visited. In Philadelphia, Mifflin was a frequent guest of Gibson's mother; he was welcome to sleep in James's bed whether or not James was at home. Mrs. Gibson enclosed Mifflin's letters to her son inside her own (Lorenzo 40). When Mifflin failed to write, Gibson would ask his mother for news of him (J. Gibson to "Mama"). Mary Parker Norris, the mother of Mifflin's friend Isaac, also welcomed Mifflin into her house and her son's bed. She mentions Mifflin's new friendship with Gibson in letters to family and friends (to H. Thomson; to Isaac, 28 October 1785) and goes so far as to call Mifflin "my adopted son" (to C. Thomson, 16 May 1786). In fact, Mrs. Norris was so far from disapproving of Mifflin's influence that she encouraged him to take her youngest son, Charles, under his wing. "I am greatly obliged to J Mifflin for the notice he takes of him," she wrote to Isaac, "as I think it is of advantage to Charles, and introduces him to proper acquaintance" (17 June 1785). The middle brother Joseph was also "happy to hear of Leanders kind Attention to Charles" (J. Norris to Logan, 11 September 1785). The experiment failed, however. "Charles is too volatile," Mrs. Norris wrote to Isaac several months later, "to engage his attention and friendship" (9 September 1785). Unable to accept Mifflin's guidance, poor Charles eventually made a misstep that got him written out of his mother's will and shipped off to Asia as a sailor.

And yet despite the lack of overt censure, a sense persists in the modern reader that there was something odd about Mifflin. This may be an effect of perspective—of looking at one man's story closely rather than a set of case studies. Smith-Rosenberg deliberately moved away from scrutiny of the psychic pathologies of the particular women she studied.

The scholar must ask if it is historically possible and, if possible, important to study the intensely individual aspects of psychosexual dynamics. Is it not the historian's first task to explore the social structure and the world view that made intense and sometimes sensual female love both a possible and an acceptable emotional option? (59)

Her shift in focus avoided the anachronism of judging early personalities by late psychosexual standards and recovered some of her subjects' dignity. But it also had a cost. In tossing out psychopathology's foul bathwater, Smith-Rosenberg also lost the baby of individualism. As Kierkegaard observed, it is error—departure from the norm—that flushes the self out of abstraction: "The category of sin is the category of individuality" (119). As a piece of the historical record, the Mifflin and Gibson diaries give evidence that at the height of sympathy's reign, American men could express emotions to each other with a fervor and openness that could not have been detached from religious enthusiasm a generation earlier, and would have to be consigned to sexual perversion a few generations later. But Mifflin's diary, in particular, is also the record of an individual, a distinctive personality, who seems to be pushing against the limits, admittedly broader then than later, to male-male emotions.

What makes Mifflin a vivid character is that he wants a friend desperately, and that he holds onto the men he finds tenaciously. What makes his diary a good read is that Gibson is not the only man he is courting. In fact, the story is a love triangle even before the diaries begin. Mifflin met Gibson "at a time when Castalio [Isaac Norris III] was in Europe, & I being left rather friendless & forlorn without a *confidant,* was more open & disposed to be impressed with his merit" (Leander 2: 214). As early as day three of his journal, either oblivious to or solicitous of the jealousy he might be provoking in Gibson, Mifflin notes that he "recieved [*sic*] letters from my dear Castalio; & sat up very late talking about him—hope soon to welcome him to his native shore" (1: 1–2).

Repeatedly, Mifflin invites Gibson to worry about whether Mifflin will remain faithful. In the same entry that Mifflin remembers Gibson fondly in the pear grove, Mifflin notes that he "drew a comparison between him [Gibson] and the young squire" (1: 8). The burden of the comparison seems to be that the young squire would make just as good a friend. A few days later, Mifflin returns to the pear grove with Ascanius (Samuel Rhoads III), and they discuss "many plans & schemes [. . .] respecting his [Samuel's] destination" (1:17), the same sort of amicable paternalism Mifflin indulged with Gibson. A week later, he praises Gibson's younger brother

John, this time making explicit the game he is playing: "Think he will stand a chance to rival the negligent inattentive Lorenzo in my affections" (1: 20).

Add to the number of young men Mifflin pursues, the intensity with which he seems to need their affection. Mifflin may not have been much more labile than the people around him, but he was undoubtedly more aware of his volatility. "I wonder if every body thinks as much & as *constantly* as I do," he once complained (2: 154). Mifflin's thinking was in no way profound, but he did monitor his fluctuating feelings with a vigilance that amounted to an innovation. On some days he treated the matter with a light touch borrowed from Sterne: "It is *inconsistent* to pretend to be always *the same*" (1: 30). But on other days it perplexed and annoyed him: "Rather in dull spirits & did not talk much there is no accounting for these taciturne moods" (1: 42). Usually, though, Mifflin did know how to account for his moods, or at least how to solace them: he turned to his young male companions. They became fetishes that could protect him from depression. If Mifflin grew sad, he could remind himself, in terms of almost Biblical rapture, "Have I not my Castalio left [. . .] & have I not acquired my Lorenzo! [. . .] In them have I cause to rejoice" (1: 100–11). When they failed him, he was left miserable. "I was in wretched spirits & wanted him [Isaac Norris III] to come home with me—but he would not —& I do not remember when I wanted more the exhilarating society of a friend" (2: 183).

Mifflin's raw neediness cut against the grain of contemporaneous political rhetoric. When Mifflin falls, he wants someone else to catch him. He longs to be vulnerable under the protection of another man. In 1787 Philadelphia, these were counterrevolutionary desires. Reciprocal but unequal relations had guided colonial society, but the American Revolution began to upset that deferential system. Christians no longer advocated submission and independence; ministers such as Jonathan Mayhew equated freedom from British authority with freedom from sin (Fliegelman 174–80). Mifflin's emotions, however, betray a nostalgia for hierarchy. As mentioned above, Mifflin liked to play the role of Gibson's patron. The role moved him deeply and passionately. Once, while discussing James's career options with Mrs. Gibson, Mifflin's "heart was so full I was obliged to go into the other room to give it vent" (Leander 2: 5). Something of a valetudinarian himself, Mifflin was happy when Gibson came down with a toothache, because it gave Mifflin a chance to nurse his friend. "Never do I feel the calls of friendship stronger than in sickness" (2: 3). The tenderness possible between a stronger and a weaker party aroused Mifflin. Exchanges between equals of mutual benefit to both parties could be left to the unsentimental marketplace.

The physical maintenance of the diaries reflects Mifflin's and Gibson's unequal statuses. Gibson is the diaries' servant and caretaker. During one of Mifflin's visits to Princeton, Gibson "marked Leander's Journal by placing the names of the months on the top of each page" (Lorenzo 52). He also sewed the journal leaves together into fascicles (Lorenzo 60). When Mifflin complained that it was "very troublesome" to cut paper to fit in his book (Leander 1: 89), Gibson helpfully "added four blank leaves to my dear Leander's journal and trimmed it" (Lorenzo 70). He further promised that "I will always agree to make Leander's journal papers provided he pays me well and my price is that he will not grow tired but always continue to write *long* journals" (Lorenzo 73). Ever so gently, and even as he affirms he likes the game they are playing, Gibson is ribbing his older friend. He is reminding Mifflin that according to the economic terms that prevail in the world at large, the disparity of their roles is something of a joke, a relic of hierarchy that cash (which labor could easily purchase) would quickly dissolve.

At the start of Mifflin's diary, Mifflin was living not in his own quarters on Second Street[10] but at the Norrises.' All of Mrs. Norris's children were away from home; Isaac and Joseph were touring Europe, Charles was banished to Asia, and married Deborah had retired to Stenton. At Mrs. Norris's invitation, Mifflin had taken up residence as "gaurd of the house" (Leander 2: 92). The Gibsons lived next-door. The Norris property—Deborah Norris Logan once jokingly called it "Norris Castle" (Derounian 511)—cast a long shadow, and Mifflin at first saw Gibson only in his shadow. Gibson was a fallback friend. Mifflin first loved Isaac, also known as Castalio, scion of the Norris family. Although Mifflin began his diary for Gibson, what gives it an almost novelistic drive is the question of whether it will continue Gibson's. The rise of Gibson's star is nearly eclipsed by Isaac's rather spectacular demise.

Less than a year younger than Mifflin, Isaac Norris III was Mifflin's emotional and intellectual peer, and ever so slightly his social superior. In 1779, Isaac and Mifflin were already so close that when Mifflin came down with a fever, Isaac spent the night to "condole" him; "I wonder what they will dream!" Isaac's sister Deborah commented (Derounian 509). Isaac's nom de plume Castalio appeared in a children's handwritten newspaper *Amusement for the Circle* as early as 1780 (No. 2, 19 August 1780). He may have been nicknamed after the lover who ended unhappily in

Thomas Otway's play *The Orphan*—"the gentle lover who was all tenderness," as Boswell called him (136)—but his name might also have been a
masculinized version of Castalia, the spring on Mount Parnassus sacred to
the Muses, named for the woman who plunged into it to avoid rape by
Apollo.[11] The alias suited Isaac. He would never marry, and he was a poet.
In a cartoonish watercolor of him, probably painted by one of the Rhoads
girls, his face is childlike and abstracted, his delicate figure perched cau-
tiously in his seat.[12] His cousin Mary Dickinson, admittedly partial, wrote
that he was "without exception the handsomest young man I know"
(Dickinson to Logan, 18 April 1789).

The same cousin encouraged Isaac to send her his poetry. "Thy little
pieces of poetry soothe my soul," she wrote him; "I have a small collection
shall be happy if thee will enlarge it" (Dickinson to I. Norris, n.d.). To one
of her letters he appended a note listing which poems he had already
mailed her, to avoid repeating himself: "Ode. when February / Sonnets. To
thee O pity & Down a sloped hill / Inscription for Queeny [?]" (Dickinson
to I. Norris, 28 March 1791). One of his poems survives, probably saved by
his sister Deborah, in a manuscript blotched with what may be tears. "Say
what is Life if Frenzy clouds the Mind," the poem asks, and its confused
attempt to answer this question seems to come from a heart that couldn't
quite bear the ups and downs of human luck or emotion. "Passions wreck
him with continual War," the poet despairs. Since neither pleasure, power,
nor wealth can bring peace to "the compound creature Man," the poet
longs for the moment of release when his "Nobler Part" will "leave the
shattered Tennement behind." Werther's embrace of death was defiant and
rebellious, but Isaac's case resembles that of Harley, the emotionally fragile, aristocratic hero of *The Man of Feeling*. He gives the impression of not
having been altogether of this world.

Cousin Mary Dickinson asked Castalio for poetry, but on other occasions she used her privilege as an intimate to remind Isaac of his nonfic-
tion duties as a Norris. Isaac had been named after an illustrious uncle
(1701–66) and grandfather (1671–1735). As the eldest son of the eldest son
in a great house, Isaac III was expected to rise to meet formidable expectations. "I do believe thy bearing the name that I have *always* so loved, &
reverenced, is a cause of my loving thee yet more," Mary wrote, in a saccharine tone that would make any young man queasy and evasive (Dickinson to I. Norris, 28 March 1791). She could threaten more directly and
ominously when she wanted to: "Consider the station in which thy Cre-
ator has placed thee among the creatures here—the Eldest son of a worthy

Father and family, who fixed their hearts on thee—God has showered great Blessings on thee—where my Child are the returns—He expects fruits" (Dickinson to I. Norris, 2 February 1790). Isaac was trapped by his inheritance; it raised the stakes while skewing the psychological odds against him. America no longer followed Norrises just because Norrises had been accustomed to lead. Isaac could not live on the estate that came with his name except by selling it off. If he entered the world, he had a great deal to lose—his pride, as well as his money—and thanks to his patrician ethereality, it was very unlikely he stood to gain anything.[13] Like Harley, Isaac would never find a way out of his socioeconomic predicament, but his aporia would attract the sympathy of everyone around him.

On 5 June 1783, Isaac set off to take the Grand Tour of Europe. Travel was "the last Step to be taken in the Institution of Youth," as *The Spectator* put it (Steele 368). The trip was supposed to teach Isaac gracious and cosmopolitan manners, give him knowledge of the wider world, and welcome him into manhood. Mifflin expected to follow his friend soon; they planned to rendezvous in England. Mifflin "is extreamly anxious to go," Deborah wrote her brother two months after his departure. "I think nothing is wanting but his Father's consent, it would cement your Friendship and you would lay in a kind of joint stock of ideas to serve you in future life" (Logan to Norris, 7 August [1783?]).

It was a time for both congratulation and admonition. Charles Thomson, secretary of the Continental Congress and a cousin by marriage, did Isaac the favor of supplying letters of introduction to Thomas Jefferson and John Jay. In exchange, Thomson had license to inflict on Isaac some grandiose advice:

> You are now in the situation of Hercules, just stepping into life and left to yourself to follow unrestrained where passion leads or prudence points the way. Before you, lie the rough ascent of virtue on the one hand, and the flowery path of pleasure on the other. I hope and trust you will with him make the glorious choice. (19 June 1784)

To Isaac, Thomson wrote of prospects. To Jefferson, however, Thomson wrote of fears. "As he is a young man of an amiable disposition and considerable fortune, I am anxious he should return as uncorrupted as he went" (18 June 1784; Jefferson 518–19). Jefferson thought he knew exactly what sort of danger Thomson was hinting at. "It is difficult for young men to refuse it where beauty is a begging in every street," Jefferson commiserated (11 November 1784; Jefferson 518–19). Overall, at least for others if not for himself, Jefferson assessed the education Paris had to offer as not worth its risk to morals.

Even Isaac's mother fretted over the chance that away from home, Isaac might marry or start a liaison with someone inappropriate. "I have a Confidence in my dear Child that he will not form any plan for his future life without the knowledge of his affect: mother, I think thee will comprehend my meaning" (M. Norris to Isaac, 15 May 1784). None of these people knew Isaac very well. If the family had heard the rumors circulating in Philadelphia even before Isaac embarked, they would not have worried about Isaac's id but his superego. According to a report filed years later by a committee of the Arch Street Monthly Meeting, while still in Philadelphia, Isaac "had joined with the People called Roman Catholics." Although Isaac did not advertise the fact and may have deceived his family to hide it, "previous to his leaving this Country he had been initiated into that society by the Ceremonies they make use of for that Purpose" (*Philadelphia* 308–9; 30 March 1787).[14]

It was no small matter for a Quaker to defect to Catholicism. The Norrises were lax churchgoers, but they were prominent in the Friends community. Once abroad, Isaac ceased to conceal his conversion, and the scandal spread quickly back across the Atlantic. When Robert Morton reported the news to a friend in Philadelphia, he commented, "I believe its the first instance of a person who had known anything of the principles of friends, changing them for Romish—I am sorry he is so deluded, and in hopes he will shortly see his errors" (letter to Pemberton, 21 November 1783). Isaac's conversion sent the Norrises into a panic, chronicled in the family letters. In the end sympathy (and blood) triumphed over doctrine. Mary Norris's 30 October 1784 letter to Isaac presented the family's final consensus on the issue: capitulation. When she had rebuked her son mildly, he had responded with silence. Now she wrote to retract her criticism:

> I have been greatly disappointed that I had no letter, if in any of my late letters to thee I may have wrote any thing concerning thyself my dear Son must attribute what I have wrote to my anxious concern for what I think is for his happiness, but altho' wee may differ in our religious sentiments, I hope that will not lessen our affection, & love, and my dear Child may depend on it that his mother will leave him to his Christian liberty at his return which She hope[s] will be by the next Spring.

The Norrises were too afraid of losing Isaac to want a quarrel.

In the end, the Norrises would lose Isaac anyway, to something rather darker than Catholicism. His conversion seems to have been only one component of a nervous breakdown. A censorious voice emerged in Isaac. All of England came under its interdict: "it is an expensive, dissipated place," he wrote, and he fled to a monastery in Liège (letter to Logan, 29 July 1783). This aspect of Isaac judged all pleasures harshly. Explaining his changed travel plans to his sister, he wrote that "from various circumstances on a nearer view I conceived a disgust to the pleasures which formerly my imagination had drawn a false picture of,—& this disgust is since improved into an entire conviction of their falsehood and vanity, and an entire adieu to them" (I. Norris to Logan, 4 February 1784). In another letter, he was at pains to correct any notion she might have that "we travellers live in perpetual rounds of amusement" (18 April 1784); to set the record straight, he meticulously catalogued his increasingly rare sallies into public. When he gave his sister the reasons for his conversion, he omitted any points on which Catholicism and Quaker doctrine differed. What brought him to Roman Catholicism, in his telling, was a new awareness of his sinfulness—"we are not placed in this world for nothing, or merely to amuse ourselves" (4 February 1784)—couched in the terms a young heir might use to reproach himself for failing to live up to the family name. Perhaps, as Isaac's boyhood ended and he realized he would never satisfy manhood's demands, his ego-ideal became crueler. What Erikson would have called his "psychosocial moratorium" was drawing to a close (Erikson 119–20), and he may have felt more and more acutely how far he was going to fall from his forefathers' standard. He himself admitted that if he had felt more confidence, he would not have needed to convert: "more satisfied with myself I might have placed happiness in myself" (I. Norris to Logan, 4 February 1784).

For all his new austerity, however, Isaac stayed in Paris because he liked it. "I find by Isaac's letter that he is in good spirits and says that he prefers one week in Paris to a year in London," Isaac's cousin Hannah Thomson gossiped to Mifflin (12 May 1785). Even though Isaac had chosen his new religion with ascetic logic, in his daily routine while abroad he consulted nothing but his pleasure. His brother Joseph wrote home that Isaac

> still preserves the same Whims, Notions, likes & Dislikes as formerly—this Day he eats heartily—to morrow he will only take Tea or some such Slop —this Night he sleeps remarkably well, the next some great Noise has

> prevented him from closing his Eyes—& he still preserves the old Custom
> of taking things going to Bed to make him sleep—With regard to his time
> of rising it is not regular sometimes at 10, he shows himself & often am told
> it is near twelve— (J. Norris to Logan, 4 February 1786)

Isaac detached himself from everything worldly, but the enthusiastic
young convert did not realize that this detachment was itself a pleasure
and temptation. "The less one goes out, and sees of the world, the more I
think what we do see interests us," Isaac wrote to his sister (12 March 1786).
Joseph could not wait to get back to Philadelphia, but Isaac postponed
his return again and again. As Joseph reported, Isaac's "attachment to this
vile *dirty hole* is astonishing—Without friends, without Acquaintances,
cubbed up in a little pittiful dark Chamber he prefers it to his native place"
(J. Norris to Logan, 4 February 1786).

The amused tone with which Joseph relayed his brother's eccentricity
sounds somewhat forced. Isaac's sleep pattern suggests depression, as does
the social isolation he more and more preferred. Isaac's "old Custom of
taking things going to Bed to make him sleep" likely refers to use of opi-
ates. Mifflin describes in his diary how with only a fever and mild dysen-
tery, he practically had to fight off prescriptions of laudanum from Dr.
Hall and Dr. Rush. Once when Mifflin explicitly "desired there might be
no opium in" his medicine (Leander 1: 150), Dr. Hall duped him. Dr. Rush
laughed when he heard about his colleague's behavior; "he said it was one
of those things which the physicians termed 'pious frauds'" (1: 151). It
would have been easy for Isaac to start taking opium; confused about his
goals and lacking in self-discipline, he would have found it difficult to stop.

Mifflin had intended to follow his friend Isaac to Europe, but soon after
Isaac's departure, Mifflin delayed the transatlantic voyage in order to woo
a young woman in Maryland (M. Norris to Isaac, 23 April 1784; Leander
2: 148). The courtship came to nothing, but just as it ended Mifflin came
down with the ague (M. Norris to Isaac, 7 August 1784). Because of his
poor health, Mifflin decided not to travel to Europe at all. By 1786, the two
had been "separated longer than thrice the annual coarse of the sun" (Leander 1: 152), and Mifflin was awaiting Isaac's return so eagerly as to compose corny verse in anticipation.

> Fly swift ye hours, you measure time in vain
> Till ye bring back Castalio again:

Be swifter now & to redeem that wrong
When he & I are met, be twice as long (Leander 1: 50)

Mifflin knew his friend had converted; he may have had some inkling of his other troubles, too. Just before they were reunited, Mifflin dreamed the reunion in anticipation. In Mifflin's dream, Isaac "was so altered both in person & manners that he appeared quite a new being to me—his face was flat & sallow, his figure long & gangling—& he had a careless swaggering air" (Leander 1: 150). Mifflin's unconscious was afraid that the sensitive poet had turned into someone with jaundiced skin and selfish manners—an opium eater, perhaps.

Mifflin's anxiety about Isaac prompted him to take the strange precaution of testing his friendship with Gibson. No other episode in the Mifflin and Gibson diaries shows so markedly the peculiar, vivid attention Mifflin devoted to his friendships.

In July Mifflin dropped a mysterious hint: "Mem-Something to break to Lorenzo, which perhaps he little dreams of—however it must be borne" (Leander 1:50). Gibson suspected nothing. When Mifflin visited Princeton several days later, innocent Gibson was ecstatic. "Very happy on seeing him," Gibson wrote on 29 July. "Spent the morning till Dinner in rumaging his trunk—talking to him, and in reading his journal—how time flies away when a person is engaged in such a manner!" (Lorenzo 51); faced with Gibson's unambiguous good will, Mifflin took to bed on 31 July with a suspiciously vague complaint.[15]

Mifflin diagnosed his sickness as caused "from low spirits" (Leander 1:58), but Gibson sensed there was more to it. After noting that he was "very sorry" to hear about Mifflin's headache, Gibson confided to his diary that "I conceit he has not quite as much regard for me now as he had some time ago—returned to college but could not study on account of thinking of him" (Lorenzo 55–56).

The next day, Mifflin "wrote a long letter to Lorenzo, with a plan which my heart did not dictate—a trial of his affection—& almost wept at the conclusion of it" (Leander 1: 59). The delivery of this letter is worth quoting at length. Mifflin

sent word by [Mr. Brown] to Lorenzo that a letter was at Mrs. Knox for him —I placed it on the table up stairs with a candle by it & then shut myself in the back room to wait his arrival—

When Gibson failed to respond to this summons, Mifflin left his hiding place to send another messenger to Gibson.

> I resumed my Station & he soon made his appearance—there was something mild & uncertain when he looked at the letter, he seemed to open it hesitatingly & his eyes flew precipitately over every page & then to the cover before he began to read—he had perused but a few lines when his countenance fell & he deliberately drew a chair & sat down—as he read I believe he heard me breathe & lookd for a few seconds earnestly at the door—all was hush'd. & he again returned to his letter—when he had finished, he folded all up slowly—& as he went down I thought I heard a sigh-My heart felt a melancholy sadness & I almost repented of my scheme—I followed & overtook him just as he had enterd the college gate—the sound of my voice so unexpected made him still more at a loss to account for what he had read —I asked him to return & told him I would explain the whole affair—when we had retired, I told him my fears about Castalio & that in case they should be realized that all my hope would rest on him & that the letter was only a trial what dependance I might have on his friendship & affection—the dear fellow seemed hurt at the experiment, but gave me the fullest assurances of his attachment—& I felt mine doubly renewed to him by the consciousness he testified of his own sincerity. (Leander 1: 59–60)

If one takes Mifflin at his word, he felt some compunction over toying with his friend's feelings, but not enough to stop. His guilt was outweighed by his desire, which he felt to be a need, to know how strongly Gibson was attached to him. The modern reader sees at once Mifflin's voyeurism and the narcissistic reward he engineered to have delivered to himself, at the cost of Gibson's pain. (Mark Twain understood that Tom Sawyer had to stumble into hearing his own funeral elegy; to have calculatedly managed it would be inexcusable even in a rascal.) Mifflin's fictional letter must have been cruel, perhaps announcing a rupture or end to the friendship. There is something unschooled about Mifflin's sadism here, like a child's torture of an animal. The strength of his own emotions preempted consideration of the emotions he was provoking. But whether or not Mifflin's explanations speak well of his character, the episode does show that the pleasures and dangers of friendship between men were compelling enough in the eighteenth century to motivate some rather elaborate behavior.

As with his pining in the pear grove, Mifflin staged the scene at Mrs. Knox's inn not only for his immediate gratification but also for the revisitable pleasure he would find in recording it as a tableau vivant. Fixed in Mifflin's diary, the scene testifies forever to Gibson's sweet, gullible loyalty. But it also testifies, without Mifflin's intending or entirely recognizing it, to the inadvertent damage caused by artists who work with human emotion. Charles Brockden Brown would discover similarly ambiguous results when his ventriloquist hero Carwin on a whim experiments with the feelings of the Wieland family, by eavesdropping and by counterfeiting their voices. Mifflin's manipulations do not lead to anything as dire as psychosis or murder; his case more closely resembles the delicate negotiation of asking a lover who does not like to pose to stand still for a snapshot. A photographer who bullies his lover and ignores her discomfort procures a sentimental token that is unreal, but time and a sort of economics are on the photographer's side. The snapshot will outlast the lover's annoyance. A photographer with a strong faculty of forgetting will be able to enjoy the still image of his lover for years, cherishing it for the happy concord she at that moment could hardly bear to represent.

Gibson, however, never gave Mifflin's tableau the lie. Later that month, Mifflin recorded that Gibson had written "informing me (& oh! how consolatory) that I 'need not labour under any apprehension from him on the score of rivalship'" (Leander 1: 137). Mifflin had not made any attempt to put Gibson at ease on this issue. It didn't occur to either party that Gibson might resent Mifflin for lording over him his status as Mifflin's second choice. The lopsided arrangement seems to have suited Gibson; he preferred not to challenge those who adopted a fatherly attitude toward him. Years later, a lawyer colleague would notice this deference in Gibson and regret it as a handicap: "Mr. Gibson is afraid of Tilghman [with whom Gibson had read law]. He believes him infallible, and dare not risque opposition to him, but if he means to be a *great lawyer* he should glory in opposing the whole *Bar,* and of all men his *old Master*" (Morris to Nicholson,14 December 1797).

Secure in Gibson, Mifflin was prepared to face the return of Isaac. Mifflin rose to the occasion with a flurry of unhealth. "My sickness comes very untimely for his arrival—but he has arrived very opportunely for my sickness," Mifflin noted, with almost too much insight to qualify him as a hysteric (1: 153). When Isaac reached Philadelphia, the Norrises sent their carriage to fetch Mifflin from his sickbed. He dashed into the Norris parlor feverish and sweating, "with all my invalid drapery flowing after me." In the happy flush of reunion, Mifflin felt that Isaac "was the same Castalio he was three years & three months ago," an assessment time would show to be untrue. As soon as the two men were left alone, Isaac "told me he was determined we should never part again—'I will give myself up to you' said he 'I will go wherever you go—& one shall not go without the other.'" Mifflin could not leave this avowal alone, of course; for Gibson's benefit he added this query to his diary entry: "Have I another friend that would make such a declaration?" (Leander 1: 156–58)

Fortunately for Mifflin, he did. In the Norris family letters, paragraphs referring to Isaac after 1786 have been systematically crossed out. Whatever was troubling Isaac in France persisted, and probably worsened, when he returned to America. Isaac continued to sleep late. "I am indeed very uneasy at his leading such an inactive life," Mifflin wrote when he discovered Isaac still in bed at one in the afternoon (2: 2–49). "I went up & talked to him—I found he had taken an anodyne the night before—a practice I have repeatedly reprobated." New rumors circulated about Isaac in town; Mifflin attributed some of them to the scandal caused by Isaac's conversion, but others seemed blacker, though Mifflin spelled nothing out (1: 184; 2: 73, 75, 93–94, 125). Only several weeks after his return, Isaac was already hinting that he wanted to go back to Paris (Leander 1: 192). It became difficult to persuade Isaac to leave the house. "I think if he would exert himself more, & mix a little more in the world he would be better," his mother wrote a friend, "but he excludes himself too much, he converses with nobody hardly, but his friend John Mifflin" (M. Norris to C. Thomson, 15 November 1787). Isaac's silent spells began to exasperate even Mifflin. "He seems never easy but when I am with him," Mifflin observed, "& frequently when we are together he will not talk" (2: 120). Gibson was often quiet, a trait Mifflin saw as of a piece with his charming modesty, but Isaac "was uncommonly mute—[. . .] almost as if he had been *stricken*" (Leander 2: 17).

Isaac's decline, however, was gradual. When Gibson returned home from school at the end of the month, it briefly looked as though the three young men—Leander, Lorenzo, and Castalio—might join in musketeers-style unity. Mifflin flitted between the Norris and the Gibson houses in a game of musical beds that sometimes found all three men spending the night together (Leander 1: 218). But when Isaac asked if he could read the journal Mifflin kept for Gibson, Mifflin seems to have made a choice (Leander 1: 214). He refused. A week later, as if to cement his decision, Mifflin admitted Gibson to his "sanctum sanctorum": he showed Gibson "some of the letters of my dear departed Eugenius—to whom he has succeeded" (Leander 1: 223). Isaac would remain a close friend; no matter what the whisperers said, Mifflin stayed loyal. But Mifflin never opened his sanctum sanctorum for Isaac. Mifflin and Gibson by contrast grew more and more intimate.

The expression of their intimacy took several forms. Gibson gave Mifflin "*a to[ken] of friendship*," and when they were apart, Mifflin remembered his friend by "putting it to my lips" (Leander 1: 95, 163). When they were together, intimacy between the two could take the form of a shared, inviolate space. During a visit to Gibson's Princeton quarters, they walled themselves off from Gibson's classmates to achieve this. "We locked ourselves in my study," Gibson wrote, "and I fixing my gown across the window (to prevent the students seeing us) we looked over papers and talked till the dinner bell rang" (Lorenzo 79). Whenever the two spent the night together, the hours of talk that came between retiring to the bedroom and falling asleep were precious; a second bout of intimate conversation always took place the next morning, before leaving the bedroom for breakfast (Leander 1: 121). Sometimes the men did more than talk during these private moments. On a trip with Gibson to Nottingham, Mifflin recorded that "In the evening as I was wrestling with Lorenzo I fell on the side of my head & hurt myself a little" (1: 239). A few days later this injury blossomed into a black eye (1: 241).

"I love & esteem him,"—Mifflin wrote of Gibson (1: 85). Whether or not the two expressed their affection in sex, they held each other in a regard that we would call *a fortiori* sexual. Mifflin dreamed of Gibson often (Leander 2: 41); in one of his dreams, he appears to have been struggling with images of shame and loss of control that a direct relation between the two men's bodies would have brought on:

> Dreamt a very odd dream last night—I thought Lorenzo & I (& I know not whether there was another person or not) were in a very small boat inside of a long kind of pier-wharf which was a great way into the river—I thought we had neither oar paddle or anything else to guide our course & we were driving fast into the current which was very strong but just as we got almost to the outside of the pier I caught hold on something to stop ~~up~~ us & then pushed our boat from one thing to another till we reached the wharf—the people on shore all the time hallowing to us & very anxuous for our safety —I climed up the pier (which was very high) & then drew Lorenzo up after me—he seemed to be Stark naked & as we were [?] running along hand in hand to the place where his cloaths were—I awaked—greatly agitated by the danger from which we seemed to have escaped (Leander 2: 35)

If the river in Mifflin's dream represents the sentiments carrying the men along, then the lack of an "oar paddle or anything else" might represent an attempt to navigate their passions without recourse to what makes their bodies sexual and male. Rudderless, they find the current dangerously unmanageable. Once Mifflin finds something to hold on to, they are saved, but then the pier rises to a massive height, and Gibson and Mifflin are exposed—"hand in hand"—on the very thing that saved them.

A dream is not evidence of sexual conduct, but there is enough detail to the story of Lorenzo, Leander, and Castalio to make the question of did they or didn't they somewhat irrelevant. It is not inconceivable that they did, but they never said so. Nor is it inconceivable that they didn't. An eighteenth-century friendship felt like a bold experiment because it was not subject to the compromises of either marriage or commerce. "Is friendship in love more to be depended on than friendship in trade?" Mifflin asked. "Not so much perhaps" (2: 30). Mifflin thought his friendship with Gibson was purer than love as well as purer than trade; it was friendship for its own sake, freed from the duties and compensations a man looked for in either a wife or a business partner.[16]

More interesting is the evidence Mifflin's pier-wharf dream gives of his evolution as a writer and self-analyst. He has moved far beyond his early elliptic comments; he tells the dream with a thoroughness and honesty that leaves him vulnerable. It is not easy to become intimate with the page, but Mifflin has learned how to. Mifflin recognized that the journal gradually ceased to be only a means for communicating with Gibson. After several months of diary-keeping, Mifflin noted that "it has now become an amusement to me" (1: 84). The writing process itself began to offer rewards, which was unexpected. It gave shelter, for example, from unsentimental company. "Indeed this journal of mine is a resource in lonely hours & against stupid people" (2: 66). With a journal to compose, Mifflin could retreat from society without fear of ennui. It bothered and fascinated Mifflin that his spirits were "subject to such extremes" (1: 210), and so it pleased him to discover that the regular examination and statement of his emotions had the effect of both amplifying and taming them. In the end, the intermediary of writing served as a more reliable solace than the friend it stood in for. It acted "to counterbalance many things I have to displease & trouble me," including Gibson's occasional inattention (2: 288). It steadied Mifflin by letting out the unsteadiness that his sympathies made him subject to. "It hath served as a barometrical diary of my hopes & fears my distresses & happiness—Many have been their vicissitudes, &

at this moment I feel a gratitude for being preserved thro' such a variety of moods & dispositions."[17]

Gibson was not married to Mifflin nor was he apprenticed to him. No writing bound them to each other. But their writing, like the sympathy that played between them, was not altogether free, either. It was decorous, nostalgically deferential, and unselfconscious about artifice. It was not common but it was decidedly not radical. Yet Mifflin's diary does unburden itself of something as it moves forward. In the pear grove and at Mrs. Knox's inn, Mifflin struggled to represent the sentiments between Gibson and himself in scenes he could not quite stage-manage smoothly. But by the time he records the pier-wharf dream, he has left this struggle behind. Maybe he felt sure, at last, of Gibson's love, sure enough to realize that sympathy could not be proved by any display he engineered, ornamented, and transcribed, but was best enacted by writing itself. The diary showed sympathy, barometrically; Mifflin only had to learn how to let it take a reading. Sharing a dream about sex was risky and intimate, riskier and more intimate than sex itself would have been, because the dream, unlike sex and unlike Mifflin's scenes, could never have been scripted beforehand. Like a literary fiction and like love for another person, a dream is both under and escaping its author's control. As he dreams about losing his oar or paddle, Mifflin is almost ready to ride the current. His diary is moving from a notion of sympathy as sentimental control toward a style of writing that invites sympathy by the sincerity and open-endedness of its attention.

## NOTES

I would like to thank Michael Hardy of the University City Historical Society in Philadelphia for sharing his discovery of the Leander and Lorenzo diaries with me, Linda Stanley and the staff of the Historical Society of Pennsylvania for their knowledgeable assistance, and the Andrew W. Mellon Foundation for a grant that made this research possible. The Historical Society of Pennsylvania, the Seeley G. Mudd Manuscript Library and Firestone Rare Books and Manuscripts Library of Princeton University, the Friends Historical Library of Swarthmore College, and the owner of the first volume of the Mifflin diary have graciously granted permission to quote from their collections.

1. For Mifflin's age and genealogy, see Merrill and Leach. For his trust fund, see E. Gibson 110. The American Philosophical Society holds one of the receipt books that Mifflin took with him on his dunning errands (16 January 1800 to 10 March 1813, catalogued as B:M585). Other details in this paragraph are from Leander as

follows: weight (1: 226 and 1: 246), cane (2: 142), hair style (2: 124), snowball (2: 154), and nearsightedness (1:106).

2. For accounts of sympathy and the changes it wrought in society, see Crane, Radner, Fiering, Barker-Benfield, Silver, Wood, and Fliegelman.

3. Moyes's blindness and the size of audience are mentioned in an unsigned Letter to SE [Samuel Emlen?].

4. For Gibson's weight, see Leander 2: 226 and 2: 246. For age at puberty, see Kett 44. For Gibson's hair, see Leander 2: 124 and Lorenzo 20. For the bargain with Barlowe, see Lorenzo 31. For Gibson's father and childhood home, see "John Gibson, Mayor of Philadelphia, 1771–1772," in *Genealogies* 652–53.

5. For an overview of Gibson at Princeton, see Woodward and Craven 187–91.

6. For more on the Cliosophic Society, see McLachlan and Looney.

7. "S Rhoads is amost agreeable friend & neighbor, I am sorry she meets with the difficultys she has to encounter settling her affairs.—I have another excellent neighbour, the Widow Gibson" (M. Norris to Dickinson, 4–6 March 1[786?]). For genealogical information on the Norris family, see *Norris Family* 2–13 and Jordan 88–89. For proof that Castalio is Isaac Norris III, see M. Norris to Isaac, 22 December 1785, which includes a postscript from "J M Jr" to "my dear Castalio" in Mifflin's hand. For the Rhoads family, see Castner 9–13. The identification of the Rhoads children as Maria, Eliza, and Ascanius is based on comparison of details in Leander with two letters: M. Rhoads to Samuel, 9 September 1786, and E. Rhoads to Samuel, 29 August 1786. Also see S. Rhoads, which includes poems commemorating the deceased "Eliza" and "Maria." For thumbnail biographies of many of the people mentioned in Mifflin's diary, including servants, see [J. Norris,] "Register." Leonora might be Clementina Ross, Mifflin's future wife, and Eugenius might be Jabez Maud Fisher (see Sweeney, 200 n. 27), but there is no firm evidence for either guess. "Eugenius" is the name Laurence Sterne gave to his friend John Hall-Stevenson in his fiction.

8. For a masterly overview of the evolution of the trope of "separate spheres" in the last three decades of women's history, see Kerber. Most of the refinements and shifts Kerber discusses, however, focus on the nineteenth and twentieth centuries. The romantic friendships in the Norris circle took place in an eighteenth-century beau monde that was not yet the exclusive province of either gender. Like the European court that was its ultimate model, the American beau monde gave special place to women but until well into the Federalist era welcomed both sexes (Shields 11–14, 99–122). Mifflin and Gibson may have slipped through a closing door; men who thrived in the beau monde were becoming suspect. John Adams registered the emerging distrust when he found the attention that his daughter's cosmopolitan suitor Royall Tyler paid to Mrs. Adams fishy: "I don't like this method of Courting Mothers" (John Adams to Abigail, 22 January 1783).

9. The Hamilton-Laurens friendship is discussed in Katz 451–56; the Webster-Bingham friendship is discussed in Rotundo 77–80.

10. White lists a "Mifflin John, Esq; counsellor at law, Second b. Walnut & Spruce streets," which corresponds to the address on the verso of H. Thomson to Mifflin, 15 September 1785.

11. I owe the second suggestion to Robert A. Ferguson. See Sterne 85 for a mention of Castalia that the Norris circle would have been familiar with. Charlotte Cibber Charke put Otway's play to a gender-deviant use in her 1756 novel, *The History of Henry Dumont, Esq.* When the sodomite Billy Loveman made a pass at the hero Henry, Billy dressed up "in a female rich dishabille" and cried out to Henry, "I come, I fly to my adored Castalio's arms! my wishes lord! [. . .] Do my angel, call me your Monimia!" (20).

12. The figure labeled "I Norris" in "A Party to Virginia." This fanciful watercolor portrays many of the young people in the Norris circle, labeled as follows, with conjectural identifications in brackets: BJ [Becky Jones], SD [Sarah Drinker, 1761–1807], JPN [Joseph Parker Norris, 1763–1841], NE [Nancy Emlen, 1755–1815], CL [Charles Logan, 1754–94], P[olly] Jackson, N[ancy] Drinker [1764–1830], PF [Polly Fishbourne, 1760–1842], T[homas] Lloyd, M[ary] Pleasant[s, 17??–1794], Capt D—e, S[ally] Jones [1760–], DN [Deborah Norris, 1761–1839], Betsy Wister [1764–1812], J[onathan] Jones [1762–1822], Sally Wister [1761-1804], SW [Woods' infant daughter?], Mrs Wood, Col [James] Wood [1750–1813].

13. Cf. Erikson 33: "These men, of the once highest strata, join those from the very lowest ones in being the truly disinherited in American life; from where they are there is no admission to free competition, unless they have the strength to start all over."

14. See also minutes for 29 December 1786 (p. 295) and 25 May 1787 (p. 320).

15. A separate essay could be written on the timing of Mifflin's illnesses. He himself admitted that "My complaints are not constitutional—they are adventitious & have arisen out of the inauspicious turns of my fate" (Leander 1: 218). They seem to coincide often with Mifflin's displeasure at the kind or degree of attention he is receiving from one of his friends.

16. Discussing eighteenth-century romantic friendships between British women, Lillian Faderman found that to focus on the sexual act led her to an interpretive dead end. About the famous Ladies of Llangollen, she wrote, "We do not know whether or not their relationship was genital, but they were 'married' in every other sense" (125). The puzzling contrast between the richness of the relationships Faderman described and her profound uncertainty about the women's sexual conduct prompted Foucault to speculate that in the eighteenth century, sex between friends had not yet become problematic: "As long as friendship was something important, was socially accepted, nobody realized men had sex together. You couldn't say that men *didn't* have sex together—it just didn't matter. . . . Whether they fucked together or kissed had no importance" (171).

17. Leander 11 May 1787, unnumbered page out of chronological order following 2: 52.

WORKS CITED

Adams, John. Letter to Abigail Adams. 22 January 1783. *The Book of Abigail and John: Selected Letters of the Adams Family, 1762–1784.* Ed. L. H. Butterfield, Marc Friedlander, and Mary-Jo Kline. Cambridge: Harvard Univ. Press, 1975. 336–39.

*Amusement for the Circle.* Norris Family of Fairhill Manuscript Books, case 37, vol. 45. Historical Society of Pennsylvania.

Barker-Benfield, G. J. *The Culture of Sensibility: Sex and Society in Eighteenth-Century Britain.* Chicago: University of Chicago Press, 1992.

Boswell, James. *Boswell's London Journal, 1762–63.* Ed. Frederick A. Pottle. New Haven: Yale Univ. Press, 1992.

Bushman, Richard L. *The Refinement of America: Persons, Houses, Cities.* New York: Knopf, 1992.

Cadbury, Sarah. "Extracts from the Diary of Ann Warder." *Pennsylvania Magazine of History and Biography* 18 (1894): 51–63.

Castner, S., Jr. *The Rhoads Family of Pennsylvania.* Philadelphia: George H. Buchanan, 1901.

Charke, Charlotte Cibber. "From *The History of Henry Dumont, Esq.*" *Pages Passed from Hand to Hand: The Hidden Tradition of Homosexual Literature in English from 1748 to 1914.* Eds. Mark Mitchell and David Leavitt. New York: Houghton Mifflin, 1998. 16–21.

Cicero. *Selected Letters.* Trans. D. R. Shackleton Bailey. New York: Penguin Books, 1986.

Crane, R. S. "Suggestions Toward a Genealogy of the 'Man of Feeling.'" *ELH* 1 (1934): 205–30.

Delia [Deborah Norris Logan]. "Again the sun recalls the vernal year." April 1780. Maria Dickinson Logan Papers, folder 1. Historical Society of Pennsylvania.

Derounian, Kathryn Zabelle. "'A Dear Dear Friend': Six Letters from Deborah Norris to Sally Wister,1778–1779." *Pennsylvania Magazine of History and Biography* 108 (1984): 487–516.

Dickinson, Mary. Letter to Deborah Norris Logan.18 April 1789. Robert R. Logan Collection, box 12, F # 12. Historical Society of Pennsylvania.

———. Letter to Isaac Norris. N.d. Norris Papers, Family Letters 1: 82. Historical Society of Pennsylvania.

———. Letter to Isaac Norris III. 2 February 1790. Norris Papers, Family Letters 1: 74. Historical Society of Pennsylvania.

———. Letter to Isaac Norris III. 28 March 1791. Norris Papers, Family Letters 1: 78. Historical Society of Pennsylvania.

Ditz, Toby L. "Shipwrecked; or, Masculinity Imperiled: Mercantile Representations of Failure and the Gendered Self in Eighteenth-Century Philadelphia." *Journal of American History* 81 (1994): 51–80.

Erikson, Erik. *Identity and the Life Cycle.* New York: Norton, 1980.

Faderman, Lillian. *Surpassing the Love of Men: Romantic Friendship and Love Between Women from the Renaissance to the Present.* New York: William Morrow, 1981.

Fiering, Norman S. "Irresistible Compassion: An Aspect of Eighteenth-Century Sympathy and Humanitarianism." *Journal of the History of Ideas* 37 (1976) 195–218.

Fliegelman, Jay. *Prodigals and Pilgrims: The American Revolution against Patriarchal Authority, 1750–1800.* New York: Cambridge Univ. Press, 1984.

Foucault, Michel. "Sex, Power, and the Politics of Identity." *Ethics: Subjectivity and Truth.* Ed. Paul Rabinow. New York: New Press, 1997. 163–73.

*Genealogies of Pennsylvania Families: From the Pennsylvania Genealogical Magazine.* Vol. 1. Baltimore: Genealogical Publishing, 1982.

Gibson, Elizabeth Bordley. *Biographical Sketches of the Bordley Family, of Maryland, for Their Descendants.* Vol. 1. Philadelphia: Henry B. Ashmead, 1865.

Gibson, James. Letter to "Mama," typescript. 28 December 1785. James Gibson, Class of 1787, undergraduate alumni records, box 46. Seeley G. Mudd Manuscript Library, Princeton University.

Hamilton, Alexander. "To Lieutenant Colonel John Laurens." [April 1779.] *The Papers of Alexander Hamilton.* Ed. Harold C. Syrett. Vol. 2. New York: Columbia Univ. Press, 1961. 34–38.

Jefferson, Thomas. *The Papers of Thomas Jefferson.* Ed. Julian P. Boyd. Vol. 7. Princeton: Princeton Univ. Press, 1953.

Jordan, John W., ed. *Colonial and Revolutionary Families of Pennsylvania: Genealogical and Personal Memoirs.* Vol. 1. Baltimore: Genealogical Publishing Co., 1978.

Katz, Jonathan Ned. *Gay American History: Lesbians and Gay Men in the U.S.A.* New York: Thomas Y. Crowell, 1976.

Kerber, Linda K. "Separate Spheres, Female Worlds, Woman's Place: The Rhetoric of Women's History." *Toward an Intellectual History of Women.* Chapel Hill: Univ. of North Carolina Press, 1997. 59–99.

Kett, Joseph F. *Rites of Passage: Adolescence in America, 1790 to the Present.* New York: Basic Books, 1977.

Kierkegaard, Søren. *The Sickness unto Death: A Christian Psychological Exposition for Upbuilding and Awakening.* Trans. H. and E. Hong. Princeton: Princeton Univ. Press, 1980.

Lawrence, D. H. *Studies in Classic American Literature.* New York: Penguin, 1977.

Leach, Frank Willing. *The Mifflin Family.* Philadelphia: Historical Publication Society, 1932.

Leander [John Fishbourne Mifflin]. *A Journal, Volume 1st.* 12 May 1786 to 11 November 1786. Private collection.

———. *Leander's Journal, Volume 2nd.* 12 November 1786 to 11 May 1787. Historical Society of Pennsylvania. (Bound with Lorenzo and catalogued as James Gibson, "Journal of Lorenzo and Leander," Am .069.)

Letter to SE [Samuel Emlen?]. 4 March 1785. Miscellaneous items, Bringhurst Manuscripts (J). Friends Historical Library, Swarthmore College.

Logan, Deborah Norris. Letter to Isaac Norris. 7 August [1783?]. Norris Papers, Family Letters 2: 94. Historical Society of Pennsylvania.

———. Letter to Sally Fisher. 10 November 1779. Charles Smith Ogden Papers, Scrapbooks, series 4, p. 76. Friends Historical Library, Swarthmore College.

———. *The Norris House*. Philadelphia: Fair-Hill Press, 1867.

Looney, J. Jefferson. *Nurseries of Letters and Republicanism: A Brief History of the American Whig-Cliosophic Society and Its Predecessors, 1765–1941*. Princeton: Trustees of the American Whig-Cliosophic Society, 1996. Lorenzo [James Gibson]. *A Journal*. 6 February 1786 to 1 October 1786. Historical Society of Pennsylvania. (Bound with Leander, vol. 2, and catalogued as James Gibson, "Journal of Lorenzo and Leander," Am .069.)

McLachlan, James. "The *Choice of Hercules*: American Student Societies in the Early 19th Century." *The University in Society*. Vol. 2. Ed. Lawrence Stone. Princeton: Princeton Univ. Press, 1974. 449–94.

Merrill, John Houston. *Memoranda Relating to the Mifflin Family*. Printed for private distribution, 24 April 1890.

Morris, Robert. "To John Nicholson." 14 December 1797. "Original Letters and Documents," no. 3. *Pennsylvania Magazine of History and Biography* 6.1 (1882): 112.

Morton, Robert. Letter to John Pemberton. 21 November 1783. Pemberton Papers, vol. 39, folder 17, p.167. Historical Society of Pennsylvania.

*The Norris Family, Reprinted from the Provincial Councillors of Pennsylvania*. Trenton: Wm. S. Sharp, 1882.

Norris, Isaac. Letter to Deborah Norris Logan. 29 July 1783. Robert R. Logan Collection. Historical Society of Pennsylvania.

———. Letter to Deborah Norris Logan. 4 February 1784. Robert R. Logan Collection. Historical Society of Pennsylvania.

———. Letter to Deborah Norris Logan. 18 April 1784. Robert R. Logan Collection. Historical Society of Pennsylvania.

———. Letter to Deborah Norris Logan. 12 March 1786. Robert R. Logan Collection. Historical Society of Pennsylvania.

———. "Poem ['Say what is Life if Frenzy clouds the Mind']." Logan Papers 9: 71. Historical Society of Pennsylvania.

Norris, Joseph Parker. Letter to Deborah Norris Logan. 11 September 1785. Robert R. Logan Collection. Historical Society of Pennsylvania.

———. Letter to Deborah Norris Logan. 4 February 1786. Robert R. Logan Collection. Historical Society of Pennsylvania.

[———.] "Register of Deaths in the Lloyd & Norris Families, with some of their near & particular Friends." *Extracts from the Letter Books of Isaac Norris*. Norris of Fairhill Manuscript Books, case 37, vol. 3. Historical Society of Pennsylvania. 249–72.

Norris, Mary Parker. Letter to Mary Dickinson. 4–6 March [1786?]. Loudoun Papers. Historical Society of Pennsylvania.

———. Letter to Isaac Norris. 23 April 1784. Norris Papers, Family Letters 1: 50. Historical Society of Pennsylvania.

———. Letter to Isaac Norris. 15 May 1784. Norris Papers, Family Letters 1: 51. Historical Society of Pennsylvania.

———. Letter to Isaac Norris. 7 August 1784. Norris Papers, Family Letters 1: 54. Historical Society of Pennsylvania.

———. Letter to Isaac Norris. 30 October 1784. Norris Papers, Family Letters 1: 56. Historical Society of Pennsylvania.

———. Letter to Isaac Norris III. 17 June 1785. Norris Papers, Family Letters 1: 63. Historical Society of Pennsylvania.

———. Letter to Isaac Norris III. 9 September 1785. Norris Papers, Family Letters 1: 65. Historical Society of Pennsylvania.

———. Letter to Isaac Norris III. 28 October 1785. Norris Papers, Family Letters 1: 66. Historical Society of Pennsylvania.

———. Letter to Isaac Norris. 22 December 1785. Norris Papers, Family Letters 1: 69. Historical Society of Pennsylvania.

———. Letter to Charles Thomson. 16 May 1786. Maria Dickinson Logan Papers, case 35, shelf 4, p. 6. Historical Society of Pennsylvania.

———. Letter to Charles Thomson. 15 November 1787. Maria Dickinson Logan Papers, case 35, shelf 4, p. 15. Historical Society of Pennsylvania.

———. Letter to Hannah Thomson. 18 October 1786. Maria Dickinson Logan Papers, case 35, shelf 4, p. 11. Historical Society of Pennsylvania.

"Party to Virginia, A." Watercolor sketch. *Rhoads Family Manuscripts,* E-95, 1: 60. Historical Society of Pennsylvania.

*Philadelphia Monthly Meeting (Arch Street) Minutes, 1782–1789.* Microfilm. Friends Historical Library, Swarthmore College.

Philander [Joshua Fisher]. Letters to Cleora [Hannah Pemberton]. 24 November 1781 and 1 June 1783. Pemberton Papers 36: 28 and 39: 8. Historical Society of Pennsylvania.

Radner, John B. "The Art of Sympathy in Eighteenth-Century British Moral Thought." *Studies in Eighteenth-Century Culture* 9: 189–210.

Rhoads, Elizabeth. Letter to Samuel Rhoads. 29 August 1786. Rhoads Family Manuscripts, E-95,1: 76. Historical Society of Pennsylvania.

Rhoads, Mary. Letter to Samuel Rhoads. 9 September 1786. Rhoads Family Manuscripts, E-95,1: 70. Historical Society of Pennsylvania.

Rhoads, Sarah. "Account of my beloved Daughters." Manuscript Commonplace Books. Historical Society of Pennsylvania.

Rotundo, E. Anthony. *American Manhood: Transformations in Masculinity from the Revolution to the Modern Era.* New York: Basic Books, 1993.

Shields, David S. *Civil Tongues & Polite Letters in British America.* Chapel Hill: Univ. of North Carolina Press, 1997.

Silver, Allan. "Friendship in Commercial Society: Eighteenth-Century Social Theory and Modern Sociology." *American Journal of Sociology* 95 (1990): 1474–1504.

Smith, John Rhea. *Journal at Nassau Hall.* 1 January 1786 to 22 September 1786. Bound photostat. Firestone Rare Books and Manuscripts Library, Princeton University. (Catalogued as "Diary of an Anonymous Student," General Mss. Bound, C0199, P02 .503, Am 12800.)

Smith-Rosenberg, Carroll. "The Female World of Love and Ritual: Relations Between Women in Nineteenth-Century America." *Disorderly Conduct: Visions of Gender in Victorian America.* New York: Oxford Univ. Press, 1985.

Steele, Richard. "Spectator No. 364." *The Spectator.* Ed. Donald F. Bond. Vol. 3. London: Oxford, 1965. 366–71.

Sterne, Laurence. *A Sentimental Journey.* New York: Penguin, 1986.

Sweeney, John A. H. "The Norris-Fisher Correspondence: A Circle of Friends, 1779–82." *Delaware History* 6 (1955): 187–232.

Thomson, Charles. Letter to Isaac Norris. 19 June 1784. *The Life of Charles Thomson, Secretary of the Continental Congress and Translator of the Bible from the Greek.* By Lewis R. Harley. Philadelphia: George W. Jacobs, 1900. 200.

———. Letter to Thomas Jefferson. 18 June 1784. Boyd 305–6.

Thomson, Hannah. Letter to John Mifflin. 12 May 1785. Manuscript Collection, Yi2 7295 F, p. 126. Library Company of Philadelphia.

———. Letter to John Mifflin, Jr. 15 September 1785. Manuscript Collection, Yi2 7295 F, p.184. Library Company of Philadelphia.

Thoreau, Henry David. *A Week on the Concord and Merrimack Rivers.* Princeton: Princeton Univ. Press, 1980.

Webster, Daniel. "To James Hervey Bingham." 3 April 1804. *The Papers of Daniel Webster.* Ed. Charles M. Wiltse. Vol. 1. Hanover: Univ. Press of New England, 1974. 50–51.

White, Francis. *Philadelphia Directory.* Philadelphia: Young, Stewart & McCulloch, 1785.

Wood, Gordon S. *The Radicalism of the American Revolution.* New York: Knopf, 1992.

Woodward, Ruth L., ed. "Journal at Nassau Hall: The Diary of John Rhea Smith, 1786." *Princeton University Library Chronicle* 46 (1985): 269–92 and 47 (1985): 48–70.

Woodward, Ruth L., and Wesley Frank Craven, eds. *Princetonians,1784–1790: A Biographical Dictionary.* Princeton: Princeton Univ. Press, 1991.

Wordsworth, William. *The Prelude, 1799, 1805, 1850.* New York: Norton, 1979.

Young, Edward. *The Complaint: Or, Night Thoughts.* Hartford: S. Andrus & Son, 1847.

# Chapter 10

# The Swan of Litchfield
## *Sarah Pierce and the Lesbian Landscape Poem*

## *Lisa L. Moore*

One of the most important documents of love between women in early America is a poem by Sarah Pierce. Pierce is a well-known figure in the early Republic as the founder of the Litchfield Female Academy, often called the first American institution of higher education for women. Among her students were Catherine and Harriet Beecher, and her four-volume *Sketches of Universal History Compiled from Several Authors, for the Use of Schools* (1811–18), was one of the first history textbooks written in the United States. Yet very little is known about Pierce's relationship with Abigail Smith, the young woman to whom she addressed her poem. Abigail was the sister of another major figure, Elihu Hubbard Smith, whose voluminous diaries tell us much of what we know about the Connecticut Wits and New York and New Haven social life at the turn of the century. Elihu Smith recorded Sarah Pierce's poem to his sister in his diary in 1798, along with the intriguing story of how it came to be written. This essay is the first to place Pierce's poem in the history of same-sex relationships in the early United States.

Sarah Pierce was born in 1767 in Litchfield, Connecticut. She lived all her life in Litchfield and died there in 1852. In addition to the widely used *Universal History,* she composed short plays for her students to act in the early years of her school, before drama came to seem a suspect pursuit for young ladies; she wrote commencement addresses that deserve to be ranked not only with some of the earliest feminist writing in the United States but also as documents presaging Transcendentalism in their understanding of the relations between spirit and intellect; and she wrote lyric verse, including the poem considered here, a pastoral, in which she suggests that rather than marrying, she and Abigail Smith should set up house together and live in idyllic harmony in a beautiful landscape.[1]

The practice of seeing a landscape, whether a literal or a literary one, as a woman's body is well-established in the eighteenth-century Anglo-American tradition of the "sister arts" of painting, poetry, and garden design.[2] Pierce's poem renders the visual landscape as an embodiment of her desire for a particular beloved woman, the addressee of the poem. And it extends this trope to an understanding of the relation between the natural and built landscapes as a relation of power, and thus brings the desire between the two women, the speaker and addressee of the poem, into the political and economic mainstream of the new republic. The poem links the female-headed household it envisions to a critique of slavery and of received religion, two topics of enduring interest to intellectual and political life in the early United States. Reading this document as part of lesbian history helps demonstrate that intimacy between women was a sustaining feature of eighteenth-century New England intellectual life.

The lesbian reading offered here is not quite the same as arguing that Sarah Pierce was—or was not—a lesbian. There are several barriers to reconstructing Sarah Pierce's interior and affective world. First, few of Sarah Pierce's personal writings—letters or journals—survive. Although she was a frequent correspondent of many notable New Englanders, and although keeping a journal was part of the curriculum she set for her own students, Sarah Pierce has come down to us primarily as a public figure. Her *Sketches of Universal History,* composed as a textbook for her own students, was first published in 1811 and was her best-known work. A few unpublished sources remain. Several of her students transcribed and thus memorialized the plays she wrote for them to perform at school exhibitions, including a drama about the famous female friendship in the Bible entitled "Ruth." Many of the commencement addresses she composed for graduation exercises at Litchfield Female Academy have also survived. And finally, the "Verses" addressed to Abigail Smith, the focus of this essay, survived because it was recorded in the journals of Abigail's brother and Sarah Pierce's friend and correspondent, Elihu Hubbard Smith. The poem is perhaps the most personal of all the extant writings of Sarah Pierce, a crucial item in the "archive of feelings" that makes up lesbian history.[3]

This chapter seeks to reconstruct a context within which it is possible to read the lesbian form and content of Pierce's poem, rather than attempting to precisely define the nature of Pierce's historical relationship with Abigail Smith. My assumption is that we can take what the poet says about her desires—that she wishes to spend the rest of her life with her friend rather than marrying a man—at face value, and also that we can reconstruct the sexual, romantic, political, religious, literary, and artistic meanings of that desire in Pierce's distinctive 1790s moment, attending both to alterities and continuities between the present and the past. Whether or not Sarah Pierce was a lesbian, her poem is part of lesbian history; just because so little information survives about her relationship with Abigail Smith is no reason to assume that it was not a romantic and erotic relationship. Pierce's lifelong personal avoidance of marriage, the anti-marriage views she apparently shared with Abigail's brother Elihu, and her interest in the biblical story of Ruth all suggest that her primary attachments were to women. Even more intriguing, Pierce chose to write her poem to Abigail in a genre—the landscape poem—that in the late eighteenth century was coming to be identified with erotic views of female bodies and with love between women. It is this latter, less obvious, and well-known context that I want to fill in here.

### Pierce's "Verses"

The title by which Pierce's poem is known may not have been hers. It appears as "Verses, written in the Winter of 1792, & addressed to Abigail Smith Jr.—by Sally Pierce" in Elihu Smith's diaries. According to Elihu, who recorded the poem in December 1795, the verses were written three years earlier, when his sister Abigail was seventeen years old and Sarah Pierce twenty-five. The poem consists of nineteen quatrains of iambic pentameter verse, including an "Epitaph" clearly modeled after Gray's famous "Elegy Written in a Country Churchyard." The verses start with a description of the house Sarah Pierce imagines building for her beloved and then moves to a description of the surrounding landscape, including not only the fruits and vegetables the two women will grow but also the views they will cultivate and the walks they will take. At the end of the poem, Pierce depicts the tombstone of the two women being visited by neighboring "maids and matrons," who read the epitaph and shed a tear for the beauty of the relationship between Sarah and Abigail. Elihu prefaces his transcription with a brief anecdote about how the poem came to be written, saying that "the knowledge of a few circumstances, connected with the following little Poem, is necessary to it's [sic] being understood." [Please see the Appendix for the full text of Pierce's poem.]

Smith goes to some lengths to establish the importance of the "strict in-timacy" which had subsisted for "some years, between Miss Sally Pierce & my two eldest sisters, Mary and Abigail."[4] Mary, Smith tells us, had just an-nounced her plans to get married, and the "conclusion" of Sally and Abi-gail was that "when Mary left them, the other two should unite, & spend their lives, together, 'in single blessedness.'" Smith tells us the discussion was pursued "sportingly," but he also considers the poetic product of the discussion serious enough to have kept a copy of it for three years and to record it for posterity in his journals.[5] Smith was very much interested in the promulgation of American letters and probably valued Pierce's poem as an addition to an emerging canon of poetry by New Englanders; but his preface suggests that he also considered it important as a document of a powerful and productive intimacy between women. The relationship also seems to have been remarkable enough that Smith has to explain it. Was Smith trying to downplay the potentially unconventional aspects of his sister's relationship for posterity? Given his own celebration of same-sex friendship and critique of marriage, discussed below, it seems more likely that he recorded the poem to memorialize an intimacy that might other-wise go unrecorded, and which he thought was noteworthy and admirable.

Smith tells us that the verses had their origins in a failed drawing. Here is the evening as imagined by Pierce's friend, during which his sisters Mary and Abigail provide inspiration:

Sally Pierce was, at the time of writing these lines, just beginning to acquire, by her own exertions, some feeble knowledge of Drawing. The three young women were together; it was evening; Sally had shewn them some of the productions of her pencil. . . . Before separating, it was agreed that Sally, should design a house suitable for each, & sketch the surrounding scenery. This, as soon as my sisters were gone, she sat down to do. Her first care was directed towards accomplishing a plan for Mary; whose lot being more cer-tainly decided, demanded the earliest attention. The inexperience of Miss Pierce, in the art of design, made her progress both slow & painful; so that, when she had effected her first picture, by the aid of the pencil, she had re-course to a readier instrument, & relied on the pen for a sketch of the sec-ond. And lo! this is the landscape which she drew.[6]

Smith literally calls Pierce's poem a drawing. One of the challenges facing the American landscape artist attempting to adapt European aesthetic conventions was that of scale. Unlike the hinterlands of the British Isles, the American wilderness was "limitless and therefore unpaintable."[7] The landscape artist's first task, then, was to manage the overwhelming scale of the prospect. Pierce registers this sense of visual overwhelm in literary terms when she says "The various landscape rushes on my view" (14). This "rush" is managed by sorting the landscape into "various" categories, arranging it into that "mixture of wild and improved nature which gave the promise of progress and bore the trace of civilization" which characterizes the American picturesque:[8]

> The cultivated farm, the flowery lawn, (15)
>
> . . .
>
> The fertile "meadows trim with daisies pied";
> The garden, breathing Flora's best perfumes; (17–18)
>
> . . .
>
> See yonder hillock, where our golden corn
> Waves its bright head to every passing breeze;
> Yon fruitful fields our sportive flocks adorn,
> Our cows at rest beneath the neighboring trees. (25–8)

The poem goes on to name a "distant Town," a "mount," a "Wood," a "river," and a "Village." The first half of the poem offers the reader/viewer a "prospect" of these sights, all from the same vantage point, the one that "rushes" on the speaker's "view" in the fourth stanza. In stanza ten the speaker's surveying eye comes to rest, and we withdraw with her into the wood or "grove" where she imagines that herself and her friend will "oft retire."

The grove, grotto, or other secluded garden space was often associated with female intimacy, even female sexual intimacy, in the metropolitan tradition of eighteenth-century English landscape design. For example, the English botanist Mary Delany designed a grotto for her intimate friend the Duchess of Portland on the Duchess's estate at Bulstrode, and also dedicated a portico (a sheltered seat) on her own Delville estate to her friend.[9] While stanza ten tells us that the activity pursued by the friends in this retreat is "Contemplation," the next stanza plunges us into a multisensory experience that alludes to female sexual pleasure. The silence of the previous stanza is broken by intimate "murmurs," "whispering" and "echoes soft" emanating from the river and the pines. The noises rise to a "hoarse" crescendo as the water passes over rocks, and we are left with a vision of "a rain-bow in the moistened sky." The curving shape of the rainbow is echoed by the arch of the sky, moistened like the arch-shaped interior of a woman's body. The best-known tradition of such erotic landscape description, going back at least to *A New Description of Merryland* (1740), sees the "Air, Soil, Rivers, Canals &c" from the ribald perspective of the heterosexual male rake. Landscape features are thinly veiled allegories for women's body parts, and the "geography" of Merryland is a catalogue of sexual practices.[10] But in the latter part of the century a group of women botanists, garden designers, and writers, including Mary Delany and Anna Seward, began to adopt this trope to create representations of intimacy between women. Pierce's poem is the first known American contribution to this genre, which I call "lesbian landscape." We will return to this theme in a moment, after completing Sarah Pierce's circuit tour.

The poem then follows "a river solemn," giving us a tour of the remainder of the poem's landscape that works like a circuit garden. The circuit garden, an eighteenth-century three-dimensional narrative form, was an influential exemplar of the notion that poetry, painting, and gardens could all tell stories or make arguments in similar ways. Circuit gardens such as the Elysian Fields at Stowe, a famous English example designed by William Kent and Stowe's early eighteenth-century owner William Cobham, includes a Temple of Ancient Virtue, featuring busts of classical philosophers and built in the Ionic style, a Temple of Modern Virtue built as a Gothic ruin, and a Temple of British Worthies, containing busts of famous Englishmen, placed downhill from their ancient predecessors so that they look up to them literally and symbolically.[11] The idea, of course, was that visitors would take a walk around the circuit and enjoy a visual narrative comparing the ruins of modern virtue to the classic beauty of its ancient counterpart, and noting that the best of contemporary British culture could only seek to emulate the heights of the classical past. Pierce describes such a circuit in her "Verses" but uses it to come to much more radical conclusions. Circuit gardens were known in America but were often too expensive to re-create. Many American landscape parks anticipated the picturesque aesthetic of the late eighteenth century in their use of natural wildness as a design feature. One of the most complete such gardens was Graeme Park in New Jersey, where the natural wetlands were framed by a series of views from the imposing stone house. Graeme Park was the setting of Elizabeth Graeme Fergusson's "Attic Evenings," an important series of salons that attracted major figures in Philadelphia and colonial society prior to the Revolution. But American circuit gardens were more likely to be found in literature than landscape.

In Pierce's poem, we are taken past various symbolic views and objects that make up a narrative of moral progress. The circuit concludes, of course, with a view of the graves of the friends; the poem, in stanza sixteen, becomes a temporal as well as spatial tour as "swift-winged Time" flies by.

The final object in the circuit is the "plain, smooth stone" beneath which the friends lie together, crowned with a "simple Epitaph":

> Beneath this stone two female friends interr'd
> Who past their lives content, in solitude;
> They wish'd no ill, yet oft, thro' ignorance, err'd;
> Reader! Depart, reflect, and be as good. (73–6)

The intimacy of the two women even in death dignifies and memorializes their relationship in life. Their "content" with their lives as a female couple is related to their "solitude," that is, their separation from the world in a utopian natural landscape that they are uniquely positioned to cultivate and enjoy.

The final apostrophe to the "Reader!" raises once again the relationship between visual and literary art, and even adds the element of three-dimensional landscape design. Of course, the "reader" of the epitaph in the poem would also be a "viewer" of the two-dimensional visual composition, the engraved stone itself, as well as an appreciator of the place of the women's monument in the surrounding landscape. We learn that "Matrons and maids shall often stoop" to read the words on the tablet, telling us that it has been carefully placed low to the ground to emphasize the moral meaning of the poem's circuit. From the erotic interior of the grove to the privacy of the grave, we have followed the journey of the two friends through time and space, imbibing their values of simplicity, compassion, and community along the way. Thus, intimacy between women is inscribed in the landscape of the poem as part of nature, an inevitable feature of the American pastoral.

## The Swan of Lichfield

As noted earlier, another important source for Pierce's lesbian pastoral vision is a literary one. While imbuing the landscape with the characteristics of an erotic female body had a prominent history in English garden design, it was also a feature of the widely circulated poetry of the English Romantic Anna Seward. Seward participated in a community of artists, physicians, and educators in Lichfield, England, a community with direct ties to Pierce's circle in Litchfield, Connecticut via Elihu Smith, a correspondent and later editor of Seward's patron Erasmus Darwin. Known as "the swan of Lichfield" after her birthplace near Bristol, Seward was one of the first biographers of another Lichfield native, Samuel Johnson, and a prolific and well-known poet by the time of her death in 1809. She was a visitor and correspondent of Mary Delany, the designer of garden grottos for female friends referred to above, and wrote a critique of Erasmus Darwin's representation of Delany's botanical illustrations in his 1789 epic poem, *The Botanic Garden*.

Darwin, another Lichfield resident, was, like Smith, a physician and botanist. His long poem, *The Botanic Garden*, gives a detailed and anthropomorphic account of the reproductive life of plants. Influenced by Linnaeus, Darwin categorizes plants in terms of how they reproduce, personifying this process in terms of human "desires," speaking of certain species as "eunuchs," others as "feminine males," still others as "masculine ladies."[12] Seward defended this explicitly sexual tome as reading matter for young women in her 1804 *Memoirs of the Life of Dr. Darwin*, arguing: "do not suppose that a virtuous girl, or young married woman, could be induced, by reading the Botanic Garden, to imitate the involuntary libertinism of a fungus or a flower."[13] Viewing the natural world as erotically charged and anthropomorphic (capable, for example, of "libertinism") was characteristic of English Linnaeans such as Darwin, Delany, and Seward.

Unlike Sarah Pierce, Seward left a copious record of her interior life, especially her feelings of disappointed love for another woman. Seward, born in 1742 in Lichfield, was a full generation older than Sarah Pierce but a protégé of Darwin's, who moved to Lichfield when Seward was twelve years old and took a keen interest in the poet's early writings. When Seward was fourteen, her family took into their home the daughter of a friend, a five-year-old girl named Honora Sneyd. By the time Honora became an accomplished and beautiful young woman, she and Anna Seward were inseparable. Honora had several male suitors, but the only one Seward approved of was Major John André, whom Honora had rejected, and her approval waxed warmest after André's death in 1780 in the American Revolution. "Monody on the Death of Major André" (1781) was one of Seward's earliest publications.[14] By that time, Honora was already dead, having sealed her fate, Seward believed, when she married Richard Lovell Edgeworth, whom Seward described in a poem as "that specious false-one, by whose cruel wiles / I lost thy amity."[15] Edgeworth was the widowed father of four children, including the future novelist Maria, when the pair met. Seward experienced Honora's marriage as a profound betrayal from which she was never to recover, and her feelings provided the topic for many of her best poems of the 1770s and 1780s. Strikingly, these are also landscape poems in which the pastoral space is pictured as imbued with the desire of the speaker and the body of the lost love. Among these "lesbian landscape poems" is the "Epistle to Miss Honora Sneyd. . . . from the Grave of a Suicide," which can be productively compared to Pierce's "Verses."[16]

All of these poems begin with the speaker situated in a beautiful outdoor setting. In "Grave of a Suicide," the tone of loss and mourning is established by this setting: the grave "where the love-desperate maid, of vanish'd years / Slung her dire cord between the sister trees" (4–5). The source for Seward's poem is the story of a young woman, disappointed in love, who kills herself and thus enters local mythology. We learn that the suicide died and was buried on the very spot the poet chooses for her "fond, fruitless plaints" (2). Seated on "the bank that screens" the "mouldering form" (7) of the corpse, the poet surveys the prospect. She notes its lack of conventional pastoral adornment: "No labouring hinds on yonder meads appear" (17)—"yet," (19) she says:

> The nearly-meeting trees, with plenteous spray,
> Arch oe'r the darkling land that winds away
> Far to the right. (21–3)

Some characteristic images for this group of lesbian landscape poems are at work here. The arch, the notion of plenitude, and the synaesthetic appeal of "spray" as both a visual and a tactile image (a spray of branches and a spray of moisture) are common to Seward's other poems in this group. The conceit of the poet as landscape painter is also key to this kind of poem. As she looks "to the right," she constructs a little landscape painting of words with the conventional image of the road dwindling away into the distance as in a Salvator Rosa painting. She then looks "in front" (23) and "to the left" (25) in turn, establishing small pictures in a few lines with each new perspective point. Another feature of these poems is their appeal to all the senses, both with the kind of overladen multisensory imagery noted above and with attention to the landscape's "rich perfume" (28) and "fragrance" (30)—here rendered ironic and sad by its proximity to "the hapless grave" (30). Moisture—"balmy dews" (34), "tearful eye" (53)—is another common conceit in Seward's lesbian landscape poems. The final stanza of this poem contains the most explicit version of Seward's reshaping of the landscape in the image of her own desire. The final vista is of a landscape where

> each object seems array'd
> In the fair semblance of the absent maid;
> Where bowers and lawns her stamp and image bear,
> At once, alas! so distant, and so near!
> And, to the aching heart, and tearful eye,
> Stand the mute spectres of departed joy. (49–54)

The poet's desiring gaze shapes the pastoral world such that it reflects back to her the form and face ("stamp and image") of her lost love. Imaging the landscape is important in Seward's poems to Honora, then, because it allows her to remake the world before the Fall. Her pastoral ideal, her unattainable Eden, is one in which the beloved woman remains with her, as familiar and accessible as "Lichfield" itself.

### Transatlantic Connections

Seward's intellectual and artistic community of writers and botanists was tied to Pierce's circle of writers, educators, physicians, and clergymen through the medium of transatlantic correspondence. Recent scholarship on women's writing in eighteenth-century North America has revealed the extent to which publication as such was only one medium, and not always the most important one, for the transmission of literature, especially writing by women. For the women poets of the generation preceding Pierce's, "the writers were known to one another and passed manuscripts among themselves—thus receiving a public notice like 'publication,'" according to Carla Mulford.[17] Taking seriously manuscript poetry such as Pierce's, Mulford argues, reveals "a culture more close to the oral and sociable networks that actually seem to have existed in the era of revolution."[18] For these coterie poets, "the handwritten manuscript, circulated among friends and family, was their preferred form of publication."[19] It is evident from the form in which Pierce's poem survived—copied into the journal of her friend Elihu Smith—that it was in wide circulation, not only among the men of Smith's all-male Friendly Club but no doubt also among the women with whom they regularly corresponded and conversed.[20] While there is no direct evidence that Pierce knew Seward's Honora poems, the similarities between her "Verses" and these well-known earlier examples of lesbian landscape poetry indicate the existence of a transatlantic feminist culture of which both were a part.

Seward's was a well-known name in New England by the time the *Lady's Magazine* declared in 1793: "The FEMALES of Philadelphia are by no means deficient in *those talents,* which have immortalized the name of a *Montague,* a *Craven,* a *More,* and a *Seward,* in their inimitable writings."[21] Seward was an important influence on a group of well-known women poets, including Elizabeth Graeme Fergusson, Annis Boudinot Stockton, Susanna Wright, and Milcah Martha Moore, who wrote in the mid-Atlantic region before and during the Revolutionary War and were well-known to literate Litchfielders in the 1790s.[22] Other than her general celebrity, however, Seward had a particular link to the Litchfield circle in which Pierce's poem was circulating. Elihu Smith, long an admirer of Seward's mentor Erasmus Darwin, wrote to Darwin in 1798 asking permission to bring out the first American edition of *The Botanic Garden.* Smith had been an enthusiast of the work since its publication in 1789; he purchased a copy of the first American edition when it became available in the fall of the same year.[23] Whether or not Seward's Honora poems were published in the 1770s and 80s, the years in which "Major André," "Elegy on Captain Cook," her verse novel *Louisa,* and other works appeared in both English and American editions, they certainly circulated in manuscript in the Lichfield circle of which she and Darwin were among the most prominent members. Seward's lesbian landscape poems, then, could well have formed part of the transatlantic correspondence and manuscript public culture that linked the Swan of Lichfield with the foremost female intellectual of Litchfield, Connecticut.

When we look again at the imagery of Pierce's poem, both Darwin's sexualization of the landscape and Seward's eroticization of it as female seem to be at play. The poem begins with one of the most common images used by eighteenth-century landscape gardeners to represent a woman's breast, belly, or buttock: "On rising ground we'll rear a little dome," an image repeated later as a "hillock" and "mount." The sensual imagery of the poem contributes to the construction of an eroticized, feminized landscape that not only "swells" with curvaceous mounds and

cleft-like vales, but also smells "fragrant," of "Flora's best perfumes," enabling the ravished senses of the observer to "delighted mark new beauties
as they stray," from convention perhaps, or from propriety. This imagery
of playful straying is repeated later as "sportive" and "play." The "flowery
lawn" is a Darwinian description of pubic hair, especially as it "sucks the
fragrance of the honied dew" in an image of combined smell and taste.
(Liquid secretions are also imaged as "tear" and "dew"). The flowered
meadow is "fertile," "fruitful" and "plenteous," the "garden, breathing." The
curving "rain-bow in the moistened sky," noted above, can now be seen in
context as part of a network of images of strong-smelling, curvaceous,
moist, and dripping shapes in the poem that do much to convey the erotic
intimacy to which the speaker never directly refers.

This reading suggests that whether or not Sarah Pierce was articulating
the direct influence of Anna Seward's poem, both poets were responding
to a moment in literary and cultural history when imbuing the landscape
with the lineaments of a beloved woman's body was a plausible and powerful way to represent lesbian desire. Eighteenth-century erotic literature,
as noted above, had long exploited the comic potential of seeing hills and
valleys as "mounds of Venus" and "doors of Life"; the Romantic poets who
were so important to 1790s New England radicals turned from ridicule to
respect and even reverence in their personification of the natural world.[24]
But when erotic gaze that rests on the feminized landscape is that of another woman, we begin to glimpse a less prominent tradition, in which
women's understandings of their own and one another's bodies were
shaped by the particular status of gender, land, and labor in New England.

## The Litchfield World of Love and Friendship

Pierce's use of landscape also allows her to engage in issues of public importance and articulate a new vision for society, a vision she shared with
her friend and correspondent Elihu Hubbard Smith. In Smith's diaries, we
have a unique window into the sexually progressive world of 1790s Litchfield he shared with Sarah Pierce. Elihu Hubbard Smith, like Sarah Pierce
(whom he always called Sally, as did all her intimates), was a native of
Litchfield. Smith was born in 1771 to Reuben Smith, an apothecary, and
Abigail Hubbard. Elihu Smith graduated from Yale College in 1786 at the
age of fifteen, by far the youngest "man" in his class, and returned to Litchfield to study medicine, work in the family shop, and pursue his literary

interests. He later moved to Philadelphia and then New York to further his studies, and it is from these locations that his letters to Sarah Pierce are dated. He is said to have authored the first sonnets ever published by an American, and was the author of magazine verse and essays. Both Smith and Pierce remained unmarried, though Smith died at the age of twenty-seven, passing his last moments in the arms of his friends and fellow-physicians Samuel Latham Mitchill and Edward Miller, while Pierce lived out her old age as a New England "spinster." Both challenged the economic norm of the male-headed household and the reproductive norm of republican motherhood, substituting in their place a vision of egalitarian same-sex unions and the production of education and writing as the basis for an enlightened republic.

The detailed, passionate essays Smith wrote about his friends Reuben Hitchcock and Thomas O'Hara Croswell attest to the power of the institution of romantic same-sex friendship between men as well as between women in the 1790s. Nancy Cott argues that the 1790s saw the invention of a new American ideology of same-sex friendship because "relations between equals—"peer relationships"—were superseding hierarchical relationships as the desired norms of human interaction."[25] Both the revolutionary politics and the religious iconoclasm of the period also encouraged sexual experimentation, according to historians John D'Emilio and Estelle B. Freedman.[26] The late eighteenth century also saw increased geographical mobility and the growth of towns, fostering greater physical freedom and anonymity in a more mobile, porous, and urban New England world.[27]

It is in this context of post-Puritan, pre-Victorian social loosening and experimentation that Elihu Smith articulates his closeness to other men. Smith's understanding of these relationships tells us something about the conventions of friendship at work in Sarah Pierce's Litchfield circle, among both men and women. For example, Smith writes of himself and his school friend Thomas O'Hara Croswell: "Never, I believe, were two hearts more united in each other, more unreserved in their communications, in every respect more One."[28] And in a letter to another friend, Theodore Dwight, Smith sets out to clear himself of the charge of being "deficient in affection" toward his friend, one

> towards whom my heart has always gone forth in the
>     full vigor of attachment; &
> in respect to whom—if it be—

in heaven a crime to love too well—
I am certainly chargeable with guilt.[29]

Smith's use of the terms "crime" and "guilt" in relation to his friendship with Dwight suggest a sexual element to their friendship. In its original context in Pope's "Elegy to the Memory of an Unfortunate Lady" ("Is it, in Heav'n, a crime to love too well?"[30]), the quoted line refers to the bloody ghost of a woman who committed suicide rather than marry the man of her uncle's choice. She is buried "without a stone, without a name."[31] Something about Smith's relationship with Dwight caused him to compare himself to Pope's fictional sexual outlaw. Finally, the romantic aspects of the friendships between men in Smith's coterie can be glimpsed in the fact that his friend Mason Cogswell, another poet-physician, adopted as noms de plume for himself and a friend the names of the lovers from a play Smith wrote, denoting himself "Edwin" and his male correspondent "Angelina."[32] The erotic aspects of same-sex intimacies were clearly part of the Litchfield world shared by Elihu Smith and Sarah Pierce.[33]

Throughout his diaries and correspondence, Smith expresses skepticism about the possibility of happiness in heterosexual marriage. Smith and Pierce shared an especially intense correspondence around the time of Abigail Smith's proposed marriage. Although Smith had confided to his diary after a visit with his sister that "her heart is too sensible: a husband firm, yet tender, is necessary for her,"[34] he and Pierce agreed that the man Abigail chose was highly unsuitable, and their remarks about the proposed match make it seem unlikely that the younger woman could have chosen anyone that the confirmed bachelor and the passionate spinster would have approved. Smith assures Pierce that "your apprehension" is well warranted: "Whatever good qualities, & whatever great talents & attainments, Mr. Bacon may possess, it is a serious deduction from the pleasure of having my sister form such a connection, that she must be so remotely separated from us."[35] Smith tells Pierce in a tone of doleful anticipation: "there are a hundred ways in which a man may contrive to break the heart of a wife, with such a heart as Abby's."[36] In a letter to Abigail herself, he warns that for the most part, young people are motivated by lust rather than good judgment in forming marital attachments: "Instant gratification is all the parties pant after," resulting in nothing but "the groans of connubial anguish, & din of domestic discord."[37] Later letters to Pierce mention Mr. Bacon's "little, occasional asperities of temper," "faults," and "error."[38]

## Public Feelings

Smith's record is especially helpful in reconstructing the affective context of Pierce's poem because the poem itself is rather reticent on the subject of the relationship between the poet and the addressee. Though the poem opens with an apostrophe to the sharer of the poet's future life, it speaks not of the feelings the lovers share but rather of their economic and political values. In this way the poem links the possibilities of a household headed by a female couple to the utopian vision of a politically, economically, and morally renovated Republic:

> On rising ground we'll rear a little dome;
> Plain, neat, and elegant, it shall appear;
> No slaves shall there lament their native home,
> Or, silent, drop the unavailing tear. (1–4)

The epithets "plain, neat, and elegant" speak to the moral value attached by New England Congregationalists such as Pierce to material simplicity. This language recurs later in the poem (the Village is characterized by "simple elegance, in neat array" [46], and the ladies will lie beneath a "plain, smooth, stone" [65] with a "simple Epitaph" [69]), suggesting the importance of this value for the poet as she conducts a muted argument against luxury ("pomp" and "wealth") throughout.

In this poem, female friendship is understood not as a refuge from the public world, but as the source of an alternative public sphere that would engage with social issues in an emancipatory way. Although this utopian landscape will be ideal, then, it will be no isolated retreat; rather, in its engagement with political debates on such issues as slavery, it will provide a much-needed corrective to the corruption of public institutions as the poet sees them. This corruption is a result of the betrayal of Revolutionary ideals of equality and freedom, ideals the poet aims to create in her relationship with her beloved. This political understanding of women's friendship perhaps accounts for the rather cool tone of the poem. The invocation of affect in this first stanza is reserved not for the lovers, but for Sarah Pierce's slave neighbors, to whose "silent" "unavailing" tears she here bears witness. Litchfield had an active Manumission Society of which Elihu Smith was a member in the 1790s.[39] Questions of slave and free labor and their relation to Revolutionary politics and the local economy are an important context for the vision of female intimacy put forward by Pierce's poem.

The economic undergirding of this household is so important that the poet gives it another stanza before turning to the more conventional topic of the pastoral landscape. In this household, she tells us in the second stanza, "Content and cheerfulness shall dwell within, / And each domestic serve thro' love alone." Pierce obviously imagines a household where mistresses and domestic servants share labor. The idea that "love alone" will be enough to compensate her servants may be another expression of the ideal of peer relationships referred to by Cott; as von Frank observes, this idea "may seem sentimentally at odds with economic realities," but "what is better worth noticing is simply the substitution, in this utopian vision, of love for force."[40] The basis for this altered economic and political reality is "meek Religion" which will "build her throne" in the household. No conventional expression of piety, this assertion links Pierce's vision of transformation to the radical social rearrangements of the Second Great Awakening.[41]

This massive social movement, which was to last for the next fifty years, was characterized by a movement away from a Calvinist theology of innate human depravity and toward an emphasis on the importance of personal faith and the inner life. Ultimately, these changes were to give rise to the radical anti-institutional tenets of Transcendentalism. Pierce was at the center of these movements and controversies, but she offers her own urbane and synthesizing response to them, readable in the term "meek Religion"; religion that, rather than seeking a high place in a social hierarchy or making a bid for institutional power, sees its place more modestly as the interior of the human heart and its mission as the connection of one heart to another through equality, compassion, and love.

Pierce's more conventional employment of such references for picturesque effect occurs in her reference to a "Wood" behind the visionary house in the poem, which she says is

> Like those where Druids wont, in days of yore,
> When Superstition wore Religion's form,
> With mystic rites their unknown Gods adore. (34–6)

The poet imagines a landscape in which the indigenous non-Christian religion would be Druidism, rather than the spiritual practices of the indigenous people who were her northwestern Connecticut neighbors.[42] Such an obvious blind spot serves to underline the fictional status of the landscape in the poem; it is a utopian vision rather than a concrete plan of action. The same picturesque effect is sought in the reference to "Fairies" who, "(if Fairies e'er have been,) / Will featly foot the moonlight hours away." The echo of Ariel's song from *The Tempest* ("foot it featly, here and there / And sweet sprites the burden bear") brings the political utopia decisively into the greenworld of pastoral convention.

As at Stowe in England, the circuit laid out by following the river in Pierce's poem is also enhanced by architectural features, but here, in line with the poem's republican valuing of simplicity, we see not purpose-built classical temples but a "Village":

> Where simple elegance, in neat array,
> Might teach even pomp that, not to wealth confined,
> Genius & taste might to a cottage stray. (46–8)

The poet's appreciation of simplicity extends to the features of the view such as the village's "level grass-plot, smooth & green" (49). Next the river takes us to the hall where the friends reside, whose architectural features are delineated by their usefulness:

> Our plenteous store we'll freely give to all;
> Want ne'er shall pass, in sorrow, from our door;
> With joy we'll seat the beggar in our hall,
> And learn the tale of woe that sunk his store. (53–6)

The "door" and "hall" here are humble enough to receive the beggar and easy of access to those in need—not removed from the village scene but of it, spaces through which needy and fortunate alike may pass.

### Sarah Pierce and Lesbian History

Sarah Pierce contributed to the new importance of landscape in a post-revolutionary, early nationalist context in which one's point of view on land tenure, development, and exploration were decidedly urgent issues worked out both visually and in literary terms. Her lesbian pastoral absorbed these transatlantic influences and in turn gave back to the discourse of romantic friendship a vision of freedom and equality that was distinctly American and also distinctly of the 1790s. For the following decades were not to see the enfranchisement of enslaved people or the spread of democracy envisioned in Pierce's "Verses." Indeed, it was to be another fifty years before her radical vision of female sexual freedom could be as well articulated again. The poem looks forward to the scientifically informed, otherworldly, and homoerotic verses of Emily Dickinson, whose Transcendentalist generation Pierce influenced not only by her own writing but also as the principal of Litchfield Female Academy and hence the educator of the Beecher sisters and other important nineteenth-century women intellectuals.

Sarah Pierce's "Verses" to Abigail Smith, then, is an important document in both the history of romantic friendship, imagined as a chaste and virtuous alternative to marriage, and in the history of lesbian erotic writing, in which the landscape itself takes on the lineaments of the beloved woman's body. This double function is only a paradox if we assume that the two modes of relationship are mutually exclusive. In fact, this poem encourages us to see how a relationship between two women could be imagined in several different ways, just as it was probably lived. Sarah Pierce and Abigail Smith doubtless did not decide how and when to love each other, based on a rigid adherence to a particular model, any more than the rest of us do. The utopian landscape of Pierce's poem offers us a continuum between progressive political striving and utopian visions on the one hand, and individually gratifying erotic intimacy on the other, that we could say is characteristic not only of lesbian relationships but also of lesbian history itself.

## Appendix

"Verses," written in the Winter of 1792, & addressed to Abigail Smith Jr.— by Sally Pierce.

> On rising ground we'll rear a little dome;
> Plain, neat, and elegant, it shall appear;
> No slaves shall there lament their native home,
> Or, silent, drop the unavailing tear.

Content and cheerfulness shall dwell within,
And each domestic serve thro' love alone;
Coy Happiness we'll strive, for once, to win,
With meek Religion there to build her throne.

And oft our friends shall bless the lonely vale,
And, social, pass the wintry eves away;
Or, when soft Summer swells the fragrant gale,
Delighted mark new beauties as they stray.

Pleased with the scene, by Fancy's pencil drawn,
The various landscape rushes on my view;
The cultivated farm, the flowery lawn,
That sucks the fragrance of the honied dew.

The fertile "meadows trim with daisies pied";
The garden, breathing Flora's best perfumes;
And stored with herbs, whose worth, by Matrons tried,
Dispels disease, and gives health's roseate blooms.

Here vines, with purple clusters bending low,
And various fruit-trees loaded branches bear;
There roots of every kind profusely grown,
Bespeaking plenty thro' the circling year.

See yonder hillock, where our golden corn
Waves it's bright head to every passing breeze;
Yon fruitful fields our sportive flocks adorn,
Our cows at rest beneath the neighboring trees.

As misty clouds from silent streams arise,
Yon distant Town attracts the gazer's view;
Yon mount, whose lofty summit meets the skies,
Shelters the Village on the plain below.

Behind our lot, a Wood defies the storm,
Like those where Druids wont, in days of yore,
When Superstition wore Religion's form,
With mystic rites their unknown Gods adore.

Within this grove we'll oft retire to muse,
Where Contemplation builds her silent seat;
Her soothing influence she will ne'er refuse
To those who wander in this blest retreat.

A river solemn murmurs thro' the shades,
The whispering pines, in echoes soft, reply,
Then, hoards o'er rocks, it seeks the distant glades,
Forming a rain-bow in the moistened sky—

Nor leaves us hear—but thro' the Village winds,
Where simple elegance, in neat array,
Might teach even pomp that, not to wealth confined,
Genius & taste might to a cottage stray.

In front, a level grass-plot smooth & green,
Where neighboring children, pass sweet hours at play,
And Fairies oft, (if Fairies e'er have been,)
Will featly foot the moonlight hours away.

Our plenteous store we'll freely give to all;
Want ne'er shall pass, in sorrow, from our door;
With joy we'll seat the beggar in our hall,
And learn the tale of woe that sunk his store.

But chiefly those who pine, by sickness prest;
Whose merit, known to few, unheeded lies;
How sweet, to banish sorrow from the breast,
And bid fair hope shine sparkling in the eyes.

Thus, humbly blest, when youthful years are flown,
(Proud to be good, not wishing to be great,)
And swift-wing'd Time proclaimed our moments run,
Resign'd to heaven, we'll cheerful bow to fate.

Placed in one grave, beneath a plain, smooth, stone,—
Where oft the tear unfeign'd shall dew the face,
The sick, the poor, shall long our fate bemoan,
But wealth and grandeur never mark the place.

This simple Epitaph the stone adorns—
Which calls, from artless eyes, the frequent tear—
Matrons and maids shall often stoop to learn,
And all the Village think it passing rare.

## The Epitaph

Beneath this stone two female friends interr'd,
Who past their lives content, in solitude;
They wish'd no ill, yet oft, thro' ignorance, err'd;
Reader! Depart, reflect, and be as good.

### NOTES

1. In the only scholarly article on the poem, Albert J. von Frank cites Pierce's artistic debts (sometimes in the form of quoted lines) to canonical English poets Milton, Pomfret, and Gray (von Frank 53). "Sarah Pierce and the Poetic Origins of Utopian Feminism in America," *Prospects: An Annual Journal of American Cultural Studies* 14 (1989): 45–63.

2. See, for example, Carole Fabricant, "Binding and Dressing Nature's Loose Tresses: The Ideology of Augustan Landscape Design," *Studies in Eighteenth-Century Culture* 8, ed. Roseann Runte (Madison: Univ. of Wisconsin Press, 1979): 109–35, 111, and James Turner, "The Sexual Politics of Landscape: Images of Venus in Eighteenth-Century English Poetry and Landscape Gardening," *Studies in Eighteenth-Century Culture* 11, ed. Harry C. Payne (Madison: Univ. of Wisconsin Press, 1982): 357.

3. The term is Ann Cvetkovich's. See Cvetkovich, *An Archive of Feelings: Trauma, Sexuality, and Lesbian Public Cultures* (Durham: Duke Univ. Press, 2004).

4. James E. Cronin, ed., *Diary of Elihu Hubbard Smith* (Philadelphia: American Philosophical Society, 1973), 112.

5. Smith, 113.

6. Smith, 113.

7. Edward J. Nygren with Bruce Robertson, *Views and Visions: American Landscape Before 1830* (Washington, DC: Corcoran Gallery of Art, 1986), 32.

8. Nygren, 32.

9. See Lisa L. Moore, "Queer Gardens: Mary Delany's Flowers and Friendships," *Eighteenth-Century Studies* 39: 1 (2005): 50–51.

10. A modern edition of this work can be found in Patrick Spedding, ed., *Eighteenth-Century British Erotica*, Vol. 3 (London: Pickering and Chatto, 2002).

11. See Stephanie Ross, *What Gardens Mean* (Chicago: Univ. of Chicago Press, 1998) pp. 59–63, for a detailed description of how this circuit garden functioned in the eighteenth century.

12. Erasmus Darwin, *The Botanic Garden, A Poem, in Two Parts; containing The Economy of Vegetation and the Loves of the Plants. With Philosphical Notes* (London: Jones and Company, 1825), Canto IV line 304; Canto I note to line 69; Canto I note to line 183; Canto IV note to line 138, 142, 184, 285.

13. *Memoirs of the Life of Dr. Darwin* (London: 1804), vol. 6, 144–145.

14. In his important history of male friendship in early nineteenth-century America, Caleb Crain notes the romantic aspects of the legend of Major André as it circulated in Revolutionary America. *American Sympathy: Men, Friendship and Literature in the New Nation* (New Haven: Yale Univ. Press, 2001), pp. 1–15.

15. Anna Seward, "Sonnet XXXII," lines 2–3. *Original sonnets on various subjects; and odes paraphrased from Horace: by Anna Seward*. Second ed. London: 1799. *Eighteenth Century Collections Online*. Gale Group. http://galenet.galegroup.com/servlet/ECCO (January 9, 2006).

16. I would nominate the following poems as belonging to this group: "Elegy, Written at the Sea-side, and Addressed to Miss Honora Sneyd" (1773); "Epistle to Miss Honora Sneyd" (1770); "Honora: An Elegy" (undated); "The Anniversary" (1769); "Time Past" (1773); and the poem discussed above, "Epistle . . . from the Grave of a Suicide." References to the latter in this essay are to this edition: Seward, Anna. "Epistle to Miss Honora Sneyd, May 1772. Written in a Summer Evening, from the Grave of a Suicide." Theobald, R., ed., *The Poetical Works (1810)*. London: 1855. http://gateway.proquest.com/openurl?ctx_ver=Z39.88–2003&xri:pqil:res_ver=0.2&res_id=xri:lion-us&rft_id=xri:lion:ft:po:Z400482004:4 (January 9, 2006).

17. Carla Mulford, ed., *Only for the Eye of a Friend: The Poems of Annis Boudinot Stockton* (Charlottesville: Univ. Press of Virginia, 1995), xv.

18. Mulford, xv.

19. Catherine La Courreye Blecki and Karin A. Wulf, eds., *Milcah Martha Moore's Book: A Commonplace Book from Revolutionary America* (University Park: Pennsylvania State Univ. Press, 1997), xii.

20. Frederika Teute argues that women such as Pierce, Idea Strong, and Susan Bull Tracy were important participants in the intellectual culture of the all-male Friendly Club. "The Loves of the Plants; or, the Cross-Fertilization of Science and Desire at the End of the Eighteenth Century," *Huntington Library Quarterly* 63: 3 (2000): 320.

21. "Biography, Miss Anna Seward," *The Weekly Magazine of Original Essays, Fugitive Pieces, and Interesting Intelligence* (Philadelphia: May 18, 1799), 68; APS Online p. 169.

22. Elizabeth Fergusson, in particular, publicized the work of Seward and her associates in poems circulated in the 1780s. According to Susan Stabile, the poet

"sees the Litchfield group as a model for American arts and letters." *Memory's Daughters: The Material Culture of Remembrance in Eighteenth-Century America* (Ithaca: Cornell Univ. Press, 2004), 233.

23. Teute, 332.

24. Both these terms were used to describe features of the infamous West Wycombe erotic garden designed by Francis Dashwood. See Ross, 67. Mary Delany may have adapted these features for the garden spots she designed for her friend Margaret Harley. See Moore, 59–61.

25. Both the libertarian rhetoric of the American Revolution and the renewed emphasis on the equality of persons before Christ in the religious revivals hastened this process, according to Nancy Cott. *The Bonds of Womanhood: "Woman's Sphere" in New England, 1780–1935* (New Haven: Yale Univ. Press, 1977), 187.

26. They argue that "individual choice, rather than parental or state control, became more important, whether in courtship, marriage, or the treatment of sexual deviance . . . at a time when "the pursuit of happiness" became a political ideal, individual pleasure, and not simply the duty to procreate or to give comfort to one's spouse, came to be valued as a goal of sexual relations. *Intimate Matters: A History of Sexuality in America* (New York: Harper and Row, 1988), 40.

27. D'Emilio and Freedman, 43.

28. Smith, 40.

29. Smith, 174.

30. Alexander Pope, "Elegy to the Memory of an Unfortunate Lady." In Quiller-Couch, Arthur Thomas, Sir. *The Oxford Book of English Verse*. Oxford: Clarendon, 1919, [c1901]; Bartleby.com, 1999. www.bartleby.com/101/ . [7 August 2005], line 6.

31. Pope, 69.

32. Smith, 273 n. 82.

33. Elihu Smith's close friend, Charles Brockden Brown, was a central figure in early national homosocial networks and much of the information we have about this aspect of his life comes from Smith's diaries. See Crain, 53–97.

34. Smith, 134.

35. Smith, 231.

36. Smith, 231.

37. Smith, 276.

38. Smith, 277.

39. Edgar J. McManus notes, "Connecticut's lawmakers were extremely cautious about moving against slavery. Negroes were more numerous in the state than in the rest of New England combined, and racial anxieties were correspondingly more acute." *Black Bondage in the North* (Syracuse: Syracuse Univ. Press, 1973), 169–70.

40. von Frank, 52.

41. As Nathan Hatch argues, despite the attempts of mainline Protestantism to coopt the religious energies of this movement, especially at its moment of origin in the 1790s, it could be a powerfully iconoclastic force. *The Democratization of American Christianity* (New Haven: Yale Univ. Press, 1989), 222.

42. In this period these would probably have been Mahican, Schaghticoke, and Paugusset peoples. Personal communication from Joanna Brooks, 25 August 2005.

# Part IV

# Reformers in the New Nation

# Chapter 11

# Sexual Desire, Crime, and Punishment in the Early Republic

## *Mark E. Kann*

The American Revolution ushered in a "sexual revolution" that lowered restraints on sexual desire but heightened fears that youths would fail to exhibit republican virtue.[1] One indicator of impending failure was the perceived growth of crime in cities such as Boston, New York, and Philadelphia. Beginning in the 1780s, penal reformers argued that the primary means for preventing crime was to encourage people to discipline desire and the preferred method for curing criminality was to rehabilitate convicts by incarcerating them for long periods. Importantly, disciplining desire meant restraining sexual desire and rehabilitation required enforcing prisoner sexual abstinence.

Penal reformers prided themselves on their enlightened advocacy of liberty and independence but they were uneasy about reduced restraints on sexual desire. They believed that excessive passion was the basis of many crimes, including sex crimes ranging from adultery and bigamy to prostitution and rape. They also identified excessive passion as the source of same-sex desire and sodomy—which they considered particularly sinful and subversive of the biological, social, and political order ordained by God, nature, and reason. Where individuals failed to discipline desire, their promiscuous, lawless behavior needed to be punished lest sexual impunity undermine social stability.

Penal reformers' recommended punishment was long-term imprisonment in penitentiaries that were specifically designed to dampen men's passions, enforce sexual abstinence, and teach redeeming self-discipline. Ideally, penitentiaries were designed so that the sexes were segregated; each man was isolated from other men; and panoptic systems of surveillance ensured that prison life was passionless. In reality, constant over-crowding in penitentiaries meant that men and women inmates occasion-ally found each other; and male inmates, boys and men, shared cells and beds with one another. Reformers' main priority was to keep men and women apart, eventually, by calling for the creation of separate institu-tions for each sex. Furthermore, reformers feared that young male inmates were being seduced and raped by older men and, once fallen from virtue, these boys could never be rehabilitated. This fear gradually gave rise to a movement to protect delinquent boys from adult criminals by placing youths in their own facilities. Finally, although reformers complained about persistent sexual behavior among adult male prisoners, prison offi-cials had neither the logistical ability nor the political motivation to pre-vent it. Officials' grudging toleration of same-sex behavior suggested that the state's power over prisoners found its limits in same-sex desire.

## The Context for Penal Reform

Dr. Benjamin Rush was an early leader in American penal reform. In his medical practice and public service, he dwelled on men's sexual excesses. He wrote that the "solitary vice" of masturbation fixed "physical and moral evils . . . upon the body and mind." Additionally, "The morbid ef-fects of intemperance in sexual intercourse with women" ruined male mental and physical health. Moreover, in schools where boys lodged to-gether and shared beds, "the venereal appetite prevails with so much force and with such odious consequences" that youths were permanently dam-aged. Rush claimed that male masturbation, promiscuity, and sodomy produced debilities ranging from insanity to criminality.[2] His anxiety about same-sex experimentation among boys in boarding schools antici-pated later reformers' apprehensions about the sexual vulnerability of young boys in adult prisons.

Rush joined other civic leaders and intellectuals to urge Americans to restrain sexual desire. In her literary study of the early Republic, Karen Weyler observes that fiction, advice literature, and education theory, along with medical writings, routinely prescribed "self-knowledge, self-disci-pline, and self-control." Liberty had to be wed to self-restraint to sustain an orderly republic.[3] Elites agreed that liberty led to licentiousness when-ever self-restraint failed to neutralize excessive desire. Religious realists and enlightenment idealists long recognized that a degree of sexual licentiousness was predictable. But was it tolerable? The American answer was mixed. In colonial New England, for example, officials legislated capital punishment for sexual deviancy but rarely hanged men convicted of sodomy. Magistrates even allowed some exhibitions of same-sex desire. Nicholas Sension's sexual aggression toward other males was well known to his seventeenth-century Connecticut neighbors, but it did not diminish "the general esteem in which he was held."[4] Overall, post-Revolution officials scaled down the practice of prosecuting sexual offenses. Quiet adultery was usually allowed. Bigamy, often a product of self-divorce followed by remarriage, was rarely prosecuted. Prostitutes plied their trade with little fear of arrest. Sexual offenses sometimes generated less official concern than public gambling and drunkenness.[5]

Still, civic leaders and leading citizens were ambivalent. They supported individual rights but retained doubts about sexual license. Penal reformers fed their doubts by condemning men's lack of sexual self-discipline as a cause of crimes, ranging from rape and sodomy to theft and murder. They urged public officials to prosecute sexual criminals, particularly those who flaunted sexual improprieties. Such open wrongdoing undermined respect for law and set a bad example for youths. Urged on by penal reformers and other moral reformers, civic leaders waged culture wars against "sporting-male" youths, who made unregulated sex their "categorical imperative." These licentious youths were most visible in New York City, where they "patronized gambling and animal blood sports, billiards, brothels, gangs, aggressive volunteer fire brigades, political clubs," but their passions and crimes also wreaked havoc in villages and small towns across the American landscape.[6]

Thomas Jefferson epitomized this ambivalence. Like other enlightened thinkers, he encouraged self-discipline and civic virtue as the primary means for restraining individual desire and maintaining social order. Furthermore, he supported the liberalization of punishments. He advocated the elimination of the death penalty for most crimes, including sex crimes such as sodomy. Simultaneously, Jefferson doubted men's ability to discipline desire, especially sexual desire. Thus, he supported replacing the death penalty with castration for men found guilty of "rape, polygamy, or sodomy with man or woman." Public vengeance apparently demanded cutting off the member rather than curing the criminal.[7] Like many reformers, Jefferson spoke the language of rehabilitation but nevertheless suspected that men who were moved by excessive sexual desire were more incorrigible than salvageable.

## Passions and Crimes

In the early Republic, ministers and magistrates began to construe crime less as a by-product of innate wickedness than as a result of excessive desires unleashed by adverse circumstances. They reported that wrongdoers' powerful passions first surfaced in childhood. The typical criminal began his career of mischief "as an unfilial child, who throws off the yoke of parental guidance to pursue willfully vicious courses, usually involving sexual promiscuity or precocity."[8] For Dr. James Mease, biology was the basis of childhood vice. Criminals sired children "destined to succeed to the hereditary vices of their parents." Most commentators attributed childhood offenses to adverse circumstances, particularly bad parenting. John Griscom blamed "the profligate example of parents." Francis Lieber especially reproached the mother "given to intemperance" or to "violence and immoral conduct" for bringing up "as many vagabonds and prostitutes as she has male and female children."[9] Even in childhood, passion, sex, and crime seemed to come wrapped in a single package.

Whether the source was nature or nurture, children's unruly passions matured into adults' criminal tendencies. Philadelphia's William Bradford claimed that men sometimes experienced "a violence of temptation" that drove them to crime. Thomas Eddy, a leader in New York penal reform, felt that otherwise innocent men could be "blinded by passion" or "allured by present temptation" only to fall "into the depths of vice and criminality." Reform warden Gershom Powers felt that "moments of frenzy" motivated many crimes. Edward Livingston, who drafted a major revision of Louisiana's criminal code, attributed numerous offenses to the individual who sought to "gratify the strongest passion of his soul" during an "intoxicating moment."[10]

Convicts commonly confessed that intoxication was a catalyst for their crimes. Johnson Green blamed "drunkenness" for his wrongdoing. John Dixon warned spectators at his execution to avoid "hard drinking" lest they end up like him. Counterfeiter William Stuart observed, "All rogues drink. Every vicious man loves rum. Every gross, vulgar man loves the bottle. A rogue cannot persist in roguery without it." Former inmate John Reynolds claimed that a ban on alcohol would leave "half the rooms in our prisons . . . without an inhabitant." Religious reformers also linked liquor to crime. Quaker Thomas Eddy wrote that "the greater number of crimes originate in the irregular and vicious habits produced by intoxication, and by the idle, low, and dissipated practice encouraged in taverns and tippling-houses."[11] The Reverend Nathan Strong was convinced that the overabundance of "tippling houses and dram shops" fostered crime. He wanted "habitual drunkards" confined and liquor sales limited.[12]

More often than not, penal reformers resisted efforts to decriminalize sexual offenses lest individuals' inner desires generate outer disorders. For example, Edward Livingston worried that if lawmakers did not punish adultery, "the injured party will do it for himself." A husband who discovered his wife's infidelity would be driven by rage to seek vengeance by "assaults, duels, assassinations, [and] poisonings." Should the husband kill his wife's lover, most juries would acquit the husband. Livingston argued that outlawing adultery and attaching a modest punishment to it would avert the disorders associated with private vengeance.[13] Historian Hendrik Hartog reports that a man's "right" to kill his wife's lover was generally judged by the state of his passions. If a husband discovered another man with his wife and killed him immediately, *in the heat of passion,* the husband could expect to be exempted from a murder charge.[14] Tapping Reeve, a domestic law scholar in the early Republic, argued that the husband's inflamed passions did not affect his culpability but should mitigate his punishment. He ought to get prison time, not the noose.[15]

William Bradford applied a similar logic to rape and sodomy. Rape was a crime that arose from "the sudden abuse of a natural passion" and was "perpetrated in a frenzy of desire." A rapist experienced a momentary lapse in reason, not "irreclaimable corruption." Sodomy, the "crime against nature," also stemmed from such excessive sexual desire. Its perpetrator was so enslaved by his passions that he was in no mind to think clearly or reflect on the terrible consequences of his actions. Had he done so, "the infamy of detection" would have been as sufficient a deterrent as the threat of capital punishment. Ultimately, sex criminals acted out of inflamed passions rather than malicious calculation or incorrigible viciousness. They should be punished with prison time rather than with hanging. In prison, Bradford suggested, they should be rehabilitated and reclaimed for law-abiding society.[16]

The growing belief that "the greater part of crimes against persons are acts committed in rashness" enabled penal reformers to argue that nearly all criminals, including men convicted of sex crimes, could be rehabilitated to citizenship if they were taught to discipline desire.[17] This focus on rehabilitation through education enabled reformers, legislators, and other public officials to rethink the purposes of punishment. They began to claim that it was unrepublican to view punishment as a mode of vengeance; it was enlightened to use punishment as a means to teach self-restraint to immature men who had failed to harness their passions sufficiently. Reformers began to design penal institutions and punishment regimens that would encumber criminals with values and habits conducive to self-restraint. And although reformers rarely spoke openly about the need to teach criminals to tame sexual desire, they did address that need in two ways. First, they used the language of "filth" to speak the unspeakable. Second, they designed penal institutions and punishment regimens to dampen convict passions by enforcing sexual abstinence among them.

## Speaking the Unspeakable

Colonial ministers often employed the language of filth to discuss men's inability to control sexual desire (lest they suffer debasement to the level of beasts). The Reverend John Cotton referred to deviant sex as "unnatural filthiness." The Reverend Samuel Danforth described a convicted sodomite as a man of "carnal uncleanness" who committed "abominable filthiness," including the "self-pollution" of masturbation.[18] Similarly, secular writers tied filth to sexual wrongdoing, for example, by referring to a prostitute as a "dirty venereal trollop." The early Republic anticipated a Victorian prohibition against explicit public sex talk. In the 1810 case of *Davis v. Maryland,* for example, the court referred to sodomy as "that most horrible and detestable crime (among Christians not to be named)." Justice Nicholson wrote in his commentary, "The crime of sodomy is too well known to be misunderstood, and too disgusting to be defined, farther than by merely naming it."[19]

Michel Foucault points out that such reticence to speak about sex did not mean a suppression of expression. Jody Greene explains why civic leaders and public officials in England felt compelled to express their disgust for acts of sodomy. On the one hand, they considered sodomy a crime not to be named or mentioned because it was infectious. Merely speaking about it or drawing attention to it would inflame the passions of audiences. On the other hand, same-sex desire and sodomy had to be denounced publicly and made known objects of punishment lest men indulge excessive desire with impunity. Sodomy became what Greene calls a "public secret": officials expressed grave reservations about uttering the word but they then proceeded to do just that.[20]

Many penal reformers and officials in the United States expressed their public secret indirectly, using the language of filth to allude to illicit sex. New York's Society for the Prevention of Pauperism declared, "Every person that frequents the out-streets of this city must be forcibly struck with the ragged and uncleanly appearance, the vile language, and the idle and miserable habits of great numbers of children" engaged in drinking, theft, promiscuity, and prostitution. Street urchins grew up into "uncleanly" delinquents. Reformers wanted a clean republic. Rush announced, "Too much cannot be said in favor of cleanliness as a physical means of promoting virtue." Cleanliness fostered self-discipline and sexual integrity, whereas "uncleanness" signified the "unrestrained passions" that generated social grime and public crime.[21]

Sending criminals to filthy jails was no solution. Reformers complained that New Hampshire's jails exposed inmates to "lasciviousness." Many jails were "half-way houses of drunkenness and ill fame." In New York City's municipal jail, individuals awaiting trial, vagrants, and petty offenders resided in a state of filth and intoxication. Inmates suffered an exacerbation of "bad passions," rendering them "an hundred-fold more vicious and untractable."[22] In a Pennsylvania jail, inmates included "the disgusting object of popular contempt, besmeared with filth from the pillory—the unhappy victim of the lash, streaming with blood from the whipping post—the half naked vagrant—the loathsome drunkard—the sick suffering from various bodily pains." A former convict described the accommodations in one Connecticut jail in this way:

> The rooms were only lighted with a small heavily grated window pane, overstocked with lice, fleas and bed bugs, and the floor five inches deep of slippery stinking filth. . . . Loathsomeness and putridity, united with billions of entomological living specimens, shower the senses of a man uninured to filth, and he instinctively feels that in such cases nothing but fire can act successfully as a purifier and health preserver. . . . Armies of fleas, lice and bed bugs nightly covered every inch of this polluted prison.[23]

Boston's Prison Discipline Society reported an instance "in which an old negro, who was covered with sores, whose clothes were filthy rags, and on whom were seen afterwards swarms of vermin, was thrust into . . . prison, and locked up, night after night, and week after week, in a narrow and filthy dungeon, with blacks and whites, old and young, and made their constant companion."[24] Traditional jails were physically and morally unhealthy. They caged men but uncaged men's most pernicious passions.

Reformers were particularly dismayed to discover men and women co-habiting and fornicating in jails. A 1787 Philadelphia County Grand Jury denounced the "general intercourse between criminals of the different sexes" in the local jail. It also condemned the prostitutes who plied their trade inside that facility. The Society for Alleviating the Miseries of Public Prisons demanded that this "mixture of the sexes" be remedied. Reformers succeeded to make the separation of the sexes a typical expectation but not a pervasive reality. In the 1820s, Boston reformers reported several cases "in which men and women have been found in the different prisons confined in the same apartment, whose guilty countenances indicated their character and habits." In one jail in Charleston, South Carolina, "The necessities of nature must be done by both sexes in the presence of each other." Some reformers promoted the separation of female inmates from male guards, who were prone to abuse and prostitute the women.[25]

On rare occasions, penal activists expressed concerns about young servant and slave girls who were confined by their masters and mistresses only to be "seduced from their original innocence" by "the most abandoned of the sex." Reporting that young female inmates were being corrupted by older female felons, New York's Society for the Prevention of Pauperism condemned the women's quarters at Bellevue as a "great school of vice." This condemnation more likely indicated reformers' concern for girls' fall from virtue rather than grave anxiety about their seduction or rape by older women.[26]

More frequently, reformers vocalized agreement with the Chief Magistrate of Massachusetts who, in 1827, examined the presence of "unnatural crime" in the state's penitentiary system and found that the "horrible offense is here committed between wretches, who are alike destitute of moral sentiment, and without the reach of physical restraint. Nature and humanity cry aloud for redemption from this dreadful degradation." The same year, commissioners appointed by the Connecticut legislature observed "that in some of our penitentiaries, if not all, in which the convicts are placed in large numbers together in the cells, the crime of sodomy has been perpetuated, in numerous instances, with entire shamelessness and notoriety." Commissioners attributed this "shamelessness and notoriety" to "hoary headed convicts condemned to long imprisonment . . . whose passions and principles have been corrupted and degraded to the lowest point of debasement, and who are at night, in numbers from four to thirty-two persons, locked together in cells which are not subject to official inspection."[27] These reports indicated that officials recognized same-sex desire as a problem for prison administration, blamed older convicts for instigating sodomy in prisons, but identified overcrowding as the main obstacle to eradicating same-sex encounters and enforcing abstinence behind bars.

## Penitentiaries and Punishments

From the 1780s onward, penal reformers persuaded legislators to replace traditional punishments such as hanging, whipping, and detention in jails with long-term incarceration in penitentiaries—with new institutions specifically designed to encourage and teach inmates to restrain their passions. Penitentiaries were expensive. New York built its first penitentiary in 1799 for $208,846, the state's largest expenditure. Pennsylvania's Eastern Penitentiary, which opened in 1829, was the most expensive structure in the nation.[28] These institutions were costly for two reasons. First, they had to accommodate growing numbers of inmates serving long prison sentences. Second, they were designed to keep inmates separated from one another. Traditional jails housed many men in a single cell; the new penitentiaries were to house one man in each cell.

Reformers demanded clean penitentiaries. South Carolina's Robert Turnbull praised Philadelphia's Walnut Street Prison, where cleanliness was "a very principal physical cause in correcting the vices of [prisoners]." Thomas Eddy, who ran New York's first penitentiary, claimed that the effect of cleanliness on physical health was well understood "but its less striking but equally certain effect on the mind has been nowhere more fully experienced than in this prison." Cleanliness tended to "soften the temper, meliorate the disposition, and produce a regard to temperance, order, and industry and . . . conduce to [prisoners'] future amendment." Dissipated, sickly inmates became sober, healthy men. Boston's Prison Discipline Society praised the New York State Prison at Auburn for being "a specimen of neatness from the gate to the sewer." Penitentiaries in Connecticut and Maryland prided themselves on housing inmates who exhibited "cleanliness in their persons, dress, and bedding."[29]

Enforcing physical and mental hygiene demanded extensive control over inmate lives. Incarceration prevented male inmates from experiencing further corruption from bad parents, vicious friends, and fallen women as well as vices associated with taverns, theaters, gambling halls, and brothels. Warden Gershom Powers felt that sequestering inmates in penitentiaries forced them "to reflection and communion with their own hearts." Enforced silence helped. Inmates who were "free from the sound of a human voice" were also free from the crude language that inflamed men's passions. Ideally, penitentiaries were stripped of "everything calculated to inflame the passions and sharpen the evil propensities of men."[30] To this end, Sean McConville writes, officials sought to control "every aspect of daily life: sleeping, eating, working, associating with others, reading—and in religion, dress, and exercise."[31] Every aspect of daily life included sexual desire and behavior.

Reformers' implicit theory was that male convicts could learn to restrain sexual desire if they were shielded from sexual stimulation. The first rule for managing prisoner sexual desire was to separate male and female inmates. This rule appeared to be relatively easy to administer because America's first penitentiaries housed few women. The early Republic had few female felons and, often, they were kept out of penitentiaries because, as William Torrey explained to New York State Prison inspectors in 1814, women prisoners were "very refractory."[32] Worse, their sexuality and filthy language had an unsettling effect on male inmates. Nevertheless, some women resided in most penitentiaries. Officials confined them to isolated quarters to prevent all contact with male inmates. The Massachusetts State Prison locked women in a single room. The New York State Prison at Auburn enclosed them in an attic above the kitchen "to prevent any communication with the men."[33] During religious services, the women sat "behind wooden grates" to remain unseen by men. Some reformers argued for separate women's penitentiaries. In 1828, New York Governor DeWitt Clinton called for a state prison for women and, a decade later, the state constructed the nation's first women's prison.[34]

The second rule for managing prisoner sexual desire was to separate male inmates from each other. Although reformers were rarely explicit about male inmates' same-sex relations, Foucault's description of eighteenth-century secondary schools applies with equal force to early American penitentiaries:

> On the whole, one can have the impression that sex was hardly spoken of at all in these institutions. But one only has to glance over the architectural layout, the rules of discipline, and their whole internal organization: the question of sex was a constant preoccupation. The builders considered it explicitly. The organizers took it permanently into account. All who held a measure of authority were placed in a state of perpetual alert, which the fix-

tures, the precautions taken, the interplay of punishments and responsibilities, never ceased to reiterate.[35]

American penal reformers' constant warnings against mutual contamination among male prisoners and their extraordinary efforts to keep male prisoners separated from each other suggest a concerted strategy to eliminate opportunities for sodomy.

Penal reformers regularly complained about the "promiscuous association" of men incarcerated together in large jail cells. Hardened criminals were able to corrupt the untried prisoners, witnesses, debtors, vagrants, disorderly persons, misdemeanants, and young, first-time offenders residing among them. These jails were "high schools of iniquity," where a "master" trained the untutored and plotted "diabolical purposes" with them. Corrupted youths became "intimately acquainted with the arts of villainy," hastening their graduation from vagrancy to felony. The promiscuous association of inmates initiated youths "to scenes of debauchery, dishonesty, and wickedness of every sort." These "scenes of debauchery" likely included the filth associated with same-sex desire, sodomy, and sexual abuse among male inmates.[36]

Reformers developed two primary systems of penitentiary architecture and discipline, both aimed at isolating male prisoners from each other. Under the Pennsylvania system, all inmates were confined in solitary cells for the duration of their sentences. Their only human contact was with guards and chaplains. Pennsylvania reformers believed that solitude was the best means to eliminate contact and corruption among vicious men. Under the Auburn system, prison officials isolated prisoners in single cells at night and then enforced (with a whip) total silence when the inmates congregated for work and meals during the day. Separation and silence were meant to prevent all communication and contact, including sexual contact, among the men.[37]

Reformer rules for managing sexual desire worked better in theory than in practice. The goal of separating men and women housed within the same penitentiary and preventing contact among male inmates was nearly impossible to achieve. Overcrowding defeated virtually all attempts to separate inmates. Men and women inmates devised ways to engage each other. Investigating committees reported that "the means of communication are not entirely cut off between the males and females." Stories about prison romances were common. Boston's Prison Discipline Society noted a liaison at the New Hampshire State Prison where, somehow, a male and female occupying opposite ends of the building "formed an acquaintance and carried on a courtship." Occasional pregnancies among long-term female prisoners belied assertions of successful sexual segregation.[38]

Filth made its way into the cleanest institutions. Philadelphia's Walnut Street Prison became an international showcase of enlightened punishment but visitors still found "idle, some dirty, and some ragged" inmates in the facility. Warden Gershom Powers sought to keep his Auburn penitentiary spotless but complained that new arrivals brought in "filth and vermin" from local jails. Meanwhile, reformers understood that clean bodies did not necessarily produce clean minds and good behavior. Prison overcrowding meant that two men often shared a bed. Thomas Eddy complained that this unfortunate practice produced poor health and immoral behavior among inmates. Indeed, "the separation of criminals from each other during the night is a matter of so great importance that it is desirable that an immediate improvement should be made"—regardless of the added expense.[39] Overcrowding urged superintendents to assign top priority to prisoner discipline and prison-labor revenues, give lip service to prisoner rehabilitation, and tolerate deviant behavior that did not directly threaten good order or revenue streams.

Where full-time solitary confinement kept men from having sex with each other, the "self-pollution," "secret vice," or "solitary vice" of masturbation was a concern. Seen as a by-product of "excessive sensuality" and "filthiness," masturbation was thought to produce physical debility, immorality, insanity, and death. Decades of warnings resulted in the "masturbation scare" of the 1830s. Writers published anti-masturbation tracts that "began by an announcement ritual in which each author proclaims that, moved by a sense of righteous calling, he or she will speak the unspeakable" because the evil was so enormous.[40] If inmates indulged sexual desire in solitary confinement, their chances of learning sexual self-restraint and achieving rehabilitation were reduced if not lost.

Prison chaplain Barrett Gerrish suggested that the problem was not so much solitary sexual activity as it was lascivious thoughts. He explained, "Much the greater portion of convicts are not only ignorant but extremely groveling and sensual. Their prevailing sentiments are sexual and these are extremely gross. They spend hours in the silence and solitude of their cells, forming in their minds pictures of these acts of sin."[41] Rather than dampen men's sexual desires, solitude invited sexual fantasies. In *A Lecture to Young Men*, health reformer Sylvester Graham warned that "lascivious daydreams" and "amorous reveries" were sources of "debility, effeminacy, disordered functions, and permanent disease, and even premature death" as well as a "current of crime."[42]

Knowing that male and female prisoners found each other, male inmates had sex with each other, and masturbation and sexual fantasies persisted, reform wardens devised surveillance regimens aimed at "unceasing vigilance." They directed architects to design cells "in such a manner as they can be inspected while the prisoner is ignorant of the fact that he is under inspection [and] the keeper can inspect the convicts without being himself inspected." In some prisons, guards wore socks or moccasins at night, enabling them to move silently, observe inmates, and note infractions. The Massachusetts State Prison strategically placed sentinels to "hear a whisper from the most distant cell" and ascertain that "all is order and silence." Some reformers wanted a matron to supervise female prisoners because, they believed, a woman would be better able to exercise "unceasing vigilance" over female prisoners, perform "a constant inspection," and communicate to the women that they were always "under her eye."[43] Prisons officials tried to enforce sexual abstinence by enforcing segregation and eliminating privacy.

### Sodomy in Prisons

The logistical reality in persistently overcrowded prisons was that men could not be separated from one another and no amount of surveillance could stop the practice of sodomy among inmates. Beginning in the 1820s, the Reverend Louis Dwight, founder and leader of the Prison Discipline Society of Boston, became the nation's most vocal critic of sodomy behind bars. He treated sodomy as a public secret. It was a "crime which is not fit to be named among Christians" as well as a subject "so revolting that we should gladly omit the further consideration of it." However, because it stood "above all" evils that occurred in prisons, it was necessary to "meet the evil and remove it [and] give our attention to the facts."[44] He chose to speak the unspeakable.

Dwight certainly condemned "the crime of sodomy" when committed among the immoral "wretches" and hardened felons who filled the cells in most state penitentiaries. However, he was especially concerned about the victimization by seasoned prisoners of the young males with whom they shared quarters. Dwight reported, "Children have been found in some of our prisons under twelve years of age . . . intimately associated with the most profligate and vile of the human race. The loathsome skin, the distorted features, the unnatural eyes of some of these boys, indicate, with a clearness not to be misapprehended, the existence of unutterable abominations, which it were better for the world if they had been foreseen and avoided." These unfortunate youths were "attentive pupils of old villains by day" and "their injured companions by night." To make matters worse, when "old offenders corrupt juvenile delinquents," the next step was for "vicious youths of seventeen [to] corrupt innocent boys of eight or nine." Like Benjamin Rush before him, Dwight worried that the same spiral of sexual corruption took place in boarding schools, where "impurity" found its beginnings in night chambers occupied by two to five unsupervised boys. There, "idle, profane, and vicious youths" took advantage of the opportunity to introduce younger boys to sexual vice.[45]

Still, Dwight's greatest apprehension was reserved for man-boy sex in prisons, where "Sodom is the vice of prisoners and boys are the favorite prostitutes." Older, hardened prisoners attempted to seduce and rape one another but they fought especially viciously and violently over a new boy with "a fair countenance." These "grey headed villains" used bribery and force to get young boys "into the same room and into the same bed." They fought to keep the boys for themselves or they traded boys as if they were sexual commodities. Dwight reported that it was difficult, if not impossible, for boys to retain their sexual innocence in penitentiaries. He recounted the story of a former inmate who had witnessed boys so brutalized that they came to "glory in every species of abomination" and constantly engage in sodomy. Dwight implied that a boy, once sexually corrupted by a man, was forever stained with sin and lost to rehabilitation. That was why it was so urgent to legislate the complete separation of "juvenile delinquents from hardened offenders." Only complete separation could prevent the "unnatural crime" of man-boy sex and its terrible, enduring consequences.[46]

For the first three decades of nationhood, penal reformers repeatedly advised public officials to separate older male criminals from youthful wrongdoers. A 1786 Pennsylvania law directed that "the old and hardened offenders be prevented from mixing with and thereby contaminating and eradicating the remaining seeds of virtue and goodness in the young and unwary." This injunction was explicitly intended to prevent delinquents from becoming felons; it also was likely meant to thwart sexual relations between men and boys. It was not until the early 1820s that reformers were sufficiently concerned and convinced that incarcerated boys could not be protected from adult prisoners unless they did something about it. John Griscom crusaded to save delinquents from further contamination by attacking the penitentiary as "an unhallowed abode," where boys' innocence was destroyed by "old and fearless offenders." He led New York's Society for the Reformation of Juvenile Delinquents, which made the recommendation to legislators that only a separate institution for juvenile delinquents, a house of refuge, could protect delinquent boys from older, predator inmates.[47]

Several states heeded the recommendation, built houses of refuge, and gave administrators broad discretion to detain and retrain at-risk children. New York State delegated to refuge managers the authority to take custody of destitute, abandoned, vicious, vagrant, and convicted children. Once inside the house of refuge, boys remained wards of the state until age 21, girls until age 18. Refuge records indicated that police and commissioners of the poor regularly committed boys for vagrancy and suspicion of theft. Occasionally, refuge managers were proactive. They wanted to take custody of "a young female, who, though well known in the haunts of vice, had never rendered herself absolutely amenable to the criminal laws." They asked that the police "have her secured and placed in the house of refuge as soon as they could find a lawful occasion." The police soon found, or manufactured, such an occasion. Reformers' impulse toward preventive incarceration was strong. Between 1826 and 1829, Boston's House of Reformation detained 192 children. Few had been convicted of a crime. Forty-nine were committed "for being stubborn and disobedient," twenty-nine for being vagabonds, eleven for leading idle lives, and four for lascivious conduct.[48]

Prescribed methods for rehabilitating juvenile delinquents were virtually identical to prison regimens for rehabilitating adult convicts. Youths were removed from free society and sequestered in controlled environments. Males and females were separated. Strict rules about personal hygiene were followed, with the children being "marched in order to the wash-room where the utmost attention to personal cleanliness is required and enforced." Solitude, labor, and schooling combined with surveillance were instituted to promote self-discipline, industry, and obedience. A matron supervised female delinquents. She was to "endeavor to unfold to those under her charge the advantage of a moral and religious life." Philadelphia's house of refuge also appointed "twelve judicious females to assist . . . by imparting advice to the youth confined therein and by bestowing their attention and care upon the domestic economy of the establishment." Lady visitors tried "to excite in the girls a sense of virtue and piety." The likelihood of their success was enlarged by the "soothing and persuasive language which so peculiarly belongs to their own sex." The authentic female voice was both passionless and regenerative.[49]

Juveniles remained in custody until placed in apprenticeships. Refuge managers sought placements conducive to virtue. A boy might be sent to the countryside to learn farming or be bound to a whaling ship, where he "is abstracted from his bad associates and has no opportunity of returning to his former habits." Long voyages and shipboard discipline were to hasten a boy's journey "to manhood." Managers did not allow boys to be apprenticed to tavern keepers or distillers of spirits and denied girls placements with single men or in boarding houses.[50] They did not want to put delinquents into sexually charged environments, where they would be vulnerable to temptation or abuse.

The practice of apprenticing boys to seagoing vessels was curious. On the one hand, rigid taskmasters "who demanded disciple, obedience, and even sobriety" governed ships. In theory, such discipline would deny boys the opportunity for indulging sexual desire. On the other hand, middle-class citizens perceived whalers and sailors as "exemplars of vice and deviance." At sea, they constituted an all-male subculture with "older and more powerful men initiating sexual relations with younger subordinates." Ashore, they were given to "whoring, drinking, and drifting about."[51] Reformers' willingness to place boys on ships raises a question about how anxious they were about eradicating sexual desire and same-sex relations among delinquent males. Unlike Louis Dwight, who feared that same-sex experiences in prison forever ruined a boy, the child-savers who ran houses of refuge may have felt that illicit sex at sea was rare and, when it did occur, it was situational and therefore temporary. Regardless, refuge officials could not have overlooked the practical reality that placing boys on ships opened up space for new admits to their institutions.[52]

## Passionless Penitentiaries?

Penal reformers believed that undisciplined sexual desire was a primal force that directly or indirectly drove men to crime. They argued that long sentences carried out in passionless penitentiaries offered hope for rehabilitating criminals to self-control and law-abiding behavior. Officials sought to dampen inmate sexual desire and promote sexual self-restraint by requiring sexual abstinence. This requirement was enforced by inmate separation and guard surveillance. The segregation of the sexes, the isolation of men from each other by day and especially at night, and proposals to build separate penal facilities for female felons and for at-risk youths and delinquents were part of a systematic strategy to manage sexual desire among the inmates of state penal institutions.

Although the white, middle-class penal reformers who advocated passionless penitentiaries hoped to rehabilitate wayward white males to virtue and citizenship, they had little to say about the disproportionately lower-class, black, and immigrant men who filled penitentiaries in the early Republic. For the most part, reformers considered these marginal Americans slaves to sexual desire and virtually incorrigible.[53] Simultaneously, white middle-class reformers began to elevate the significance of freedom from sexual desire. They attached this freedom to idealized middle-class women, whose exemplary passionlessness served as "the archetype for human morality."[54] Accordingly, penal reformers who demanded that marginal men be sentenced to spend years in passionless penitentiaries, where they would be "forced to be free" from sexual desire, condemned inmates not only to sexual abstinence but also to emasculation and feminization.

Reformers' commitment to passionless penitentiaries encountered three problems. First, to the extent that officials succeeded to create chaste penal environments, they failed to prepare the prisoner for the moment when he would be released back into free society—where desire, temptation, and corruption were ubiquitous. Reporting on the typical American penitentiary prisoner, Gustave de Beaumont and Alexis de Tocqueville noted, "He was dead to the world, and after a loss of several years he reappears in society, to which, it is true, he brings good resolutions, but perhaps also burning passions, the more impetuous, from their being the longer repressed."[55] Prison rehabilitation was a false promise to the degree that penitentiaries exacerbated rather than reduced a man's passions. It was only a matter of time before excessive desire fueled by intoxication and adverse influences would again set him on a pathway to crime.

Second, reformers encountered critics who pointed out that traditional punishments such as hanging and beating (which reformers considered cruel and suitable only for monarchies) were in some respects more enlightened, humane, and republican than incarceration. Hangings were quick affairs. Beatings were over in minutes. Neither a hanged man nor a beaten man had to cope with long-term exposure to prison fevers, the psychological terrors of prolonged solitude, or draconian and arbitrary prison discipline. Furthermore, traditional punishments did not inflict on wrongdoers long-term sexual deprivation and emasculation enforced by constant surveillance.

Third, by their own reckoning, penal officials never succeeded to create passionless penitentiaries. With constant prison overcrowding, men and women found each other; same-sex relations and relationships persisted; masturbation was unstoppable; and sexual fantasies formed in prisons continued to have unknown but unsettling effects on discharged prisoners. Reformers and officials lowered their expectations about prisoner rehabilitation and began to develop implicit priorities in managing prisoners' sexual desire. Their foremost concern was to separate women and men in prison. Their second concern, emerging in the 1820s, was to remove delinquent boys from the sexual reach of older inmates by moving them into houses of refuge. Ultimately, preventing sodomy and masturbation within prisons became a tertiary concern. On the one hand, there was not much officials could do to stop sodomy in overcrowded prisons. On the other hand, officials were more interested in maintaining prison order and enhancing prison revenues than in policing same-sex desire.

This relative neglect of same-sex desire among adult prisoners probably stemmed from a combination of post-Revolution tolerance, lowered expectations, and political paralysis. American ministers and legislators often supported draconian punishments for what they considered deviant sexual acts, but American citizens and officials tended to tolerate discreet expressions of illegal sexuality such as fornication, adultery, bigamy, prostitution, and sodomy. If Americans did not decriminalize sodomy as some continental European nations did, neither did they emulate the English by vigorously prosecuting sodomy.[56] It appears that American prison officials mostly tolerated expressions of same-sex desire among male prisoners and could do so because the new walled-in penitentiaries, like discreet houses of prostitution, were not accessible to public viewing.

Furthermore, the first wave of penal reformers in the 1780s and 1790s, who expressed remarkable optimism about prisoner rehabilitation, gave way to a new generation of reformers with lower expectations. The later group was less likely to expect prisoners to be rehabilitated in their souls and more apt to settle for prisoners' good behavior upon their discharge. Good behavior could mean being discreet by practicing one's vices in private rather than flaunting them in public.[57]

Finally, reformers faced a political challenge that made it imprudent for them to problematize and publicize same-sex desire in prisons. Reformers' argument to legislators and taxpayers was that they should support the expensive new penitentiaries because these institutions provided a clean, controlled environment that would rehabilitate criminals, deter would-be criminals, and thereby prevent future crime. This made imprisonment seem palatable in an otherwise liberty-loving republic. However, reformers would have had difficulty promoting the image of clean, passionless penal institutions if they publicized the fact that the men within them engaged in "filthy" sex. This might explain why Louis Dwight's efforts to publicize sodomy within prisons attracted few followers.

Gustave de Beaumont and Alexis de Tocqueville observed during their 1831 travels, "While society in the United States gives the example of the most extended liberty, the prisons of the same country offer the spectacle of the most complete despotism." Inmate memoirs from the early Republic agreed that stripping men of liberty, incarcerating them, and destroying their privacy constituted despotism. Henry Tufts "incessantly pined after that liberty of which . . . I saw myself so totally divested" and W. A. Coffey "ardently sought a restoration to liberty." If inmate regrets over lost liberty were in good measure a function of the deprivation and degradation they suffered within penitentiaries that sought to enforce sexual abstinence, it was penal reformers' obsession with what Michael Meranze calls "the threat of sexual contact"—which "transgressed disciplinary limits and expressed [prisoners'] ungoverned desires"—that encouraged and perpetuated despotism but also limited it. Penal despotism could not be complete as long as transgressive, ungoverned same-sex desire persisted and prison personnel were compelled to tolerate same-sex behavior among adult male inmates.[58]

NOTES

1. Richard Godbeer, *Sexual Revolution in Early America* (Baltimore: Johns Hopkins University Press, 2002); see also John D'Emilio and Estelle B. Freedman, *Intimate Matters: A History of Sexuality in America* (New York: Harper and Row, 1988), 44–45, 49–50.

2. Benjamin Rush, *Medical Inquiries and Observations Upon the Diseases of the Mind* (New York: Hafner, 1962 [1812]), 32–33, 347, 351; Benjamin Rush to David Ramsay, March or April 1788, in Benjamin Rush, *Letters of Benjamin Rush,* ed. L. H. Butterfield, 2 vol. (Princeton: Princeton University Press, 1951), 1:454.

3. Karen Weyler, *Intricate Relations: Sexual and Economic Desire in American Fiction, 1789–1814* (Iowa City: University of Iowa Press, 2004), 33.

4. Rudi C. Bleys, *The Geography of Perversion: Male-to-Male Sexual Behaviour Outside the West and the Ethnographic Imagination, 1750–1918* (New York: New York University Press, 1995), 68–69; Richard Godbeer, " 'The Cry of Sodom': Discourse, Intercourse, and Desire in Colonial New England," in this volume, 95; see also D'Emilio and Freedman, 30; Leila J. Rupp, *A Desired Past: A Short History of Same-Sex Love in America* (Chicago: University of Chicago Press, 1999), 31–32.

5. Nancy F. Cott, *Public Vows: A History of Marriage and the Nation* (Cambridge, MA: Harvard University Press, 2000), 30, 38–40; Mary P. Ryan, *Women in Public: Between Banners and Ballots, 1825–1880* (Baltimore, Johns Hopkins University Press, 1990), 89, 97–98; Michael Stephen Hindus, *Prison and Plantation: Crime, Justice, and Authority in Massachusetts and South Carolina, 1767–1878* (Chapel Hill: University of North Carolina Press, 1980), 52.

6. Lawrence M. Friedman, *Crime and Punishment in American History* (New York: Basic Books, 1993), 201; Howard P. Chudacoff, *The Age of the Bachelor: Creating an American Subculture* (Princeton: Princeton University Press, 1999), 35–36; Christine Stansell, *City of Women: Sex and Class in New York, 1789–1860* (Urbana: University of Illinois Press, 1987), 23, 27–28; Timothy J. Gilfoyle, *City of Eros: New York City, Prostitution, and the Commercialization of Sex, 1790–1920* (New York: Norton, 1992), 99, 115.

7. Thomas Jefferson, "A Bill for Proportioning Crimes and Punishments," in Thomas Jefferson, *Writings*, ed. Merrill D. Peterson (New York: Library of America, 1984), 355–56.

8. Richard Slotkin, "Narratives of Negro Crime in New England, 1675–1800," *American Quarterly* 25, 1 (March 1973): 7.

9. James Mease, *Observations on the Penitentiary System and Penal Code of Pennsylvania with Suggestions for their Improvement* (Philadelphia: Clark and Raser, 1828), 29; John Griscom, "The Memorial of the Managers of the Society for the Reformation of Juvenile Delinquents in the City of New York to the U.S. Congress [1826]," in John H. Griscom, ed., *Memoir of John Griscom, LL.D.* (New York: Robert Carter, 1859), 189–90; Francis Lieber, "Translator's Preface," in Gustave de Beaumont and Alexis de Tocqueville, *On the Penitentiary System in the United States and Its Application in France,* tran. Francis Lieber (Carbondale: Southern Illinois University Press, 1964 [1833]), 8–9, 14.

10. William Bradford, *An Enquiry How Far the Punishment of Death is Necessary in Pennsylvania,* [1793] in *Reform of Criminal Law in Pennsylvania: Selected Inquiries, 1787–1819* (New York: Arno Press, 1972), 8–9; Thomas Eddy, *An Account of the State Prison or Penitentiary House in the City of New York* (New York: Isaac Collins and Son, 1801), 51; Gershom Powers, *A Brief Account of the Construction, Management, and Discipline &c. &c. of the New York State Prison at Auburn* (Auburn: U. F. Doubleday, 1826), 49; Edward Livingston, *A System of Penal Law for the State of Louisiana* (Union, NJ: Lawbook Exchange, 1999 [1833]), 23.

11. Johnson Green, "The Life and Confession of Johnson Green [1786]," in Daniel E. Williams, *Pillars of Salt: An Anthology of Early American Criminal Narratives* (Madison, WI: Madison House, 1993), 259; John Dixon in "The American Bloody Register [1784]," in Ibid., 251; William Stuart, *Sketches of the Life of William Stuart: The First and Most Celebrated Counterfeiter of Connecticut* (Bridgeport, CT: W. Stuart, 1854), 13–14; John Reynolds, *Recollections of Windsor Prison; Containing Sketches of Its History and Discipline* (Boston: A. Wright, 1834), 174; Eddy, 59.

12. Daniel A. Cohen, *Pillars of Salt, Monuments of Grace: New England Crime Literature and the Origins of American Popular Culture, 1674–1860* (New York: Oxford University Press, 1993), 97.

13. Livingston, 173.

14. Hendrik Hartog, *Man and Wife in America: A History* (Cambridge: Harvard University Press, 2000), 218–19, 224–26.

15. Tapping Reeve, *The Law of Baron and Femme* (New York: Source Book Press, 1970 [1816]), 300.

16. Bradford, 21, 29.

17. Lieber, 23.

18. John Cotton, "Unnatural Filthiness," in Jonathan Katz, ed., *Gay American History: Lesbians and Gay Men in the U.S.A.* (New York: Harper and Row, 1976), 20; Samuel Danforth quoted in Ronald A. Bosco, "Lectures at the Pillory: The Early American Execution Sermon," *American Quarterly* 30, 2 (Summer 1978): 156–57; See also Godbeer, "The Cry of Sodom," 284; Thomas Foster, "Antimasonic Satire, Sodomy, and Eighteenth-Century Masculinity in the *Boston Evening-Post*," *William and Mary Quarterly*, 3rd Ser., 60, 1 (January 2003): 178.

19. Clerk quoted in Godbeer, *Sexual Revolution*, 321; Rush, *Medical Inquiries*, 353; Davis v. State, 3 H & J 154; 1810 Md. Lexis 31.

20. Michel Foucault, *The History of Sexuality, Volume 1: An Introduction*, tran. Robert Hurley (New York: Vintage Books, 1990), 3–35; Jody Greene, "Public Secrets: Sodomy and the Pillory in the Eighteenth Century and Beyond," *The Eighteenth Century: Theory and Interpretation* 44, 2–3 (June 2003): 203–32.

21. Society for the Prevention of Pauperism, *Report of a Committee Appointed by the Society for the Prevention of Pauperism in the City of New York on the Expediency of Erecting an Institution for the Reformation of Juvenile Delinquents* (New York: Mahlon, Day, 1823), 7; Benjamin Rush, "An Enquiry into the Influence of Physical Causes upon the Moral Faculty," in Benjamin Rush, *Two Essays on the Mind* (New York: Brunner/Mazel Publishers, 1972), 22.

22. *Reports of the Prison Discipline Society of Boston*, 6 vol. (Montclair, NJ: Patterson Smith, 1972 [1855]), 1:438–39; Eddy, 62.

23. Roberts Vaux, *Notices of the Original and Successive Efforts, to Improve the Discipline of the Prison at Philadelphia and to Reform the Criminal Code of Pennsylvania: with a Few Observations on the Penitentiary System* (Philadelphia: Kimber and Sharpless, 1826), 13–14; Stuart, 165–66.

24. *Reports of the Prison Discipline Society of Boston*, 1:10–11.

25. *The Pennsylvania Gazette*, September 26, 1787, quoted in Negley K. Teeters, *The Cradle of the Penitentiary: The Walnut Street Jail at Philadelphia, 1773–1835* (Philadelphia: Pennsylvania Prison Society, 1955), 132; Memorial No. 2, "Describes the Terrible Conditions Existing in the Walnut Street Jail, January 12, 1789," in Negley K. Teeters, *They Were in Prison: A History of the Pennsylvania Prison Society (Formerly The Philadelphia Society for Alleviating the Miseries of Public Prisons), 1787–1937* (Chicago: Winston, 1937), 29–30, 449–50; *Reports of the Prison Discipline Society of Boston*, 1:11; 37, 64; Report on South Carolina jail conditions quoted in Friedman, 50.

26. Society for the Prevention of Pauperism managers cited in Estelle B. Freedman, *Their Sisters' Keepers: Women's Prison Reform in America, 1830–1930* (Ann Arbor: University of Michigan Press, 1981), 7.

27. Chief Magistrate and Commissioners quoted in *Reports of the Prison Discipline Society of Boston*, 1:64–65.

28. Mark Colvin, *Penitentiaries, Reformatories, and Chain Gangs: Social Theory and the History of Punishment in Nineteenth-Century America* (New York: St. Martin's Press, 1997), 42, 55, 80; Scott Christianson, *With Liberty for Some: 500 Years of Imprisonment in America* (Boston: Northeastern University Press, 1998), 96, 133; Edward L. Ayers, *Vengeance and Justice: Crime and Punishment in the 19th-Century American South* (New York: Oxford University Press, 1984), 34–35; see also William Crawford, *Report on the Penitentiaries of the United States* (Montclair, NJ: Patterson Smith, 1969 [1835]), xi.

29. Robert J. Turnbull of South Carolina, *A Visit to the Philadelphia Prison* (Philadelphia: James Phillips and Son, 1797), 19–20, 22; Eddy, 53; Thomas Eddy to Patrick Colquhoun, June 5, 1802, in Samuel L. Knapp, *The Life of Thomas Eddy* (New York: Arno Press, 1976 [1834]), 179; *Reports of the Prison Discipline Society of Boston*, 1:100–01, 348; Crawford, Appendix, 72, 95.

30. Powers, *Brief Account*, 1–2, 16; Society for the Prevention of Pauperism in the City of New York, *Report on the Penitentiary System in the United States* (New York: M. Day, 1822), 46, 58–59; "A View of the New-York State Prison," in William Roscoe, *Observations on Penal Jurisprudence and the Reformation of Criminals* [1819], in *Reform of Criminal Law in Pennsylvania: Selected Inquiries 1787–1819* (New York: Arno Press, 1972), Appendix, 40; Eddy, 36; Gershom Powers, *Letter of Gershom Powers, Esq. in Answer to a Letter of the Hon. Edward Livingston in Relation to the Auburn State Prison* (Albany: Croswell and Van Benthuysen, 1829), 16.

31. Sean McConville, "Local Justice: The Jail," in Norval Morris and David J. Rothman, eds., *The Oxford History of the Prison: The Practice of Punishment in Western Society* (New York: Oxford University Press, 1998), 276.

32. William Torrey to the Inspectors of the [NY] State Prison, February 12, 1814, in Roscoe, *Observations on Penal Jurisprudence and the Reformation of Crimi-*

*nals* [1819], in *Reform of Criminal Law in Pennsylvania*, Appendix, 71; "Visiting Committee of the Society for Alleviating the Miseries of Public Prisons Report, January, 1799," in Teeters, *They Were in Prison*, 59; see also Orlando F. Lewis, *The Development of American Prisons and Prison Customs, 1776–1845* (Montclair, NJ: Patterson Smith, 1967 [1922]), 263.

33. W. David Lewis, *From Newgate to Dannemora: The Rise of the Penitentiary in New York, 1796–1848* (Ithaca: Cornell University Press, 1965), 162.

34. Powers, *Brief Account*, 15; *Reports of the Prison Discipline Society of Boston*, 1:261–62; Beaumont and Tocqueville, 188.

35. Foucault, *The History of Sexuality, Volume 1*, 27–28.

36. Beaumont and Tocqueville, 48; Memorial No. 2, "Describes the Terrible Conditions Existing in the Walnut Street Jail," in Teeters, *They Were in Prison*, 29–30; Eddy, 62; *Reports of the Prison Discipline Society*, 1:11, 61–66; Stephen Burroughs, *Memoirs of the Notorious Stephen Burroughs* (New York: Cornish Lamport, 1852), 177; Memorial No. 5, "A Petition for a Bridewell for Vagrants, January 25, 1803," in Teeters, *They Were in Prison*, 454; Vaux, 29.

37. For an early comparison of Pennsylvania and Auburn systems, see Beaumont and Tocqueville, ch. 2.

38. Crawford, 18, Appendix, 95; *Reports of the Prison Discipline Society of Boston*, 1:101–02; Livingston, 695.

39. Powers, *Brief Account*, 4; "The Visiting Committee of the Society for Alleviating the Miseries of Public Prisons Report, January, 1799," in Teeters, *They Were in Prison*, 59–60; Eddy, 38.

40. Helen Lefkowitz Horowitz, *Rereading Sex: Battles over Sexual Knowledge and Suppression in Nineteenth-Century America* (New York: Vintage, 2003), 86, 94, 100.

41. *Reports of the Prison Discipline Society of Boston*, 1:11; Barrett Gerrish quoted in Lewis, *The Development of American Prisons*, 185.

42. Sylvester Graham quoted in Horowitz, *Rereading Sex*, 97.

43. Powers, *Brief Account*, 3, 7; *Reports of the Prison Discipline Society of Boston*, 1:7, 243, 297, 336–37; Crawford, 10, 16; Livingston, 697, 705; see also Michel Foucault, *Discipline and Punish: The Birth of the Prison*, tran. Alan Sheridan (New York: Vintage, 1977), 201.

44. *Reports of the Prison Discipline Society of Boston*, 1:37; Louis Dwight, "The Sin of Sodom is the Vice of Prisoners," in Katz, 27.

45. *Reports of the Prison Discipline Society of Boston*, 1:11–12, 64, 66, 289–90.

46. Dwight, "The Sin of Sodom is the Vice of Prisoners," in Katz, 27–28.

47. Law quoted in Harry E. Barnes, *The Evolution of Penology in Pennsylvania: A Study in American Social History* (Indianapolis: Bobbs-Merrill, 1927), 119; Griscom, *Memoir*, 167, 169; Society for the Reformation of Juvenile Delinquents in the City of New York, "Second Annual Report," in *Documents Relative to the House*

*of Refuge, Instituted by the Society for the Reformation of Juvenile Delinquents in the City of New-York, in 1824* (New York: Mahlon Day, 1832), 76; "Third Annual Report," in Ibid., 132.

48. Society for the Reformation of Juvenile Delinquents in the City of New York, "First Annual Report," in *Documents Relative to the House of Refuge,* 47, 57; "Second Annual Report," in Ibid., 89, 93–95; "Fourth Annual Report," in Ibid., 175; "Fifth Annual Report," in Ibid., 187; "Sixth Annual Report," in Ibid., 240; *Reports of the Prison Discipline Society of Boston,* 1:245.

49. Griscom, *Memoir,* 165; Society for the Reformation of Juvenile Delinquents in the City of New York, "First Annual Report," in *Documents Relative to the House of Refuge,* 45–46; "Second Annual Report," in Ibid., 83, 85, 107–08; "Third Annual Report," in Ibid., 138–41; "Seventh Annual Report.," in Ibid., 253–54; Livingston, 714–16; Crawford, Appendix, 150, 154; *Reports of the Prison Discipline Society of Boston,* 1:297.

50. Society for the Reformation of Juvenile Delinquents in the City of New York, "Fifth Annual Report," in *Documents Relative to the House of Refuge,* 189; "Sixth Annual Report," in Ibid., 217, 229–30; Beaumont and Tocqueville, 149–50; "Rules of the House of Refuge in Philadelphia," in Crawford, Appendix, 153.

51. Margaret S. Creighton, "Fraternity in the American Forecastle, 1830–1870," *The New England Quarterly* 63, 4 (December 1990): 531–32; Rupp, *A Desired Past,* 20–21.

52. For a discussion of the concept of "situational homosexuality" in prisons, see Regina G. Kunzel, "Situating Sex: Prison Sexual Culture in the Mid-Twentieth-Century United States," *GLQ: A Journal of Lesbian and Gay Studies* 8, 3 (2002): 253–70.

53. See Mark E. Kann, *Punishment, Prisons, and Patriarchy* (New York: New York University Press, 2005), ch. 9; Rupp, 41.

54. Nancy F. Cott, "Passionlessness: An Interpretation of Victorian Sexual Ideology, 1790–1850," in Nancy F. Cott and Elizabeth H. Pleck, eds., *A Heritage of Her Own: Toward a New Social History of American Women* (New York: Simon & Schuster, 1979), 165.

55. Beaumont and Tocqueville, 84.

56. See Bleys, 68–69, 81; A. D. Harvey, "Prosecutions for Sodomy in England at the Beginning of the Nineteenth Century," *The Historical Journal* 21, 4 (December 1978): 939.

57. See Kann, ch. 8.

58. Beaumont and Tocqueville, 79; Henry Tufts, *The Autobiography of a Criminal* (New York: Duffield, 1930 [1807]), 284; W. A. Coffey, *Inside Out; or An Interior View of the New-York State Prison* (New York: J. Costigan, 1823), iii, 67, 92, 98; Michael Meranze, *Laboratories of Virtue: Punishment, Revolution, and Authority in Philadelphia, 1760–1835* (Chapel Hill: University of North Carolina Press, 1996), 184.

# Chapter 12

# The Black Body Erotic and the Republican Body Politic, 1790–1820

## John Saillant

An eroticized black male body appears in a number of antislavery writings published and republished in America between 1790 and 1820. In these writings arose two entirely new elements in American writing. First is an erotic representation of the black male body—its visage, hands, muscle, skin, height, sex—unparalleled by the representation of any other body, black or white, male or female. Second is a *communitas*, blending sentimentalism and homoeroticism, shared by black men and white men who unite in opposition to slavery. Earlier than the polemics of the antebellum abolitionists, these writings express an alternative to the republican racialism of postrevolutionary America in a time when ideas about race and slavery were in flux, not yet settled into the extremes of a proslavery view presupposing black inferiority and a liberal, sometimes perfectionist abolitionism. The eroticized black male body figures in antislavery variations on eighteenth-century sentimentalism and revolutionary republicanism, two strains of thought linked by the sentimentalist reconstruction of the classical ideal of martial virtue into an ideal of affection, benevolence, sentiment, and sympathy shared among men, the virtuous citizens of the American republic.[1] The black man who appeared between 1790 and 1820 in antislavery narratives, essays, and poems is the "poor negro," deserving benevolence but denied it by his white masters.[2] This sentimentalized poor negro, on American soil, became an eroticized "friend," echoing the homoeroticism of classical martial virtue as well as gesturing toward nineteenth-century blackface and its interracial homoerotics.[3] Rooted in the eighteenth century, the sentimentalized and eroticized black friend of the turn of the nineteenth century predates the eroticized figures of antebellum sentimental women's writing concerned with race and slavery.[4]

White men eroticized black men in antislavery writings because in American ideology sentimentalism and republicanism grounded their vision of the body politic in a fundamental likeness among men that produces benevolence.[5] Republicans believed some fundamental likeness to be required in a free society like postrevolutionary America. This notion of likeness echoed some prominent elements of the American past—Puritan covenant theology, the Calvinist doctrine of a benevolent providential design inhering in all people and things, the idealized communalism of farming communities, and the idealized unity of the patriots in the War of Independence. It also echoed some prominent elements in eighteenth-century European thought—both Montesquieu's notion of a "spirit" uniting a society and British sentimentalism and commonsense philosophy.[6] Republicans lacked a proslavery argument, accepting merely the Montesquieuian view that any group that could not join in the spirit of a society should be enslaved or banished. Colonization, the expatriationist effort to remove black Americans to Africa or the Caribbean, flowed from this view of the black man as alien to the unifying likeness required in a republic.[7] Still, Montesquieu, one of the greatest European influences on revolutionary and postrevolutionary American thought, had made it clear in 1750 that one "likeness" white men share with black men is precisely a sexual likeness.[8] Attacking "Negro slavery," Montesquieu savaged the making of "eunuchs" as a way of depriving "blacks of their likeness to us in a more distinctive way."[9] In a counter discourse to American republicanism, interracial likeness and interracial benevolence were understood by antislavery writers to be rooted in physical similarities between the black male body and the white male body. The eroticization of black men in antislavery writing confirmed this likeness by uniting black men and white men in an affectionate and physical bond. Indeed, antislavery writing introduced the body in American writing, for no figure other than the black male is represented in such bodily detail and in such a sexualized fashion before 1790.

Eighteenth-century republican thought, like all systems of ideas and values, led its adherents into beliefs about their own sexuality as well as the sexuality of those defined as "other." The sexuality attributed to black men, the republican "other," was sometimes a wild rapaciousness and sometimes a sentimental adhesiveness. Republicanism provided a crucible in which antislavery thought sentimentalized and eroticized black men. The sentimentalization and eroticization of black men by white men functioned in a counter discourse to republican ideology, rubbing against one of its sorest points, the persistence of an enslaved, oppressed class in a republic founded by a liberty-loving people. The persistence of slavery placed leading republicans in an uncomfortable position, one impossible to sustain. Colonization, which men like Thomas Jefferson and James Madison viewed as essential to republicanism, was impractical, while republican discourse could disdain but not quell the notion that oppressed black men were like white men and thus were worthy of liberty and dignity. Republicans freed themselves from this uncomfortable position only by freeing themselves from the eighteenth-century underpinnings of republican thought. The impulses to enslave blacks and to deny them an equal place in the social order, North as well as South, proved to be stronger than the commitment to revolutionary ideology. As liberal thought transformed the republican commitment to likeness, benevolence, and unity into a commitment to Protestant pluralism, economic freedom, and individualism, the dialectic between the view of the black man as an alien and the view of the black man as a sentimental friend came to an end. The writings examined in this essay were printed and reprinted in the decades in which it seemed that revolutionary republicanism would determine the character of American culture and its race relations. These writings were part of a debate, sometimes lively and sometimes desperate, about race, but insofar as their nexus is a black man and a white man in a sentimental friendship, they lost their potency after 1820 in a new, liberal America.

In the postrevolutionary decades, republican leaders promoted various strategies for fortifying likeness among white men—universal common education, the division of society into small "ward-republics," and an empiricism that would unite people in common sense, not divide them by a fissiparous idealism. The black male, in the republican mind, threatened such unity not only because he was in some sense outside it—by slavery whites had already alienated blacks, reasoned republicans, while by nature the races were divided—but also because he had a claim to benevolence that white Americans at large were unwilling to recognize.[10] This claim to benevolence was made explicit by black spokesmen of postrevolutionary America, who modulated their claims through religious doctrine, republican principles, and reminders of the virtuous service of blacks in difficulties like the revolutionary battles and the yellow fever epidemic.[11] Certain that the black man threatened the republic because he was both socially and naturally "heterogeneous," republican leaders planned to maintain slavery until blacks could be expatriated, a plan that simply paralleled other republican strategies for creating white unity. No leading republican conceded that the benevolence required in a republic could cross the race line, so blacks, reasoned republicans, must be enslaved until the expatriation to Africa. So dogmatic was this notion that when James Monroe suggested that a settlement far in the west might suit both America and its blacks, Jefferson scolded him that even there blacks would be a "blot" and reminded him that the time to commence the expatriation was short."[12]

Essential to white thought on race and slavery in the early republic is the opposition between the schemes of the republican literati to remove blacks physically from America and the newspaper essays and pamphlets in which white men eagerly embraced black men and their claims to benevolence. Antislavery writings centering upon benevolent relations between a black man and a white man were not anti-republican but, rather, the issue of a different understanding of the connections among race, sentiment, and republicanism. Unlike the republican literati, white men who could imagine interracial benevolence had no place in the central republican discourse of postrevolutionary America; they published their thoughts anonymously in pamphlets and newspapers, creating an almost subterranean republican commentary on race. As the Jeffersonians and other expatriationists monopolized political philosophy and religious discourse, other men with a vision of interracial benevolence modulated their ideas and values through the erotics of masculine relationships. In other words, when it became all but impossible to address interracial benevolence, which was the heart of the matter, in republican political philosophy and religion, a handful of white men turned to a union of bodies. Eros, one urge behind sentiment, became an eroticism of black men and white men when American ideology condemned interracial benevolence.

A French Montesquieuian provided Americans a model for eroticization in antislavery writing. Joseph LaVallée's *Le nègre comme il y a peu de blancs*, published in Paris in 1789, appeared almost immediately in English.[13] Two different English translations appeared in London in 1790, *The Negro As There Are Few White Men* and *The Negro Equalled by Few Europeans*. A Philadelphia periodical, the *American Museum, or Universal Magazine*, carried *The Negro Equalled by Few Europeans* in installments in 1791. Finally, in 1801, an American edition appeared in Philadelphia.[14] The status of LaVallée's *Negro* as an important antislavery text is suggested by the long list of subscribers for the American edition, including two eloquent spokesmen for black rights and dignity Richard Allen and Absalom

Jones.[15] The novel, presented as an autobiography of the African Itanoko, seems to have directly influenced American thought about slavery as well as capturing the spirit of the republican age in which slavery became a problem in political philosophy. The language and the incidents of the novel are echoed in later writings about slavery, while two of LaVallée's themes—the beauty of the black male body and the value of intimate, benevolent relations between a black man and a white man—became central in newspaper and pamphlet writings about race and slavery. Although its male protagonists love women, LaVallée's *Negro* both valorizes an erotic relationship between Itanoko and a white man intent on securing his enslaved friend's liberty and condemns sexual connections between enslaved black men and white men who exploit them sexually but are uninterested in their freedom. In its homoeroticism, LaVallée's *Negro* presented Americans with a new object of representation—the black male body. The most remarkable element in postrevolutionary American periodical essays and religious tracts concerning slavery is the emergence of the black male body as an object of representation—a new object framed by the sentimentalism, republicanism, and Christianity that defined American ideas and values. As white Americans wrestled with the problem of slavery in a new democratic and Christian republic, they were thrust by their ideas and values into this new zone—the black male body.

An announcement that whites must accept blacks either as "slaves" or as "friends" sounds the opening note of LaVallée's *Negro*, which chronicles the African's adventures with men who seek to enslave or to befriend him.[16] Whatever their intention, the men who encounter Itanoko are immediately enthralled by his pulchritude. In its antislavery sentiments and its tales of black-white relationships, the novel casts the black male body as the supremely important object of representation. Itanoko is first heard in the narrative as he addresses the "beauty" he shares with the black "nation": "I have not to complain of Nature. She endowed me with a robust form, a distinguished height. To that she added the beauty of my nation: a jet black, a full forehead, piercing eyes, a large mouth, and fine teeth."[17] Constant elements in the narrative, Itanoko's "height and muscle" are admired by all the men he meets, both black and white.[18] Not content with height and muscle, the translator of the first London edition emphasized the nudity of Itanoko, who lacks "pudicity"—modesty concerning his genitalia.[19] When Itanoko is seized by a neighboring African prince who seems to desire him as a caged companion—Itanoko is given free run of the palace but is forbidden to leave the premises—these circumstances are explained thus: "My height, my air, my figure struck him."[20] When Itanoko escapes from the palace by means of a prodigious swim to a ship anchored off-shore, a ship's officer, upon pulling him out of the water and first glimpsing the African's physique, exclaims, "This is the finest negro I have ever seen."[21] As the ship's captain admires him, Itanoko notes, "My fine figure struck him."[22] Again the first translator emphasized Itanoko's sexuality, by indulging in a double entendre on "bodily parts" and "bed." Itanoko swims to the French slaver at night and when he climbs nude into the light he reports, "If the reader observed what I said above respecting my bodily parts, he will not wonder at the air of astonishment with which they received me. Zounds! cries the officer on watch, with an energetic oath, that's the finest black I ever clapt my eyes on; how lucky is the captain, why, fortune hunts him even in bed."[23]

Itanoko's beauty distinguishes him not only from the white characters of his narrative, whose bodies are almost never represented, but also from the white figures who appear in American writing of the late eighteenth century. In American writing, informed by sentimentalism, republicanism, and Christianity, a white man appears ideally as a neighbor, brave citizen, loyal family man, or pious believer, but never as a body endowed with remarkable beauty. "The good husband, the good father, the good friend, the good neighbour," announced *American Museum, or Universal Magazine,* "we honor as a good man worthy of our love and affection."[24] LaVallée's identification with Itanoko's beauty—the narrator's projection into a beautiful black male body as well as the whites' frank appreciation of the African—engendered a subgenre of American writing in which Itanoko's black sons displayed their beauty.

Itanoko's brave swim makes him a slave, since he has unknowingly swum to a French slaver, but it sets him in the benevolent relationship that dominates the rest of his narrative. Itanoko's capacity for male-to male benevolence is well established by the time he swims to the slaver, since he has two such connections in his past. One was with his boyhood friend Otourou, his "friend" and "brother," with whom Itanoko shared "one soul" and, as boys, "one cradle."[25] Mutual devotion and disinterestedness characterize their friendship. The other was with Dumont, a Frenchman who survived a shipwreck on the Senegalese coast to become Itanoko's tutor in French and Christianity. "Sympathy," "analogy," "sentiment," "love," and "the ties of the heart" unite Itanoko and Dumont, while Christianity shapes their intimacy. Finding Dumont in prayer, for instance, Itanoko reports, "I threw myself into his arms. 'Inform me,' said I, 'why do you do this.' He embraced me. Tears of joy sprang from his eyes."[26] Yet, Otourou and Dumont merely prefigure the man whose friendship Itanoko comes to value most, the slave ship captain's son, Ferdinand. Hungry after his great swim to the ship, Itanoko is fed European food for the first time, but he finds even the "pleasing" new tastes overwhelmed by the young man who feeds him. "Nothing," Itanoko declares, "gave me such pleasure as the sight of Ferdinand. Tall and finely formed, he possessed also an ingenuous countenance, which ever attaches to the heart in the first instance. I could not resist it."[27]

The intimacy that immediately burgeons between the young black man and the young white man seems to be blighted when Ferdinand's father has Itanoko chained in the hold with the other captives. Having remarked several times on the African's beauty, the slave ship's captain plots to sell Itanoko into a servitude particularly suited to his appearance, presumably a position of sexual service.[28] Associating Ferdinand with the slave traffic, Itanoko locks his heart against the young white man who nevertheless visits him in the hold. "Many times during the day did Ferdinand approach me," Itanoko recalls, but "my heart was entirely shut up."[29] Only when Ferdinand declares himself against slavery can Itanoko reopen his heart. For, undaunted by the African's coolness, Ferdinand undoes the leg irons of the friend he desires and promises Itanoko that things will be better, despite his current pain. "I answered not a word," Itanoko states. "I could not speak. If I had possessed that power, resentment alone would have furnished my expressions. But, as no one was then near us, he seized my irons, and threw them into the sea with such indignation, that this action, which did not escape me, instantly disarmed me. I took his hand and pressed it to my heart. He understood my language, and answered with sobs."[30] As Ferdinand's "tears" serve to resurrect their mutual benevolence, Itanoko reports that these entreaties "penetrated me."[31] Ferdinand keeps his promise to Itanoko by giving him money with which to buy his freedom; they will be separated soon, but Itanoko, Ferdinand explains, can pass the money to a confidant in St. Domingue, who will buy the African from his new master and orchestrate a reunion between the two friends. The gold coins exchanged between Ferdinand and Itanoko are themselves homoerotically charged, since they are given while the African is chained and are to be hidden while he is in the hold, in the slave market in St. Domingue, and on a plantation, until he can meet Ferdinand's confidant. Only by secreting the gold coins in his rectum can Itanoko secure the liberty Ferdinand provides him.[32]

If Ferdinand loves Itanoko, Ferdinand's father, Urban, it seems, rapes Itanoko. Urban's plan to sell Itanoko into a position of sexual service seems to require that the white slaver rape the black man. Calling Urban a "ravisher" and then a "perfidious ravisher," Itanoko reports that the slaver "was struck by my comeliness" and pushed into a state of "covetousness." Urban was led to "violate, what is most sacred among men," forcing Itanoko into this position: "I bore resemblance to a man, who, weary with struggling against a tiger, that threatened his life, would fall into a voluptuous sleep, between the clutches of the monster." As several white men examine Itanoko, Urban leers, in what is probably an eighteenth-century version of a phallic joke, "He will be taller yet."[33]

Commitment to the black man's liberty fosters intimacy between Itanoko and Ferdinand. However, in St. Domingue in his quest for liberty and reunion with Ferdinand, Itanoko encounters a different sort of young white man. As the slavers zero in on Itanoko, Ferdinand's friends spirit him off to a sugar cane plantation where he will be cached, surrounded by slaves. On the plantation, Itanoko encounters Theodore, whose "criminal complaisance with the overseer" allows him to give "free scope to his irregular passions" with the plantation slaves, who were around 1790 mostly male.[34] These "irregular passions" apparently include sexual activity with black men, which LaVallée calls "crime," "vice," and "rapine," all "enormities" resulting from "unbridled disorders" and "passion."[35] Moreover, Itanoko discovers, Theodore seems intent on the new African on the plantation: "Theodore at first regarded me only as a young man who would serve as a companion for his irregularities. He had not the usual prejudice of the Europeans who think they dishonor themselves by admitting us to their society; but it was debauchery alone which gave him this apparent philosophy. . . . His amusements were too far removed from my taste to permit me to accept an equality to which my principles must have been sacrificed."[36] As the first British translation has it, Theodore indulged "shameful pleasures, only fit for darkness" on the plantation, far from those who might hear "the moans of the victims of his violence"; he "at first, saw in me but a young man, whose inexperience gave him hope of complaisance."[37] When Itanoko proves not to be complaisant, Theodore plots the African's death.

LaVallée condemns Theodore not for desire, but for refusal to join desire for black men to an opposition to slavery. Itanoko and Ferdinand embrace precisely because the white man opposes slavery. Their intimacy reflects their commitment to freedom. When they embrace upon parting,

Ferdinand reminds Itanoko of that commitment. Itanoko recalls that "melting into tears, I precipitated myself into his arms. 'Cherish,' cried he, 'the principles which we have cultivated together.' . . . We held each other long embracing without speaking."[38] Sentimentalist opposition to slavery, presupposing that the black man is either slave or friend of the white, assures us that Itanoko must resist the advances of a white man who desires the slave's body but not his liberty. Indeed, LaVallée uses the very man who spirits Itanoko away from the slavers to emphasize that a man's desire for black males is immoral only if joined to a toleration of slavery. Itanoko immediately notes that his new companion, the middle-aged Frenchman Dumenil, is unmarried—LaVallée's cliffhanger leads the reader to believe that Dumenil has purchased the African for sexual service—and so queries the white man's servants about his marital status. Dumenil "has never taken a companion to his bosom," reply the servants laconically.[39] After such suggestions of homosexuality, Dumenil is revealed to be a Christian helpmate of Itanoko and Ferdinand, not a sexual predator like Theodore. LaVallée could hardly have more strongly emphasized that white men's interest in black men and love of them leads to black liberty, while white men's exploitation of black men and passion for them leads to black slavery.

As an originating text, LaVallée's *Negro* reads like a textbook of the themes appearing in American writing about slavery in the 1790s and early 1800s. Its forthright republicanism is evident in the notion that slavery is unlawful because "the liberty of man is an inalienable right."[40] Avarice, passion, and a desire for luxury lead to the enslavement of some human beings by others, according to LaVallée's republicanism.[41] Extending both antislavery and proslavery thinking into a zone centered on the black male body, LaVallée's antislavery characters develop intimacy across the race line, while his proslavery characters reveal their obsession with the black male body even within their desire to enslave and break it. The homoerotic feeling that apparently receives LaVallée's blessing is one elevated by republican brotherhood and Christian love, not one vitiated by passion. LaVallee's naturally benevolent black men, moreover, help one another escape slavery and its cruelties. This notion is well represented in the natural benevolence shared by Itanoko and Otourou, who disinterestedly places his friend's interest before his own and seeks his friend's liberty out of a spirit of "friendship alone."[42] Finally, LaVallée penned a scene that would be replicated in American antislavery writing: a black man and a white man go off alone into a sublime setting, at which point, the writer turns to a rhapsody about the beauty that the two men together encounter. For instance, Itanoko and Dumont retreat, as the "sun [descends] toward the horizon," to a beautiful spot in Senegal, where they breathe in the "sweet perfumes" of flowers under a "serene" sky. This scene "ravishes my senses," cries Itanoko. With nightfall they return, the African finding that his "heart was full."[43] In general, this scene of two people going off alone into a sublime setting is highly eroticized in writings about race and slavery; whether the two are a black man and a black woman or a black man and a white man, the same turn to a rhapsody about beauty appears.

A new Itanoko appeared in American newspapers as "Quashi; or, The Desperate Negro," in the 1790s.[44] His narrative itself is simple. Quashi and his master share benevolent affection, based in boyhood intimacy, but fractured by the master when he wrongly credits an accusation made against his devoted slave. The meaning of Quashi's narrative is that benevolence can characterize black-white relations, while slavery is essentially a violation of benevolence. Quashi's narrative ends improbably in his suicide after he reproaches his master for the white man's abandonment of their mutual "attachment."[45] Within this series of events, Quashi's beauty is joined to benevolence, while the violation of his beauty by the whipping his master plans is joined to slavery and its abnegation of benevolence. Quashi's body, in his skin and even his thighs, is central to the narrative, while his master, a typical white character, hardly appears as a body.

Reared as "playfellow to his young master," Quashi, "a lad of parts," became as a man the "driver" or "black overseer, under his master." (One newspaper here substitutes "companion" for "master.")[46] Within this master-slave relationship, Quashi retains "the tenderness" and "the affection" for his master that had been nourished in "their boyish intimacy." Within this benevolent connection, Quashi "had no separate interest." "The most delicate, yet most strong, and seemingly indissoluble tie that could bind master and slave together" seemed to be the fruit of their lifelong intimacy.[47] However, when the master wrongly believes Quashi guilty of a minor infraction of plantation discipline, slavery is revealed as a violation of benevolence and Quashi's beauty enters the narrative. The master resolves to whip Quashi, who, never having been whipped, has maintained "the smoothness of his skin"—in the original, "the glossy honours of his skin" —precisely because of his benevolent connection with his master. This scourging of black skin rivets attention on the black man's body and his beauty: "A Negro, who has grown up to manhood, without undergoing a solemn cart whipping (as some by good chance will), especially if distinguished by any accomplishment among his fellows, takes pride in what he calls the smoothness of his skin, and its being unrased by the whip; and would be at more pains, and use more diligence to escape such a cart-whipping, than many of our lower sort would to shun the gallows."[48] Quashi responds to his master's resolution by avoiding the white man and seeking a white "mediator" or "advocate" to intercede, since he himself feels unable to speak.

After Quashi is unable to secure a mediator and unable to speak directly to the friend who is betraying him, the black man and the white man struggle on the ground in a morbid travesty of sexual intercourse:

> Quashi ran off, and his master who was a robust man, pursued him. A stone, or a clod, tripped Quashi up, just as the other reached out to seize him. They fell together, and struggled for the mastery; for Quashi was a stout man, and the elevation of his mind added vigor to his arm. At last, after a severe struggle Quashi got firmly seated on his master's breast, now panting and out of breath, and with his weight, his thighs, and one hand, secured him motionless. He then drew out a sharp knife, and while the other lay in dreadful expectation, helpless and shrinking into himself, he thus addressed him:—"Master, I was bred up with you from a child; I was your playfellow when a boy; I have loved you as myself; your interest has been my own. I am innocent of what you suspect; but had I been guilty, my attachment to you might have pleaded for me; yet you condemn me to a punishment of which I must ever have borne the disgraceful marks,—thus only can I avoid it." With these words, he drew the knife with all his strength across his own throat, and fell down dead, without a groan, on his master, bathing him in his blood.[49]

While benevolence is possible between black and white, Quashi's narrative instructs, slavery violates black beauty as well as benevolence. Indeed, a newspaper that reprinted Quashi's narrative made explicit, one week before the appearance of the black man's tale, the value of the benevolence his master violated: "The *social* principle in man is of such an expansive nature, that it cannot be confined within the circuit of a family, of friends, or a neighborhood; it spreads into wider systems, and draw [sic] men into larger confederacies, communities and commonwealths. It is in these only that the higher powers of our nature attain the highest improvement and perfection of which they are possible."[50]

Other young black men replicated Itanoko's and Quashi's beauty in

American writing of the late eighteenth century and early nineteenth. One was Selico, whose narrative began appearing in 1798, in the *American Universal Magazine* and the *Philadelphia Minerva*.[51] "Of all the negroes of Juida," the narrator assured his readers, "Selico was the blackest, the best made, and the most amiable."[52] Zami, who also appeared in the *American Universal Magazine* in 1798, was "aged eighteen, beautiful in shape as the Apollo of Belvedere, and full of spirit and courage." Zami's associate, Makandal, who is quite self-conscious about his allure and sexual prowess, states to his fellow slave, "Zami, you know the formidable power of my image."[53] Zembo appeared in the *Monthly Anthology and Boston Review* in 1807, "Tall and shapely as the palm, / A storm in war, in peace a calm; / Black as midnight without moon, / Bold and undisguised as noon."[54] This string of valorizing adjectives culminating in "undisguised" (i.e., nude) is an early example of what Eric Lott identifies as "white men's investment in the black penis."[55] The vibrant sexuality of such young black men arises in their narratives. The white men who penned these tales clearly identified with the sexual prowess they attributed to black men; even a prim condemnation of sexual excess does nothing to mask the enthusiastic language used to describe black men's sexual exploits.

In his adventures, Selico "penetrates" a sultan's seraglio and launches himself into a rollicking series of events in which he is rescued from torture and immolation only when he explains to the sultan that he is not a rapist but a votary of love.[56] Zami is linked to the Apollo of Belvedere, a male nude of the young god known as the lover of Daphne, Coronis, and Cassandra. Significantly, perhaps, Apollo was the god of divine distance, who warned from afar of humankind's guilt and who spoke through oracles of the future and the will of his father, Zeus. Also, Apollo was a victim of his brother Hermes' thievery, but became reconciled to Hermes through Zeus's judgment. The significance of a black American Apollo —erotic brother, betrayed and prophetic—is easy to see, whether or not this anonymous writer was fully aware of the resonance of his analogy. Makandal's remarkable sexual prowess began early, according to the narrator of his tale:

> At the age of fifteen or sixteen, love began to inflame his breast, and to rule with the most astonishing impetuosity. He did not, however, entertain an exclusive passion for one object, but any woman who possessed any charms, received part of his homage, and inflamed his senses. His passion acquired energy and activity in proportion as the objects which inspired it were mul-

tiplied. In every quarter he had a mistress. It is well known, that among the negroes, enjoyment soon follows desire; and that satiety and indifference are the usual consequence; but Makandal, on the contrary, appeared always to be more enamored of those who had contributed to his felicity.[57]

Zami shares his fellow slave's avid sexuality, for Zami and his lover, Samba, meet "at a private place, where, amidst a grove of odiferous orange trees, on the turf, ever crowned with verdure, under a serene sky, never obscured by clouds, in the presence of the sparkling orbs of heaven, and favored by the silence of night, they renewed the ardent testimonies of their affection and comforted each other by the tenderest caresses." Unsurprisingly, "this happiness" leads Samba to discover that "she was about to become a mother."[58] Recalling LaVallée's men paired before nature's ravishing beauty, this scene involves two characters paired in a beautiful natural setting and a turn of the writer away from explicit description of the characters to an evocation of the sublimity of nature. The manly young Zembo, after slaying a tiger, similarly envelops a woman with "his eager arms" in "the broad palmetto shade."[59] Sometimes the characters are a black man and a white man, sometimes a black man and a black woman. The former encounter is more or less clearly homoerotic, while even the latter is homoerotic since it is written by a white man who identifies with both the black male in sexual intercourse and the female with whom he shares his "happiness."[60]

Itanoko, Otourou, Quashi, Selico, Zami, Makandal, and Zembo are revived in William, another young black man who becomes a white man's object of representation. In 1815 appeared an Anglican minister's account of his conversion of a black servant, William; the account equally describes the minister's conversion to an erotic Christian love for the young black man. First a pamphlet, the story of William's conversion was reprinted as a newspaper account soon afterward.[61] William's story opens with an association of benevolence, liberty, and Christianity. The minister encounters William because, in the words attributed to the black man, his "master" is "good" and has made him "free" by awarding him his "liberty." William resides with his former master, who has noticed a spark of Christian faith in his black protégé and thus asks the minister for guidance. The minister visits William, discovering that he can read the Bible and that he is "a very young looking man with a sensible, lively, and pleasing turn of countenance." William, the minister discovers, is seeking "Christian friends" and is prone to "cry" upon contemplating Jesus. The manumitted

slave's desire for friendship and his Christian sentimentalism not only recall LaVallée's distinction between slave and friend, but also augur a benevolent consanguinity between the minister and the black man. Yet not
everyone, the minister also discovers, regards William benevolently, for
when he speaks of his love for Jesus, some white people call him "negro
dog, and black hypocrite." The minister's interest in William intensifies
when the black man describes his idea of Christian love, a straightforward
version of universal benevolence: "Me love all men, black men and white
men, too."[62]

After this first interview, the minister reports, he found himself drawn
to visit William again soon. Mounting his horse, the minister soon finds
himself in a scene echoing Itanoko and Dumont before the ravishing
beauty of nature in Senegal, Zami and Samba "on the turf," and Zembo
with his lover in his eager arms under the tropical trees. Choosing a scenic
route along the coast in order to admire the beauties of nature, the minister discovers William solitary there, an object in nature's beauty yet also an
apparent soul mate who has likewise come out along the coast on a Christian mission—reading his Bible. In the minister's words: "The road which
I took lay over a lofty down or hill, which commands a prospect of scenery
seldom equalled for beauty and magnificence. It gave birth to silent but
instructive meditation. I cast my eye downwards a little to the left, towards
a small cove, the shore of which consists of fine hard sand. It is surrounded by fragments of rock, chalk cliffs, and steep banks of broken
earth. Shut out from human intercourse and dwellings, it seems formed
for retirement and contemplation. On one of these rocks, I unexpectedly
observed a man sitting with a book." Peering down, the minister recognizes William. "The black color of his features, contrasted with the white
rocks beside him," reports the minister, reveals the man as "my Negro disciple. . . . I rejoiced at this unlooked-for opportunity of meeting him in so
solitary and interesting a situation." Roping his horse to a tree, the minister scrambles downhill to meet William. Even the description of the path
suggests that the minister finds William in a masculine paradise, for the
way to the black man was "formed by fishermen and shepherds' boys in
the side of the cliff." The minister's inference that he has found a soul mate
who shares his appreciation of nature and his Christian commitment is
soon amply confirmed.

Their talk immediately turns to religion, leading William and the minister to address their likeness. "Me wish me was like you," declares William.
"Like me, William? Why, you are like me, a poor helpless sinner," responds

the minister. Both agree that the black man should fly to the minister who represents God. "Come to Jesus," says the minister. "'Yes, Massa,' said the poor fellow weeping, 'me will come: but me come very slow; very slow, Massa, me want to run, me want to fly.—Jesus is very good to poor Negro, to send you to tell him this.'" After this positive evidence of William's faith, the minister uses a religious trope to broach the subject of William's semen and helps William fill his heart with God in a conversion experience. God's promise, asserts the minister, is that "he will not only 'pour water upon him that is thirsty,' but 'I will pour my Spirit upon thy seed, and my blessings upon thine offspring.'"[63] The understanding of blessing that the minister attributes to William is rooted in the body and its orifices, for the black man desires, he says, that God "purge me with hyssop, and I shall be clean." William's purgation is that of the body as well as that of the spirit (Psalms 51:7). The biblical hyssop was probably a type of caper, but the hyssop long known to European and American folk medicine, a variety of mint, indeed purges the body. After purgation, William is filled with God: "This was a new and solemn 'house of prayer.' The sea-sand was our floor, the heavens were our roof, the cliffs, the rocks, the hills, and the waves, formed the walls of our chamber. It was not indeed a 'place where prayer was wont to be made;' but for this once, it became a hallowed spot: it will by me ever be remembered as such. The presence of God was there. —I prayed—The Negro wept. His heart was full. I felt with him, and wept likewise." The praying finished, William and the minister must leave. The minister finds that he must trust in William's body as he ascends to his horse. "It was time for my return, I leaned upon his arm, as we ascended the steep cliff on my way back to my horse, which I had left at the top of the hill," reports the minister. "Humility and thankfulness were marked in his countenance. I leaned upon his arm with the feeling of a *brother*. It was a relationship I was happy to own—I took him by the hand at parting." As he rides out of the woods, the minister muses that his experience with William "produced a sensation not easy to be expressed." Still, the minister advances hopefully, "The last day will shew, whether our tears were not the tears of sincerity and Christian love."

The minister again is unable to be apart from William. Riding to the home of William's master, he finds the black man awaiting him in a grove. "Ah! Massa," cries William, "me very glad to see you, me think you long time coming." The minister then begins to call William "brother from Africa." Both William and the minister rivet their attention on the black man's body, William humbly claiming that his "soul" is "more black" than his "body" and the minister borrowing from the Bible to add new verses to a hymn featuring William: "Though he's black, he's comely too." Even the saintly William seems inevitably physicalized in the imagination of the minister, who declares of the black man, "He was a monument to the Lord's praise."[64] The point of William's tale is that the affectionate, eroticized consanguinity shared by the black man and the white man overturns the violent seizure that brought the African to America: "Me left father and mother one day at home, to go to get sea shells by the sea shore; and, as I was stooping down to gather them up, some white men came out of a boat, and took me away."[65]

White men opposed to slavery seem to have been captive to the black man's body and to the physical likeness between black and white. In 1803, Rhode Island slaveholder turned abolitionist Moses Brown interpreted a black man with white marks on his skin as "evidence of the sameness of human nature and corresponding with the declaration of the Apostle, that, 'God hath made of one blood all nations of men.'" Brown found likeness to the "easy and agreeable" Henry Moss through the black man's body: "His back below his shoulders is mostly as white as white people of his age, as are parts of his breast and even his nipples. The white parts of his skin and especially his anus are so transparent as to show the vains [sic] as distinct, as a white mans [sic]." Julie Ellison has accurately noted that "sensibility" encouraged attention to "the body [of] color," along with hope for an encounter defined by "interpersonal transparency." Here in the writings of white antislavery men on black men is invoked a transparency of the body as well as of the consciousness. The white man's benevolence to the black man seems inevitably to involve the latter's body.[66]

Revolutionary republicanism taught Americans that benevolence is the unifying force of society and that benevolence helps gird the virtuous man to fight against oppression. Republican ideology, liberal religion, and Calvinist orthodoxy all led Americans to believe that while monarchy had traditionally united society through authority, cruelty, and force, a new society in the United States could cohere by means of the natural benevolence inherent in humankind. The same newspapers that printed white-penned narratives of young black men in the 1790s told readers that "society being formed, it becomes essentially necessary that universal benevolence founded on the true principle of friendship should be its base and support."[67] "Friendship," Americans were encouraged to believe, "is the grand tie of society."[68] An analogy between black loyalty and republican loyalty reveals the heart of the matter. The tale of "Scipio" told of a teen-aged slave so "greatly attached" to his master's son, with whom he had been reared, that he presciently refuses to trust a nurse hired to care for the sick white boy.[69] When the nurse fails in her duty, Scipio, concealed under the boy's bed, comes to the rescue. Scipio's loyalty is likened to that of the "Patriots" during the War of Independence—the heart of the matter in white thinking about blacks and benevolence.

Between 1790 and 1820, antislavery writings represented intimacy between a black man and a white man with the sentimentalist vocabulary of benevolence: affection, attachment, brotherhood, disinterestedness, friendship, heart, intimacy, love, sentiment, sympathy, and tenderness. This antislavery writing usually noted that while slavery violates a natural right to liberty, it is also an abnegation of benevolence. According to this critique, which shared little with the individualistic abolitionism of the antebellum decades, the black must be either the slave or the friend of the white. Lamenting the cruelty of slavery, a 1791 newspaper article stated the essence of this critique: "The Negro has no friends."[70] Anti-slavery writers of the 1790s, moreover, sought to emphasize an irony they perceived in slavery. Blacks, they were often convinced, are especially benevolent and sympathetic, but are not accepted within the circuit of society. Thus, white Americans in the post revolutionary decades were in the remarkably complex situation of hearing that republican society could cohere only through benevolence, while they were living with blacks, whose enslavement and oppression surely violated benevolence and likeness and yet who were like whites in language, religion, and sex and were even commonly believed to be especially benevolent.

Defenses of slavery of the revolutionary era and the early republic shared with antislavery writing the sentimentalist presuppositions about the unifying force of benevolence but presupposed that affection and the other ties that unite individuals could not cross the race line. This defense of slavery was not an abandonment of sentimentalism—indeed, its major spokesman, Jefferson, was both slaveholder and sentimentalist, but rather it was a revelation of the grim face of sentimentalism. Society must enslave or banish those who cannot join it benevolently, reasoned Jefferson as he affirmed Montesquieu's arguments of the middle of the eighteenth century. The accumulated cruelties of slavery and the seemingly natural differences between black and white suggested to a critical mass of Americans that blacks were better slaves than free. Almost never did eighteenth-century Americans defending slavery claim that slavery is ultimately just. Rather, they claimed that blacks and whites, separated by past cruelties and by nature and, thus, unable to coexist benevolently in a free society, would turn on each other. Slavery's justice, therefore, was provisional. For only colonization—the expatriation of black Americans to Africa or the Caribbean—would allow manumission, reasoned the American defenders of slavery. Such Americans could reveal their concern with black sexuality, whether in the notion that black men are more "amorous" or in the fear that miscegenation would become even more widespread in a free society in the Southern states than it was in a slave society. It was a commonplace of the day that liberating American slaves would lead to "a general commixture" and "Ethiopians [in] sexual intercourse with the whites" were the freed slaves to remain in the United States."[71] Indeed, this fear of future miscegenation, especially in the South, was a tacit affirmation of the desirability of the black male, since a slave society already offered white men considerable access to black women and any great increase in miscegenation would likely then be intercourse between black men and white women.

Erotic representations of black men by white men are not records of sexual activity but, rather, records of beliefs and feelings.[72] The beliefs and feelings inscribed in these representations resulted from an encounter of white men, who were heirs and affiliates of sentimentalism, republicanism, and Christianity, with black men, who represented to white men a peculiar "other"—like yet unlike, compatriot yet slave, masculine by nature yet by society restricted as lovers, husbands, fathers, and citizens. Erotic representations of black men by white men resulted from a rupture in the national (or hegemonic) discussion of race and slavery in postrevolutionary America. The major spokesmen for white America proclaimed that benevolence could never exist between black and white in America. Democratic-Republican or Federalist, deist or orthodox, Americans, like Thomas Jefferson, James Monroe, James Madison, Samuel Hopkins, and Jonathan Edwards, Jr., believed that blacks and whites could never share the likeness and the unity of common sense and experience required for benevolent relations.[73] Separation of the races, not benevolent association, was the standard of white leaders in postrevolutionary America. The means of this separation was to be the expatriation of black Americans to Africa or the Caribbean, and its fruit was the American Colonization Society. Despite this standard, there is considerable evidence that white Americans saw a likeness within black Americans, a likeness whose recognition they usually suppressed, perhaps because of guilt about slavery, or a reluctance to share with an underclass the benefits of their new society, or ambivalent feeling about blacks as at once near and far, an "other" to white Americans. Even Jefferson, for instance, considered blacks to be natural republicans and Benjamin Banneker to be a true scientist—an ideal to which Jefferson himself aspired.[74]

As a new object of discourse, the black male body entered through a rupture in republican discourse about slavery. The white experience of likeness in blacks—feeling benevolence for them, recognizing their republican desire for liberty, worshipping the same God—could not be entirely suppressed, even if it could be barred from standard forms of social thought and religion. One participant at a revival well indicated how the presence of blacks could be marginalized but not suppressed. He "cried out . . . 'God is among the people'" as he saw "prostrate on the ground . . . the learned pastor, the steady patriot, and the obedient son, crying 'Holy, holy, holy, Lord God Almighty.'" Then he listed those he saw in succession as he cast his "eyes a few paces" on and on. After the men were the women praising God, after the women were the worst sinners now converted, and after the worst sinners, at the limit of the sanctified, was "the poor oppressed African with his soul liberated, longing to be with his God."[75] Neither in black writing nor in the white imagination would the figure of the black male remain at the margin, but came instead to the center to address the issue of masculine likeness. When William's minister brought the black man bodily as well as spiritually into the circle of benevolence, he emphasized their sameness: "The religion of Jesus is everywhere the same. Its real possessors, whether black or white, all use the same language—all are actuated by the same love and animated by the same hopes through faith in the same Savior."[76] Like William's minister, some white American men, even a determined expatriationist like Jefferson, found black men "like" themselves, an experience of likeness "not easy to be expressed" precisely because it was effectively barred from white discourse. Blurring the line between benevolent and erotic feelings, representations of the black male body became the means of saying what otherwise could barely be said, for the body of one man possesses an undeniable likeness to that of another. Representations of the black male body allowed physical equality to hint of political equality, while homoeroticism hinted of the likeness and benevolence that might join black and white.[77]

This black male, eroticized and republicanized, reveals something essential in postrevolutionary American ideology. Black and masculine, the first body to be so fully represented in American publications revealed the masculine likeness on which revolutionary republicanism was grounded, the likeness that became either threatening or inviting when it crossed between black and white. The republican literati recognized this likeness by acknowledging black men's natural republicanism and their alleged desires for white women, but explained the threat such likeness posed to the republic by arguing that the historic cruelties of slavery would always undermine a black-and-white republic. Republicans sought to expatriate blacks precisely to preserve the likeness required by American republicanism, but the figure of the black man himself—oppressed, like white men, and impossible to banish—helped to upset the precarious balance of late eighteenth-century American thought.

Long noted by historians, this precariousness has been attributed to the republican effort to balance civic virtue and commercial development as well as natural aristocracy and participatory democracy.[78] But this precariousness derived also from the republican insistence on setting black against white in a sentimentalist system of ideas and values. As antislavery pamphlets and newspaper writings of the era demonstrate, this balance could not be maintained in a slave society nor, as leading republicans apprehensively recognized, in a postslavery republic. The black man served to disrupt republican ideology because he was too close to white men— too close to the affections, too much a republican—in a system of ideas and values demanding that he be separate. The response of leading republicans to the existence of the black man—expatriate him and other blacks to Africa—was so impractical that some other adjustment, ideological if not geographical, was seemingly required.

Liberal individualism, well known as a response to new economic, political, and geographical circumstances in the new republic, was also a readjustment of thought about slavery, race, and the future of a multiracial America. Liberal individualism recast the abolitionist understanding of slavery—no longer a violation of benevolence, but an infringement upon an individual's natural liberty. Liberal individualism allowed Americans to jettison the notion, on which eighteenth-century thought about race rested, that the black man is inevitably either slave or friend to the white by replacing it with the notion that an ex-slave rather would be another atomistic individual in a free society.[79] As Americans came to realize that blacks and whites would inhabit the same continent but could share little of the benevolence esteemed in eighteenth-century theology and social thought, revolutionary republicanism died and liberal individualism quickened.

The black man stirred questions about the possibilities of sentiment and liberty. Leslie A. Fiedler has argued that the "relationship between a white man and a colored one" has been homoeroticized because the colored man represents white men's desire for uncivilized freedom, "a life of impulse and instinct," a life that cannot be conceived heterosexually. This, in relation to black men, is wrong, and it has led to Fiedler's error in writing that "the Negro is a late comer to our literature, who has had to be adapted to the already existing image of the original Noble Savage. Our greatest Negro characters, including Nigger Jim, are, at their most moving moments, red men in blackface."[80] In his own right and in the white imagination, the black man is his own figure in American writing and thought, not a derivative of the Indian. At the transition from the eighteenth century to the nineteenth century, the black man represented in one part of the white imagination not uncivilized freedom but the eros and union of sentiment. William and his minister in the cove yearn for union, not a wild freedom. Paradoxically, the black man stirred questions about sentiment and liberty in a time when white Americans were not only developing a new notion of freedom, free from the sentimentalist conditions of republicanism, but also groping toward a new, liberal ethos of race relations, one made inevitable by the impracticality of expatriation.

### NOTES

Editor's note: From "The Black Body Erotic and the Republican Body Politic, 1790–1820," by John Saillant, from the *Journal of History of Sexuality* 5:3, pp. 403–28. Copyright © 1995 by the University of Texas Press. All rights reserved. Reprinted by permission.

1. Sentimentalism, republicanism, and Christianity in late eighteenth-century and early nineteenth-century America are well treated in the following works: A. Owen Aldridge, *Thomas Paine's American Ideology* (Newark, NJ, 1984); Bernard Bailyn, *The Ideological Origins of the American Revolution* (Cambridge, 1967); James T. Kloppenberg, "The Virtues of Liberalism: Christianity, Republicanism, and Ethics in Early American Political Discourse," *Journal of American History* 74 (1987): 9–33; Adrienne Koch, *The Philosophy of Thomas Jefferson* (New York, 1943); Mark Valeri, "The New Divinity and the American Revolution," *William and Mary Quarterly* 46 (1989): 741–69; Garry Wills, *Inventing America: Jefferson's Declaration of Independence* (Garden City, NY, 1978); Gordon S. Wood, *The Creation of the American Republic, 1776–1787* (New York, 1969), and *The Radicalism of the American Revolution* (New York, 1992); and Conrad Edick Wright, *The Transformation of Charity in Post Revolutionary New England* (Boston, 1992). Republicanism is a contentious issue in American historiography. A recent overview appears as

"Special Issue: The Republican Synthesis Revisited: Essays in Honor of George Athan Billias," *Proceedings of the American Antiquarian Society* 102 (1992): 69–224. My goal here is less to take a side in the republican/liberal debate than to suggest that the evolution from republicanism to liberalism was driven not only by economic factors (as is commonly accepted) but also by racial and sexual factors in which the black man is a commanding presence. For recent examples of the emphasis on economic factors, see the following: Robert E. Shalhope, "Republicanism, Liberalism, and Democracy: Political Culture in the Early Republic," *Proceedings of the American Antiquarian Society* 102 (1992): 117; Carroll Smith-Rosenberg, "Discovering the Subject of the 'Great Constitutional Discussion,' 1786–1789," *Journal of American History* 79 (1992): 847–49; and Steven Watts, *The Republic Reborn: War and the Making of Liberal America, 1790–1820* (Baltimore, 1987).

2. These writings share in the eighteenth-century "centrality of sentiment and pathos" (Janet Todd, *Sensibility: An Introduction* [New York, 1986], pp. 1–9). Part of an Americanization of British sentimentalism, the "poor negro" is a black, American variation of "virtue in distress," prey to racism and economic exploitation. Remodeling conventional representations of distressed women, the sentimentalist depictions of black men were meant to elicit "humanity" from the reader (G. J. Barker-Benfield, *The Culture of Sensibility: Sex and Society in Eighteenth-Century Britain* [Chicago, 1992], pp. 219–34). The British background of sentimentalism is discussed in John Mullan, *Sentiment and Sociability: The Language of Feeling in the Eighteenth Century* (Oxford, 1988). I agree with a recent argument that the use of the term "Age of Sensibility" has been too narrow because it has not included the way in which "race relations and sexual relations [were] represented in terms of sympathetic transactions" (Julie Ellison, "Race and Sensibility in the Early Republic: Ann Eliza Bleeker and Sarah Wentworth Morton," *American Literature* 65 [1993]: 446).

3. Paul Rahe, *Republics Ancient and Modern: Classical Republicanism and the American Revolution* (Chapel Hill, NC, 1992), pp. 128–33, 154–55; Eric Lott, *Love and Theft: Blackface Minstrelsy and the American Working Class* (New York, 1993).

4. Karen Sánchez-Eppler has noted the way in which a sentimentalism attributed to women led in the 1840s and 1850s to alluring depictions of black bodies, since "sentimental fiction constitutes an intensely bodily genre." "Miscegenation," she thus argues, "provides an essential motif of virtually all antislavery fiction" ("Bodily Bonds: The Intersecting Rhetoric of Feminism and Abolition," in *The New American Studies: Essays from Representations*, ed. Philip Fisher [Berkeley, 1991], pp. 235–40).

5. For some of Jefferson's statements on "benevolence," "emulation," "imitation," and "virtue," see the following: *The Writings of Thomas Jefferson*, ed. Andrew A. Lipscomb and Albert Ellery Bergh (Washington, DC, 1903), 1:116–19, 2:121, 177, 3:318, 12:393–94, 16:73; *The Papers of Thomas Jefferson*, ed. Julian P. Boyd et al. (Princeton, NJ, 1950–92), 1:76–77, 8:637.

6. "How to attach people to one another and to the state? That was one of the central obsessions of the era," Gordon S. Wood has written of the revolutionary and postrevolutionary years. "The Enlightenment came to believe that there was 'a natural principle of attraction in man towards man,' and that these natural affinities were by themselves capable of holding the society together" (*The Radicalism of the American Revolution*, p. 214). See also Gordon S. Wood, "Illusions and Disillusions in the American Revolution," in *The American Revolution: Its Character and Limits*, ed. Jack P. Greene (New York, 1987), p. 358. For Montesquieu on sentiment and social unity, see Ann M. Cohler, *Montesquieu's Comparative Politics and the Spirit of American Constitutionalism* (Lawrence, KS, 1988), pp. 45–55. For Montesquieu's influence on Jefferson, see Garrett Ward Sheldon, *The Political Philosophy of Thomas Jefferson* (Baltimore, 1991), p. 67. For the "ward-republics," see Richard K. Matthews, *The Radical Politics of Thomas Jefferson: A Revisionist Approach* (Lawrence, KS, 1984), pp. 81–89.

7. Lipscomb and Bergh, eds., 2:192, 201. Colonizationist efforts arc discussed in the following works: Robert McColley, *Slavery and Jeffersonian Virginia*, 2d ed. (Urbana, IL, 1973), esp. pp. 129–30; Duncan J. MacLeod, *Slavery, Race, and the American Revolution* (New York, 1974), pp. 78–85; John Chester Miller, *The Wolf by the Ears: Thomas Jefferson and Slavery* (New York, 1977), pp. 164–70; P. J. Staudenraus, *The African Colonization Movement, 1816–1865* (New York, 1961); and Larry E. Tise, *Proslavery: A History of the Defense of Slavery in America, 1770–1840* (Athens, GA, 1987), esp. pp. 190–91, 356–61.

8. For Montesquieu's influence in America, see the following: Thomas L. Pangle, *The Spirit of Modern Republicanism: The Moral Vision of the American Founders and the Philosophy of Locke* (Chicago, 1988), pp. 89–94; and Paul Merrill Spurlin, *Montesquieu in America, 1760–1801* (Baton Rouge, LA, 1940).

9. Charles-Louis de Secondat, baron de La Brède et de Montesquieu, *The Spirit of the Laws*, trans. and ed. Anne M. Cohler, Basia Carolyn Miller, and Harold Samuel Stone (New York, 1989), p. 250.

10. Lipscomb and Bergh, eds., 1:72–73; Rahe, pp. 619, 636–37, 648; Dumas Malone, *Jefferson and His Times: The Sage of Monticello* (Boston, 1981), pp. 341–42.

11. Indeed, articulate black Americans of the postrevolutionary years, whether sophisticated ministers like Richard Allen and Lemuel Haynes or societies that left their beliefs inscribed in constitutions and proclamations, set their claims for black dignity exactly in the circle of benevolence. Richard Allen, *The Life Experience and Gospel Labors of the Rt. Rev. Richard Allen, To Which Is Annexed the Rise and Progress of the African Methodist Episcopal Church in the United States of America, Containing a Narrative of the Yellow Fever in the Year of Our Lord 1793, With an Address to the People of Color in the United States* (New York, 1960)—see pp. 19–26, 50, 72, 75–89 for comments on benevolence; Ruth Bogin, "'Liberty Further Extended': A 1776 Antislavery Manuscript by Lemuel Haynes," *William and Mary Quarterly* 40 (1983): 85–105 (see 98–104 for Haynes's use of "natural

Effections" and "Disinterested Benevolence"); Lemuel Haynes, *The Nature and Importance of True Republicanism, with a Few Suggestions Favorable to Independence: A Discourse Delivered at Rutland (Vermont) the Fourth of July 1801, It Being the 25th Anniversary of American Independence* (Rutland, VT, 1801), pp. 7–13; *Laws of the African Society, Instituted at Boston, Anno Domini, 1796* (Boston, 1802); *The Proceedings of the Free African Union Society and the African Benevolent Society, Newport, Rhode Island, 1780–1824*, ed. William H. Robinson (Providence, RI, 1976), pp. 145–46.

12. Lipscomb and Bergh, eds., 10:294–97.

13. Joseph LaVallée, *Le nègre comme il y a peu de blancs* (Paris, 1789). The work was reprinted in France in 1795 and 1800. "Antislavery" deserves a comment here that applies to all the texts examined in this chapter. The antislavery thought expressed in these texts is at least as much sentimental and paternalistic as fraternal and egalitarian. The African American antislavery thought of its day, such as that of Lemuel Haynes and John Marrant, rejected its paternalism. Lacking interest in the self-determination of African Americans, the authors of the texts examined here partook of a white paternalism that would come to be important in antebellum proslavery thought. A belief in sentiment as the force that would alleviate slavery led the authors examined here into a paternalism in which the white man frees the black as the two come to recognize their sentimental ties. Thus, even the claims of black superiority in beauty and sentiment could serve to subordinate the black man waiting for the recognition of his sentiments and for his liberation.

14. Joseph LaVallée, *The Negro As There Are Few White Men*, trans. J. Trapp (London, 1790); I read this translation in the Rare Book Room of the Boston Public Library. The other versions mentioned include Joseph LaVallée, *The Negro Equalled by Few Europeans* (London, 1790; Dublin, 1791; Philadelphia, 1801), and "The Negro Equalled by Few Europeans," *American Museum, or Universal Magazine* 9 (January-June 1791): 53–60, 99–107, 145–53, 205–13, 257–65, 313–24; 10 (July-December 1791): 29–40, 77–88, 129–44, 185–200, 241–56, 285–303. All quotations are from the 1801 printing, except as noted.

15. LaVallée, *The Negro Equalled by Few Europeans*, 2:239–44.

16. Ibid., 1:5.

17. Ibid., p. 8.

18. Ibid., p. 87.

19. LaVallée, *The Negro As There Are Few White Men*, 1:14.

20. LaVallée, *The Negro Equalled by Few Europeans*, 1:40.

21. Ibid., p. 48.

22. Ibid., p. 61.

23. LaVallée, *The Negro As There Are Few White Men*, 1:61. By the end of the eighteenth century, the word "parts" had a well-established sexual connotation in "privy parts" (*Oxford English Dictionary*, 2d ed., s.v. "privy parts").

24. *American Museum, or Universal Magazine* 9 (1791): 275. Jefferson's republi-

can "good man" is "he whose every thought and deed by rules of virtue moves," who assumes a "neighbor's" role, "not stranger-like" but integrated into his community and uninterested in profiting from his peers (Lipscomb and Bergh, eds. [n. 5 above], 16:110–11). For Timothy Dwight's Federalist ideal of masculine neighborliness, see *Greenfield Hill*, in *The Major Poems of Timothy Dwight*, ed. William J. McTaggart and William K. Bottorff (Gainesville, FL, 1969), pp. 481–95. Neither Jefferson nor Dwight includes any notion of masculine beauty in these representations of white men.

25. LaVallée, *The Negro Equalled by Few Europeans* (n. 14 above), 1:21–22. This notion of black benevolence was probably related to a belief that blacks were likely to participate in what modern social scientists describe as "same-sex dyadic ties," which, some scholars speculate, were extensions of " 'shipmate' relationships" formed in transport from Africa (Sidney W. Mintz and Richard Price, *An Anthropological Approach to the Afro-American Past: A Caribbean Perspective* [Philadelphia, 1976], pp. 22–23).

26. LaVallée, *The Negro Equalled by Few Europeans*, 1:12–14.

27. Ibid., p. 51. The first translation takes a slightly different approach to this meeting: "Well shaped, straight, endowed with the happiest and sweetest countenance, he was possessed of those secret charms which conquer the heart at first sight. I did not hold out. . . . Sit by me, said I, so beautiful a face, cannot be without a noble soul" (*The Negro As There Are Few White Men* [n. 14 above ], 1:65).

28. LaVallée, *The Negro Equalled by Few Europeans*, 1:61–75.

29. Ibid., p. 58.

30. Ibid., p. 59.

31. Ibid., p. 63.

32. Ibid., pp. 76–77.

33. LaVallée, *The Negro As There Are Few White Men*, 1:80–98. By the end of the eighteenth century, the word "embrace" had a long history of association with sexual intercourse, the word "violate" had a long history of meaning rape, and the word "voluptuous" had a long history of meaning sensual. "Ravish" had a long history of meaning rape, while "ravisher" meant in particular rapist (*Oxford English Dictionary*, 2d ed., s.v.v. "embrace," "violate," "voluptuous," "ravish," and "ravisher").

34. Caribbean plantation owners preferred buying new stocks of young African men to encouraging indigenous slave families, since the cost of buying a young man was considered less than the cost of rearing a child to be a slave.

35. "LaVallée, *The Negro Equalled by Few Europeans* (n. 14 above), 1:86, 109–11.

36. Ibid., p. 111.

37. LaVallée, *The Negro As There Are Few White Men* (n. 14 above), 1:152, 155. Itanoko also reports that when Theodore chose a man-servant, "One may sufficiently guess that luxuriance of shape had been more consulted, than personal qualifications" (p. 156).

38. LaVallée, *The Negro Equalled by Few Europeans,* 1:93.

39. Ibid., pp. 101–2.

40. Ibid., p. 67.

41. Ibid., pp. 63, 66, 69.

42. Ibid., p. 153.

43. Ibid., pp. 15–18.

44. Two periodical versions are "Quashi, or the Desperate Negro," *Massachusetts Magazine, or Monthly Museum of Knowledge and Rational Entertainment* 5 (1793): 583–84; and "Quashi the Negro, a True Story," *Vergennes Gazette* 1 (October 18, 1798): 4. A pamphlet version is *The Story of Quashi; or, The Desperate Negro* (Newburyport, MA, 1820). This pamphlet, which nearly duplicates the 1793 version, is the source of all references here, except as noted. The source of the Quashi stories is apparently Reverend James Ramsay, *An Essay on the Treatment and Conversion of African Slaves in the British Sugar Colonies* (London, 1784), pp. 248–53.

45. *The Story of Quashi,* p. 8

46. "Quashi the Negro, A True Story," p. 4.

47. *The Story of Quashi,* p. 5.

48. Ibid., p. 6. Ramsay, p. 251. The 1820 version (*The Story of Quashi*) substitutes "unrased" for the "unraised" of the 1793 ("Quashi, or the Desperate Negro"). This change could be an error or else a self-conscious effort to use "unrased" (a variant of "unrazed") to suggest even more of the violence of whipping than does "unraised." Since there are no other misspellings in the pamphlet, and since it is a well-produced, illustrated booklet, I suspect that the change was made self-consciously.

49. *The Story of Quashi,* pp. 8–9.

50. "Duties of Society," *Vergennes Gazette* 1 (October 11, 1798): 4.

51. "Selico, an African Tale," *American Universal Magazine* 4 (1798): 183–92. Selico's tale was also printed in the *Philadelphia Minerva* 4 (1798): 13–21.

52. "Selico, an African Tale," p. 185.

53. "Account of a Remarkable Conspiracy Formed by a Negro on the Island of St. Domingue," *American Universal Magazine* 4 (1798): 196–97. This was reprinted in the New York *Minerva* 2 (1823): 74–75. The 1798 version is the source of all references here.

54. James Montgomery, "Zembo and Nila: An African Tale," *Monthly Anthology and Boston Review* 4 (1807): 603–4.

55. Lott (n. 3 above), p. 121.

56. "Selico, an African Tale," pp. 188–89. By the end of the eighteenth century, the word "penetration" had a well-established sexual meaning in penile penetration (*Oxford English Dictionary,* 2d ed., s.v. "penetration").

57. "Account of a Remarkable Conspiracy Formed by a Negro on the Island of St. Domingue," pp. 193–94.

58. Ibid., p. 197.

59. Montgomery, p. 604.

60. In *White over Black: American Attitudes toward the Negro, 1550–1812* (Chapel Hill, NC, 1968), pp. 136–78, Winthrop D. Jordan has explored the sexual implications of the fact that white "desire and aversion rested on the bedrock fact that white men perceived Negroes as being *both alike and different* from themselves" (p. 137). Jordan's interest is in explaining both miscegenation and the "fundamentally sexual" character of "white men's insecurity vis-à-vis the Negro" (p. 156). My interest, however, is in white men's eroticization of black men as an extension of sentiment, part of a counter discourse to republicanism that still shared the sentimentalist presuppositions of leading republicans.

61. I have used "Narrative of a Negro Servant," *Christian Messenger* 1 (November 13, 1816): 59–61 and (November 20, 1816): 65–66. This narrative is attributed to Legh Richmond (1772–1827). At least nine other printings appeared before 1820: *The Negro Servant, and the Young Cottager* (New York, 1815); *Annals of the Poor: Containing the Dairyman's Daughter (with Considerable Additions), the Negro Servant, and the Young Cottager* (New Haven, CT, 1815); *The Negro Servant, an Authentic and Interesting Narrative* (Andover, MA, 1815; Boston, 1815; New York, 1815); *The African Servant* (Andover, MA, 1816; Andover, MA, 1818); *The Negro Servant: An Authentic Narrative* (Boston, 1816[?]); *The Negro Servant* (Philadelphia, 1817).

62. "Narrative of a Negro Servant," pp. 59–61.

63. By the end of the eighteenth century, the word "seed" had a long history of meaning semen (*Oxford English Dictionary*, 2d ed., s.v. "seed," definition 4).

64. "Narrative of a Negro Servant," pp. 65–66.

65. Ibid., p. 60.

66. Moses Brown Anti-Slavery Papers, 1803 folder, Rhode Island Historical Society; Ellison (n. 2 above), pp. 447–49. For Moses Brown and other Quaker opponents of slavery, see David Brion Davis, *The Problem of Slavery in the Age of Revolution, 1770–1828* (Ithaca, NY, 1975), pp. 213–54.

67. "On Friendship," *Herald of Vermont* 1 (July 23, 1792): 4.

68. "Friendship," *Vergennes Gazette* 2 (February 27, 1800): 4.

69. "Fidelity; or, Scipio, the Negro Boy," *Christian Messenger* 1 (March 12, 1817): 196; also printed in *Boston Recorder* 2 (January 7, 1817): 38.

70. "A Fragment," *Morning Ray* 1 (November 29, 1791): 3.

71. "On the Moral and Political Effects of Negro Slavery," *Middlebury Mercury* 2 (July 6, 1803): 1–2. See also Jonathan Edwards, Jr., *The Injustice and Impolicy of the Slave-Trade and of the Slavery of the Africans* (Providence, RI, 1792), pp. 35–37, for the necessary choice between miscegenation and separation after the end of slavery.

72. Thomas W. Lacqueur is obviously right in noting that discourse about sexual activity is quite different from the activity itself ("Sexual Desire and the Market Economy during the Industrial Revolution," in *Discourses of Sexuality: From Aristotle to AIDS*, ed. Domna C. Stanton [Ann Arbor, MI, 1992], p. 200).

73. Drew R. McCoy, *The Last of the Fathers: James Madison and the Republican Legacy* (New York, 1989), pp. 277–303.

74. For Jefferson on blacks' natural republicanism, see Lipscomb and Bergh, eds. (n. 5 above), 1:72–73. An excellent analysis of Jefferson's ambivalent feelings about blacks, touching on his thoughts about Banneker, is Frank Shuffelton, "Thomas Jefferson: Race, Culture, and the Failure of the Anthropological Method," in *A Mixed Race: Ethnicity in Early America,* ed. Frank Shuffelton (New York, 1993), pp. 257–77.

75. "Religious Intelligencer," *Vermont Mercury* 1 (May 10, 1802): 2. Albert J. Raboteau notes that worship of the same God implied an egalitarianism across the race line ("Slave Autonomy and Religion," *Journal of Religious Thought* 38 [1981–82]: 51–64, and "The Slave Church in the Era of the American Revolution," in *Slavery and Freedom in the Age of the American Revolution,* ed. Ira Berlin and Ronald Hoffman [Charlottesville, VA, 1983], pp. 196–211).

76. "Narrative of a Negro Servant," p. 59.

77. Smith-Rosenberg (n. 1 above) has argued that the idea of the black slave was used by white Americans to define and stabilize, by way of contrast, the idea of a middle-class individual, free and productive (pp. 861–62). The likeness recorded in the texts I discuss here threatened to subvert that contrast, so discussion of black-white likeness was pushed out of postrevolutionary white discourse.

78. The most distinguished commentary on commercial development and participatory democracy in postrevolutionary America is that of Joyce Appleby: "The Social Origins of American Revolutionary Ideology," *Journal of American History* 54 (1978): 935–58; "What Is Still American in the Political Philosophy of Thomas Jefferson?" *William and Mary Quarterly* 39 (1982): 287–309; "Commercial Farming and the 'Agrarian Myth' in the Early Republic," *Journal of American History* 58 (1982): 833–49; *Capitalism and a New Social Order: The Republican Vision of the 1790s* (New York, 1984); "Republicanism and Ideology," *American Quarterly* 37 (1985): 461–73; and "Republicanism in New and Old Contexts," *William and Mary Quarterly* 43 (1986): 20–34.

79. Louis S. Gerteis, *Morality and Utility in American Antislavery Reform* (Chapel Hill, NC, 1987), pp. 20–22; and Daniel J. McInerney, " 'A Faith for Freedom': The Political Gospel of Abolitionism," *Journal of the Early Republic* 11 (1991): 374–75.

80. Leslie A. Fiedler, *Love and Death in the American Novel,* rev. ed. (New York, 1966), pp. 159, 339, 366, 375–77.

*Chapter 13*

# What's Sex Got to Do with It?
## *Marriage versus Circulation in* The Pennsylvania Magazine, *1775–1776*

### *Laura Mandell*

The "It" of my title is the United States. Americanist scholarship has focused on the uneven development of American nationalism as it emerged well after the Revolution, in the antebellum period.[1] But nonetheless, as devotees to the cause of Revolution well knew, a sense of group cohesion was needed not only for mustering the patriotism necessary for overturning British colonial rule but also for maintaining order in the newly independent Republic. Historian Benedict Anderson describes the imagined sense of belonging to a group ("imagined community") that emerged before and during the American Revolution. The sense of community in America was produced by the circulation of early newspapers, Anderson argues, focusing especially on the paper produced by Philadelphia printer Benjamin Franklin.[2] But recently, historical scholar Ed White has called for "sustained engagement with Anderson's narrative" about printing in the United States which he finds flawed partly because Anderson does not take into account how much colonial printing endeavors actually "bridged the Atlantic" rather than creating colonial identity.[3] The monthly magazines that I examine here, I would argue, do both, exploring the transatlantic circulation of printed matter and ideas as they participate in forging a sense of American community.

Intellectual transactions with old England were needed even though—or perhaps, especially because—the colonies were about to sever political ties. "The problem of forging a unified national identity began," Cecilia O'Leary insists, "with the War of Independence" when newspapers rallied Americans to "Join, or Die." In this essay, I argue that discussions of human sexuality at the revolutionary moment were involved in maintaining cultural connections with England as well as facilitating "[t]he requisite transference of allegiance from the British crown to an independent United States."[4] Though more concerned with delineating how same-sex desire was categorized at the revolutionary moment, and with the political interests served by representing certain features of sexual communication, this essay, as its title suggests, proposes a preliminary answer to the question, how does representing sexuality as analogous to politics in 1775–1776 affect our culturally bound understanding of same-sex desire?

Here I look at essays by "the Old Bachelor" and friends, published in the *Pennsylvania Magazine* in the Philadelphia of 1775 and early 1776, authored primarily by Thomas Paine, but also by Francis Hopkinson and others. In this series of articles, the bachelor is a figure of and for circulation itself. *The Pennsylvania Magazine* achieved "a greater circulation than any magazine had achieved up to that time."[5] Moreover, as is visible in essays such as that written by "The Twelve United Colonies, by their Delegates in Congress, to the Inhabitants of Great-Britain," contributors to this magazine imagined an audience of readers on both sides of the Atlantic, thus presupposing transatlantic circulation.[6] The bachelor figure was very cosmopolitan; he traveled to the metropole and frequented London clubs for men.[7] The essays about him were addressed especially to the inhabitants of Philadelphia of the revolutionary decades, a city characterized by cosmopolitan print promiscuity: huge numbers of books and magazines from England and Europe arrived in Philadelphia, some of them exemplars of the high culture to which American colonists could not yet aspire, some quite pornographic.[8]

As historians have shown, the "American founders" advocated marriage as a way of containing the "disorderly men," and the Bachelor and the sodomite were seen as particularly dangerous. Unharnessed sexual energy threatened to subvert the emerging Republic.[9] In their satirical attacks on the bachelor, Paine and his cohort at the *Pennsylvania Magazine* tried to turn national sentiment against transatlantic circulation of goods as well as magazine articles and other cultural artifacts, promoting instead the North American colonies' own independent business activities and cultural production. They did so by allying this disruption of cosmopolitan circulation with the curtailment of bachelor sexuality.

In these essays, as I demonstrate below, "the Old Bachelor" is a figure for both old-world aristocratic hauteur and revolutionary energies, for gallantry and libertinism, as well as deviance and unmitigated radicalism or continuous revolution. His sexuality is envisioned as ambiguous precisely in the ways that the threats to the new Republic are seen as inchoate, approaching from multiple fronts. Smoking him out, and, more important, distinguishing bachelor sexuality from the Philadelphian male clubbishness fostered by production of this early magazine, precipitates a sense of national cohesion immediately before the emergence of a Republic— before, that is, the emergence of nationalism properly speaking.[10] Thus, though appearing at an early moment, articles about the bachelor appearing in the *Pennsylvania Magazine* during 1775 and 1776 show us in at least one instance and at one crucial moment *how* "'National Defense' and 'Heterosexual Defense' [became] interdependent projects of boundary maintenance."[11] French sociologist Michel Foucault has described modern power structures as not top-down but rather disciplinary: we are all controlled by the discipline instilled in us by social structures as well as by self-discipline. Therefore, the question to ask about how people are controlled is not "who" or "why," but "how?" Taking a leaf from Foucault's analysis of "power," I take it as axiomatic that "how" is much more interesting than "that": this is not an argument *that* our national identity depends upon reasserting national heterosexuality, but a cultural poetics, showing *how* in one historically crucial moment two concerns, nation and sex, became allied.

### The Revolutionary Bachelor

Much has been written about the American bachelor: "the antebellum bachelor" as well as "the early national bachelor"; the literary character who features in "bachelor sentimentalism."[12] The bachelor of British Victorian literature "desexualized the question of male sexual choice" for British society.[13] That figure differs from the bachelor of colonial culture who posed "one of the worst threats to nineteenth-century bourgeois and sexual ideology" insofar as he opened up "the anarchic sexual possibilities of solo masculinity."[14] In an important article that later became a chapter of his book, historian Mark Kann describes the American bachelor as participating in "an 'epidemic' of premarital sex and children conceived out of wedlock in the last half of the eighteenth century."[15] In his description of this figure, Kann sums up writings by the founders of the United States— Franklin, Jefferson, Adams, and Madison—as well as those printed in American magazines, and his summary is worth repeating here.

Associated with a kind of literal infectiousness, with venereal disease, the bachelor was also seen as corrupting in a figurative sense as well: "the Bachelor's perversity was infectious." Both a 1763 Boston newspaper article and a 1785 sermon, Kann discovered, worry that contact with bachelors will produce "'a smooth-speaking class of people who mean to get their living out of others' and, in the lower ranks, 'a disrespect to every personage in a civil character.'" A predatory libertine, the bachelor's deepest crime was "selfishness": the predatory libertine wanted to have all the women he wished, ruining their chastity and giving them nothing in return. Putting bachelors into the same category as "the strolling poor," "the founders saw bachelorhood, libertinism, rape, sodomy, itinerary, pauperism, frontier violence, slave unrest, and military disorder as the crest of a weave of male degeneracy" threatening national order. Kann argues that the founders wrote about the bachelor as a "grown boy" or "half a man," who can therefore, like North American colonists themselves, be castigated for his lack of independence:

> [T]he Bachelor and other disorderly men [. . .] were destroyers, not procreators. They congregated in the democratic mobs that elevated passion over virtue and they filled the ranks of libertine suitors who manipulated, deceived, and abused women rather than loved, governed, and protected them. They were the Other—what young males had to outgrow to gain respectability as family men and to attain civic standing as citizens.[16]

In Kann's description, the bachelor "foster[s] disorder among men" for reasons that are contradictory if not mutually opposed: "The Bachelor symbolized the dangers of democracy and the corruption of patriarchy."[17] Democracy certainly can be patriarchal, but in the revolutionary context, democratic impulses undermined a paternalistic old England. The bachelor is, as literary critic Leonard Tennenhouse argues, an "import," a "European libertine," and therefore as committed to an aristocratic social order as to monarchic, patriarchal political structures. "American fiction," Tennenhouse argues, "incorporates the libertine in order to have him act on natural desires forbidden by an older [British, aristocratic] system for exchanging women." American seduction stories that do not punish libertine seducers of women implicitly argue that "men refuse to adhere to rank in the new United States."[18] So we could without injury to his evidence change Kann's last term from "patriarchy" to "aristocracy" in order to make the contradictory claims about bachelors more apparent. Indeed, the bachelor figure is either deeply democratic, and so too wild, or deeply entrenched in the old system, and so too corrupt.

## Ambiguous Promiscuity

In "The Speech of Polly Baker" published in his newspaper in 1747, Benjamin Franklin accuses bachelors of selfishly "leaving hundreds of their posterity to the thousandth generation."[19] However, bachelors are also accused of avoiding women altogether out of preference for same-sex relationships.[20] As historian Thomas Foster puts it:

> In the colonial context, bachelors were considered disruptive male types with a particular sexuality, who demonstrated the frustration of marital, moderate, heterosexual masculinity. The foppish, effeminate bachelor was also associated with deviant sexual desires and practices, including masturbation and sodomy.[21]

While "disruptive" male sexuality might produce too many children, deviant practices involve selfishly not leaving any children, leaving none of their posterity, at all. In "Mapping an Atlantic Sexual Culture," included in this collection, historian Clare Lyons lists the types of same-sex relationships formulated during the eighteenth century. The Bachelor is not clearly identifiable as a libertine rake, nor fop, nor sodomite, the main types on Lyons's list.[22] A series first published in 1810–1811 in the Richmond *Enquirer,* in 1814 as a book, written primarily by William Wirt, gives us a sense of the bachelor character in its opening paragraph:

> Alas! it is too true: I can no longer hide the melancholy fact, even from myself: I am, indeed, an Old Bachelor[. . . .] But [. . .] no narrow and sordid cast of character, no selfish love of solitude and silence, no frost of spirit, nor (what is more frequent) habits of low and groveling vice, have kept me so long a bachelor. No, gentle and friendly reader, I am a bachelor [. . .] *in spite of myself.* For the last five and twenty years of my life, I have not failed to dispute this point of dying a bachelor, once a year, with some charming woman or other: but [. . .] I lost my suit.[23]

This paragraph gives us the set of questions one would ask upon meeting an old bachelor: Is he selfish, miserly, celibate, monkish, salacious (with prostitutes or men), or simply unlucky?

The idea of the bachelor is riddled with uncertainty. "Celibacy" is a term used to define the bachelor that can either mean abstention from sexual encounters or uncontrolled indulgence in them because of its association with the priesthood, as can be seen in a poem called "An Old Batchelor's Reflections on Matrimony" published in *The Columbian Magazine* in 1789:

> Let moping monks, and rambling rakes,
>    The joys of wedded love deride:
> Their manners rise from gross mistakes,
>    Unbridled lust, or gloomy pride.[24]

Monks and libertines are subjected to "unbridled lust" or "gloomy pride": though gloom and moping connect the monk to proud abstinence, the placement of these choices in the last sentence of the stanza connects, by parallel structure, monk with "lust" and rakes with "pride." In a similar confusion of priestly celibacy with worldly lust, "celibacy" clearly means indulgence in rather than abstinence from sexuality in the "Marriage or Celibacy?" debate in 1860s England which was about the causes of prostitution. Throughout the nineteenth century, the bachelor is typically depicted as a libertine responsible for causing prostitution, and marrying bachelors is seen as a nostrum for society's cure (prostitution's eradication). Yet, contradictorily, demographers from the nineteenth century to our own time have claimed that the clients of brothels have been primarily married men.[25] So visibly a logical contradiction, the bachelor is said to produce both innumerable illegitimate children and zero population growth, often within the space of just a few sentences.[26]

Uncertainty over his promiscuity or abstinence points to one difference between the bachelor and the libertine. A bachelor can be a libertine rake embroiled in promiscuity, but libertinism is not identical with bachelorhood simply because it can include celibacy. The libertine is seen as unequivocally predatory, sometimes with men, sometimes with women. One of the first literary bachelors to appear on the scene is the ex-libertine, the hero of William Congreve's *The Old Bachelor*, first produced in 1693 at Theatre Royal, Durry Lane and performed in London as late as 1789. According to Congreve's own "Dramatis Personae," Heartwell is "a surly old Bachelor, pretending to slight Women, but secretly in love with Sylvia," a woman half his age, at least. Joseph Addison writes of this play:

> In the character which gives name to this play there is excellently repre-
> sented the reluctance of a battered debauchee to come into the trammels of
> order and decency; he neither languishes nor burns, but frets for love.[27]

The bachelor is a retired libertine, one who is burned out, and his "fret-ting" is curiously undefined except by its inefficacy.

The bachelor figure as depicted in American magazines is similarly dis-tinct from the libertine, first by age—he is almost always "old"—and second by a settled and habitual preference for men to the exclusion of women rather than a predatory interest in either. One of the poems ap-pearing in *The American Magazine*'s "Poetical Essays for March, 1769" is ti-tled "The Batchelor's REASONS for taking a WIFE":

> Let sinful batchelors their woes deplore,
> Full well they merit all they feel and more.
> Unawed by precepts, human and divine
> Like birds and beasts, promiscuously they join;
> Nor know to make the present blessing last,
> To hope the future or esteem the past;
> But vainly boast the joys they never try'd,
> And find divulg'd the secrets they would hide.[28]

This poem defines bachelors as men who "join promiscuously," boasting of their conquests of women as a way of hiding their "secret" desires for other men. Unlike the libertine, bachelors abjure sex with women: those are "joys they never try'd." We find another such connection in a satire ap-pearing in the weekly paper for women, published in Philadelphia from 17 November 1814 to 30 December 1815, *The Intellectual Regale; or Ladies' Tea Tray*:

> TO BE DISPOSED OF BY A LOTTERY,
> Forty old Bachelors from the age of 29 to 50. Some are misanthrops, some
> misers, some what are commonly denominated cots, some worn out rakes,
> and some disappointed lovers, and a few men.[29]

By ending "and a few men," the essay implies that the rest are not men, not masculine, and the name "cot" specifies sexual preference. Bartlett's *Dictionary of Americanisms* does not (as the O.E.D. does) list "cot" but rather "cotbetty," "a man who meddles in the woman's part of household affairs." Bartlett adds, "Halliwell and Wright give both *cot* and *cot-quean* with the same meaning. See *Betty*."[30] The meaning of "queen" as domestic goddess is given most clearly in "An Old Batchelor's Reflections on Matrimony": "A queen is she, and he's a king, / And their dominion is their home."[31] And the O.E.D. offers two meanings for "Betty": "a female pet name" or a name "given in contempt to a man who occupies himself with a woman's household duties. (So Molly.)" And of course the latter term refers to "an effeminate man or boy; a male homosexual. Also: a man who performs work typically associated with women, or who concerns himself with women's affairs."[32] The bachelor's sexual preference for men is allied with an effeminate concern with domesticity.

However, the lottery ad says only that the bachelor *may* be a cot. Unlike the libertine who decidedly does pursue both men and women, the early American old bachelor might or might not; he may be potent or impotent, merely "disappointed" or completely "worn out." Ambiguity has its uses. As Eve Sedgwick insists in working with the British, Victorian bachelor figure, fictional representations of the bachelor constitute "recuperation as character taxonomy"[33] of deep ideological contradictions. Of course the one in which Sedgwick is interested is the contradictory injunction that men must work together in close contact, developing inalienable bonds, but also not love each other, sexually or emotionally. Sedgwick calls this contradictory imperative the "double bind." And such a worry is certainly prominent in a revolutionary era that puts primary importance upon the bonds of fraternity. But another ideological contradiction dominates the colonial American scene.

According to Richard Godbeer, fear and hatred of sexually voracious women dominate colonial ephemeral literature of the early eighteenth century. The example he reproduces in total is "The Batchelor's Soliloquy" that appeared in a Philadelphia almanac published in 1767: here the bachelor refuses to marry in order to avoid being cuckolded by the sexually voracious women lampooned by the essay. A different worry emerges, Godbeer contends, in newspapers, magazines, and almanacs published in the United States during the latter half of the eighteenth century. Here one finds instead a fear of masculine sexual depravity.[34] Both types of representations, Godbeer emphasizes, depict men as helpless; but, in the former case, they are beset by external forces (women), and in the latter case, by internal forces (degeneracy).

Political parallels are clear. In the earlier literature, women demanding money and satisfaction of desire stand in for a voracious mother-country. But as the century wore on, as independence from Britain came to be seen as a viable possibility, people began to wonder what colonial self-rule would be. An anonymous essay published in Boston in 1763 calls for the government to "suppress" libertines. However, says Mark Kann, "The Bachelor could not be wholly suppressed because he existed within all men. Most founders saw males as inherently passionate creatures whose sexual propensities were emblematic of their overall inability to resist temptation" including violence.[35] Godbeer agrees: the anxiety dominating the revolutionary colonial press is a worry about constraining male desire. Colonial leaders needed *restrained* revolution, one that overthrew British rule but didn't go too far in overturning the established order. Worrying about sexual self-restraint allows expression of anxieties that revolution could turn into out-and-out pillage by the dispossessed. "Bachelor Hall" discussed in so much ephemeral satire and poetry becomes a figure for the United States as a country.

## *The* "Old Bachelor" *Essays*

Before writing his most famous American work, *Common Sense,* Thomas Paine was editor of the *Pennsylvania Magazine* for at least half of its nineteen-month run, beginning his editorship of the magazine with its second issue and finishing between August and September the same year.[36] According to biographer Frank Smith, Paine arrived from England in Philadelphia and almost immediately wrote two articles that appear in the first, January 1775 issue of the *Pennsylvania Magazine,* "The Publisher's Preface" and "To the Publisher of the *Pennsylvania Magazine.*[37] Publisher Robert Aitken must have asked Paine to formulate the plan for launching the *Pennsylvania Magazine:* it was to provide a place "for the improvement of the arts and sciences in America" while adhering to a "strict impartiality" as to political issues of the day.[38] And yet, of course, the Declaration of Independence made its first public, printed appearance in this magazine's last number.[39] "Most of the material" published in the magazine, Frank Mott asserts confidently, in 1958, "was non-political, however. An extraordinary amount of comment on marriage was printed[. . . .]"[40] But of course we now know better than to so confidently separate the private from the public sphere. Feminist critic Carroll Smith-Rosenberg has carefully examined articles and essays in what she calls "the urban press," the "monthly political and literary magazines" published in Philadelphia, New York, and Boston during the mid-1780s. She notices that, for instance, in Noah Webster's essays of 1788 that appeared in his *American Magazine*, "the act of participating in [a Republic] becomes the analogue of the act of participating in the marriage contract." Though she doesn't discuss the bachelor specifically, Smith-Rosenberg notices the recurring gender distinctions and confusions typical of discussions of the bachelor figure:

> [T]he urban press repeatedly fused male and female subjectivities, refusing the male political subject virility, virtue and power. The nature of political representation lay at the very heart of these fusions and refusals, as, indeed, it lies at the heart of all discussions of republican government, and, most tellingly, of the constitution of the United States.[41]

I will now show how the bachelor figure came to represent political issues through his ambivalent relationship to marriage.

According to literary historian Edward Larkin, Paine preserved the printer's need for "political impartiality" (aka a large circulation) by writing about political issues indirectly, through fable and allegory.[42] Paine's portraits of domestic life have less to do with his biography, with the fact that Paine had separated from his wife through legal means before leaving England, and more to do with his grappling with American independence as a political problem.[43] As historian Jay Fliegelman puts it, "Paine favored articles about marriage not only in justification of his own marital separation, but because domestic politics addressed the same domestic issues as international politics."[44] In the "Old Bachelor" essays, the use of marriage to figure political events is pronounced and dramatic. Before examining that use in detail, we should look at the features of this persona, the bachelor, as developed in this particular magazine during 1775–1776.

The twelve essays comprising the "Old Bachelor" series in the *Pennsylvania Magazine* create what is clearly a persona. Possible writers of the "Old Bachelor" essays (Robert Aitken and John Witherspoon) as well as Francis Hopkinson, who definitely wrote essays VII and VIII, were all married. Thomas Paine was the only one among certain and possible authors of the series who comes close to being a bachelor as a widower and divorcee.

In essay number I, the bachelor is portrayed as a sexual predator. He maintains that he has been "as great a benefactor to the province of Pennsylvania [. . .] as any man," but then continues:

> I don't know what are become of [my offspring], some are here, and some
> are there, and some are no where, some are black, and some are white, and
> some are neither, some are gone to the English, and some to the French, and
> some, perhaps, are beyond the Styx; [. . .] Perhaps I have made sale of part
> of myself, and converted my own flesh and blood into property.[45]

This conversion of self to property connects the bachelor to the prostitute whose fall he caused, according to reports by the Magdalene Society of Philadelphia published from 1826 to 1831: she is not essentially corrupt but corrupt by contagion with the allegedly unmarried libertine who first deflowered her.[46] This rant might allow Kann's "founders" to proclaim the bachelor's productivity fundamentally unproductive: he produces no legitimate children, which is to say, no Americans: these offspring are English, French, or dead. Moreover, insofar as this old bachelor begot them in "the gay world," he is associated with and contaminated by marital infidelity; he is aristocratic and corrupt.[47]

In the next number of the series, this one definitely written by Paine, the bachelor becomes even more clearly a figure for old-world libertinism and corruption.[48] That gay, aristocratic world is described in a poem:

> Fair Venus so often was miss'd from the skies,
> And Bacchus as frequently absent likewise,
> That the synod began to enquire out the reason,
> Suspecting the culprits were plotting of treason.
> At length it was found they had open'd a ball,
> At a place by the Mortals call'd Bachelor's Hall;
> Where Venus disclos'd ev'ry fun she could think of,
> And Bacchus made nectar for mortals to drink of.
> Jove highly displeased at such riotous doings,
> Sent Time to reduce the whole building to ruins.
> But time was so slack with traces and dashes
> That Jove in a passion consumed it to ashes.[49]

The British-born Paine sees post-Restoration, libertinism as "treason"—against what? Not certainly against the British monarchy or aristocracy who deserve no protection as far as he is concerned: "The Honourable plunderer of his country, or the Right Honourable murderer of mankind" deserve none of the respect due to those who "have justly merited the address of The Honourable Continental Congress," he will say, under the pseudonym Vox Populi, in the "Reflections on Titles."[50] In the poem, then, Jove, insofar as merely hastening the ruin of time, figures the Continental Congress or really any new-world antagonist of old-world aristocratic corruption in which "Old" bachelors participate. That this corruption involves myriad kinds of sexual activities is clearly stated: "Venus disclos'd ev'ry fun she could think of" in "Bachelor's Hall." Here the Bachelor figures English/French/old-world aristocratic promiscuity and corruption, allied with unspecified sexual behaviors, that must be expelled from the "Hall" or the newly coalescing nation.

In "The Old Bachelor (Number III)," the bachelor stands for same-sex desire. Here the character proclaims, "I have a good mind to marry now I am old, out of revenge upon myself." "But the misfortune is," he continues,

> that if I take a wife by way of a duel, I don't know who to choose for a second—A man; no that will not do.—A woman; that will be worse still.[51]

In engaging in a duel against himself (taking revenge), he needs a "second"—that is, someone bearing a weapon that he can use against himself, which is to say, a partner with spousals in hand—but he cannot decide whether to marry a man or a woman. The man will not do for social reasons, the woman, perhaps because he is old and so social decorum is violated in that case as well, but "worse still" suggests that she will not do because of his predilections.

Hints about his desire for men are dislodged in "The Old Bachelor [Number VII]" and VIII where, in a bachelor's will (a friend is marrying, and so is leaving his state of bachelorhood to the Old Bachelor), bachelors are referred to as "Mr. W. N.," "Mr. W. M.," and "Mr. L. D.": will not (marry), will maybe/marry, and Mr. Long Delay.[52] Same-sex predilections are reversed in "The Old Bachelor (Number VIII)," in which he claims to have fallen in love with a young woman and requests that readers desist from calling him "old" so that he might more effectively court her.[53] The last essay in the series of "Old Bachelor" essays published in the *Pennsylvania Magazine* is a letter to the bachelor by an "Old Maid." She has, since reading his first number, she claims, fallen in love with him: "Your first paper gave me the first wound, your last completed the business, and left me bleeding at your feet."[54] Here the bachelor's heterosexual potential is, how-ever humorously, reasserted. Implicit in that reassertion is a desire to sepa-rate from "Old England," as an Oneida correspondent calls it in the last is-sue to be published in 1775.[55] This semiconversion only hints at the politi-cal purposes to which the bachelor's characterological ambivalence and sexual ambiguity be put.

## Political Problems at Home

"The Old Bachelor" essay number IV was reprinted over a decade later, during the Constitutional Congress. There, it appears after an anonymous essay advocating the domestic production of silk (as against importation) which concludes,

> Citizens of America,
> Now you are gloriously emancipated from the political thraldom of Eng-land, disdain to be held to her by commercial chains. . . . [T]he new govern-ment . . . happily for our native land is soon to be perfected.[56]

The "Old Bachelor (Number IV)" immediately following this exhortation and encomium in 1788 is reprinted exactly from the 1775 version because it provides a fantasy or allegory of political and economic emancipation.[57] Number IV enumerates types of infidelity-producing aristocratic mar-riages and then concludes with "the sentiments of an American savage on this subject."[58] As Aitken had indicated in his Publisher's Preface, unlike a British production, an American magazine "cannot be expected to" pre-sent any "Discoveries of the curious remains of antiquity": "We can look no farther back than to rude manners and curious customs of the savage Aborigines of North America."[59] The sentiments presented by the "savage" therefore form part of national history:

> [A]n American savage on . . . being advised by one of our countrymen to marry according to the ceremonies of the church . . . briskly replyed [*sic.*], "That either the Christian's God was not so good and wise as he was repre-sented, or he never meddled with the marriages of his people. . . . [A]s soon as ever you meet you long to part; and, not having this relief in your power, by way of revenge, double each other's misery: Whereas in ours, which have no ceremony than mutual affection, and last no longer than they bestow

mutual pleasures, we make it our business to oblige the heart we are afraid to lose; and being at liberty to separate, seldom or never feel the inclination. But if any should be found so wretched among us, as to hate where the only commerce ought to be love, we instantly dissolve the band.[60]

This passage so clearly echoes the yet-to-be-written Declaration of Independence, its first paragraph, as to be uncanny: "When, in the course of human events, it becomes necessary for one people to dissolve the political bands which have connected them with another . . . , a decent respect to the opinions of mankind requires that they should declare the causes which impel them to the separation."[61] The savage of "Old Bachelor IV" describes political union based upon "mutual affection" and the bestowing of "mutual pleasures"; held together by no ritual or ceremony or respect for the past should that mutuality cease, "we instantly dissolve the band" "being at liberty to separate."[62]

While a figure for aristocratic corruption in number II, here in number IV the bachelor figures something else entirely, the opposite one might almost say. Similarly, number III, author unknown, meditates upon what the bachelor has lost and preserved by not marrying. By staying single, he has made himself over into, he says, "a little state." But he finds no pleasure in ruling this state, in "being called master of the house" because "[a] bachelor must inevitably be the prey of his servants."[63] In this number, the bachelor describes in detail how his servants stole fine linen from his household and a set of china and stemware by pretending his dogs had broken it all—a "magistrate" helps him recover the china. This essay delineates the bachelor's character as effeminate: wifeless, he is forced to take on her tasks and interests. But as a fantasy of master-servant relations, it does more. Expressing anxieties about the colonies' ability to govern the hoi poloi later expressed by the Philadelphia Board of Guardians whose attempt to restructure the poor-relief system in the 1820s reflected their anxieties that American "society itself was menaced by an alien form [pauperism] within its boundaries."[64] Unable to prevent his servants from stealing from him and then selling back to him his goods, the bachelor of this Old Bachelor essay fuels readers' anxious fantasies about establishing a standing police force:

[T]he gap is so great between me and my servants, that we act towards each other like armies of observation,—in which they have the better ground. . . . If a bachelor had as many eyes as Argus he would be cheated.[65]

Dana Nelson finds similar fears expressed in the writings of John Adams which she sees as "precocious," given that they surface during "the early years of the revolution."[66] And yet surely the colonists must have wondered if, after a "divorce" from the crown, lacking its ritual prestige and military support, they could indeed maintain order in civil society. How far would the desire for democracy extend? Would "all men are created equal" be interpreted radically enough to include "every man that has not a farthing"?[67] Would the iconoclasm destroying the prestige of titles and crowns lead perhaps to the "unblushing effrontery" of the "unmarried mothers," who later approach Philadelphia's Board of Governers, "arrogantly exacting as a right" the outrelief that "ought never have been granted, even as a charity"?[68]

The bachelor represents liberation from ritual-based oppression, as is made clear, albeit facetiously, in a debate about bachelors which arose in England precisely on the eve of the Reform Bill, the bill that would significantly extend the right to vote:[69]

["Wilhelmina Wanter" of "Celibacy Terrace":] [W]hen once the men began to ponder upon any sort of emancipation, it was easy to see that the parson's business in the knot-tying line would be apt to suffer. . . .

[Reply by the "Dominie":] That marriage has gone out of fashion, in a general sense, . . . I do not mean to deny; but that the Reform Bill is the entire cause of this, I think, . . . may admit of question.[70]

Earlier, in the United States, the anonymous author of "Arguments in Favor of Celibacy" makes a similar kind of connection:

Marriage is confinement, and confinement is misery. Liberty is essential to happiness; for without it, the world and all its enjoyments are insipid. Ask French republicans the value of liberty; they say that life without liberty is contemptible, and existence a curse. "Liberty or death!" is re-echoed by a thousand ghosts of Columbian heroes who have sealed their testimony with the richest blood of America.

There is no happiness but in liberty, nor liberty but in celibacy. The batchelor is the only free man, free from family expense, [. . .] free to make love and marry if a charming object strike his fancy; not tied to a piece of antiquity he has been loving these twenty years; free from the torture of jealousy

[. . .]; free to forsake a peevish companion; would he emigrate, or change business, he meets no opposition from a wife and family; if he incur disgrace, he involves no wife, nor children in infamy; at death, free from the pain of parting with his family, left perhaps to be starved in a pitiless uncharitable world.[71]

Here are invoked two revolutions, and this bachelor is allied with the apparently continuous fund of revolutionary freedom fighters, French and American. His is a continuous revolt against "antiquity" which he finds revolting, in the person of an old wife. He is as free to abandon old or "peevish" companions as he is to "emigrate, or change business": life for him is continuous revolution, mimicking the world's political upheavals.

Anxieties about radical democracy evoke the conservative fantasy articulated by Edmund Burke in his *Reflections on the Revolution in France* of 1790, the catalyst for Paine's *Rights of Man* (Part I, 1791). According to Burke, the desacralizing process set in motion by any revolution cannot be stopped; revolution will be continual, each leader being immediately deposed after ascending his "throne," unless he prevents his demotion through the use of terror.[72] In the *Federalist* No. 10, James Madison similarly articulates his worry that "a pure democracy" would be beset by continuous "spectacles of turbulence and contention."[73] Madison will thus invoke a certain kind of political structure, a Republic based on political representation of the masses by their superiors, as a stopgap for revolutionary violence. But Burke worries about continuous "intractability" or incessant criminality if "the body of the people . . . find the principles of natural subordination . . . rooted out of their minds," potentially articulating an anxiety that would not be fully exorcised even by Madison's plan.[74]

As a figure for the emancipated, the bachelor partly figures the United States as it is coming into existence through its separation from England. But this bachelor figure is not master of a family estate, only master of a "little state." Caring too much about what his servants do to his china when there is no wife to monitor it, he fits into the character description of a "cotquean." Once feminized, the bachelor figure can be easily scapegoated, the "dominion" or "state" that he figures given the eventualities too unpleasant to imagine for a fledgling nation. A bachelor (not a country of married men) takes emancipation from ritual too far, these writers wish to pretend. It's really the "little" bachelor "state," lacking masculine leadership, and not the united colonies, the *Pennsylvanian Magazine* insists, that will be dominated by the lowest classes who, had we the eyes of Argus, we wouldn't be able to contain. It is precisely here that we find ambiguous bachelor sexuality connected to the representation of anxieties over the intractability of humanity if radical democracy is achieved, a fantasy as prevalent in America of the 1770s as in Britain of the 1790s. Here we can see a specific example of Christopher Newfield's contention that homophobia is allied with "a phobia about equality."[75]

## *Literary Ambiguity*

The opening essay in the "Old Bachelor" series adds yet another item to the list of what bachelors figure. The narrator speaks of "my brother bachelor, Dr. Johnson." Given that Samuel Johnson had been married for 17 years (1735–1752), what makes him qualify here as a bachelor rather than a widower, for instance? It may have to do with the fact that his union was childless, or it could have to do with something else. The essay continues, about Johnson:

> —O! he's the prince of ill-nature—he's an excellent fellow. I should like to see some of his best quarrelling faces, when he is maulling and tearing your poets, and your players, and your authors of all works to pieces. They tell me that he cuts up a critic like a goose [. . . . ] I have just seen a print of him in one of the English magazines. O! he's a rare hand at a surly face—He frowns so emphatically, that every muscle is a sentence. [. . .] [I]f you have any taste for looks, look at Dr. Johnson, he looks as logically as he writes.[76]

Here what seems to make Johnson into a bachelor is his ugliness, his meanness. But also, as writer of and star in British periodicals, he figures the male clubbishness as well as same-sex sexuality characterizing the cadre of men who produce periodicals—characterizing the "Nonsense Club," for instance, of London's Inner Temple.[77] How will the male collective constituting the persona of the "Old Bachelor" in the *Pennsylvania Magazine* deter associations with Britishness, aristocracy, and same-sex love? How will it cauterize itself, as it were, from transatlantic circulation? These two questions, I argue, become in the *Pennsylvania Magazine* one and the same.

In his first essay in the Magazine, Francis Hopkinson contrasts this periodical to the newspapers:

You may perhaps wonder I have not tried my hand in some of the public papers; but the truth is, that what with your *Citizens,* your *Philadelphians,* your *Lovers of liberty,* and your *Lovers of no liberty at all,* your *Moderate men,* and your *Immoderate men,* there is no such thing as getting a word or two in edge-ways amongst them. Now I look on your proposed Magazine as a pleasant little path, where a man may take an agreeable walk with a few quiet friends, without risk of being jostled to death in a crowd.[78]

The community of contributors and correspondents who will provide the magazine's "matter" is smaller than those servicing a news-driven coalition of colonies; magazine contributors in contrast are above the crowd, both in terms of class and intellect.

Hopkinson's community is all male. One can see this community carefully constructed in the minds of male and female readers, especially in the anonymous "Arguments in Favour of Celibacy" appearing in the *American Universal Magazine*:

If there were any thing to marry but women, if we could make it convenient [. . .] to marry one another, perhaps the married state might be less tormenting[. . . .]

The persona who ostensibly "writes" this essay appeals to a male audience ("one another" is contrasted against "women"), but appended to it is a message allegedly from someone else, the editor:

We hope this naughty creature will not frighten our female readers; we beg they would not be alarmed, and assure them, that our only motive in inserting this wicked production, is, to give an opportunity of refuting whatever can be urged against charming matrimony: and we doubt not, but in our next number, he will receive a sound drubbing.[79]

The editor allegedly wishes to stimulate correspondence for the sake of increasing the matter he has to publish. But that matter may already be written by his staff, and his real concern to stimulate readers to keep purchasing and perusing the periodical out of curiosity over counterattacks. He wants to bolster sales. So, for instance, the published attacks on the bachelor in the "Old Bachelor" series in the *Pennsylvania Magazine* were signed by female figures and obviously written by men.[80] The letter "To the Bachelor" from "Aspasia" was written by Hopkinson himself.[81]

Hopkinson's male club of producers for the *Pennsylvania Magazine,* his "few quiet friends," are less driven than the news-mongering hoi polloi by events for their topics—they are more reflective—but they are also distinct from the aristocratic world of knowledge. In the dream-allegory that follows the above-quoted paragraph, Hopkinson attempts "the choice of subject" for his essay. Encountering the labyrinthian excesses of the European Garden—so far from Eden that it is a garden of knowledge with a tree of religion in the middle—Hopkinson decides to frequent only "a pleasant corner," in which he found "a neat little fountain, of simple architecture, from which issued several streams of pure water," "THE PENNSYLVANIA MAGAZINE" written on its pediment.

Recently, the feminist literary theorist Lisa Moore has demonstrated that there is "an eighteenth-century tradition of erotic garden design."[82] Hopkinson's images, quiet friends in a pleasant corner issuing streams of periodical ink, evoke in the context of this male club of writers a sublimated version of some kind of phallic or homoerotic issuing of seminal fluids. The argument that homoerotic activity is this imagery's repressed content seems less of a stretch, I believe, if juxtaposed to the introductory essay by the magazine's editor, Paine, that directly precedes it.

In the first part of his essay, Paine compares the American "Press" to "a fountain [from which] the streams of vice or virtue are poured forth over a country," and to "a lover [who] woos its mistress with unabated ardour, nor gives up the pursuit without a conquest," thus sexualizing both periodical production and sales. And yet his opening gambit in selling a specifically American periodical is to attack the British periodical press as corrupt because it is sexually licentious:

> The British magazines, at their commencement, were the repositories of ingenuity: They are now the retailers of tale and nonsense. From elegance they sunk to simplicity, from simplicity to folly, and from folly to voluptuousness. The Gentleman's, The London, and the Universal Magazines, bear yet some mark of their originality; but the Town and Country, the Covent-Garden, and the Westminster, are no better than incentives to profligacy and dissipation.[83]

Philadelphians at the moment, as Lyons's research presented in chapter 7 of this volume shows, were purchasing a great deal of explicitly sexual and often same-sex erotic literature available to them through transatlantic circulation. When Paine inveighs here against "the importation of foreign vices," he refers to specific printed texts available in circulating libraries as well as for purchase:[84]

> European wit is one of the worst articles we can import. It has an intoxicating power with it, which debauches the very vitals of chastity[. . . .] We soon grow fatigued with the excess, and withdraw like gluttons sickened with intemperance.[85]

The only press that won't pour vice from its fountain of ink is the American press: instead of "infect[ing]" like British periodicals, it will "attract" by "improv[ing] (10). To frighten us away from "attraction" to British periodicals, the ocean is turned into an infectious (seminal) fluid; the only possible response is a nationalistic one because defensive participation in Philadelphia and its periodicals will act as a bulwark against European contamination. Effete, culturally astute, brothers with Johnson, "Old" (though only 29), Bachelors are connected to that promiscuous transatlantic circulation of ink. Imagining a transatlantic intellectual community united by water is like imagining periodical writers such as Johnson on one side of the Atlantic and Hopkinson and Paine on the other exchanging fluid, inky or otherwise, "brother bachelor[s]."[86] Such an antinationalistic picture must be abhorrent, and so one must also abhor the male-to-male sexual exchanges that such circulation implies.

## Conclusion: The Bachelor's Ideological Function

In the *Pennsylvania Magazine,* the bachelor is complicated, expressing ambivalent desires, representing ambiguous sexuality, and thus able to represent political passions at the highly fraught and traumatic moment of revolutionary war. Because the bachelor figure was able to carry so many often conflicting identities, it served well to express the contradictory hopes (revolutionary) and anxieties (conservative) of "the founding fathers" who manipulated it, whether or not they were conscious of employing the figure in those ways. In the *Pennsylvania Magazine* essays about the bachelor, that femininized figure becomes associated with the propensity for promiscuous transatlantic and cross-class circulation so threatening to the new Republic. Let me end by suggesting that this association partly comprises the genealogy of present-day homophobia. In one of his more feminine identities, the bachelor was a cosmopolitan "cotquean." Ambiguous and indeterminate sexualities (i.e., those lying outside the pale of traditional heterosexual marriage), alternative sexualities once represented by the politically suspect bachelor, were at some later moment reduced to the "queen" type. Scapegoating, anthropologist Mary Douglas insists, occurs in order to reduce ambiguity and secure order.[87] Modern-day homophobia, I would like to suggest in closing, emerges from a political desire to clarify order. The "Old Bachelor" essays in the *Pennsylvania Magazine* participate in the revolutionary-era project of creating a dependable, stable national identity by ejecting the bachelor within the emerging nation. Here we can see the alliance of heterosexual with national defense. And here we can also see how U.S. national history has rendered discussion of same-sex marriage so threatening.

NOTES

I would like to thank Sheila Croucher, Martha Schoolman, and especially Thomas Foster, for careful readings and criticism of this essay in its early stages.

1. In *Nationalism and Modernism: A Critical Survey of Recent Theories of Nations and Nationalism* (New York: Routledge, 1998), Anthony Smith surveys those "modernist theories" according to which American nationalism emerged after the French Revolution in 1789, as well as those "perennialist theories" that contradict it. See Eric Kaufman, "Modern Formation, Ethnic Reformation: The Social Sources of the American Nation," *Geopolitics* 7, no. 2 (2002): 99–120, 99, 117 note 2.

2. *Imagined Communities: Reflections on the Origin and Spread of Nationalism,* rev. ed. (New York: Verso, 1983, 1991), 61–63. Richard L. Merritt provides a systematic, empirical analysis of exactly when U.S. newspapers began designating the colonies with symbols of implicit and explicit "American common identity," dating its emergence as dominant in 1773 (*Symbols of American Community, 1735–1775* [New Haven: Yale Univ. Press, 1966], 115, 131).

3. Ed White, "Early American Nations as Imagined Communities," *American Quarterly* 56, no. 1 (2004): 49–81, 58–59.

4. Cecilia Elizabeth O'Leary, *To Die For: The Paradox of American Patriotism* (Princeton, NJ: Princeton Univ. Press, 1999), 11.

5. Frank Luther Mott, *A History of American Magazines,* 5 vols. (Cambridge, Mass: Belknap Press, Harvard Univ. Press, 1958–1968), I.87, cited hereafter in the text by volume and page number.

6. *Pennsylvania Magazine* 1 (August 1775): 376, cited hereafter in the text.

7. The "metropole" is the country that governs the colony, here Britain, but also sometimes its metropolitan center, here, London. For the other side of the coin, the effects of colonies on Britain and specifically its self-definition as a

nation or empire, see Stephen Conway, *The British Isles and the War of American Independence* (Oxford: Oxford Univ. Press, 2000); Eric Hinderaker, *The Persistence of Empire: British Political Culture in the Age of the American Revolution* (Chapel Hill, NC: Univ. of North Carolina Press, 2000); Bernard S. Cohn, *Colonialism and Its Forms of Knowledge: The British in India* (Princeton, NJ: Princeton Univ. Press, 1996); Catherine Hall, *Civilising Subjects: Metropole and Colony in the English Imagination, 1830–1867* (Chicago: Univ. of Chicago Press, 2002).

8. See Clare A. Lyons, "Mapping an Atlantic Sexual Culture: Homoeroticism in Eighteenth-Century Philadelphia," in this volume.

9. Mark Kann, *A Republic of Men: The American Founders, Gendered Language, and Patriarchal Politics* (New York: New York Univ. Press, 1998), 52–66.

10. My reading of the ideological function of the bachelor, insofar as the figure enables relocating clubbishness from London to Philadelphia rather than completely overturning cosmopolitanism as an ideal, fits in with White's location of the "colonial origins of nation-ness" with "the ambivalent, imperiographic nationalism of the early United States" (76); see also Ed White, *The Backcountry and the City: Colonization and Conflict in Early America* (Minneapolis: Univ. of Minnesota Press, 2005).

11. Lauren Berlant, Elizabeth Freeman, "Queer Nationality," *boundary 2* 19, no. 1 (1992): 149–180, 161.

12. Vincent J. Bertolini, "Fireside Chastity: The Erotics of Sentimental Bachelorhood in the 1850s," *American Literature* 68, no. 4 (1996): 707–737, 707–710; Bryce Traister, "The Wandering Bachelor: Irving, Masculinity, and Authorship," *American Literature* 74, no. 1 (2002): 111–137, 114; Lisa Spiro, "Reading with a Tender Rapture: Reveries of a Bachelor and the Rhetoric of Detached Intimacy," *Book History* 6 (2003): 57–93, 61.

13. Eve Kosofsky Sedgwick, *Epistemology of the Closet* (Berkeley: Univ. of California Press, 1990), 188.

14. Bertolini, 708.

15. Kann, 57.

16. Kann, 58, 57, 64, 72, 59, 78. Historian Thomas A. Foster agrees: "Bachelors, as individuals who had not yet achieved full manliness given their unmarried state, worried those who saw a marriage and household order as critical for a virtuous, stable social order." See *Sex and the Eighteenth-Century Man: Massachusetts and the History of Sexuality in America* (Boston: Beacon Press, 2006), 528. Foster links procreative pressures, discussed in more detail below, to anxieties about the increased "geographic mobility" of men in the colonial and revolutionary context (105), and, in the postwar context, to the desire for "the growth and development of stable households on which to build a virtuous nation" (109). Also, queer theorists Henry Abelove and John D'Emilio have linked the pressure for sexual reproduction to emergent capitalism, the need for a plentiful and so cheap labor force

(Henry Abelove, "Some Speculations on the History of Sexual Intercourse during the Long Eighteenth Century in England," *Genders* 6 [1989]: 125–130; John D'Emilio, "Capitalism and Gay Identity," in *Powers of Desire: The Politics of Sexuality*, ed. Ann Snitow, Christine Stansell, Sharon Thompson [New York: Monthly Review Press, 1983], 100–117).

17. Kann, 52.

18. Leonard Tennenhouse, "Libertine America," *Differences* 11.3 (1999/2000): 1–28, 15, 23, 12. This association between bachelors and corrupt European aristocrats is especially visible in the proceedings of the National Convention in France: "The Dunkerque society of the people applauds a decree limiting the freedom of the men of the convention by making them reject any truce with tyrants. The decree demands the exclusion of priests, nobles, and bachelors from all public functions" (14 ventôse, an II, qtd. in Jean Borie, *Le célibataire français* [Paris: Le Sagittaire, 1976], 5, my translation).

19. Benjamin Franklin, "The Speech of Polly Baker," 1747, in *Writings*, ed. J. A. Leo Lemay (New York: Viking Press, 1987), 305–308, qtd. in Kann, 56.

20. Kann, 63–64.

21. Foster, *Sex and the Eighteenth-Century Man*, 102.

22. Lyons, this volume, p. 169.

23. William Wirt, *The Old Bachelor*, ed. Bruce Graver (Delmar, NY: Scholar's Facsimiles, 1985), 1.

24. Anonymous, *Columbian Magazine* 3.3 (March 1789): 197–198, 197.

25. John M. Robson, *Marriage or Celibacy? The Daily Telegraph on a Victorian Dilemma* (Toronto: Univ. of Toronto Press, 1995), 23, citing Francis W. Newman, *The Cure of the Great Social Evil* (London: Trubner; Bristol: Arrowsmith, 1869), 12; Fernando Henriques, *Modern Sexuality* (London: MacGibbon and Kee, 1968), 125, 259.

26. Traister, 114; Kann, 64; see also Benjamin Franklin, note 19 above.

27. William Congreve, *Complete Plays*, ed. Eric Bentley (New York: Hill and Wang, 1956), 42; Joseph Addison, *Tatler* 9, qtd. in Congreve, 35.

28. Anonymous, "The Batchelor's REASONS for taking a WIFE," in "Poetical Essays," *The American Magazine* (1769): 91.

29. Ariel, "To Be Disposed of by a Lottery," *The Intellectual Regale* 2, no. 6 (24 June 1815): 506, quoted in Traister, 114.

30. John Russell Bartlett, *Dictionary of Americanisms: A Glossary of Words and Phrases Usually Regarded as Peculiar to the United States*, 4th enlarged ed. (Boston: Little, Brown, 1896), 151.

31. Anonymous, *Columbian Magazine* 3.3 (March 1789): 197.

32. *Oxford English Dictionary Online*, 3rd ed. (Oxford: Oxford Univ. Press, 2005). See also Lyons, this volume.

33. Sedgwick, 189.

34. Richard Godbeer, *Sexual Revolution in Early America* (Baltimore: Johns Hopkins Univ. Press, 2002), 264–288.

35. Kann, 59; Kann quotes an unspecified source found in Charles Hyneman, Donald Lutz, eds., *American Political Writings during the Founding Era, 1760–1805*, 2 vols. (Indianapolis: Liberty Press, 1983), 1:33–37.

36. Edward Larkin, *Thomas Paine and the Literature of Revolution* (New York: Cambridge Univ. Press, 2005), 13–14, 34, 46, cited hereafter in the text.

37. Frank Smith, "New Light on Thomas Paine's First Year in America, 1775," *American Literature* 1, no. 4 (1939): 347–371, in Larkin, 35 note 13. (This essay is concerned with Paine's literary biography, life events that shed light on Paine's writings.)

38. "The Publisher's Preface," *Pennsylvania Magazine* 1 (January 1775): 3; see also Lyon N. Richardson, *A History of Early American Magazines, 1741–1789* (New York: Thomas Nelson, 1931), 174–175. In particulars about the *Pennsylvania Magazine*, I also consulted Edward W. R. Pitcher, *The Pennsylvania Magazine, or American Monthly Museum, Philadelphia 1775–1776: An Annotated Index of Sources, Signatures, and First Lines of Literary Articles* (Lewiston, NY: Edwin Mellen Press, 2001).

39. *Pennsylvania Magazine* 2 (July 1776): 328–330.

40. Mott, 1:90.

41. Carroll Smith-Rosenberg, "Political Camp or the Ambiguous Engendering of the American Republic," in *Gendered Nations: Nationalisms and Gender Order in the Long Nineteenth Century*, ed. Ida Blom, Karen Hagemann, Catherine Hall (New York: Berg, 2000), 271–292, 276, 274, 281, 276.

42. Larkin, 33.

43. Divorce at this time in Britain required an act of Parliament, and separations were ultimately not legally binding, though everyone pretty much adhered to the common law that allowed for them (see Lawrence Stone, *Uncertain Unions: Marriage in England, 1660–1753* [New York: Oxford Univ. Press, 1992]).

44. Jay Fliegelman, *Prodigals and Pilgrims: The American Revolution Against Patriarchal Authority, 1750–1800* (New York: Cambridge Univ. Press, 1982), 124, quoted in Larkin, 37.

45. "The Old Bachelor. (Number I.)," *Pennsylvania Magazine* 1 (March 1775): 111–113, 113.

46. Michael Meranze, *Laboratories of Virtue: Punishment, Revolution, and Authority in Philadelphia, 1760–1835* (Chapel Hill: Univ. of North Carolina Press, 1996), 275.

47. "Old Bachelor No. I," 113.

48. On Paine's authorship, see Richardson, 183.

49. *Pennsylvania Magazine* 1 (April 1775): 168.

50. *Pennsylvania Magazine* 1 (May 1775): 209–210.

51. *Pennsylvania Magazine* 1 (May 1775): 213.

52. *Pennsylvania Magazine* 1 (November 1775): 512, 1 (December 1775): 554.

53. "The Bachelor [Number VIII.]," *Pennsylvania Magazine* 1 (December 1775): 551–554.

54. *Pennsylvania Magazine* 2 (June 1776): 268.

55. "A speech of the Chiefs and Warriors of the Oneida Tribe of Indians, to the four New-England Provinces; [. . .]," *Pennsylvania Magazine* 1 (December 1775): 601–602, 601.

56. *American Museum* 3.1 (January 1788): 89–91, 89.

57. Larkin, 39–40.

58. *Pennsylvania Magazine* 1 (June 1775): 265.

59. *Pennsylvania Magazine* 1 (January 1775): 4.

60. *Pennsylvania Magazine* 1 (June 1775): 265.

61. *Pennsylvania Magazine* 2 (June 1776): 328.

62. The fantasy of a marriage that persists because of continuous reiterated consent fits into the attempt of the Constitution to be a continuously spoken document, (re)iterating in the mouth of every reader that person's consent to be governed, as described by Anne Norton (*Alternative Americas* [Chicago: Univ. of Chicago Press, 1986], 20).

63. *Pennsylvania Magazine* 1 (May 1775): 213.

64. Meranze, 272.

65. *Pennsylvania Magazine* 1 (May 1775): 214–215.

66. Dana D. Nelson, *National Manhood: Capitalist Citizenship and the Imagined Fraternity of White Men* (Durham, N.C.: Duke Univ. Press, 1998), 30.

67. Adams to James Sullivan, *The Works of John Adams, Second President of the United States,* 10 vols. (Boston: Little, Brown, 1850–1856), vol. 9, 378, qtd. in Nelson, 29.

68. Meranze, 269.

69. In 1832, after passage of the Bill into an Act, "217,000 voters were added to an electorate of 435,000. . . . Approximately 1 in 5 adult men now had the vote in England and Wales in a population of 16 million" (Catherine Hall, "The Rule of Difference: Gender, Class and Empire in the Making of the 1832 Reform Act," in *Gendered Nations,* ed. Blom, Hagemann, and Hall, 107–135, 107; Hall cites E. L. Woodward, *The Age of Reform, 1815–1870,* 2nd ed. [Oxford: Clarendon, 1971], 88, and N. Gash, *Aristocracy and People: Britain, 1815–1865* [London: Edward Arnold, 1970], 152).

70. Anonymous, *The Lady's Magazine* (December 1832): 245.

71. Anonymous, *American Universal Magazine* 1.7 (6 March 1797): 304.

72. Edmund Burke, *Reflections on the Revolution in France,* 1790, ed. Conor Cruise O'Brien (New York: Viking Penguin, 1968), 172.

73. James Madison, "The Same Subject Continued: The Union as Safeguard

Against Domestic Faction and Insurrection," *The New York Packet* (Friday, 23 November 1787), rpt. *Library of Congress, Thomas* <http://thomas.loc.gov/home/histdox/fed_10.html> 2 June 2006.

74. Burke, 372.

75. Christopher Newfield, "Democracy and Male Homoeroticism," *Yale Journal of Criticism* 6, no. 2 (1993): 29–60, 30.

76. "The Old Bachelor. (Number I.)," *Pennsylvania Magazine* 1 (March 1775): 111–113, 111–112.

77. Lance Bertelsen, *The Nonsense Club* (New York: Oxford Univ. Press, 1986).

78. *Pennsylvania Magazine* 1 (January 1775): 15.

79. "Misogamous," *American Universal Magazine* 1.7 (6 March 1797): 301–305, 303, 305.

80. "Aspasia," 2 (January 1776): 28–32; "An Old Maid," 2 (June 1776): 267–268.

81. Pitcher, 54.

82. Lisa L. Moore, "Queer Gardens: Mary Delany's Flowers and Friendships," *Eighteenth-Century Studies* 39.1 (2005): 49–70, 50.

83. *Pennsylvania Magazine* 1 (January 1775): 10.

84. Lyons, this volume.

85. *Pennsylvania Magazine* 1 (January 1775): 12.

86. "The Old Bachelor. (Number I)," *Pennsylvania Magazine* 1 (March 1775): 111–113, 111.

87. Mary Douglas, *Purity and Danger: An Analysis of the Concepts of Pollution and Taboo* (New York: Ark/Routledge, 1966), 168–179.

# Chapter 14

# In a French Position

### Radical Pornography and Homoerotic Society in Charles Brockden Brown's Ormond or the Secret Witness

## Stephen Shapiro

Charles Brockden Brown's *Ormond or the Secret Witness* (1799) is the most radical novel written by an American until perhaps Melville's *Moby Dick* (1850). Brown's narrative rejects middle-class aspirations of individual merit and commercial success by looking to nurture a community based on the values of rational cooperation and mutual betterment. Though these collectivist ideals are rooted in the Quaker worldview of Brown's family background, *Ormond* breaks from the Society of Friends' pacifism by exploring violence as a catalyst for liberation, especially for homoerotic relations. Inspired by a brief moment of renewed revolutionary activity throughout Europe in the late 1790s, Brown's novel differs from the period's emerging descriptions of same-sex sexuality as it conceptualizes homoeroticism more in terms of its group politics, rather than those of aberrant biological sex or its codification in gender roles. Instead of wondering what sexual acts reveal about an individual's personality, their "identity," Brown's romance considers homoerotic desire and an enlightened, democratic ethics as mutually enabling. This consideration of sexuality as defined by the striving for social justice appears remarkably modern, but the historical context of Brown's perspective belongs to eighteenth-century arguments surrounding the concept of civil society, which was developed as a counterweight against the early modern institutions of the absolutist state and doctrinal church.

Locating Brown within the period's definition of civil society, rather than the consecration of personal "individuality," will prove tremendously useful to students of pretwentieth-century (homo)sexuality, as it breaks out of a current impasse in sexuality studies regarding the self-aware emergence of groups associated with certain erotic modes of pleasure. After Foucault, the dominant paradigm for analyzing same-sex sexuality has been his distinction between sexual acts and identities.[1] Anglophone cultural historians consequently often argue that a homosexual identity was only possible after the concept of personhood, defined by a subject's interior psychology of quasi-genetic drives, arose and became consolidated throughout the nineteenth century. In the early modern period, roughly between the fifteenth and eighteenth centuries, same-sex activity was punished if it violated the traditional hierarchies of rank and gender submission, but it was not held to signify a truth about one's self, mainly because the period's elites could not allow the potentially dangerous notion that the lower ranks might have a private life worth noticing, let alone policing.

The acts-versus-identities model has had ambiguous effects for recovering sexual cultures. For the notion that conceptions of sexuality are socially conditioned and historically mutable has frequently meant that even otherwise gay-friendly critics often deny that pretwentieth-century agents gave meaning to their sexual practices. The initial problem with an overly dogmatic use of Foucault is that his work concentrates on tracking the changing terms used by officials to describe sexual activity. He never attempted to develop a method for discerning how the subjects covered by terms like "sodomy" or "homosexuality" may have conceptualized their own erotic behavior. Likewise, his work never acknowledged the belatedness of bourgeois professional knowledge, where middle-class writers and publicists usually begin discussing cultural matters long after these formations have already existed, especially if they were initiated by the laboring-class or other groups on the margins of middle-class expectations. The fact that early modern authorities refused to acknowledge the presence of alternative attitudes and semicovert communities in their midst does not mean they did not exist before 1800.

A tendentious use of Foucault has resulted in sexuality studies policing itself in ways far more rigid and unimaginative than is the case for other kinds of social history. We acknowledge the presence of a middle class before 1800, even while we understand that the particular bourgeois ideal of antagonistic individualism protected by the refuge of nuclear family domesticity does not fully exist then because the middle classes have different traits that they emphasize as defining themselves. Defoe's Robinson Crusoe does not have the rich interiority of a nineteenth-century Bildungsroman's hero, but the novel begins by clearly nominating Crusoe as belonging to the mercantile, middling class. It would be nonsensical to argue that, just because Crusoe does not fit the particular form of middleclass behavior dominant in the nineteenth century, the bourgeoisie, and the larger category of capitalism, does not exist before 1800. For sexuality studies, the overly homogeneous nature of the Foucauldian paradigm does not give us critical tools that are supple enough to make sense of sexual cultures that cannot easily be slotted into the acts or identities categories. This two-stage model flattens the multiple and often uneven phases of erotic practice in the post-medieval West, especially those within the eighteenth century as a phase of transition and radical transformation between the early modern and modern periods.[2]

*Ormond*'s significance is that it indicates a late eighteenth-century response that does not mainly consider sexuality either in terms of licit/illicit acts or *personal* identity, but as a collective experience shaping a diffuse set of groups and subjects into an interactive *society*. Here Brown participates in one of the main preoccupations for eighteenth-century writers associated with the middle class: the question of how to form a nonaristocratic civil society, rather than the one about consecrating competitive individuality. In works like Adam Ferguson's *An Essay on the History of Civil Society* (1767) and Abbe Sieyres's *What is the Third-Estate?* (1789), publicists sought to articulate visions of what a nonaristocratic, nonplebian society might look like. This metropolitan, sociological imagination differs markedly from a nineteenth-century one. Unlike later ideologues, Adam Smith's defense of free trade saw the good of commerce in terms of national wealth and as a medium for fashioning a moral community among strangers, not an arena of permissible war of all against all. Unlike scholars, like Tönnies, who contrast an idealized, agrarian organic community (*Gemeinschaft*) of recognizable, traditional relationships against a modern society (*Gesellschaft*) of alienated individuals coercively administered by impersonal bureaucracies, eighteenth-century writers saw the term "society" as defining a positive emancipation from the gothic rigidities of rule by lineage elites and religious superstition. To understand the period's consideration and enactment of same-sex sexuality, we need likewise to consider this phenomena within the terms provided by these larger debates. Rather than engage in the ahistorical search for a homosexual personal identity, the terms of which would have been unavailable and uninteresting to most agents in the period, we must explore the rudiments of a homoerotic society as enacted in a variety of institutions and parainstitutions.

Much of the period's debate on the question of civil society involved discussions about the desirability of fixed institutions. An institution has managers who administer the survival and routinization of social actions with the rent or purchase of an enclosed architecture that can house the enactment of conventional beliefs and practices. On the other hand, a parainstitution is more like simple customary behavior, highly mutable because it lacks a stable mechanism for self-regulation. In the early American Republic, New York merchants transformed the parainstitutional street trading of stocks by hand gestures under certain trees and appointed a committee to institutionalize the stock market by purchasing the Tontine Coffee House, the forerunner of the New York Stock Exchange, for their use as a bourse. A cruising ground is a parainstitution because its rules of sexual behavior are fashioned by an anonymous collective whose money is not spent on its upkeep, even if the site contains financial exchanges, like prostitution. An eighteenth-century London pub of male-male encounters (a "molly house") is an institution because a specific individual, like "Mother Clap," is clearly responsible for its operation and rent.[3]

As children of modern institutions, we find it difficult not to see these as teleologically necessary. Eighteenth-century writers were uncertain about the matter, not least because the period's main examples of institutionality, the absolutist state and the Catholic Church, were negative ones. Many writers either favored parainstitutionality, as with sentimental claims for the spontaneous circulation of affect or Adam Smith's notion of the marketplace's "invisible hand," or highly limited forms of institutionality. Whatever positions writers took, the debate's parameters delineate the period's discursive field for the social question.

This tension between society as best formed by parainstitutions or institutions is our best framework for recognizing and evaluating homoeroticism in the eighteenth century, as with the writings of French novelist Pierre François Godard de Beauchamps. In *The History of King Apprius* (1728), Beauchamps divides male-male eroticists into two tribes, the Ugobars and Chedabars.[4] The Ugobars are "enemies of display and ornamentation." They dress and act modestly and conduct their activities in private, an "inviolable secrecy conceals them from the eyes and scrutiny of all those who have not been initiated into their practices." On the other hand, the Chedabars are "insensible to the repugnance of humiliation." Their appearance is "soft, effeminate, and ephemeral . . . they are recognized by the richness of their outfits and even more by their manner of handling themselves. Their glances are calculated; their gait is affected." Chedabars use perfume, curl their long hair, and "have a language of their own, full of af-fection" and nicknames for each other.

At one level, Beauchamps clearly reaffirms the period's clichés of active pederasty, with its gendered correlation to masculinity and inversion with a feminized receiver. Yet these sex-gender descriptors mask a more sub-stantive difference between the men involving their positions regarding cultural assimilation and autonomy. The Ugobars protectively closet their erotic difference against retaliation from mainstream society, perhaps due to their greater age and wealth. On the other hand, the Chedabars' osten-tation suggests that their stylized language and mannerisms are knowingly crafted to advertise their rejection of secret integration, indicate their erotic behavior as chosen and embraced, rather than felt as a burden, and consolidate erotic solidarity. Beauchamps makes it clear that these gen-dered codes are situational, rather than intrinsic, as he writes that some Chedabars become Ugobars after they lose their youthful bloom. Though Beauchamps is no friend to same-sex eroticism, his discussion of same-sex sexuality indicates an awareness about the use of gendered bodily perfor-mances as a means of representing cultural disposition rather than con-fused sexual object choice.

It does not require much pressure then to see the institutional implica-tions of Beauchamps's later narrative about the war between the Cyther-ans and the Ebugors in *Anecdotes to be Used in the Secret History of the Ebugors* (1733).[5] The heterosexual Cytherans assume that other societies are inferior deviations from their natural ideal. Against this chauvinism, the cosmopolitan Ebugors are an "enemy of prejudices and of a very socia-ble disposition." Since Beauchamps argues that one joins the Ebugors by "vanity rather than taste" (cultural choice rather than congenital predeter-mination), these furious soldiers struggle to overcome Cytheran domina-tion through the formation of a nation-state based on values of inclusion. The *Secret History* goes beyond *King Apprius* as it suggests that same-sex groups, like their cross-sex sexual contemporaries, were likewise formed by the context of debates about the political difference between modern society and the old regime.

## Brockden Brown's Sexual Romance

Brown does more than just reflect this long-lasting debate, since he sculpts *Ormond* as an inquiry into the durability of revolutionary energies and erotic possibilities in the 1790s at a time of their increasing containment with the unexpected return of political and ecclesiastic conservatism. *Ormond*'s particular contribution here is that by rehearsing a strategy about preserving homoerotic collectives through a tactical manipulation of the mediums of representation, like the novel or other aesthetic forms, it offers a vantage point on a less-remarked strand of self-reflexive lesbian and gay history.

Brown is the author who first brought same-sex sexuality explicitly into American fiction as his incompletely serialized *Memoirs of Stephen Calvert* (1800) includes a woman's condemnation of her husband's unembarrassed intercourse with other men. While Brown's writing often elliptically registers the pressures placed on homoeroticism, *Ormond* is the one most determined to overcome erotic pessimism by manipulating narrative and bodily form. On initial glance, *Ormond* can be read as little more than a conventional sentimental romance about a morally reckless libertine's siege on female sexual purity. The plot involves the trials of a merchant's daughter, Constantia Dudley, after her father becomes bankrupt in the early 1790s due to the machinations of a confidence man. Without credit or credibility, the impoverished man moves his family to Philadelphia, where it is left to Constantia to maintain him after her depressed mother dies, through his ensuing blindness and alcoholism, and their self-imposed quarantine during the yellow-fever plague. Amid these domestic and metropolitan crises, Constantia encounters two figures, the male Ormond and female Martinette de Beauvais, who enthusiastically align themselves with the spirit of international revolution, rejection of bourgeois mores, and support of the above through the use of secrecy, dissimulation, and racial and gender transvestitism.

With the entry of these two characters, never seen together even as they act similarly toward Constantia, Brown alters the generic structure of virtue in distress in three sequential ways that allegorize the rise and fall (and rise) of same-sex sexual radicalism. First, the familiar tale of cross-gender seduction, with the male rake Ormond's pursuit of Constantia, is unexpectedly matched with Martinette's frequent and seemingly rehearsed visits to Constantia. While the heterosexual libertine novel often gives the male rake a female accomplice, as with *Les Liaisons Dangereuses* (1782), the lack of contact between Ormond and Martinette suggests that Martinette is less an aide than a competitor for Constantia's attraction. While Martinette's enactment of gestures otherwise taken as the prerogative of male erotic ambition insinuates the proximity of female-female desire, Brown acknowledges the resistance to this kind of female-female sexual desire with the tale's narrative voice. The omniscient narrator reveals herself midway through the tale as Sophia Westwyn, the childhood friend of Constantia who had been separated from her in adolescence. Not only does Sophia appropriate control of the text's exposition, but she also physically arrives in Philadelphia to place herself as Constantia's protector from the influences of Ormond and Martinette in ways unusual for these tales of a woman's distress, wherein female solidarity rarely succeeds. Yet if Sophia appears to represent a different mode of female-female relations with her turn against Ormond and Martinette's linkage of bodily transvestitism with political and erotic freedom, Brown's narrative has one more turn of the screw as he refunctionalizes the period's existing ideology of universalizing sentimental vision that Sophia deploys by routing it through contemporaneous British critiques of gender and French pornographic tales of voyeurism and sexual initiation. With *Ormond*'s tale of transvestitism and other shape shifting, Brown does a conceptual trick that aligns violence to bodily markers of race and gender with his own confusion of literary genres so that the medium of literary representation can act as a surrogate institution for sustaining homoerotic sociality through an incipient long period of reaction. If Constantia's relationship to Martinette and Sophia exemplify two kinds of female-female sexuality, in ways that might index butch/femme roles, Brown attempts to resolve this tension with a third position. By fashioning an erotically suffused cultural address that simultaneously indicates trauma and supersedes it through a coding device that can be decrypted by ideal readers, Brown telegraphs the onset of the gay-associated style we today call camp in ways that arguably makes him one of the first modern-looking writers of "homosexual" literature.

## No Sex Please, We're American?

The above claims for *Ormond*'s motivation would seem to be refuted by the relative lack of mention about homosexuality in the American colonies and early Republic. Throughout Western Europe and the Atlantic basin during the eighteenth century, police prosecution of same-sex sexual acts and spaces provides an initial vantage point on a widely shared geography of homoerotic enactments.[6] Since the United States was tightly integrated within the trade circuits that shuttled men, cultural artifacts, and social codes throughout the oceanic matrix, it would be commonsensical for analogous scares and indictments to occur in the United States. Despite a few ministerial and juridical complaints about sodomy, a term which does not solely refer to sexual practices in the period but also covers any kind of dissent, there were no prolonged or significant condemnations of ongoing same-sex practices in the British American colonies. Does this mean that Americans lacked a homoerotic sensibility that was found elsewhere in the Atlantic?

The absence of court trials and police records about homosexuality need not indicate the nonexistence of homoeroticism; it simply marks a missing need for social anxieties to find the form of homophobic pronouncements. Most moral scares about immoral, secret practices emerge from the fear by petit bourgeois groups that their tenuous hold on bourgeois privileges is slipping away. In order to bolster their fading prestige, they denounce outrageous behavior as a means of reestablishing themselves on the right side of the status divide. When London East End artisans felt threatened in the 1720s by an increasingly restive and newly urbanized laboring class population that was increasingly intruding on their neighborhoods and customs, they pounced on the "molly houses," the pubs where mainly working and underclass men met for homoerotically charged sociality and sex.[7] The raids on the molly houses tell us that these clubs existed, but they offer little insight on how long these places existed before coming to the notice of the lower middle-class moral police. While there was no comparative public scare in British America, this silence may simply convey how American colonialists had an easier target than sodomites onto which to project their discontent, namely, the London court and political establishment. In contrast to the Iberian and Caribbean colonies, which aggravated fears about disestablishment with the personal intermixture among metropolitan European administrators, white creoles, and (semi-)free mestizo groups of "color," the British American colonies' strictly guarded racial divides, relative lack of absentee landowners, and limited boundary disputes between colonies, did not replicate or amplify fears of blurred status distinction as elsewhere in the New World.

Even during periods of heightened police persecution in the Old World, an episodic state repression was only successful in removing the new homoerotic institutions, like the molly houses, and not the less formalized, parainstitutional grounds of encounter that often evaded police recognition. Some of London's parks and gardens, like Moorfields, remained active sites of male-male liaison for decades, if not longer. Despite the vulnerability of same-sex sexual institutions, homoerotic collectives showed remarkable resilience in the face of danger. In his account of life in Paris at the height of the Terror, Restif de la Bretonne describes how the Palais Royale became eerily empty of its normal retinue of pornographic booksellers, female prostitutes, and promoters of staged sex acts by adolescents. Yet the men cruising for (unpaid?) sex remained.[8]

## The 1790s American Revolution of the Senses

A similar dynamic occurs when an American threshold of emergence for same-sex sexual parainstitutions and the possibility for institutionality occurs during the 1790s. As a result of the dual Francophone revolutions in France and Haiti, American merchants gained full access to the lucrative trade of Caribbean sugar and coffee.[9] The increased volume of shipping to America ports also brought a greater number of transient maritime laborers, who carried circumatlantic hetero- and homosexual mores to the harbor towns. With the ensuing economic boom, America urbanized with internal immigration into the seaboard cities, mainly New York and Philadelphia. As previously isolated hinterland Americans came into contact with the port's linkage to Atlantic experiences, the United States generated new metropolitan mixtures similar to those that London realized earlier in the century when the molly houses began to be recorded.

With deruralization came the loss of traditional artisan structures as masters increasingly paid apprentices to find their own room and board.[10] As young craftsmen were freed from the workplace's surveillance of personal behavior, the time and space for nonregulated hetero-and homoerotic contact in an increasingly anonymous city was made possible.[11] A similar process happened with an increased number of literate, college graduates who also congregated in the port towns, where they often associated and lived together in ways that ignored the regional and denominational status divides of the prior generation. This cosmopolitanism of experience was facilitated and amplified by Americans' increased contact with circumatlantic ideas regarding new experiences.

European progressive ideals about gender politics filtered into the States, especially with the popular writings of Paine, Godwin, and Wollstonecraft. These writers condemned absolutist regimes as legitimizing their coercion through obfuscation and a mythology of traditional hierarchy as unalterable. Because these writers believed personal relationships to be socially constructed, they took the reformation of intimacy as a precursor to large-scale social transformation. In this light, they condemned marriage as no more than contractual slavery and promoted the ideal of heterosexual erotic friendship as a more consensual organization of physical contact outside of the church and regal state's despotism. Part of this reformation of sexual attitudes were calls for removing the prejudice against sodomy, which was seen to be little more than another example of the old regime's irrational resistance to natural human affinities.

One other factor catalyzes the American moment for nonnormative sexual activity. Although their numbers were relatively small, the Catholic, Francophone exiles from the Jacobin terror in France and the black uprising in Haiti had a cultural influence in the 1790s United States far greater than other prior ethnic group arrivals. Unlike the Germans, the French diaspora was concentrated in the rapidly transforming seaboard cities.[12] As many exiles survived exile as dancing teachers, dressmakers, chefs, hairdressers, and fencing masters, the French exodus brought a new awareness of mutable bodily presentation in fashion, comportment, and sexual manners precisely at a time when young Americans were challenging older behavioral conventions.[13] Knowledge of sexual affairs increased as the immigrants also established Francophone newspapers and bookstores, which frequently reproduced the pornographic libels that were a mainstay of French political discourse.[14] The Haitian creoles also carried northward that boundary-disrupting object of sexual wonder—the free mulatta mistress—and both sets of French immigrants brought forward a new ease regarding the recognition of same-sex sexuality, oft-mentioned in the obscene books, after the National Assembly's 1791 decriminalization of sodomy.[15] The two elements of miscegenation and female homoeroticism were often mixed, since the beautiful mulatta's perceived transgression of racial lines was often taken to indicate analogous sexual excess.[16]

## Writing a New Erotic History: Charles Brockden Brown's Narrative of Sexual Society

As Charles Brockden Brown begins writing fictional prose in New York and Philadelphia amid the years of an internationalizing urban transformation, his tales resonate from their crucible of new life conditions and radical social ideas, especially involving a debate on social historiography. Inspired by Godwin, Brown distinguishes between the categories of historical and romance writing. "History" is simply the collection of archival facts, while romance constructs a critical narrative that attempts to explain the hidden springs that may have caused these events to occur.[17] This notion of inductive narration is congruent with Dugald Stewart's naming of Adam Smith's method as one of theoretical or conjectural history, which Stewart feels is akin to what his French contemporaries call *Historie Raisonnée*.[18] These writers developed the notion of intuitive history because it allows for a means of making history legible and pertinent to their middle-class readers, who were themselves hidden from the histories produced before the eighteenth century. This method of historiography thus belongs to a larger project by which the middle class might conceptualize and record their own social emergence and rise to power.

From a contemporary perspective, conjectural history violates the later demands for an empirical history, based on the evidence provided by official archives, as it mainly seems to reveal its authors' mentality. If prerevolutionary French historians produced romantic "secret histories" of the court and church's sexual irregularities, this may be proof less of Marie Antoinette's actual lesbian activity, than what these writers thought was a good way to condemn the court. Yet because relying on official documents as the only legitimate historical sources simply reinforces existing authorities' institutional disapproval about new types of erotic behavior, this kind of history writing is particularly unsatisfactory with regards to lives of the marginalized and victimized. Here the ostensible weakness of conjectural history can be a strength because of its preexisting dissatisfaction with archival evidence's ability to provide a fair or feasible explanation for the events it records. Because these writers believed in the power of personal relations to transcend governmental prohibitions, their work captures transformations in the culture of sexual practice in ways that other evidentiary sources cannot.

While critics have long recognized the presence of same-sex female desire in *Ormond*, Brown's purpose in representing this desire has not.[19] Brown's narratives are frequently mis- or incompletely read because they are done so outside of his self-declared intellectual context within a British radical perspective. The project in *Ormond* is not simply to document the existence of same-sex eroticism in the early American Republic, but to make a "romantic" argument about the values that lead to that presence and inform its politics. Writing while the bright prospects of institutionalized radicalism were fading under the glare of insurgent conservatism, Brown dissents from the slightly earlier Godwin and Wollstonecraft's distrust of institutions. Still beholden to a belief in the parainstituional effects of sincere, public declarations of personal desire (what we might call a politics of visibility), the British dissidents failed to conceptualize the role of counterhegemonic institutions. Brown sees their parainstitutional performances as incomplete and having left progressivism unprotected against the ensuing conservative backlash.

Considering that the moment for progressive social change is rapidly diminishing by the late 1790s, Brown produces literary narrative as a surrogate institution for erotic collectives, something that is more fixed than a parainstitution, but less vulnerable to repression than an easily located geographically fixed institution. *Ormond* breaks up generic literary and behavioral forms to reassemble them as a cultural space in between the open-air parainstitution and the enclosed institution. Brown most likely enacts this literary project of erotic communalization from inspiration by the Francophone obscene texts that were more widely available in the 1790s as a result of the French influx.[20] The French generic tale of sexual initiation and tutelage through didactic voyeurism allows him to disrupt the optics of sentimental vision with the theme of covert surveillance ("secret witness"-ing). Brown also uses the image of occluded vision as his metaphor for dominant society's limited field of social recognition and the canniness of marginal communities to transmit group-affirming encoded meaning in semipublic, semiprivate ways. Brown then deploys the theatrical imposture of transvestitism for its violence against (symbolic, textual, and anatomical) form as a new sensibility for a radically queer community. He thus moves beyond Beauchamps's opposition between careful assimilation and flamboyant refusal to argue for a third position, involving literary tales of coded gender masquerade that some ideal readers will recognize as pointing to the existence of a homoerotic society.

### In a French Position: Witnessing Homosexuality

*Ormond*'s framing narrative introduces its themes and symbols. The young painter Stephen Dudley is forced to return to New York from Italy to manage his recently died father's apothecary. The transition from art to commerce is not immediately distasteful, since even business has its own intellectual challenges. However, these are short-lived and the repetition of the shop's tasks depresses Dudley. Taking on an apprentice, Thomas Craig, Dudley has the idea of eventually returning to painting after shifting the business to his junior partner. The merchant then discovers Craig's correspondence with his American working-class mother, which reveals the youth's reference letters and English identity as forgeries, just before Dudley realizes that a suddenly vanished Craig has embezzled from and bankrupted him. When his daughter's suitor consequently loses interest in the now poor Constantia, the family moves to Philadelphia where they hide under a pseudonym. As Dudley goes blind under poverty's strain, *Ormond* argues that social constraints become embodied ones and conversely that freedom from the constraint of dominant opinion will be associated with fluid physical form. The vignette of Craig's fraudulent letters also conveys the notion that textual records barely disguise social antagonism, especially those unable to be recognized from a bourgeois perspective. Dudley's painterly eye fails to discern the forces of class difference because his middle-class aesthetic conventions cannot represent other social groups. From the normative reader's and the narrative voice's perspective, Craig is a villainous scoundrel. A slightly reversed gaze reads his deception as a working-class youth's covert resistance to the superficial civility disguising Dudley's exploitation of Craig's labor and examination of his behavior.

The dual themes of ambivalent optics and liberation through physical transformations are negatively combined in Philadelphia, where Constantia must now "square her conduct" and remain constant to expectations of female subordination by selling her personalizing books and clothes to support Dudley (the mother has died) and moving with him into progressively smaller apartments. When the Dudleys quarantine themselves during the yellow-fever plague, Constantia's retreat into tighter architectural spaces represents the ongoing restriction of her experiential domain, an asceticism that also functions as her rejection of male privilege. While Stephen wants to avoid the shame of recognition, Constantia's closeting of her self and wish for "security and solitude," or the security of solitude, conveys her desire to avoid contact with a public sphere that she understands as a "theater of suffering" scripted by invasive masculine surveillance, which simply views her as an available object of prostitution, either literally or in the matrimonial traffic of women.

Constantia's perception of heterosexuality as the combination of violence and tedium is underscored as she escapes a potential street rape only because a self-made businessman, Balfour, rescues her. An epitome of bourgeois norms, Balfour "betray[s] few marks of intelligence," lacks emotional lability, and proposes to Constantia because he admires her "economy of time and money."[21] Dudley urges Constantia to accept and realize her biology's value in the exchange between men, but she rejects the offer by equating marriage with slavery.

By resisting a generic matrimonial conclusion, Constantia transcodes an apparently conventional tale of a woman's "happy" end in domestic enclosure into one that explores the possibility of avoiding marriage's compulsory and commodified heterosexuality. This refusal forces the narrative to begin anew, a return signified by the surprise resurfacing of Craig, as if Constantia bade the narrative to go back and investigate an alternative history of female experience than the one it had so far mapped out.

The remainder of *Ormond*'s trajectory has to be understood through Brown's technique of thinking through a problem, such as the question of liberated female subjectivity, with variations on an initial question. Brown manages these forensic shifts through his use of what I call a *segmentifier*, where a narrative element, often a (minor) character or scenario, reappears to demarcate the start/stop of the fiction's internal units. The segmentifier has both a semantic value, in that it means something in itself, and a syntactic one, as part of the text's grammar of rhetoric. In *Ormond*, the segmentifier is the figure of the forger Thomas Craig, who bundles the themes of fraudulent letters, the disruption of marriage plans, the presence of hidden affectionate networks, and Brown's own self-positioning as the author of what initially seems to be a tale of conventional gender roles.

In its first post-Craig reincarnation, *Ormond* stages a series of encounters where Constantia becomes increasingly drawn emotionally to a Frenchwoman who appears under different guises and names. This spiral of intimacy begins after the plague when she hears the story of the émigré Ursula Monrose. Living alone with her father before the plague's onset, Ursula was seen tearlessly burying a man at midnight in the garden before she disappears amid the plague. Listening to the tale, Constantia feels "unspeakable regret" that she will never meet Monrose, since Constantia believes that Monrose "would prove worthy of her love," given their similarity in "principles, sex, and age," and that the midnight burial hints at a more substantive revolt.[22] While the Frenchwoman is described as living in poverty with her father, she is later seen after the plague as wealthy and surrounded by black male servants. Because Brown frequently uses images of ethnoracial passing in his other fictions and had written a short story that describes a French émigré living openly with his mixed-race wife, *Ormond* implies that Ursula and the man belong to the white Haitian exodus and black Revolution, and that Monrose, described as having a lightly dark skin, is the man's mulatta mistress.[23] Ursula may have conducted her own private revolution by assassinating her master/lover, escaping, and then performing a public fiction of white mastery to protect the man's now liberated darker-skinned slaves from recapture.

This keyhole glance at the linkage between erotic desire, emancipation, and public emergencies (plagues and revolutions) as a feature of mysterious identity is continued when Constantia shortly afterward goes to pawn a lute, her father's last item of pleasure. At the shop she finds a Frenchwoman, who buys the instrument through the merchant's translation. Since we later discover that the woman speaks perfect English, the moment is construed as a reversal of gender prerogatives, where the male trader's voice is made to be the object exchanged between the two women. Because a lute is traditionally used in the pictorial conventions that Dudley has been trained within to represent erotic passion, the moment not only provides Constantia with a glimmering of female autonomy, but also suggests how public mediums might be used to exchange homoerotic affections.

### The Drag Revolution: Cross-Dressing and Sexual Radicalism

The sexualized nature of the encounter is further insinuated as Constantia, typically the object of men's observation, reverses this erotic sight as she concentrates on "interpreting the [Frenchwoman's] language of looks and gazes." Noticing something that the narrator says a less astute observer would have missed, Constantia is electrified by how the other woman's "muscle belongs to woman, but the genius of her aspect . . . was heroic and contemplative. The female was absorbed . . . in the rational creature."[24] The meaning here is that the woman has freed herself from the prison-house of her biological sex and its assumed mores. What Constantia does not recognize, the narrator says, is the "utmost accuracy" between her and the other woman's body. The claim is superficially surprising because Constantia is a tall, light-skinned, rough-looking sixteen-year old, while the foreigner is a small, delicate, darker-skinned thirty-something. Yet the narrator insists that while Constantia herself is "probably unconscious of this resemblance," the similarity will later "influence her in discovering" its meaning.[25]

This encounter quickly passes and Constantia remains secluded until, hearing a lute once more, she discovers her new neighbor to be Martinette de Beauvais, the widow of a guillotined Girondin. After a ballet of invitation, which can be likened to the maneuvers of seduction, Martinette becomes a "frequent" visitor to Constantia's home after revealing herself as both Ursula Monrose and the lute-buyer. As Constantia listens to Martinette's complex biography of travel, education in male topics, and participation in revolutionary crises, she wonders about the difference between her own uneventful past and Martinette's cosmopolitan experience. The Frenchwoman answers that while Constantia "grew and flourished, like a frail mimosa, in the spot where destiny" had planted her, she is "better than a vegetable."[26] Refusing the fixed location of naturalized gender that delimits women, Martinette describes her own process of self-liberation through rebellion against sex-gender roles. When cross-dressing to fight in the American Revolution, she discovered that "the timidity that commonly attends women gradually vanished" as she felt "imbued with a soul that was a stranger to sexual distinction." Returning to France to cross-dress again in the Revolutionary Republic's army, Martinette explains that she discovered so many other covert militant women in the ranks that they could have filled whole regiments. Some fought alongside male lovers, some fought because of a passion for war, and some for patriotism, while others did so from "contagion of example."[27]

Constantia becomes flushed on hearing of Martinette's adventures, but hesitates at what she considers to be the final violation of passive femininity, not dressing like a man, but the bloody rupture of his flesh. Martinette's eyes sparkle, however, as she describes how two of the thirteen royalists she killed in battle were prerevolution lovers, and that she had narrowly missed passing as an émigré to assassinate a French royalist general. The plan recalls the story of that other murderous Girondin, Charlotte Corday's assassination of Marat. While Constantia initially recoils at the terror committed in "a scene of so much danger," Martinette responds, "Danger my girl? It is my element. I am an adorer of liberty, and liberty without peril can never exist . . . [as a woman of reason] my hand never faltered when liberty demanded the victim."[28]

The idea of Martinette's sublime sex, or faith in transvestite action that consumes the distinctions of gender, and how this withering away of the physical state and its implied same-sex sexuality can enact social change comes to Brown from at least two sources.

First, there is Wollstonecraft's *Vindication of the Rights of Women,* which Brown had already used in his earlier writing. By insisting that exclusion from a useful education and the division of vestimentary codes is responsible for female limitation, Wollstonecraft describes enfranchisement as a process where the acquisition of knowledge is intrinsically connected to transforming the appearance of female physique. She emphasizes this point by including D'Eon, the cross-dressing French ambassador in her list of great women.[29] Second, as she says that the mathematician Newton "was probably a being of superior order, accidentally caged in a human body," Wollstonecraft implies that the body should not be understood as the container of civil rights, but their containment.[30] Wollstonecraft's gambit here is to suggest that human rights are not inalienable, or fastened to the body, but, like that extraterrestrial Newton, are ontologically *alienable*, and best realized when disconnected from the material of naturalized gender.

In this light, Martinette's conversion of the female is not her becoming masculine, or even androgyne, but is conceptualized as the use of reason to go beyond the categories of sex and gender for the purposes of human advancement. Brown reads Wollstonecraft more radically by taking her to suggest that the rational does not lie in creating the fiction of gender's transparency, as the notion that equal rights are achieved by making distinctions invisible. Instead the liberating act of reason lies in its ability to recognize and then violate its own morphology, be these traditional containers literary or anatomical, and *Ormond*'s conceit is that the two are the same. Furthermore, reason is not simply an individual act of self-realization, but a channel for collective social action as it pedagogically encourages others into alternative life-experiences. It was exactly this expansion of autonomous female-female education that terrified the period's authorities. When women were caught cross-dressing as male soldiers on either side of the 1790s Revolutionary wars, their male interrogators did not want to know *why* the women cross-dressed, taking the benefits of masculinity as self-evident. Instead they wanted to find out *how* the women knew it was possible to cross-dress; what were the training channels that circulated this information? These were the covert tutelary networks that authorities wanted to stop.[31]

We do not have a good sense of how these mainly plebian communications operated, but the popularity of the printed narrative accounts about these women had paradoxical effects. On the one hand, they informed the women who could read, or listen to a reader, about the existence of female daring. On the other hand, they also provided a pornographic thrill to the male reader since the generic conventions of transvestite narratives require a scene of the disrobed female body as a moment of visual confirmation of her gender.[32] This dual aspect of voyeuristic secrecy and collective revelation is one that Brown partially learns through its advertisement in contemporaneous French pornography.

## Bourgeois XXX: Obscene Politics

In their research on Continental print culture, Robert Darnton and Lynn Hunt argue that the French bourgeois reading public of the eighteenth century received erotic narratives as manuals of social instruction, more than private pleasures, that encouraged the appropriation of governmental functions previously forbidden to the middle class.[33] As the bourgeoisie titilated itself with secret histories about the church's and court's sexual peccadilloes, frequently involving male and female homosexuality, to criticize the Catholic Church and the Queen, respectively, their literary voyeurism helped the middle class abandon their deference to the manners of traditional elites. A chief carrier of these energies was the literary convention of the hidden watcher, who narrated the tale in ways that the voyeur, as a metonym for the sidelined bourgeoisie, could excite the reader's own awareness of an alternative society and behavioral conventions. This dual function explains why the period's censors used "bad books" as the term for both obscene texts and philosophic critiques of absolutism.

Brown could have become aware of these codes' intermingling of eroticism and social transformation from multiple sources, including his two closest friends at the time of *Ormond*'s composition, Elihu Hubbard Smith and William Dunlap, and his French émigré publisher, Hoquet Caritat. Both Smith and Dunlap were familiar with French commentary on same-sex perversion. Smith studied Tissot's *Onanism, or Physical Dissertation on the Illnesses Caused by Masturbation* (1760), which includes accounts of "clitoral" pollution where some women appropriate "virile functions" in the salon and bedroom in order to seduce younger women into a life of homosexuality.[34] Smith typically handed his medical readings over to Brown as a usable resource for his fictions, which frequently rely on medical and psychological anomalies as plot devices. Dunlap's diary records him hearing from his French language tutor in 1798 about the "bestiality" of priests and nuns that occurs because of their isolation from the opposite gender.[35] Brown may have also encountered French sexual acknowledgment of homoeroticism as he was an inveterate searcher for French language texts among New York bestsellers. He need not have gone far since his Manhattan publisher, the bookseller Hoquet Caritat, advertised for sale titles like Restif de la Bretonne's notoriously pornographic *The Perverted Peasant,* which tells the story of a provincial youth's corruption by metropolitan immorality through scenes of secret watching, in an edition that includes plates of secretly observed lesbian orgies.[36] Given that Continental French booksellers kept two sets of catalogs, one that could be shown to authorities and another that indicated the more illicit texts on offer, Caritat might have also sold even more explicit texts than those he openly advertised.[37]

Caritat was no shady or marginal seller. His 1790s bookstore was based in New York's fashionable City Hotel, used for decades by the town's political, social, and financial elites to meet, dine, and seal contracts. The well-connected Caritat's bookstore was also a lending library, which had the largest collection in New York.[38] With its special ladies reading room, Caritat's was also one of the few secular, semipublic places for middle-class women to encounter each other outside of parental and male supervision. That a well-educated Caritat advertised Francophone pornographic texts at such a mainstream site suggests a much wider familiarity with homoerotic topics and codes in the early Republic's reading communities than has been otherwise recognized.

In *Ormond,* Brown fuses the political radicalism of an otherwise prurient Wollstonecraft with Continental obscenity to link a political critique of sex-gender codes, which assumes that their alteration leads to social betterment, with equally politicized ones about erotic free-play for the purposes of creating a surrogate institution for homoerotic society.

This dynamic first appears when Constantia asks Martinette how the latter could have survived the plague at a time when the panic about infection should have closed all doors. Martinette answers that Philadelphia's French émigrés lived without fear of the disease and continued to sing and dance "with their customary unconcern." She tells Constantia that none of them would have refused "a countrywoman, even if her name had not been Martinette de Beauvais . . . [even] without a farthing and without a name, I would not have incurred the slightest inconvenience."[39] In contrast to Constantia's grim isolation, Martinette describes an inviting city, unacknowledged by its other citizens, which would welcome you amid a general health crisis, even if you really were not a Mademoiselle, and even if you did not have a ready name with which to enunciate your subjectivity.[40]

Promising to bring Constantia her written memoirs that will more fully divulge her past transvestite exploits, Martinette disappears from the narrative, which then relies on the male figure of Ormond to continue Constantia's tutelage into a new world perspective. Like Martinette, Ormond is a master of disguise, and he first visits Constantia's house disguised as an African servant, a transgression of skinside boundaries that reiterates Brown's scripting of embodied identities as fictional categories open for revision. Belonging to a secret society advocating global Jacobinism and devoted to forming a new world utopian community, Ormond increasingly details these ideas to Constantia as if encouraging her to join. While the narrative's voice claims that Ormond and Martinette are separated siblings, no evidence supports that claim. However, their shared skill in biological masquerade, failure ever to be seen together, despite frequent visits to Constantia, and implied link through an embedded narrative about a Southern male fraud, Martynne, whose name recalls Martinette's, suggests that the two might be actually the same figure alternatively masking gender roles and that Ormond's declaration of sexual desire for Constantia ventriloquizes Martinette's as well.

Against Constantia's increasingly voluntary affiliation with radicalism, the forces of conservatism regroup, personified by the narrator Sophia Westwyn. As Constantia's childhood friend, who has returned from Europe to look for her, Sophia stands as the ideological opposite of Martinette de Beauvais. Although they share similar conditions in their upbringing, Martinette is cosmopolitan, comfortable with the adversity of historical flux, and socially and politically radical, while Sophia is provincial, resistant to alterity, and reactionary. Sophia's revelation that she has been the previously undeclared narrator has been treated in two ways by critics. Male scholars often see Sophia as merely vocalizing Brown's own cultural politics. William Hedges reads Sophia's control of the narrative voice as "the sure sign that the novel will tolerate no deviance from accepted views," and Robert Levine takes her as Brown's suggestion that "the preservation of liberty may require a 'reactionary' power."[41]

More recently, Sophia's heated description of her affinity with Constantia is read more sympathetically by female critics as Brown's welcoming of homoerotic attraction.[42] Both readings overlook Brown's purpose in contrasting Sophia and Martinette's competing models and the narrative's repeated use of masquerade at every level and scene. Sophia's emotionally saturated relationship with Constantia is an Ugobar-like one that looks to establish a privatized coupling that accepts the regulations of mainstream society, and indeed desires to accommodate heterosexual regulations in marriage as a discrete safeguard behind which female emotional relations may continue to develop. Martinette conversely looks to guide Constantia into a Chedabar-like, semipublic collective that operates within dominant society, but also manhandles its behavioral conventions as a means of telegraphing its presence, and sees homoeroticism as enabling, if not defined by, an ethical dedication to insurrection and refusal to acquiesce to dominant manners.

Brown's adjudication between the two models of assimilation versus autonomy for female-female relations appears at the narrative's end, when Sophia rushes to Constantia's home to prevent what she believes will be Ormond's rape of Constantia. Entering the house, she looks through a locked door's keyhole to see a teary and dissheveled Constantia with two male bodies lying next to her. "One of them was Ormond. A smile of disdain still sat upon his features. The wound by which he fell was secret and was scarcely betrayed by the effusion of a drop of blood."[43] The other corpse is Craig's.

When Constantia recovers, Sophia pruriently asks if anything "has happened to load you with guilt or shame," as though secretly desiring the impregnating event that would force Constantia away from public view and into her private care. After Constantia explains, in tones more like a sorry lover than an aggrieved victim, that she killed Ormond by a random knife-thrust, Sophia enlists a judge, ostensibly to acquit Constantia, but functionally to remind her of the social order's power to incarcerate her if she continues to deviate from the script of normative female submission. Favoring "the ultimate restoration of tranquility," where monotony is the abeyance of radical enthusiasm, Sophia effectively polices Constantia by distancing her from Martinette and removing her to England, where Sophia smugly says that Constantia's life now experiences "little variation."[44] Returned to the domestic enclosure in which she began the novel, Constantia is seemingly being prepared by Sophia for a tedious marriage to a German Balfour, the I. E. Rosenberg to whom the novel is addressed as an epistolary narrative.

Sophia's planned ending of social restraint is not Brown's. With Constantia standing over Ormond with a pen-knife, his secret wound, that bleeds but a little, suggests a gender reversal wherein Constantia deflowers Ormond. If Martinette claims that the boundary separating Constantia's cloistered domestication from her own transgressive mobility can be broken by violence to male anatomy, then the scene suggests that Constantia has crossed that line by completing the Corday-like gesture of symbolic castration. Yet Ormond's "disdainful smile," with its lurid postcoital air of satisfaction, suggests that what Sophia interprets as the evidence of rape may actually be his knowing performance of a "scene of danger," the staging of which Martinette says is the prerequisite to liberation. This dramatization of violence may be Constantia's entry into the affectional community represented by the tangled male bodies lying on the floorbed.

The presence of this alternative erotic geography appears when Ormond had previously revealed his knowledge of Constantia's intimate secrets. When a befuddled Constantia asks how he knows so much about her, Ormond explains that the back of her father's closet was covered by a canvas sheet that hid an entrance to a neighboring rowhouse from which he could watch her. If Constantia's home, with its backdrops, functions as the dramatic stage on which the costume-changing Ormond and Martinette have both watched and acted before her, then the narrative's subtitle, the secret witness, may refer to Constantia, who only belatedly recognizes herself as a spectator in this play. If she follows the "contagion by example" by removing the closet's membrane, she can follow Ormond into a nouveau Philadelphia, whose lack of enunciation cannot be taken as its historical absence.

The sense of this reading comes as the second male body next to Ormond belongs to Thomas Craig, the segmentifier that indicates both the end of one narrative segment and the beginning of a new one. What could this beginning look like since the novel is in its last pages? One possibility emerges from Craig's prior scrambling of Constantia's compulsory marriage and his fraudulent letters surrounding his family. This logic implies that the novel is not yet over, even as Sophia seems literally to end it with the framing letter to Rosenberg. Since Constantia has already twice before eluded bourgeois marriage in moments linked to the appearance of Craig, his resurfacing, even as a corpse, insinuates that she will soon find a similar escape from Rosenberg's embrace, an evasion that is implied in Rosenberg's name. Wil Verhoeven notes that Rosenberg is Mon(t)rose translated into German and inverted.[45] Hence, it could be that the Rosenberg who Constantia is being prepared in marriage for may be another of Martinette's disguises to enable Constantia's escape from Sophia's closet. If the supple Martinette and Ormond have already made a mockery of the corporeal limits of race and gender, then why not those of death as well?

Despite Sophia's authority, there is no reason why readers should grant that other piece of writing, which is the text of the *Ormond* itself, as substantive. If all the letters in the novel are either inauthentic or missing when called on to testify, then Craig's return encourages the reader to give over to Sophia the tangible record of the printed page and look beyond the text's canvas-like sheets to join *Ormond*'s last remaining secret witnesses, those other readers who are schooled to recognize Brown's connotations of utopia.

The ultimate message of *Ormond* is one mutually shaped by Brown's own formation by radical political science and personal sense of conservatism's rising hegemony at the century's turn, a dynamic allegorized by Sophia's late arrival and appropriation of the narrative. At this historical juncture, Brown implies that the opposition of quiet assimilation and outrageous declaration for sexual cultures is neither satisfactory nor tactically feasible. Instead, he argues for a third, "French" position of circulating codes through the framework of a publicly distributed narrative, as a means of setting up camp, in the dual sense of establishing sanctuary from attack and a modern gay rhetorical style. Rather than accept a definition of homoeroticism as a mode of dysfunctional anatomy, criminal act of confused gender assignment, or degenerate individual personality, *Ormond*'s uses a "romance" narrative about masking and unmasking the body as a means of indicating to future readers the prior existence of a spirited homoerotic society, long before Stonewall's own rebellion.

### NOTES

1. Michel Foucault, *The History of Sexuality: Volume I* (London: Penguin, 1980).

2. Stephen Shapiro, " 'Man to Man I Needed Not to Dread His Encounter': Edgar Huntly's End of Erotic Pessimism," in *Revising Charles Brockden Brown: Culture, Politics, and Sexuality in the Early Republic.* eds. P. Barnard, M. Kamrath, and S. Shapiro (Knoxville, TN, Univ. of Tenn. Press, 2004), 216–251.

3. Alan Bray, *Homosexuality in Renaissance England* (London, Gay Men's Press, 1982); Rictor Norton, *Mother Clap's Molly House: The Gay Subculture in England, 1700–1830* (London, Gay Men's Press, 1992).

4. Pierre François Godard de Beauchamps, "The History of King Apprius," in *Homosexuality in Early Modern France: A Documentary Collection*, eds. J. Merrick and B. T. Ragan, Jr. (Oxford, Oxford University Press, 2001), 127–8.

5. Pierre François Godard de Beauchamps, "Anecdotes to Be Used in the Secret History of the Ebugars," in ibid., 128–31.

6. *Queer Sites: Gay Urban Histories since 1600*, ed. David Higgs (London, Routledge, 1999); Clare A. Lyons, "Mapping an Atlantic Sexual Culture: Homoeroticism in Eighteenth-Century Philadelphia," in this volume.

7. Stephen Shapiro, "Of Mollies: Class and Same-Sex Sexualities in the Eighteenth Century," in *In a Queer Place: Sexuality and Belonging in British and European Contexts*, eds. Kate Chedgzoy, Emma Francis, E. and Murray Platt (London, Ashgate, 2002), 155–176.

8. Restif de la Bretonne, *My Revolution: Promenades in Paris, 1789–1794* (London, Allen Lane, 1971), 310.

9. The following description of the 1790s condenses arguments in Stephen Shapiro, *The Culture and Commerce of the Early American Novel: Reading the Atlantic World-System* (University Park, Pennsylvania State University Press, forthcoming, 2008).

10. Sean Wilentz, *Chants Democratic: New York City & the Rise of the American Working Class, 1788–1850* (New York, Oxford University Press, 1984), 33; Elizabeth Blackmar, *Manhattan for Rent, 1785–1850* (Ithaca, Cornell University Press, 1989), 61–63.

11. The 1790s saw an increase in New York of brothels and streetwalkers in regions near the docks. Timothy J. Gilfoyle, *City of Eros: New York City, Prostitution, and the Commercialization of Sex, 1790–1920* (New York, Norton, 1992), 25.

12. Nearly 10 percent of Philadelphians in the 1790s were recent Francophone immigrants. John L. Earl III, "Talleyrand in Philadelphia, 1794–1796," *Pennsylvania Magazine of History and Biography* 91 (1967): 282–298.

13. Howard Mumford Jones, *America and French Culture, 1750–1848* (Westport, CT, Greenwood Press, 1973), 255–7.

14. Because the main bibliographic archive, Evans, does not list foreign-language imported or printed in the early Republic, it structurally silences the impact and diffusion of these texts, a quarter of which were French. See Bernard Fäy, *The Revolutionary Spirit in France and America* (New York, Cooper Square Publishers, 1966).

15. Susan Branson and Leslie Patrick, "Étrangers dans un Pays Étrange: Saint-Dominigan Refugees of Color in Philadelphia," in *The Impact of the Haitian Revolution in the Atlantic World* (Columbia, University of South Carolina Press, 2001), 193–208. French politician Talleyrand scandalized Philadelphia natives by parading in the streets with his arm around a (French?) black woman. Earl, 291.

16. Moreau de Saint-Méry, *A Civilization that Perished: The Last Year of White Colonial Rule in Haiti* (New York, University Press of America, 1985), 82.

17. Charles Brockden Brown, "Walstein's School of History, from the German of Krants of Gotha," in *Literary Essays and Reviews*, eds. Alfred Weber and Wolfgang Schäfer (Frankfurt, Peter Lang, 1992), 31–39; Charles Brockden Brown, "The Difference Between History and Romance," in *Literary Essays and Reviews*, 83–85.

18. Dugald Stewart, Account of the Life and Writings of Adam Smith in *The Glasgow Edition of the Works and Correspondence of Adam Smith, Vol. 3*, eds. W. P. D. Wightman, and J. C. Bryce (Indianapolis, Liberty Fund, 1982), 218–86.

19. For a review of the critics on *Ormond*'s lesbianism, see Kristin M. Comment, "Charles Brockden Brown's *Ormond* and Lesbian Possibility in the Early Republic," *Early American Literature* 40 (2005), 57–78; Heather Smyth, " 'Imperfect Disclosures': Cross-dressing and Containment in Charles Brockden Brown's *Ormond*," in *Sex and Sexuality in Early America*, ed. Merril D. Smith (New York, New York University Press, 1998), 240–261.

20. While Lyons indicates that Continental pornography was already circulated earlier in the century, the increase in French booksellers in the 1790s widened the channels of textual entry.

21. Charles Brockden Brown, *Ormond; or, The Secret Witness*, ed. Mary Chapman (Peterborough, Canada, Broadview, 1999), 101–102.

22. *Ormond*, 93.

23. Charles Brockden Brown, "Portrait of an Emigrant," in *Somnambulism and Other Stories*, ed. Alfred Weber (Frankfurt, Peter Lang, 1987), 112–6; *Ormond*, 98, 187.

24. *Ormond*, 98.

25. Ibid., 97.

26. Ibid., 194.

27. Ibid., 206.

28. Ibid., 205. Paul Lewis argues for Brown's tacit endorsement of Martinette's Corday-like acts. Paul Lewis, "Attaining Masculinity: Charles Brockden Brown and Woman Warriors of the 1790s," *Early American Literature* 40 (2005), 37–55. For period accounts of Corday's politics, familiarity with male knowledge fields, like history, and gender dimorphism, see Nina Corazzo and Catherine R. Montfort, "Charlotte Corday: *femme-homme*," in *Literate Women and the French Revolution of 1789*, ed. Catherine Montfort (Birmingham, Summa Publications, 1994), 33–54. In 1796, the *New-York Magazine* praised Corday's beauty and republican stoic self-control, and her similarity to Brutus as a defender of liberty in the "Sketch of the Character of Marie Anne Victoire Charlotte Cordet, who was executed under the Reign of Robespierre, for the Assassination of Marat." For period dramatic representations of Corday, see Marie-Helen Huet, *Rehearsing the Revolution: The Staging of Marat's Death, 1793–1797* (Berkeley, University of California Press, 1982).

29. Mary Wollstonecraft, *A Vindication of the Rights of Woman; A Vindication of the Rights of Man* (Oxford, Oxford University Press, 1993), 149. For a recent history of D'Eon, see Gary Kates, *Monsieur d'Eon is a Woman: A Tale of Political Intrigue and Sexual Masquerade* (New York, Basic Books, 1995).

30. Wollstonecraft, 101.

31. Rudulf Dekker and Lotte van de Pol, *The Tradition of Female Transvestitism in Early Modern Europe* (Houndmills, Macmillan Press, 1989). See also, Emma Donoghue, *Passions Between Women: British Lesbian Culture, 1668–1801* (London, Scarlet Press, 1993). For other accounts of belligerent transvestitism, see: Alfred

Young, *Masquerade: The Life and Times of Deborah Sampson, Continental Soldier* (New York, Vintage, 2005); Judith Hiltner, " 'She Bled in Secret': Deborah Sampson, Herman Mann, and *The Female Review*," *Early American Literature* (1999): 190–220; Lynne Friedli, " 'Passing Women': a Study of Gender Boundaries in the Eighteenth Century," in *Sexual Underworlds of the Enlightenment*, eds. George S. Rousseau and Roy Porter (Manchester, Manchester University Press, 1987), 234–260; Dianne Dugaw, "Female Sailors Bold: Transvestite Heroines and the Markers of Gender and Class," in *Iron Men, Wooden Women: Gender and Seafaring in the Atlantic World, 1700–1920*, eds. Margaret S. Creighton and Lise Norling (Baltimore, Johns Hopkins Press, 1996), 34–54; and Darline Gay Levy and Harriet B. Applewhite, "Woman and Militant Citizenship in Revolutionary Paris," in *Rebel Daughters: Women and the French Revolution*, eds. Sarah E. Meltzer and Leslie W. Rabine (Oxford, Oxford University Press, 1992), 79–101.

32. Mourão argues for lesbian readerly pleasure in these scenes as well. Manuela Mourão, "The Representation of Female Desire in Early Modern Pornographic Texts, 1660–1745," *Signs* 24 (1999): 573–602.

33. Robert Darnton, *The Forbidden Best-Sellers of Pre-Revolutionary France* (London, Harper Collins, 1996); Lynn Hunt, *The Family Romance of the French Revolution* (Berkeley, University of California Press, 1993; *The Invention of Pornography*, ed. Lynn Hunt (New York, Zone Books, 1993). See also, Jean Marie Goulemot, *Forbidden Texts: Erotic Literature and its Readers in Eighteenth-Century France* (Oxford, Polity Press, 1994); David Foxon, *Libertine Literature in England, 1660–1745* (np, Book Collector, 1963); Bradford K. Mudge, *The Whore's Story: Women, Pornography, and the British Novel, 1684–1830* (Oxford, Oxford University Press, 2000); Peter Wagner, *Eros Revived: Erotica of the Enlightenment in England and America* (London, Secker & Warburg, 1988).

34. Samuel Andre Tissot, "Onanism, or Physical Dissertation on the Illnesses Caused by Masturbation," in *Homosexuality in Early Modern France*, eds. J. Merrick and B. T. Ragan, Jr., 28–29.

35. William Dunlap, *Diary of William Dunlap (1766–1839)* (New York, New York Historical Society, 1931), 335.

36. Amy Wyngaard, "Libertine Spaces: Anonymous Crowds, Secret Chambers, and Urban Corruption in Restif de la Bretonne," *Eighteenth-Century Life* 22 (1998): 104–122; David Coward, "The Sublimations of a Fetishist: Restif de la Bretonne (1734–1806)," in *'Tis Nature's Fault: Unauthorized Sexuality During the Enlightenment*, ed. Robert Purks Maccurbin (Cambridge, Cambridge University Press, 1988), 98–108; Restif de la Bretonne, *The Corrupted Ones: Le Paysan and La Paysanne Pervertis* (Bristol, Neville Spearman, 1967). Wyngaard reproduces the obscene plates from Restif de la Bretonne, *Le Paysan Perverti, Vol. 1* (The Hague & Paris, Esprit, 1776), 138. Judging by publication dates, this edition and its lascivious plates may have been the ones that Caritat advertised for sale and Brown may have handled.

37. Caritat's catalog contains numerous other Francophone titles that could indicate obscene texts, but this cannot be verified because no extant copy exists. The catalog also includes texts that are not textually obscene, but which, nonetheless, often came with lascivious plates, such as Jean-Baptiste Louvet de Couvrai's tale of cross-dressing and seduction, *The Life and Adventures of the Chevalier de Faublas,* Sophista Longus's *The Pastoral Amours of Daphnis and Cloe,* and Diderot's *La Religieuse.* George Gates Raddin, *An Early New York Library of Fiction: With a Checklist of the Fiction in H. Caritat's Circulating Library, No 1. City Hotel, Broadway, New York, 1804* (New York, The H.W. Wilson Company, 1940). Philip Stewart notes how books were sold with accompanying plates that often illustrated erotic acts not explicitly mentioned in the text. I am suggesting that *Ormond* similarly links printed word to implied vision. Philip Stewart, *Engraven Desire: Eros, Image, and Text in the French Eighteenth Century* (Durham, Duke University Press, 1992). An earlier catalog published by Caritat in the same year as *Ormond* lists pornographic titles such as *Chronique Scandaleuse, ou Histoire Secrete des Sociétés pendant ces dernières annés; Choix de poesies Erotiques; Danger d'un amour illicite; Histoire Publique et Secrete d'Henry IV; Histoire de la Vie Privee de Louix XV; Histoire Amoureuses des Gaules; Poësies de Sapho*; along with Bretonne's *Paysan Perverti* and *Pornographe.* Hoquet Caritat, *Catalogue des Livres Francais* (New York, 1799). Bretonne's work was sold in the U.S. by French booksellers as early as 1790. C. P. Raguet, *Catalogue of French, and other Books* (Philadelphia, 1790).

38. George Gates Raddin, *Hocquet Caritat and the Early New York Literary Scene* (Dover, NJ, The Dover Advance Press, 1953), 30.

39. *Ormond,* 208.

40. Brown's "Portrait of an Emigrant" has one of its narrative voices say that "the French are the only people that know how to live," based on the émigrés' habit of waking up late, working a few hours, and then spending the rest of the day in playful leisure.

41. William Hedges, "Charles Brockden Brown and the Culture of Contradictions," *Early American Literature* 9 (1974): 107–142; Robert S. Levine, *Conspiracy and Romance: Studies in Brockden Brown, Cooper, Hawthorne, and Melville* (Cambridge, Cambridge University Press, 1989), 49.

42. Smyth, 'Imperfect Disclosures'; Comment, "Charles Brockden Brown's *Ormond* and Lesbian Possibility in the Early Republic; Lewis, "Attaining Masculinity"; and Faderman in this collection.

43. *Ormond,* 273.

44. *Ormond,* 275–276.

45. Wil Verhoeven, "Displacing the Discontinuous; or, the Labyrinths of Reason: Fictional Design and Eighteenth-Century Thought in Charles Brockden Brown's *Ormond,*" in *Rewriting the Dream: Reflections on the Changing American Canon,* ed. Wil Verhoeven (Amsterdam, Rodopi, 1992), 202–29.

# Afterword

## John D'Emilio

Let's face it. For many U.S. historians who teach and research the history of sexuality, early America is an unfortunate inconvenience. It does not provide us with a route to the present. We cannot turn to it for the origins —even the distant attenuated origins—of our own world in which sexuality is bound closely to and has helped constitute a regime of mass consumption, an ethic of pleasure, and a sense of both individual and group identity. Sex in colonial North America seems firmly embedded in a marital reproductive matrix. We move quickly through it until the magical properties of the nineteenth-century demographic revolution shift sex into a sphere in which human beings are able to exercise at least some modicum of choice.

We try to make the best of the situation. We seize the opportunity at the beginning of the semester to entertain our students with stories about those odd Puritans who placed animals in line ups and executed the ones who had participated in the crime of bestiality. Early America gets cast as the unalterable other: that was then, this is now. For the history of same-sex relations, it allows us to demonstrate the acts (then) versus identities (now) paradigm. It serves almost as a form of prehistory, a starting point that precedes real history, the moment (located somewhere in the late eighteenth century) when change over time finally begins.

I know the early modernists reading the above two paragraphs must be shaking their heads in dismay or rolling their eyes as they dismiss the intellectual provinciality of someone who writes mostly about a past that is so recent that some do not even consider its history. So, alright, I admit that I am exaggerating. But, still, I would wager that many U.S. historians structure their teaching—and their understanding—of the history of sexuality in ways that give the nineteenth and twentieth century pride of place.

Part of the great value of *Long Before Stonewall* is that it takes a giant step toward redressing this imbalance. By pulling together a wide range of essays, some previously published and some brand new, it allows us to re-think both the marginalization of early America to the history of sexuality and the simplistic interpretations we have of sex over this long stretch of time. It also does more. The writers in this volume are struggling over is-sues of interpretation, significance, and method that are vital to all stu-dents of sexuality. Their essays allow us both to see new things and to see the familiar differently. They also provoke us into caring about the issues and arguing about interpretation.

Let me offer a few examples of what I mean.

1. A generation ago, Carl Degler published a very influential essay titled "What Ought to Be and What Was."[1] In it, he drew a sharp line between prescriptive literature and lived experience. The former, Degler argued, could not be used as evidence for the latter. The essay was an important milestone in the continuing effort to rethink Victorian sexuality. Since then, the cultural turn in many academic disciplines has encouraged us not so much to abandon this distinction but to move beyond the simple clarity of it. Texts cannot be read as literal transcriptions of daily life, but language does help constitute experience. Learning how people think, what people think, and how they choose to represent their experience through cultural texts is indispensable in developing sophisticated, com-plex, and nuanced understandings of how these folks might have lived.

A number of authors play with these distinctions and subtleties. By looking closely at the evidence of two different cases, Richard Godbeer is able to identify a difference between the harshly condemnatory prescrip-tions of clerical and legal authorities and the views, shaped by daily living, of ordinary people. Clare Lyons mines the content of the books that crossed the Atlantic for clues about the structure of thought and feeling in eighteenth-century Philadelphia. Lisa Moore is able to see in the conven-tions of the landscape poem an opening for the expression of desire and passion between women.

At the same time, the examination of these cultural products as a route into the past provoked in me a yearning to go beyond them. Stephen Sha-piro's characterization of *Ormond* as "the most radical novel" of its era made me want to know more about the social history that produced such sexual radicalism. What experiences generated this way of seeing and thinking? Was there a basis in day-to-day life for the eroticized friendships that white antislavery writers idealized in the generation after 1790? What was it about the sexual norms of the 1780s and 1790s that allowed "sympa-thy," in Caleb Crain's analysis, to flourish? Is it possible to move beyond the specifics of Leander and Lorenzo to construct a broad interpretation of intimacy among white middle-class men in the way that Carroll Smith-Rosenberg did for their nineteenth-century female counterparts? What sense did eighteenth-century Philadelphians make of novels produced from a very different social milieu across the Atlantic? Did their own expe-rience allow them to nod in recognition? Or were they encountering the alien in these pages? Did the availability of such texts provoke change in the social world of these North American colonials?

2. The themes of power and hierarchy have been central to the history of sexuality. Feminists and gay liberationists saw sexuality as a core com-ponent of the oppression they battled, and these social movements pro-vided the legitimating contexts for the first formative body of historical writing in the 1970s and early 1980s. As the field has grown, our under-standings of power may have grown more sophisticated and our analyses of hierarchy become more complex, but these themes remain pervasive.

Power and hierarchy are everywhere in the essays you have just read. Ramón Gutiérrez frames his revisionist interpretation of the berdache in these terms. The gender-crossing individuals whose stories Elizabeth Reis examined provoked anxiety, in part because they shook the certainty of differences that sustained a gender hierarchy. Anne Myles lets us see how the Quaker challenge to certain hierarchical distinctions unleashed fears of sexual disorder that were in turn mobilized against these rebels. Observa-tions of the sexual behavior and mores of native peoples in North America unleashed an inflammatory language of moral disapproval that justified conquest and colonization.

3. History has been an evidence-based discipline. Unlike some others (I will not name names), where vast literatures and whole theories have been generated by analysis of one movie or the administration of a question-naire to a captive group of college students, historians search and search and search, and we read and read and read. Maybe we do not examine every surviving document, but at least we keep going until the documents we are finding have stopped adding to our understanding of the subject at hand.

Historians of the twentieth century are blessed—or cursed—with an abundance of sources. For instance, to take the topic of cultural represen-tation and lesbian desire: There were dozens upon dozens of pulp novels published in the United States between 1950 and 1965. Historians can read them and study the cover art. We can read reviews and examine where and how these books were advertised. We can find consumers of these novels and elicit their recollections of acquiring them, reading them, and talking about them. We can probe the impact, if any, these works of popular fiction had on their lives. We can find out about the authors and their intentions. We can study the archival records of the publishing industry. All this, and that still leaves us with many other types of surviving evidence about same-sex love and desire in the mid-twentieth-century United States.

But what to do when one has only a handful of texts that colonial Philadelphians imported? Or when one has, as was true for Tracy Brown, only two surviving cases of sexual misconduct for New Mexico for the entire eighteenth century? None of the authors in this volume could be said to be drowning in evidence. So they combine the art of close reading with the discipline of not overreaching. Richard Godbeer finds in the two New England cases for which there is a substantial surviving record some suggestive phrases ("inward disposition" and "this trade") that open productive lines of speculation without, however, his claiming too much. Or authors widen the framework of analysis. By placing Philadelphia within the bigger context of Atlantic society and employing the concept of cultural exchange and circulation, Clare Lyons expands the body of evidence she can analyze.

4. History is, fundamentally, a story of change. Yet the paradigms that commonly explain sexuality, such as the eternal moral values of certain religious traditions or forms of popular scientific theorizing that amount to biological reductionism, render it immune to change. Everywhere in this volume, authors allude to evidence of change. John Saillant's discussion of antislavery writings points to different forms of representation earlier and later. Clare Lyons writes of "new constructions of sexuality" that traveled across the Atlantic. Lisa Moore's article has a phrase, "distinctly of the 1790s," that tells us there is a before and after that is different from that decade. Caleb Crain refers to "the height of sympathy's reign," thereby informing us that it did not always reign.

Each of these examples, as well as others, whetted my curiosity. Where does sexuality fit into the story of change across two centuries of early American history? What provokes change in mores, understandings, and patterns of behavior? Is sex only something acted upon, or is it also, itself, an independent agent of change? How is sexuality a part of the revolutionary upheavals of the second half of the eighteenth century? These are not small questions, and it may be too early to be able to explain, rather than describe, the lineaments of change. But, these essays inspire a wish to know even more about the shifting contours of same-sex love and desire in early America.

5. History may be a story of change, and the past is not the present, but the urge to find the present in the past is a powerful one. We look for heroes, for models, for forms of recognition. This, it seems to me, has been an especially powerful impulse among the generation that came of age in the couple of decades before and after Stonewall. "We are everywhere" served as political slogan and rallying cry; it was appropriated as the title of an anthology of historical documents.[2]

Some of these essays might easily serve as models for how historians generally can successfully navigate the treacherous shoals of present mindedness. Ramón Gutiérrez addresses the problem head on in his reinterpretation of the berdache. He rejects what he calls a "politics of yearning" that has trapped the berdache within "romantic webs of obfuscation." Refusing to project backward the post-Stonewall stance of visible, proud gay men, he unsentimentally analyzes the surviving accounts and places these figures within a history of conquest, rape, and servitude. Though I doubt that his piece will be the last word on the berdache (romantic illusions die slowly), his essay makes one wonder: How could this evidence have been ignored for so long?

In a different way, Lisa Moore steps around the trap created by the urge of lesbians and gay men to construct a simple usable past. She refuses the easy—and not very interesting—route of claiming Sarah Pierce as a lesbian foremother, an early American lesbian writer. But she does argue resolutely that there is value in "reading [the poem] as part of lesbian history." Her interpretation of the poem and her locating it within a tradition of landscape literature allows her to draw the powerful conclusion that "intimacy between women was a sustaining feature of eighteenth-century New England intellectual life." This is certainly not a traditionalist interpretation of the social and cultural milieu of revolutionary America and its project of nation building.

6. Part of what makes history endlessly fascinating for me is that interpretations keep changing. Just when one foolishly thinks "well, I know everything about this now," someone else brings a fresh perspective to it, and the conventional wisdom gets thrown into question.

A generation ago, the distinction drawn between acts and identities, a paradigm to which many of this volume's contributors refer, constituted a tremendously productive analytic breakthrough. While it would be an exaggeration to claim that there have been no dissenters from this framework (John Boswell was the most notable),[3] it is fair to say that it dominates much historical scholarship, and that the debate has been around how, when, and where sexual identities coalesce and a homosexual/heterosexual distinction is drawn, not whether.

While Foucault often receives credit for first articulating this mode of analysis, attributing its invention to him is a good example of intellectual imperialism: the famous claim territory that the peons were already cultivating. If I think about how I saw these ideas coalescing in the 1970s, I would trace a genealogy that includes Mary McIntosh, then a young sociologist in Britain; Jeffrey Weeks, a little known activist historian in Britain; the writings of John Gagnon and William Simon in the United States; and the animated, though unrecorded, dialogue among a far-flung group of community-based historians in several U.S. cities.[4] As I composed the essay "Capitalism and Gay Identity" near the end of that decade, these and various Marxist political economists shaped my adaptation of the acts-versus-identities paradigm.[5] To paraphrase Tina Turner, "what's Foucault got to do with it?"

But even the best, the most productive, and the most exciting ideas can grow stale or can constrain creativity. I found myself nodding in assent when Stephen Shapiro referred to a "current impasse in sexuality studies" and "an overly dogmatic use of Foucault" and "sexuality studies policing itself." At times it seems that we are reduced to repeating ourselves, to showing once again that there was a time before sexual identities, that sexual identities emerged, and then debating whether they emerged here or there, in this decade or that decade.

Can students of the history of sexuality think outside of this box? And, if we did, what would we be writing about and how would we be analyzing the documentary record of the past? I wish I had the answer to this question, but it would not surprise me if it looked something like the approach of Anne Myles in her investigation of seventeenth-century Quakers and the Puritan persecution of them. The question she posed ("What if anything can looking at a religious movement tell us about sexuality in early America?") immediately grabbed my attention. Her claim that discourses of religious conflict constituted a "symbolic space of erotic otherness" made me want to investigate other moments and places of religious upheaval to see whether her argument is confined to this particular location and time, or whether perhaps it is productive of other original insights.

Whatever the answer, *Long Before Stonewall* forces one to rethink the marginalization of early America in the history of sexuality. It makes a simple past seem far less settled and uncomplicated. It invites reconsideration and reflection of things we thought we already knew.

### NOTES

1. Carl N. Degler, "What Ought to Be and What Was: Women's Sexuality in the Nineteenth Century," *American Historical Review* 79 (December 1974): 1467–90.

2. Mark Blasius and Shane Phelan, eds., *We Are Everywhere: A Historical Sourcebook of Gay and Lesbian Politics* (New York: Routledge, 1997).

3. John Boswell, *Christianity, Social Tolerance, and Homosexuality: Gay People in Western Europe from the Beginning of the Christian Era to the Fourteenth Century* (Chicago: University of Chicago Press, 1980).

4. Mary McIntosh, "The Homosexual Role," *Social Problems* 16 (1968): 182–92; Jeffrey Weeks, *Coming Out: Homosexual Politics in Britain from the Nineteenth Century to the Present* (London: Quartet Books, 1977); John H. Gagnon and William Simon, *Sexual Conduct: The Social Sources of Human Sexuality* (Chicago: University of Chicago Press, 1973).

5. John D'Emilio, "Capitalism and Gay Identity," in Ann Snitow, Christine Stansell, and Sharon Thompson, eds., *Powers of Desire: The Politics of Sexuality* (New York: Monthly Review Press, 1983), 100–113.

# Contributors

*Tracy Brown* is an Assistant Professor of Anthropology in the Department of Sociology, Anthropology, and Social Work at Central Michigan University. She is the author of numerous articles on Pueblo ethnohistory.

*Caleb Crain* is a writer who lives in New York City. He is author of *American Sympathy: Men, Friendship, and Literature in the New Nation.* He has written essays for *The New Yorker, The New Republic,* and *The Nation.*

*John D'Emilio* is Professor of Gender and Women's Studies and History at the University of Illinois at Chicago. D'Emilio's publications include *Sexual Politics, Sexual Communities; Intimate Matters,* cowritten with Estelle Freedman; and *Lost Prophet.*

*Lillian Faderman* has published eleven books, including *Surpassing the Love of Men, Odd Girls and Twilight Lovers,* and *To Believe in Women.* Her latest book is *Gay L.A.: A History of Sexual Outlaws, Power Politics, and Lipstick Lesbians.*

*Gunlög Fur* is Associate Professor of History at Växjö University in Sweden. She is author of *Colonialism in the Margins: Cultural Encounters in New Sweden and Lapland.*

*Richard Godbeer* is Professor of History at the University of Miami. He is author of *The Devil's Dominion: Magic and Religion in Early New England* (1992), *Sexual Revolution in Early America* (2002), and *Escaping Salem: The Other Witch Hunt of 1692* (2005).

*Ramón A. Gutiérrez* is Professor of History and Ethnic Studies at the University of California, San Diego. He is author of *When Jesus Came, the Corn Mothers Went Away: Marriage, Sexuality, and Power in New Mexico, 1500–1846.* He coedited, with Richard J. Orsi, *Contested Eden: California Before the Gold Rush* (1998).

*Mark E. Kann,* Professor of Political Science and History at the University of Southern California, holds the USC Associates Chair in Social Science. His publications include *On the Man Question: Gender and Civic Virtue in America* (1991); *A Republic of Men: The American Founders, Gendered Language, and Patriarchal Politics* (1998); *The Gendering of American Politics* (1999); and *Punishment, Prisons, and Patriarchy* (2005).

*Clare A. Lyons* is Associate Professor of History at the University of Maryland. She is author of *Sex Among the Rabble: An Intimate History of Gender and Power in the Age of Revolution, Philadelphia, 1730–1830.*

*Laura Mandell* is Associate Professor of English at Miami University of Ohio. She is author of *Misogynous Economies: The Business of Literature in Eighteenth-Century Britain.*

*Lisa L. Moore* is Associate Professor in the Department of English and the Center for Women's and Gender Studies at the University of Texas at Austin. She is author of *Dangerous Intimacies: Toward a Sapphic History of the British Novel* (Duke University Press, 1997).

*Anne G. Myles* is Associate Professor of English at the University of Northern Iowa and author of numerous essays on early American dissent. Her discussion "Queering the History of Early American Sexuality" appeared in the *William & Mary Quarterly* 60:1 (2003).

*Elizabeth Reis* is Associate Professor in the Women's and Gender Studies Program at the University of Oregon. She is author of *Damned Women: Sinners and Witches in Puritan New England* and editor of several volumes, including *American Sexual Histories: A Blackwell Reader in American Social and Cultural History.*

*John Saillant* is Professor of History and English at Western Michigan University. He is author of *Black Puritan, Black Republican: The Life and Thought of Lemuel Haynes, 1753–1833* and coeditor with Joanna Brooks of *Face Zion Forward: First Writers of the Black Atlantic, 1785–1798.*

*Stephen Shapiro* is an Associate Professor in English and Comparative Literary Studies at the University of Warwick. He coedited with Philip Barnard and Mark Kamrath, *Revising Charles Brockden Brown: Culture, Politics, and Sexuality in the Early Republic.* His study *The Culture and Commerce of the Early American Novel: Reading the Atlantic World-System* is forthcoming from Penn State University Press.

# Index

Lindeström, Peter, 33
Lister, Anne, 182
Litchfield, Connecticut, 253, 267–69, 274n22; love/friendship within, 264–69
Litchfield Female Academy, 253–54, 270
Livingston, Edward, 282–83
Logan, Deborah Norris. *See* Norris, Deborah
Logan, George, 225
London, 99–100, 172, 191n7, 351n7, 365; political establishments, 364
Lorenzo. *See* Gibson, James
Lott, Eric, 314
*Louisa* (Seward), 263
Love: Christian, 115–16; expressing, 227; gay, 217; heterosexual, 214; in Litchfield, 264–69; religious, 128; same-sex, 387–88; between women, 207, 212, 253
*Love and Death in the American Novel* (Fiedler), 216n7
Lyons, Clare, 6–7, 335, 381n20, 385, 387

Mackintosh, Benjamin, 197n41
Mack, Phyllis, 119, 136n14
Madison, James, 305, 320
Magdalene Society of Philadelphia, 341
Mandell, Laura, 12
Manley, Delariviere, 182–83, 200n67
*The Man of Feeling*, 234
Manumission Society, 267
Marlowe, Christopher, 110n69
Marriage, 332; bachelors perspective on, 340, 344, 348; condemnation of sex outside, 84–85; as confinement, 345; as contractual slavery, 366; heterosexuality of, 115, 266; infidelity within, 341; between men, 21; in Native American culture, 24, 53; persistence of, 355n62; refusals, 47; resistance to, 370; same-sex, 351; of Sension, 110n65; sexuality unrestricted by, 38; Smith, Abigail, critique of, 256
Marshall, Margaret, 185
Martyrdom, 126–28, 141nn55, 57, 143n76
Masculinity, 150; crisis in, 188–90; heightened importance of, 203n88; heterosexual, 335; of Pueblo Indians, 65–72
Massachusetts, 1, 5, 89, 91, 97; courts, 109n59; laws of, 152; Salem, 124
Massachusetts Body of Liberties, 134n9
Massachusetts State Prison, 288, 291
Master-slave relationship, 312, 344

Masturbation, 91, 93, 108n51, 280; considered "self-pollution," 284, 290
Mather, Cotton, 85, 108n56
Mayhew, Jonathan, 232
McConville, Sean, 288
McIntosh, Mary, 389
McLaren, Angus, 162n29
Mease, James, 282
*A Mechanical and Critical Enquiry into the Nature of Hermaphrodites* (J. Parsons), 148
*Medicinal Dictionary* (James), 182
Meeson, John, 173–74
*Memoir* (Godwin), 209
*Memoirs of a Woman of Pleasure* (Cleland), 172, 195n30
*Memoirs of Stephen Calvert* (C. B. Brown), 362
*Memoirs of the Life of Dr. Darwin* (Seward), 260
Men, 21, 28, 44, 65, 72, 173, 187, 189, 202nn84, 86, 203n90, 231, 334; anal sex, women and, 86, 107n46; friendship between, 240, 274n14; having sex with boys, 292; relationships between, 169, 209; wearing clothing of women, 21–22, 25, 34, 42–43
*Men in Love* (Haggarty), 193n15
Meranze, Michael, 297
Merritt, Jane T., 40
Merritt, Richard L., 351n2
Michell, Edward, 90–91, 109n60
Middlesex County Court, 152, 161n20
Midwifery, 154
*The Midwives Book: or the Whole Art of Midwifery Discovered* (Sharp), 145
Mifflin, John Fishbourne, 187, 217–45; age/genealogy of, 245n1; diary of, 222–33, 238–39, 244–45; dreams of, 239, 243–44; expressing intimacy with Gibson, 243; first meeting of Gibson, 220; Norris family garden visits of, 219–20; Norris, Isaac, reunion with, 242; relationship with Norris, Isaac, III of, 232–40; sickness of, 241; status of, 233; writing style of, 226–27
*Millennium Hall*, 208
Miller, Edward, 265
Miller, Jay, 35
Ministers: defining sodomy, 85–86, 105n31, 134n8; Gorton as, 95–96; sodomy as sacrilege according to, 91
Mitchel, Jonathan, 86
Mitchill, Samuel Latham, 265

# About the Editor

Thomas A. Foster is Assistant Professor of History at DePaul University and author of *Sex and the Eighteenth-Century Man: Massachusetts and the History of Sexuality in America.*